Apple Pro Training Series

Getting Started with Final Cut Studio

Apple
Certified

Apple Pro Training Series: Getting Started with Final Cut Studio
Copyright © 2006 by Apple Computer

Published by Peachpit Press. For information on Peachpit Press books, contact:

Peachpit Press
1249 Eighth Street
Berkeley, CA 94710
(510) 524-2178
Fax: (510) 524-2221
http://www.peachpit.com
To report errors, please send a note to errata@peachpit.com
Peachpit Press is a division of Pearson Education

Contributing Writers: Mary Plummer, Klark Perez, Matthew Geller
Contributing Author, Interactive DVD: Damian Allen
Editor: Serena Herr
Production Editor: Susan Rimerman
Technical Editors: Adam Green, Estelle McGechie
Technical Reviewers: Victor Gavenda, Eric Geoffroy
Copy Editor: Karen Seriguchi
Compositor: Danielle Foster
Interior Design: Frances Baca
Cover Design: George Mattingly

ISBN 0-321-36991-2
9 8 7 6 5 4 3 2 1
Printed and bound in the United States of America

Contents

Getting Started

Welcome to the Apple Pro Training tutorials for Final Cut Studio, Apple Computer's dynamic and powerful digital video production suite.

The lessons in this book are also available in PDF format on two tutorial DVDs that ship in the box when you purchase Final Cut Studio. Because some readers prefer to have the tutorials in printed form, Peachpit Press has published them here.

This book is an introduction to Final Cut Studio. It has two aims. First, the book's "Introducing" lessons give newcomers a solid overview of Final Cut Pro 5, Motion 2, Soundtrack Pro, and DVD Studio Pro 4, and help them acquire a basic level of familiarity with the applications.

Second, the book's "Mastering" lessons, which focus on new and advanced features, give experienced users a quick way to learn about the most powerful improvements and additions to Final Cut Studio.

The Methodology

The lessons in both the book and the interactive DVD tutorial emphasize hands-on training. Each exercise is designed to help you learn the application in a real-world context, starting with the basic interface and moving on to more advanced techniques. The book assumes a basic level of familiarity with the Mac OS X operating system.

If you are new to Final Cut Studio, it would be helpful for you to start at the beginning and progress through each lesson in order, since each lesson builds on information learned in previous ones. If you are already familiar with earlier versions of the applications, you can start with any section and focus on that topic.

Course Structure

The book offers two ways to learn Final Cut Studio: an interactive DVD tutorial, and step-by-step lessons with accompanying project files. The two learning methods reinforce each other, and are designed to be used together.

Apple Pro Training Final Cut Studio Interactive DVD Tutorial

The Apple Pro Training Final Cut Studio DVD Tutorial is an interactive course that gives you an excellent overview of Final Cut Pro 5, Motion 2, Soundtrack Pro, and DVD Studio Pro 4. The tutorial takes you through the applications' interfaces and primary features, including a tour of some of the most important new features. This is an interactive teaching tool, with lesson files and media included on the DVD, so you can work through real-world projects as you learn.

Apple Pro Training Final Cut Studio Tutorials

The Apple Pro Training Final Cut Studio Tutorials are step-by-step, project-based lessons—the equivalent of about 8 hours of training—with accompanying project and media files located on the book's second DVD. Lessons are included for both new and experienced users, and cover Final Cut Pro 5, Motion 2, Soundtrack Pro, and DVD Studio Pro 4.

Lesson 1: Introducing Final Cut Pro

This step-by-step introduction to the cornerstone application of Final Cut Studio guides you through the process of editing two projects. As you edit, you'll discover the primary aspects of the Final Cut Pro interface and will become familiar with its basic operation, including navigating through a sequence, opening and marking clips, assembling clips, basic trimming and editing techniques, adding transitions and filters, and using nested sequences. Approximate lesson time: 1 hour.

Lesson 2: Mastering Final Cut Pro

This advanced lesson covers some of Final Cut Pro's most exciting new features and more advanced techniques. You'll work with multiclips to create a multi-angle montage and a multi-camera edit. Then you'll use advanced effects techniques to animate opacity, change speeds, apply basic color correction, modify a nested sequence, and composite images. You'll use all these techniques to build a promo for the show "Capturing the eXtreme" for the fictitious eXtreme Living Channel. Approximate lesson time: 1 hour.

Lesson 3: Introducing Motion

This introductory-level lesson takes you through the process of creating a Motion project from start to finish. After exploring the Motion interface, you'll work with some of Motion's most exciting features, including animated text, filters, behaviors, and particles, as you build a ten-second promo for the fictitious eXtreme Living Channel. Approximate lesson time: 45 minutes.

Lesson 4: Mastering Motion

This advanced tutorial focuses on some of Motion's most powerful new features and more advanced techniques. You'll learn to work with replicators, the 3D filter, image masks, generators, and keyframed animations to build a "Coming Up Next" bumper for the fictitious eXtreme Living Channel. Approximate lesson time: 1 hour.

Lesson 5: Introducing Soundtrack Pro

This hands-on lesson is designed to give you an overview of the Soundtrack Pro interface and some of the application's professional sound design features as you build and mix a project. You'll learn to arrange audio clips on the Timeline, synchronize audio and video, automate volume and pan levels, edit audio files, reduce noise, normalize a voiceover, add effects, and create a mix. Along the way you'll also learn some handy keyboard shortcuts and sound design tricks. Approximate lesson time: 1 hour, 15 minutes.

Lesson 6: Introducing DVD Studio Pro

In this introduction to DVD Studio Pro, you'll use the application's Basic configuration to author a simple DVD containing one track, a slideshow, and one menu. You'll learn how to modify an existing menu template to your own design, create custom buttons, and connect your assets for a DVD. By working through a few of the basics, you'll have a solid foundation and be ready to tackle your next project. Approximate lesson time: 1 hour.

Lesson 7: Mastering DVD Studio Pro

This lesson explores techniques for designing more advanced menus in DVD Studio Pro, including how to create motion menus, transitions, subtitles, and more. You'll be authoring a DVD to promote a fictitious show Shark Encounter on the eXtreme Living Channel. The project includes a slideshow of the production, a movie track, chapter index menus, and alternate angles. Approximate lesson time: 1 hour, 15 minutes.

System Requirements

Before beginning to use *Apple Pro Training Series: Getting Started with Final Cut Studio,* you should have a working knowledge of your computer and its operating system. Make sure that you know how to use the mouse and standard menus and commands and also how to open, save, and close files. If you need to review these techniques, see the printed or online documentation included with your system.

Basic system requirements for Final Cut Studio are:

▶ Macintosh Computer with a PowerPC G4 (867MHz or faster) or G5 processor; HD features require 1GHz or faster single or dual processor; authoring of HD DVDs requires a PowerPC G5 processor.

▶ Mac OS X v 10.3.9 or later; Core Image Units and 16- and 32-bit float rendering in Motion 2 require Mac OS X v10.4 or later

▶ QuickTime 7 or later

▶ 512MB of RAM. HD features require 1GB of RAM or more (2GB recommended)

▶ DVD-ROM drive required for installation

▶ AGP Quartz Extreme graphics card

▶ Motion 2 requires the standard graphics card found on any Power Mac G5 or iMac G5, a 1.25GHz or faster PowerBook G4 or a 1.25GHz or faster flat-panel iMac. Any of the following graphics cards is highly recommended: NVIDIA GeForce FX 6800 Ultra DDL, NVIDIA GeForce FX 6800 GT DDL (NV40), ATI Mobility Radeon 9700 (RV M11), ATI Radeon 9800 Pro (R350) or ATI Radeon 9800 XT (R360).

▶ Playback of HD DVDs authored in DVD Studio Pro 4 requires a PowerPC G5 processor, Mac OS X v10.4 and Apple DVD Player 4.6 (or later)

▶ 4GB of available disk space required for project and media content installation (NTSC or PAL) from Tutorials DVD.

Copying the Lesson Files

This book includes an Apple Pro Training Final Cut Studio Tutorials DVD of all the files you will need to complete the lessons. For each lesson, there are folders containing the applicable project and media files in both NTSC or PAL formats. (NTSC is used predominately in North America; PAL is used in Europe and some parts of Asia.)

The Apple Pro Training Final Cut Studio Tutorials require a certain amount of free disk space: 4 GB of available disk space is necessary for installing either NTSC or PAL tutorial media and projects (8 GB required for installing both formats).

More information regarding installation and setting up your system for each tutorial is provided at the beginning of each Lesson.

Note: If you want to use only one tutorial, you can install the tutorial media and project files for just that tutorial. Simply open the Apple_Pro_Training_Tutorials-NTSC or Apple_Pro_Training_Tutorials-PAL folder on the DVD, and copy the appropriate subfolder to your computer's hard drive by dragging the subfolder to your Desktop.

About the Apple Pro Training Series

Apple Pro Training Series: Getting Started with Final Cut Studio is part of the official training series for Apple Pro applications, developed by experts in the field and certified by Apple Computer. The series is the official course curriculum used by Apple Authorized Training Centers, and offers complete training in all Apple Pro products. The lessons are designed to let you learn at your own pace. Although each lesson provides step-by-step instructions for creating specific projects, there's room for exploration and experimentation. You can progress through the book from beginning to end, or dive right into the lessons that interest you most.

For a complete list of Apple Pro Training Series books, see the course catalog at the end of this book, or visit www.peachpit.com/applebooklet.

Apple Pro Certification Program

The Apple Pro Training and Certification Program is designed to keep you at the forefront of Apple's digital media technology while giving you a competitive edge in today's ever-changing job market. Whether you're an editor, graphic designer, sound designer, special effects artist, or teacher, these training tools are meant to help you expand your skills.

You can become a certified Apple Pro by taking the certification exam at an Apple Authorized Training Center. Certification is offered in Final Cut Pro, DVD Studio Pro, Shake, and Logic. Successful certification as an Apple Pro gives you official recognition of your knowledge of Apple's professional applications while allowing you to market yourself to employers and clients as a skilled, pro-level user of Apple products.

Apple offers training courses at Apple Authorized Training Centers worldwide. These courses, which use the Apple Pro Training Series books as their curriculum, are taught by Apple Certified Trainers and balance concepts and lectures with hands-on labs and exercises. Apple Authorized Training Centers have been carefully selected and have met Apple's highest standards in all areas, including facilities, instructors, course delivery, and infrastructure. The goal of the program is to offer Apple customers, from beginners to the most seasoned professionals, the highest quality training experience.

To find an Authorized Training Center near you, go to www.apple.com/software/pro/training.

Resources

Apple Pro Training Series: Getting Started with Final Cut Studio is an introduction to Final Cut Studio. It is not intended to be a comprehensive reference manual, nor does it replace the documentation that comes with the application. For comprehensive information about program features, refer to these resources:

▶ The User Manuals. Accessed through the Help menu, the User Manuals contain a complete description of all features, along with recommended techniques and procedures.

▶ Apple's Web site: www.apple.com.

1

Lesson Files	Apple_Pro_Training_Tutorials > Introducing_ Final_Cut_Pro > 1_Intro_FCP_Starting
	Apple_Pro_Training_Tutorials > Introducing_ Final_Cut_Pro > 2_Intro_FCP_Finished
Time	This lesson takes approximately 60 minutes to complete.
Goals	Learn the Final Cut Pro interface
	Navigate through a sequence
	Open and mark clips in the Viewer
	Assemble clips using the Canvas, a storyboard, and the Timeline
	Trim edit points using the Roll tool
	Add transitions and filters
	Import clips into the Browser
	Trim using the Razor Blade tool
	Add B-roll to an interview sequence
	Learn to use nesting sequences

Lesson **1**
Introducing Final Cut Pro

Welcome to the cornerstone application of Final Cut Studio: Final Cut Pro. This step-by-step Apple Pro Training tutorial will guide you through the process of editing two projects. As you edit, you'll discover the primary aspects of the Final Cut Pro interface and will become familiar with its basic operation.

If you want to learn more, move on to the Mastering Final Cut Pro tutorial, explore the interactive Apple Pro Training DVD, and see the About Apple Pro Training folder on this DVD for information on the self-paced Apple Pro Training Series books and the Apple Pro certified training program.

Preparing the Project

Before you start, you'll need to install the Final Cut Pro software on your hard disk. You also need to copy the applicable Apple Pro Training Tutorials folder from the DVD to your computer's desktop.

NOTE ▸ Choose either the Apple Pro Training Tutorials NTSC folder (North America), or Apple Pro Training Tutorials PAL folder (Europe and some parts of Asia), depending on which broadcast standard you'll be using.

Once you have the Final Cut Pro application and the applicable Apple Pro Training Tutorials Folder on your computer, you're ready to begin this lesson.

MORE INFO ▸ You can find more detailed installation instructions on the Final Cut Studio tutorials Read Me file included in the Tutorials DVD.

Opening Final Cut Pro

There are three ways to open Final Cut Pro:

▸ Double-click the Final Cut Pro application icon, located inside the Applications folder, on your hard disk.

▸ Click once on the Final Cut Pro icon in your Dock.

▸ Double-click any Final Cut Pro project file.

For this exercise, you'll open Final Cut Pro by opening a project file.

1   Locate the Apple Pro Training Tutorials folder on your computer's desktop. Double-click the folder to open it.

The folder opens to reveal the Apple Pro Training Final Cut Studio tutorials.

2   Open the Introducing_Final_Cut_Pro folder.

3   Double-click the **1_Intro_FCP_Starting** file to open Final Cut Pro and the project.

NOTE ► If this is your first time opening Final Cut Pro, you may encounter some dialogs.

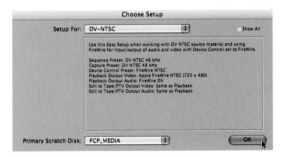

From the Setup For menu, choose DV-NTSC for NTSC, or DV-PAL for PAL, depending on which broadcast standard you are using (NTSC is used in North America, PAL is used in Europe and some parts of Asia). Click OK on the Choose Setup dialog. You can always reset your scratch disk settings (where your captured and rendered media will go) after you have launched Final Cut Pro.

External A/V

Unable to locate the following external devices:

Apple FireWire NTSC (720 x 480)

Your system configuration may have changed, or your deck/camera may be disconnected or turned off.

Please check your connections and click "Check Again", or click "Continue" to set external device selection to None.

☐ Do not warn again

(Continue)   (Check Again)

If you do not have a DV deck connected and powered, click Continue on The External A/V dialog. This dialog box lets you know that Final Cut Pro can't establish a connection with a DV deck.

You will see the main interface of Final Cut Pro, which consists of four windows, a Tool palette, and an audio meter.

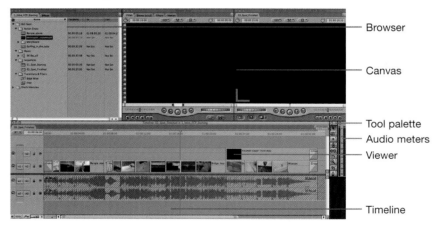

— Browser

— Canvas

— Tool palette
— Audio meters
— Viewer

— Timeline

Getting Familiar With the Interface

The interface, on first glance, might seem a little daunting, but you are look-ing at one of the most elegant user interfaces in creative computing today. Let's state a few Golden Rules to make your exploration fun and efficient.

▶ Final Cut Pro has a *contextually sensitive* interface. Many commands have multiple functions that depend on which window is active. You must select the correct window and, sometimes, the correct content within a window for a given command or tool to become available.

▶ In Final Cut Pro, there are multiple ways to perform a task. This flexibility lets you discover which way works best for you. Commands can be implemented from pop-up menus, via mouse clicks, or by keyboard shortcuts, to name a few.

▶ The Final Cut Pro main interface paradigm is *drag and drop*. Most editing functions can be achieved by dragging a file, clip, filter, transition etc. from one place to another.

▶ There are multiple levels of Undo in Final Cut Pro. If one of the steps in these exercises does not yield the result you want, just select Undo from the Edit menu, or press Command-Z. By default, you'll always be able to go back ten steps.

The Final Cut Pro Interface

Four windows make up the main interface of the application: the Browser, Viewer, Canvas and Timeline. They are shown here in their most common arrangement, with the Browser, Viewer, and Canvas from left to right across the top, and the Timeline at the bottom.

Browser

The Browser, located in the upper left of this image, is where you organize all the project elements you use when editing. You can view the different elements as a list or as icons. Here, the project is shown in list order. For each listed item, notice the icons at the left that indicate what kind of element it is: a video clip (film strip icon), an audio clip (speaker icon), or a sequence (rectangle with blue and yellow boxes). Sequences are assemblages of video or audio clips in a specific order. Elements are stored in *bins*, which are the icons that look like folders.

Viewer

Just to the right of the Browser is the Viewer. The Viewer is where you view your original, unedited source material and choose edit points. You can also edit audio, modify transitions and effects, and build titles here. The buttons at the bottom of the Viewer are used to navigate through the clip.

Canvas

The Canvas is a visual representation of the Timeline. Marked clips can be assembled into a sequence here, and this is the place where you observe the sequence as it plays. Note that its navigation controls mimic those of the Viewer.

Timeline

The Timeline is a graphical representation of all the editing decisions you make. This is your workbench area, where you edit your material, trim it, move it, stack it, and adjust it. Here you can see all you edits at a glance. The sequence begins at the left, and progresses through time to the right. The rectangular objects you see are clips that have been assembled into the sequence. Above the gray bar in the middle of the timeline are video clips (blue); below are audio clips (green).

During this tutorial, your progress through the interface will typically be from left to right, from Browser, to Viewer, to Canvas, and from there into the Timeline.

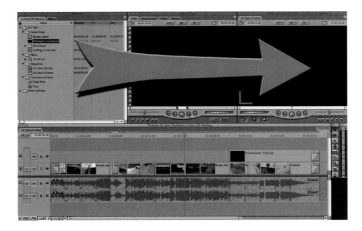

Tool Palette

The Tool palette, located on the right of the Timeline, is a collection of Final Cut Pro editing tools that can be used throughout this tutorial. Each tool has a shortcut key, so it's possible to access each tool directly from the keyboard.

Audio Meters

The Audio Meters window, also located on the right of the Timeline, displays two audio meters that reflect the volume level of whatever audio is playing. It could be a source clip that you are screening in the Viewer before editing, or the final edited piece that you are viewing in the Canvas.

Playhead Navigation

The best place to start is to learn some basic playhead navigation skills. These techniques can be used throughout the entire interface.

1 Click anywhere in the Timeline window.

An active window's title bar is a lighter gray than the others. Clicking in a window is the easiest way to make sure it's active.

2 Press the Home key on your keyboard (or the Fn and Left Arrow keys if you're on a PowerBook).

Note that the playhead (the yellow triangle with the descending line) jumps to the beginning of the sequence.

3   Press the Space bar to play and pause your video. Playback starts and stops with each press of the Space bar.

4   Press End (or the Fn and Right Arrow keys if you're on a PowerBook). The playhead jumps to the end of the sequence.

5   Click the yellow triangle of the playhead and drag it back to the beginning of the sequence. As you do, you "scrub" backward through the sequence.

6   Experiment with the arrow keys (pressed individually), and see what happens with the playhead.

The Left and Right Arrow keys move the playhead backward and forward one frame at a time. The Up and Down Arrow keys move the playhead to the boundaries of a clip. These are called *edit points*.

7   Place the three middle fingers of your right hand on the J, K, and L keys on the keyboard.

8   Press L to move the playhead forward.

9   Press J to move the playhead backward.

10   Press multiple times on either J or L to increase the speed of the playhead.

The playhead moves faster with subsequent taps of the same key, and moves slower with subsequent taps of the opposite key.

11   Press K to pause playback.

12 Click the large Play button in the Canvas.

This also starts and stops playback in the Canvas and Timeline. Remember, these two windows are always linked.

Creating a 30-Second Spot

Now that you know how to move around a little, it's time to get to work. Let's dive right into a project that creates the spot you've just been navigating through. Before we begin, you might want to play the spot all the way through to familiarize yourself with how it will look when we're done.

The sequence you've been looking at is named, 02_Spot_Finished. Both the Timeline and Canvas have tabs that reflect this name.

The sequence also exists in the Browser, inside the Sequences bin.

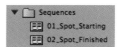

In order to assemble our own version of this 30-second spot, we'll start with an empty sequence.

1 Double-click the 01_Spot_Starting sequence, located in the Sequences bin in the Browser.

The 01_Spot_Starting sequence opens in the Timeline, with its own tab.

Notice that the 02_Spot_Finished sequence is still there. The tabbed interface in Final Cut Pro allows you to have multiple sequences open at the same time.

2 Click the 02_Spot_Finished tab in the upper left of the Timeline to bring that sequence to the front again. The finished sequence reappears.

3 Click the 01_Spot_Starting tab.

NOTE ► We created 01_Spot_Starting for you, but you could have created a brand-new sequence in the Browser and opened it up as well. We'll create new sequences later in the lesson.

Working in the Viewer

The next step is to get familiar with the Viewer controls and to learn how to mark clips by setting In and Out points. Let's start by opening a clip in the Viewer.

1 Drag the icon of the **Helicopter_snowboard** clip (the second clip in the Action Shots bin) from the Browser to the Viewer.

The clip opens in the Viewer, and the Viewer automatically becomes active, ready for you to navigate through the clip.

2 Use any of the navigation methods from the previous exercise to navigate through the clip: the J, K, and L keys, the Space bar, the arrow keys, dragging the playhead, or even pressing the Home and End keys.

Note that the same keyboard shortcuts work in the Timeline, the Canvas and the Viewer. The difference is the Viewer is now selected.

3 Observe the two Timecode fields in the upper left and right corners of the Viewer.

The upper-left field, called the Timecode Duration field, is the duration of the clip, 00:00:33:10, or 33 seconds and 10 frames, (for PAL 00:00:33:08 or 33 seconds and 8 frames).

The upper-right field, called the Current Timecode field, displays the current timecode of a clip wherever a playhead is positioned, (for PAL this will read 01:30:11:14).

Setting In and Out Points

On the keyboard above J, K, and L keys you'll see the I and O keys. In Final Cut Pro, you use the I and O keys to set the In and Out points of a clip. In this exercises, you'll mark a few seconds of video by setting In and Out points. We use material at the beginning of the clip, but for this exercise the precise location of the points is not important.

1   Navigate again through the clip, but this time, as you play forward, press I and O, to set an In and Out point for the clip.

In and Out point marks appear in the white bar (called the scrubber bar) of the Viewer. Gray areas before the In point and after the Out point indicate material you're not interested in using. These are called *handles*.

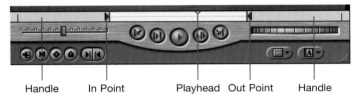

Handle   In Point   Playhead   Out Point   Handle

NOTE ▶ In and Out points can be set, deleted, and continuously renewed in Final Cut Pro. If you don't like where you've set your points, you can reset them by pressing I and O again.

2   Observe the Timecode Duration field in the upper left of the Viewer.

It now reflects the smaller duration between your In and Out points.

3   Drag the "ear" of either the In or Out point to manually reposition it.

As you do, the Timecode Duration field continuously changes to reflect the new duration between the In and Out points.

4 Keep refining your In and Out points until you have a few seconds of the clip marked.

Assembling Into the Timeline

The next step is to take this clip and place it in the sequence. You will assemble the clip into the sequence by dragging it from the Viewer to the Canvas.

1 Place your pointer in the middle of the Viewer, and click and drag the clip to the Canvas, but don't let go of the mouse button just yet.

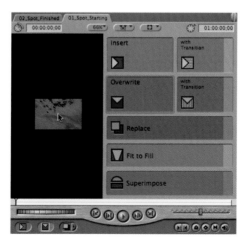

An Edit Overlay appears showing the seven types of edits one can do in Final Cut Pro. The highlight around the Overwrite overlay indicates that an Overwrite edit is the default edit when editing in the Canvas.

2   Drag the clip over the Overwrite section of the Edit Overlay, and release the mouse button.

The clip appears in the Timeline, and the *last* frame of the clip appears in the Canvas. Additionally, the playhead in the Timeline appears at the end of the clip, ready to accept the next clip into the sequence.

An overwrite edit "writes over" anything that is in the Timeline. The position Timeline playhead determines where the clip will go.

So far so good, but let's remember that the spot we're editing is set to music, and the music will obviously influence how we edit the sequence. Let's add the music into the sequence, so we can get a better feel of where and when to make our edits.

3   Double-click the **30 Sec.aif** sound file, located in the Music bin.

The audio clip opens in the Viewer.

Double-clicking a clip in the Browser is another way to open it in the Viewer. Notice also that the Viewer is not just for viewing video clips. A waveform display of your audio appears, and you can set In and Out points just as with video clips.

The pink marks in the scrubber bar are called *markers*, which are flags that indicate special frames of a clip. Markers are multifunctional: they can be used to indicate important moments in a clip, to create chapter markers for DVD authoring, among other uses. In this case, these markers indicate significant moments in the music, such as the beginning of measures and percussion hits. We've already marked your audio file to make your assembly a little easier.

4   Play the audio clip a few times, to see where the markers have been placed.

We're going to use this entire clip in our sequence; so setting In and Out points is not necessary. What is necessary, however, is to get the playhead back to the beginning of the Timeline, so when we edit this audio into the sequence, it starts from the very beginning.

> **TIP** ▶ If you marked an In or Out on your audio clip you can easily delete both marks by using the keyboard shortcut, Option-X. Option-I deletes the In mark and Option-O deletes an Out mark.

5   Click the Timeline to make it active.

6   Press Home.

Instead of editing with the Canvas overlays, we will use another method to edit the material into the sequence.

7   Click the small red Overwrite button in the lower-left area of the Canvas.

The audio clip edits into the sequence. The markers in the clip are also visible in the sequence.

The Overwrite button in the Canvas, like the Canvas Overwrite overlay, edits whatever is currently marked in the Viewer into the Timeline, overwriting any material at the position of the playhead.

> **NOTE** ► If after this step, you can't see the entire contents of your sequence in the Timeline, then click the Timeline and press Shift-Z. This command resizes the sequence so that the contents fit entirely in the window.

Simple Trimming in the Timeline

To drive the piece forward, let's time each edit to occur at four- or eight-beat increments of the music (one or two markers). You will use the "snapping" feature in Final Cut Pro to help you trim the first clip in your sequence so that it ends at the fourth beat of the music.

1   Click the right edge of the clip, and drag it to the left until it snaps to the first marker in the audio clip below.

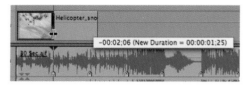

The clip now lasts for four beats of music.

Snapping is like a magnetization of elements in the Timeline. It helps you align clips to each other and to other elements such as markers.

2   Press the Up Arrow on the keyboard once, to bring the playhead to the last frame of the clip in the sequence.

Assembling the Rest of the Clips

Now you are ready to assemble other clips into the Timeline.

1   In the Browser, double-click the **Bungie_above** clip (the first clip in the Action Shots bin) to open it in the Viewer.

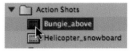

2   Drag the **Bungie_above** clip to the Canvas, and release the mouse over the Overwrite overlay.

The clip is edited into the sequence.

3   Click the Timeline, press Home, and press the Space bar to play back the sequence.

That looks good, but let's say you wanted to put another clip between these two. To do so, you'll need an Insert edit. An Inset edit inserts a clip into the Timeline at the current playhead position and moves any clips following the inserted clip further along the timeline.

Before you perform the insert edit, there's something you need to do. You have added a music audio track to your sequence, and since you don't want to split the audio while you perform an insert edit, you need to lock the audio tracks. Locking a track, whether it's video or audio, preserves the content of the track so that a clip cannot be moved or changed.

4   Click the lock icons, located in the track headers on the left, for audio tracks 1 and 2.

5   Use your Up and Down Arrow keys to get the playhead right between the two clips.

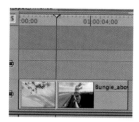

6 In the Browser, double-click the **Surfing_in_the_tube** clip to open it in the Viewer.

We'll need exactly 1 second and 25 frames of surfing clip to fit into four beats of music (for PAL 1 second and 21 frames).

> **NOTE** ▶ If you Control-click (or right-click for multibutton mice) on the first video clip in the sequence, you'll see it has a duration of 01:25 (for PAL 01:21), which lasts for four beats of our music. Control-clicking is an excellent way of learning the Final Cut Pro interface. The shortcut menu that pops up gives you all the options you have for an item you've clicked.

7 Navigate through the **Surfing_in_the_tube** clip and set an In point.

8   Click once in the Timecode Duration field in the upper left of the Viewer.

9   Type 0125 (for PAL 0121) and press Return.

An Out point is set exactly 1:25 (for PAL 1:21) after your In point.

10   Drag the clip from the Viewer to the yellow Insert section of the Edit Overlay in the Canvas.

Surfing_in_the_tube is inserted between the **Helicopter_snowboard** and **Bungie_above** clips. The **Bungie_above** clip moves further along to accommodate **Surfing_in_the_tube**.

11   Click the Timeline to activate it, and press the Down Arrow once to get the Timeline's playhead to the end of the last video clip.

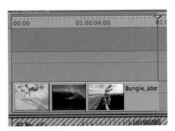

Storyboard Editing

Sometimes you'll want a more visual approach to assembling your clips. To achieve this, you can edit by arranging the clips by their icons. This is called Storyboard editing.

1   While pressing the Option key, double-click the Storyboard bin in the Browser.

The contents of the Storyboard bin opens and a tab for the bin is created in the Browser. Accessing the bin through this tab is a convenient way to save screen real estate.

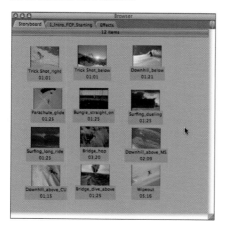

You are looking at these clips in medium icon view, instead of the list view that appears in the main tab of the Browser. This allows you to visually arrange the clips, in storyboard fashion, so you can assemble them into the sequence in the order they appear. When you select all of them and drag them to the Canvas, Final Cut Pro will assemble them as they are arranged, left to right, then row by row. You can arrange them in any order you wish, but if you want your edit to look like the final version, leave them as they are.

2   Select all the clips in this tab by pressing Command-A.

3   Drag one of the clips directly to the Edit Overlay area of the Canvas, hold the clip over the Overwrite overlay to select it, and release the mouse button.

All the storyboard clips are now assembled in the sequence.

4   Click the Timeline to activate it, press Home, and press the Space bar to play the sequence.

As you view the edited sequence, notice that the fourth, fifth, and sixth clips in the sequence don't quite relate to each other. You will need to make a few more refinements to smooth out your edited clips.

Trimming With the Roll Tool

First you will trim the edit point between then fourth and fifth clip to make the clips visually work in relation to each other.

1   Select the Roll tool from the Tool palette (the fourth one down).

The Roll tool will allow you to "roll" an edit point between two clips back and forth, making one of the clips longer, and the other shorter, by an equal number of frames. When using trimming tools such as the Roll tool, it's best to turn off the snapping feature that helped us during our assembly of the sequence.

2   Click the Snapping button in the upper right of the Timeline.

3   Press the mouse button on the edit point between the fourth and fifth clip in the sequence.

The edit point becomes highlighted.

The Canvas transforms to display the frames on either side of the edit point: the incoming and outgoing edit points.

4 Drag the mouse slightly to the left.

As you do, a yellow tooltip appears in the Timeline, indicating how many frames you've trimmed. Simultaneously, the Canvas updates to show you the new timecode for the incoming and outgoing edit points.

5 Try to roll the edit point to the left about 8 to 10 frames.

Notice that, in the Canvas, the skiers on either side of the edit point now appear in the same general area of the frame.

The clip on the left has become shorter, and the clip on the right longer.

6 Drag the playhead behind the edit point, and press L to play back the sequence.

The fourth clip flows nicely into the fifth, but we need something to emphasize the "woosh" sound in the music. Also, the direction of the skier in the sixth clip should be reversed to follow the flow of the fifth clip. Let's add a transition and a filter to make these enhancements.

Adding Transitions and Filters

Transitions help one clip flow into another and a transition is positioned on an edit point. Filters actually change the nature of the image of a clip, and they are placed directly onto a clip. The many transitions and filters in Final Cut Pro can be found in the Effects tab in the Browser, grouped into bins by type. You can save and customize transitions and filters and for this exercise, we have two saved in a bin called Transitions & Filters.

1 Click the 1_Intro_FCP_Starting tab, to return to the main contents of your project file.

2 Locate the Transitions & Filters bin.

One transition, called Edge Wipe, will create a soft wipe effect, and one filter, called Flop, reverses the image of a clip.

3 Drag the Edge Wipe transition to the edit point between the fourth and fifth clips in the sequence. Make sure to center it on the edit point.

The transition now appears between the two clips.

4 Drag the Flop filter directly over of the sixth clip in the sequence, release the mouse button once the clip is highlighted.

The filter has reversed the image, as if you were looking at the clip in a mirror.

5 Click the Timeline to activate it, press Home, and press the Space bar to play back the sequence.

NOTE ▶ Final Cut Pro has advanced RealTime playback capabilities, but the amount real time performance you experience will depend on the processing power of system you are running. If you see a "Warning – Dropped Frames" dialog you have a number of options, You can uncheck "Warn next time," click OK, and restart your playback, ignoring any dropped frames. You can Render your timeline by pressing Option-R. Or you can lower your RT Extreme settings to allow more real-time effects. To lower your RT Extreme settings from the RT pop-up menu in your Timeline, select the following settings: Unlimited RT; Playback Video Quality > Low; Playback Frame Rate > Dynamic.

The lower-third clip now appears in the second video track of the sequence.

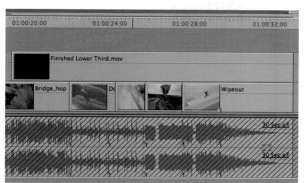

This clip was created in Motion. If you have Motion installed, you'll be able to create it in the Mastering Motion section of this tutorial book.

Next you will add a few cross dissolves to begin and end the spot. You'll use a handy contextual menu to add a default 1 second cross dissolve.

6 Control-click the left edit point of the first video clip in the sequence, and select Add Transition 'Cross Dissolve' from the shortcut menu.

7 Control-click on the right edit point of the **Wipeout** clip (the last in the sequence on video track 1), and select Add Transition 'Cross Dissolve' from the shortcut menu.

8   Control-click on the right edit point of the **Finished Lower Third.mov** clip, and select Add Transition 'Cross Dissolve' from the shortcut menu.

9   Press Home, and press the spacebar to play back your sequence.

Your edit is complete! This introductory exercise allowed you to work with video-only and audio-only clips. However most of the time, you will be working with synced material, that is, clips that have both audio and video together. In the next exercise you will begin to work with synced material.

Creating an A/B-Roll Interview Sequence

In this exercise, you'll learn some techniques typical of news package and documentary editing. To see what we're about to accomplish, take a look at the final sequence.

1   In the Browser, click the disclosure triangle next to the ELC Spot bin.

The bin closes, along with all of its contents.

2   Click the disclosure triangle next to the Shark Interview bin.

All of the elements for this next exercise appear, including a Sequences bin.

3 Double-click the 04_Shark_Interview_Finished sequence.

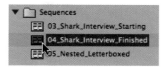

4 Press the Space bar to play the sequence.

The clips on video track 2 (V2) are called cover shots, or B-roll (an old news term referring to the second roll of film used to shoot additional items). They allow the editor to tell the story with images to which the speaker is referring. B-roll clips also cover the jump cuts between the sound bites of the speaker. Notice that when the playhead encounters the B-roll clips, they are shown in lieu of the interview clips beneath them.

The sound bites are on video track 1 (V1) and audio tracks 1 and 2 (A1 and A2). For each one, the video clip and two underlying audio clips all have the same name with an underline beneath the name. These are "synced material," or clips that have video and corresponding audio, grouped together. Synced clips are treated as a single clip.

5   Click one of the **Christy_Interview** clips in the Timeline.

The clips on all three tracks are highlighted.

Now let's take a look at synced material in the Viewer.

6   Double-click the **05_Christy_Interview** clip in the Browser.

The clip opens in the Viewer.

7   Press the Spacebar to play the clip.

Notice that there are two tabs in the Viewer, one for Video, named *Video*, and one for Audio, named *Stereo (a1a2)*. The name of the audio tab in the Viewer reflects the type of audio clip. In this case, the 05_Christy_ Interview clip has Stereo audio.

8   Click the Stereo (a1a2) tab at the top of the Viewer.

The waveforms of the audio are shown.

Let's begin by editing some synced interview clips into a sequence.

9 In the Browser, double-click the 03_Shark_Interview_Starting sequence to open it in the Timeline.

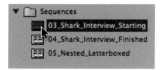

Note that the playhead is already in position for the next editing steps.

Marking Audio in the Viewer

First, we'll add two more short interview statements, from Christy to the sequence.

1 Click the Video tab in the Viewer.

2 Press I to set an In point just before Christy says the phrase "To me, it's like a once-in-a-lifetime. . ."

3 Press O to set an Out point just *after* she finishes by saying, ". . . it's very thrilling and exciting."

4   Click the Viewer's Play In to Out button to review the audio.

This button is very helpful especially for reviewing the material you've marked.

5   Drag the clip from the Viewer to the Overwrite section of the Canvas Edit overlay

The clip is edited into video track 1, and audio tracks 1 and 2.

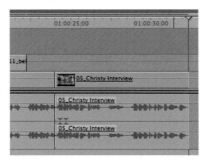

How does the clip manage to assemble itself into those specific tracks? Take a look at the track Source and Destination controls, on the left side of the Timeline.

Source controls

Destination controls

These controls work as a patch bay. When a clip is opened in the Viewer, the tracks of that clip show up as Source controls on the left, which can be patched to (or disconnected entirely from) the Destination controls, at right.

6   Click the Viewer to make it active.

7   Press I to set an In point just before Christy says, "I probably won't ever get the chance. . ."

8   Press O to set an Out point just after she says the word "...*scared*". Make sure to include the little exasperated sigh she utters right after, for dramatic effect.

9   Click the Play In to Out button on the Viewer to review the audio.

10 Click the Overwrite button on the Canvas to overwrite the clip into the sequence.

Trimming Out the "Air"
Next you will listen to how the interview audio sound clips sound in relation to each other.

1   Click the Timeline, and press Home.

2   Press the Space bar.

Concentrate on the audio as you will fix the visual jumps in the picture with B-roll later in the tutorial.

At the end of the sequence, during Christy's last sound bite, the pause between "even though I'm. . ." and "scared" is rather long.

3   Select the Razor Blade tool from the Tool palette (the sixth one down).

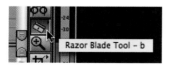

4 Move the razor blade into the Timeline over the center of the last clip.

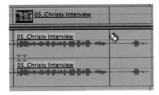

5 Using the audio waveforms as your guide, click once with the tool right *after* the phrase "even though I'm. . ."

TIP ▶ If you're having trouble seeing the audio waveform, you can zoom into the timeline. Press Command-= to zoom in and Command-- to zoom out

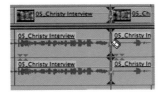

TIP ▶ If you're not familiar with the look of audio waveforms, move the playhead to the beginning of the last sound bite clip, play the sequence, and stop the playhead just after each phrase. Then, use the playhead line as a guide for where to click the Blade on the clip.

6 Click once more on the clip just before she says "scared."

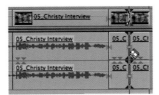

What you've done here is to create two new edit points within this clip, which now makes three clips. The small red triangles indicate that the frames before and after the edit point are contiguous. They are called *through edit indicators*. Now all we have to do is remove the center clip, which contains the pause.

7 Select the Selection tool from the Tool palette (the first one).

8 Select the 'pause' you spliced in the Timeline.

9 Press Shift, then press Delete.

The clip is cut, and the rest of the edited material ripples in to close the gap.

A ripple delete, implemented by pressing Shift-Delete, is a perfect command for removing pauses like this and allowing the rest of the material on the tracks to ripple in.

10 Press Home, and press the Space bar to listen to the audio again.

Now you can add some B-roll to cover all those jump cuts.

Adding in B-roll

In order to have the B-roll clips assemble into the correct track (V2), you'll first change the patching of your Source and Destination controls in the Timeline.

1   In the Timeline drag the v1 Source control to the V2 Destination control. Future video clips will now assemble to V2.

You'll add a few preparatory clips of Christy suiting up to cover your first jump cut. These clips have already been marked with In and Out points for you.

2   Press the Up Arrow to move the playhead to the edit point between **04_Christy_Interview** and the **05_Christy_Interview clip**.

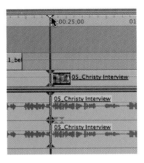

3   In the Browser, click the disclosure triangle next to the B-roll bin, to reveal the B-roll clips.

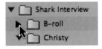

4   Starting just to the left of the **12_belt finished** clip, draw a box around clips 12, 13, and 14, to select them all.

5 Drag any one of these selected clips to the Overwrite section of the Canvas Edit overlay.

The three clips are edited into the sequence.

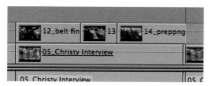

Multiple clips from a list are assembled in the order that they are sorted: in this case, alphanumerically.

6 In the Browser, drag the **15_C into water with sharks** clip into the Viewer.

7 Press I to set an In point a few moments before Christy jumps in the water.

8 Click once in the Timecode Duration field of the Viewer.

9   Type 225, (for PAL 218) and press Return.

You've set the duration at 2 seconds and 25 frames (for PAL, 2 seconds and 18 frames) for this B-roll shot, but you might not like the specific 2:25 section you've marked. Use the next step to "slip" through the material until you've found a section you like.

10   Press and hold the Shift key, drag one of the "ears" of either the In or Out points.

The space between the edit points stays consistent, and you are able to choose another portion of the clip. The Viewer is showing you the new In point of the clip, while the Canvas is showing you the Out point.

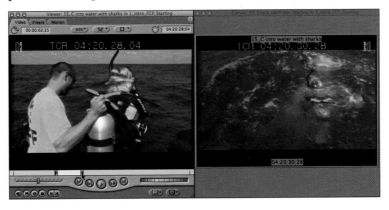

11   Release the mouse button when Christy is clearly still on the boat in the Viewer and well in the water in the Canvas.

12   Click the Play In to Out button in the Viewer to review the marked portion of the clip.

13 Drag the clip from the Viewer to the Timeline and snap the clip next to clip 14 on Video Track 2 (V2) in the Timeline and ensure the pointer has a downward arrow before you release the mouse.

Our last clip of B-roll will be used to cover the last jump cut.

14 In the Browser, double-click the **16_uw wide shark near Christy** clip to open it in the Viewer.

15 Press I to set an In point and press O to set an Out point make sure the duration of the clip is exactly 3:20 (for PAL 3:17).

16 Drag the clip from the Viewer to Video Track 2 (V2) in the Timeline. Make sure the clip covers the edit point between the last two sound bites and has enough material to end the piece as well. Remember not to release the mouse button until you see the arrow pointing down.

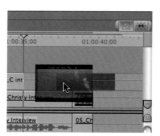

TIP You may need to turn your snapping off to avoid snapping the clip to the playhead or an edit point, which in this case is not what we want. Another way to turn snapping on and off is to simply press N at any time.

17 Press Home, and press the Space bar to play back the sequence.

Adding Some Finishing Touches

The relationship between the B-roll and the bites near the end of the sequence needs to be softened up a bit, so we'll add some cross dissolves, as we did in the previous exercise. This will transition the viewer from B-roll to Christy and back, and then finally to fade us to black.

1   Control-click the right edge of the **15** clip on Video Track 2, (V2), then choose Add Transition 'Cross Dissolve' from the shortcut menu.

2   Control-click on the left edge of the **16** clip on Video Track 2, (V2), then choose Add Transition 'Cross Dissolve' from the shortcut menu.

3   Control-click on the right edge of the **16** clip on Video Track 2, (V2), then choose Add Transition 'Cross Dissolve' from the shortcut menu.

4   Press Home, and press the Space bar to view the sequence.

Nesting Sequences

Next, you'll add a Widescreen filter to the sequence, adding black bars to the top and bottom of the frame, so we can mask out the timecode window burn-ins on the clips. This will allow us to export the sequence so we can show it to a client or other interested parties.

Instead of adding a filter to each clip, which would take a while, we're going to place this sequence inside another sequence, a process called *nesting*. When you nest a sequence, it's essentially like editing a clip. Then you apply a single Widescreen filter to the entire nested sequence.

The first step is to create a new sequence.

1   In the Browser, click the disclosure triangle next to the B-roll bin, to make some room.

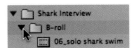

15 Click the Timeline to highlight it, press Home, and press the Space bar to view the finished sequence.

NOTE ▸ At this point, you may want to render the effects and transitions. Press Option-R to render all your effects in your currently active sequence.

Exporting a QuickTime File

Now you're ready to export a QuickTime file of your sequence, so you can copy it to another computer or use it for another application such as DVD Studio Pro or Motion.

1 Click on the Timeline to make it active then select File > Export > QuickTime Movie.

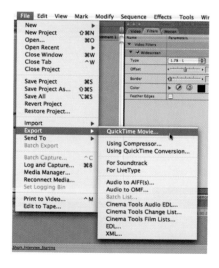

A dialog appears, asking for more information about the file you're about to export.

2 From the Where pop-up menu, choose Desktop.

3 Make sure the Make Movie Self-Contained box is checked.

Selecting this checkbox creates a QuickTime file that has all the video frames and audio samples from your original sequence in one file. If it were not checked, it would create a reference movie, which references other files on your computer to play back the movie. In general, reference movies are great for same-computer applications, and self-contained movies are perfect when you are taking the file elsewhere. For this exercise, we'll leave it self-contained.

4   Click Save.

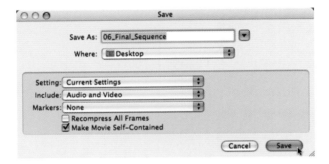

A dialog appears to show you how long it will take to make the QuickTime movie.

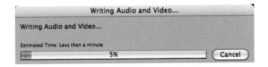

5   After the export is complete, press Command-H to hide Final Cut Pro.

You should see the **06_Final_Sequence** movie sitting on your desktop.

6 Double-click the file.

It reopens in Final Cut Pro, in its own Viewer.

7 Press the Space bar to view the sequence.

8 Close this extra Viewer by clicking its close button.

Project Tasks

Here are some additional exercises to further hone your editing skills.

Exporting the 30-Second Spot

In the Timeline, click back on your 01_Spot_Starting sequence, and use the steps above to export a self-contained QuickTime movie of that sequence.

A Custom Shark Dive Interview

Using all of your newly acquired skills in Final Cut Pro, try creating Christy's interview sequence from the beginning using a new sequence and all of the clips provided. You can tell quite a different story from the one you just did by rearranging the sound bites and B-roll, or perhaps even by substituting the music from the first exercise!

Congratulations! You've completed the Introducing_Final_Cut_Pro project and learned many Final Cut Pro skills, including marking clips, editing clips into a sequence using a host of techniques, trimming, and adding transitions and filters.

What's Next?

This Apple Pro Training tutorial was designed to teach you some fundamentals of working with Final Cut Pro as you edited the 30 Second Spot and A/B Roll Interview projects. You've learned a lot, but there is so much more to this software!

If you want to learn more, explore the interactive Apple Pro Training DVD tutorial (on the companion DVD) or go on to the next tutorial, Mastering Final Cut Pro, which uses some of the more advanced features of Final Cut Pro, such as variable speed effects, manipulating clip size and position using the Motion tab, color correction, and compositing.

For detailed information about specific features, refer to the Final Cut Pro documentation that comes with the application.

For more complete training, see page 302 for information about Apple certified training, Apple Authorized Training Centers, and the following self-paced Apple Pro Training books, which use the same project-based learning style as this tutorial:

- ▶ Apple Pro Training Series: Final Cut Pro 5
- ▶ Apple Pro Training Series: Advanced Editing Techniques in Final Cut Pro
- ▶ Apple *Pro Training Series: Advanced Color Correction and Effects in Final Cut Pro*
- ▶ Apple Pro Training Series: Optimizing Your Final Cut Pro System
- ▶ Apple Pro Training Series: Final Cut Pro for Avid Editors

2

Lesson Files	Apple_Pro_Training_Tutorials > Mastering_Final_Cut_Pro > 1_Mastering_FCP
Time	This lesson takes approximately 60 minutes to complete.
Goals	Create a multiclip
	Switch and cut multi-angle footage
	Animate clip opacity
	Work with time remapping
	Apply a color correction filter
	Modify a nested sequence
	Add volume overlay keyframes in the Timeline

Mastering Final Cut Pro

This is a self-paced, hands-on tutorial designed to guide you through some of Final Cut Pro's new features and more advanced techniques. Over the next hour you'll work with multiclips to create a multi-angle montage and a multi-camera edit. Then you'll use some some advanced effects techniques to animate opacity, change speeds, apply some basic color correction, modify a nested sequence, and composite images. You'll use all these techniques to build a promo for the show "Capturing the eXtreme" for the fictitious eXtreme Living Channel.

This tutorial builds from the skills that you learned in the Introducing FCP tutorial. If you are not familiar with the basic interface and editing features, complete the Introducing Final Cut Pro tutorial before you begin this project.

To learn more, explore the Apple Pro Training DVD tutorial (on the companion DVD). For more comprehensive training, see the About Apple Pro Training folder on this DVD for information on the self-paced *Apple Pro Training Series* books and the Apple Pro certified training program.

Preparing the Project

Before you start, you'll need to copy the applicable Apple Pro Training Tutorials folder from the DVD to your desktop. You'll be working with the **1_ Mastering_FCP** project located in the Mastering_Final_Cut_Pro tutorials folder. Take a moment to open and save the project.

1   Open the Mastering_Final_Cut_Pro tutorial folder.

   The Mastering_Final_Cut_Pro folder includes the project and a Media folder that contains the media that you'll use for the tutorial.

2   Double-click the project **1_ Mastering_FCP to open the project and Final Cut Pro**. If it requires rendering (you'll see a horizontal red line at the top of the Timeline), press Option-R to render the current sequence.

3   Choose File > Save Project As to open the Save As window.

4   Save the project to the My_Saved_Projects folder located in the Apple Pro Training Studio Tutorials folder on your desktop.

The Backup_Sequences folder in the Browser contains progressive versions of the project. If at any time you fall behind, or don't complete a step, you can open the appropriate backup project. Each backup project is numbered sequentially and named for the last completed task in the project.

Modifying the Browser

It's a good idea to familiarize yourself with the Browser so you'll know where to find the various clips and sequences that you'll be using throughout this tutorial.

All of the project elements have been sorted into bins to keep the Browser organized in list view. This is a good time to mention the new text-size feature included with Final Cut Pro 5. The text-size feature allows you to change the text size in the Browser and Timeline. This is especially useful if you are working with a large Apple Cinema display set to a high resolution.

1 In the Browser, Control-click the empty space in the Name column to open a shortcut menu.

2 From the shortcut menu, choose Text > Medium to change the size of the text in the Browser.

> **TIP** Shortcut menus, also called *contextual* menus, are a handy way to access common features and tasks while working in the interface. The menus change based on the context of where you Control-click the mouse. You can also open these menus by right-clicking on a two-button mouse.

The first sequence you'll work on is the 1 Multi Angle Montage Sharks sequence. The clips for that sequence are in the 1 Multi Angle Montage bin located at the top of the Browser. In list view, each bin has a disclosure triangle to show its contents. You can also open a selected bin by pressing the Right Arrow key.

3 Click the 1 Multi Angle Montage bin to select it in the Browser.

4 Press the Right Arrow key to view the contents of the bin.

> **TIP** The Right Arrow key opens a selected bin, and the Left Arrow key closes the bin. The Down Arrow key moves to the next bin in the list.

You can use a shortcut menu to show and hide columns in the Browser. One way to familiarize yourself with the clips in the Browser is to show the Thumbnail column.

To show or hide columns you can Control-click any column header except the Name column.

NOTE ▶ Final Cut Pro 5 includes new logging information and Browser columns for film projects, such as Film Slate, Camera Roll, Lab Roll, Key Number, Ink Number, and Daily Roll. You can also view the ruler at the top of the Timeline in Drop Frame, Feet+Frame, or Frames.

5   Control-click the Duration column header, then choose Show Thumbnail from the Show list.

The Thumbnail column appears in the Browser after the Name column.

By default, the thumbnail will show the first frame of a clip or the In point.

You can scrub through the content of a clip in its thumbnail by clicking the thumbnail and dragging the mouse.

6   Click the **Christy** clip's thumbnail and drag the mouse to the right until you see a close shot of Christy.

7   Press the Control key, then release the mouse button to set a new frame in the thumbnail.

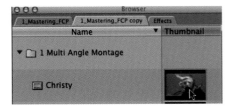

8 Repeat steps 6 and 7 to change the thumbnail frame for the **Dive_Master** clip.

9 Scrub the thumbnails for the other three clips to become familiar with the footage.

Next, you'll learn how to combine all five angles of the shark dive footage into a multiclip.

Working With Multiclips

Final Cut Pro 5 includes multiclip features that allow you to group up to 128 camera angle clips and switch or cut between them in real time. With multiclips you can edit synchronized footage from multicamera shoots, or you can group unsynchronized footage together for real-time montage editing.

In the next series of exercises you will create and edit two multiclips. First, you'll edit a multiple-angle montage with unsynchronized shark dive footage. Then you'll edit a multiclip of synchronized footage with audio from a televised hockey tournament. These projects represent real-world multiclip-editing techniques.

Creating a Multiclip

Whether the footage is synchronized or unrelated, each clip in a multiclip is known as an angle. The 1 Multi Angle Montage bin contains five clips that will become angles in the multiclip. These clips were taped on the same day but not at the same time, so they are unsynchronized footage. When you create a multiclip, all of the angles will be synchronized by timecode, In points, or Out points. For this exercise you'll synchronize the clips by In points. You'll start by selecting four of the five clips. You can add the fifth angle a little later.

1   In the Browser, select the first four clips in the 1 Multi Angle Montage bin.

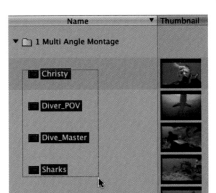

TIP You can select contiguous clips by pressing the mouse button as you drag it over the clips, or by selecting the first clip, then Shift-clicking the fourth clip.

2   Choose Modify > Make Multiclip to group the four selected clips into a multiclip.

The Make Multiclip window opens, listing all four clips.

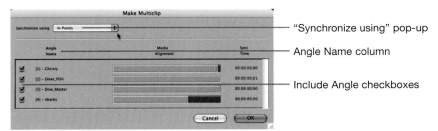

The light blue bars in the Media Alignment column show the relative alignment of each angle. Notice that the Sharks angle has a shorter blue bar that indicates that the clip is shorter in duration than the other clips.

At the top of the window is the "Synchronize using" pop-up menu, which you can use to determine how the clips will be synchronized, in this case by In points. You can click on an angle's Include Angle checkbox to deselect it if you don't want to include the angle in the multiclip.

Each clip is assigned a numbered angle in the order it appears in the Browser.

NOTE ▶ The same capture preset should be used for all footage you plan to make into a multiclip. You can also assign angle numbers to clips in the Log and Capture window, or in the Angle column of the Browser.

3   Click OK to create the multiclip.

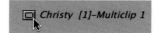

The multiclip appears in the Browser below the active angle. The multiclip name reflects the name of angle 1 because that is the active angle.

Playing a Multiclip in the Viewer

You can open a multiclip in the Viewer by double-clicking it, dragging it to the Viewer, or selecting the multiclip and pressing Return. Once you open the multiclip in the Viewer, you can choose view options from the View pop-up menu to see 1, 4, 9, or 16 angles simultaneously.

1   Double-click the multiclip in the Browser to open it in the Viewer.

All four angles of the multiclip appear in the Viewer with the active angle highlighted.

2   Press the Space bar or click the Play button in the Viewer transport controls to play the multiclip. Press the Space bar again to pause playback.

3   In the Viewer, click the lower-right angle to make it active.

The lower-right angle is highlighted, and the multiclip in the Browser changes from Christy [1] to Sharks [4], indicating that angle 4 is now the active angle.

You'll use this same technique to edit the multiclip a little later in the lesson.

Loading the Multiclip Shortcut Buttons

There are at least three means of doing virtually everything in Final Cut Pro: menus, keyboard shortcuts, and buttons. By default, most multiclip keyboard commands use the number pad with modifier keys to switch or cut between multiclip angles. Final Cut Pro 5 also includes convenient preinstalled keyboard layout and shortcut buttons for multiclip editing. Let's load shortcut buttons to use with the multiclip exercises in this tutorial.

1   Choose Tools > Button Bars > Multiclip.

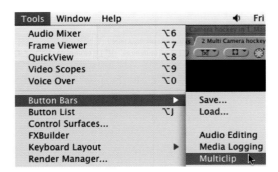

The preinstalled multiclip shortcut buttons appear in the Viewer, Canvas, Browser and Timeline button bars.

For this multiclip exercise you'll work with the four buttons on the far left of the Timeline button bar. These are the buttons for switching video angles.

TIP ▸ You can hover the mouse over any of the buttons in the button bar to see the help tag that tells what the button does and what the corresponding keyboard shortcut is.

2   Click the Switch Video to Angle 1 button (the far-left button in the Timeline button bar) to switch from angle 4 to angle 1.

NOTE ▸ The Viewer window must be active for the Switch Video to Angle buttons to switch active angles in the Viewer.

3   Click each of the three remaining numbered Switch Video to Angle buttons to switch to the corresponding active angle in the Viewer.

Next, you'll edit the multiclip into the Timeline. To edit the multiclip into the Timeline you can simply Option-drag it to the Canvas Edit Overlay and choose an editing mode, drag it to the Timeline, or click an edit button on the Canvas.

4   Click the Overwrite button on the lower-left corner of the Canvas to overwrite the multiclip to the Timeline.

Once the multiclip is in the Timeline you can view, switch, or cut the active angle in the Canvas in real time.

Choosing Real-Time Playback Options

It's a good idea to check your Real Time Effects (RT) settings to maximize the real-time performance of your system. Final Cut Pro 5 includes a new Dynamic real-time setting for playback video quality and playback frame rate. The Dynamic settings change the quality or playback frame rate as needed for maximum real-time playback. The RT pop-up menu also includes a Multiclip Playback setting that allows you to switch and edit multiclips in the Timeline.

1 Click to Open the RT pop-up menu at the upper left of the Timeline.

2 From the RT pop-up menu, select Unlimited RT, Dynamic Playback Video Quality, Dynamic Playback Frame Rate, and Multiclip Playback if they aren't already selected.

Switching Angles During Timeline Playback

Switching active angles during playback allows you to change active angles as the multiclip plays without making a cut in the multiclip. You can switch angles from either the Viewer or the Timeline. If you choose the Open playhead sync option you'll be able to see all the angles play in the Viewer while you switch the active angle in the Timeline.

1 Double-click the multiclip in the Timeline to reopen it in the Viewer.

The playhead sync can be changed to Open by choosing Open in the Playhead Sync pop-up menu, or by clicking the Playhead Sync Open button in the Viewer button bar.

2 Click the Playhead Sync Open button on the Viewer button bar.

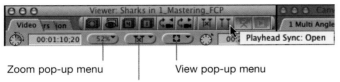

You can switch angles in the Timeline by Control-clicking the multiclip and choosing a different angle from the shortcut menu, pressing Shift and the number of the corresponding angle on the numeric keypad, or clicking the Switch Video to Angle buttons on the button bar.

3 Click the empty space above the multiclip in the Timeline to deselect the clip and make the Timeline window active.

The Open sync mode won't work if the multiclip is selected in the Timeline.

4 Press the Home key to move the playhead to the beginning of the Timeline if it's not already in position.

5 Press the Space bar to begin playback.

6 Click the Switch Video to Angle 1 button to switch the active angle to Christy [1].

NOTE ▶ If your computer keyboard includes a numeric keypad, feel free to use the Shift-1 keyboard shortcut to switch to angle 1. You can continue to use the Shift key plus the numeric keypad number to switch angles for the remainder of this switching exercise.

7   Click each of the four Switch Video to Angle buttons to switch active angles during playback.

NOTE ▶ Temporary blue markers appear in the Timeline ruler to indicate each new active angle. These will disappear once you finish your switch.

8   Continue switching between angles until the playhead stops at the end of the multiclip.

TIP ▶ Watch the angles in the Viewer to find a good shot before you switch to that angle.

9   Press the Home key, then Shift–Right Arrow to move the playhead 1 second from the beginning of the Timeline.

Adding an Angle to the Multiclip

You can insert, overwrite, and rearrange multiclip angles in the Viewer. In this exercise you'll insert the **Shark_solos** clip in the multiclip. Then you'll explore some of the additional multiclip features in the Viewer. To insert an angle, you drag the clip to the Viewer and continue pressing the mouse button until you see the Insert New Angle and Overwrite Angle overlays. Once the overlays appear, you can choose to either insert a new angle or overwrite the current angle.

1   From the Browser, drag the **Shark_solos** clip to the Viewer and press the mouse button until you see the Insert New Angle and Overwrite Angle overlays.

2   Choose Insert New Angle.

The Shark_solos angle is inserted into the multiclip.

At the moment you can only view four of the five angles at one time in the Viewer. To see the fifth angle, you'll need to move the mouse pointer over the viewer and click the downward-pointing arrow on the lower right of the Viewer.

3   Click the arrow to see the fifth angle in the multiclip.

4   Click the upward-pointing arrow at the upper right of the Viewer to return to the previous angles.

How do you know which angles are which in the Viewer? Good question. One option is to turn on the multiclip overlays from the View pop-up menu, or simply click the Show Multiclip Overlays button on the Viewer button bar.

5   Choose Show Multiclip Overlays from the View pop-up menu.

The angle number, name, and timecode for each angle appear in the Viewer.

The View pop-up menu also allows you to change the number of angles that you can view simultaneously in the Viewer.

6   Choose Multiclip 9-Up from the View pop-up menu to change the Viewer to the 9-up view.

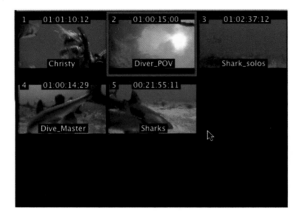

The Viewer changes to show up to nine angles simultaneously in real time.

NOTE ▶ You can include up to 128 angles in a multiclip, but you can see a maximum of 16 angles simultaneously in the Viewer.

You can rearrange angles by Command-dragging an angle in the Viewer to a different position.

7   Command-drag the Diver_POV angle to the Angle [5] position in the Viewer.

The other angles shift positions and angle numbers to accommodate the move.

Now that you've added an angle, you'll also need to add a button to Switch Video to Angle 5.

8   Choose Tools > Button List to open the Button List window.

The Button List window includes hundreds of preinstalled buttons that you can insert on the button bars.

9 Type *switch video to* (all lower case) in the Button List search field.

A list of all the "Switch Video to" buttons appears.

10 Drag the Switch Video to Angle 5 button from the Button List window to the Timeline button bar, and place it after the Switch to Angle 4 button.

11 Close the Button List window.

12 Click the new Switch to Angle 5 button on the button bar to switch to that angle.

> **TIP** It's a good idea to put the most important angle in the Angle [1] position to make it easy to find and switch to using the keyboard shortcut or button. Since Christy is the main focus of the story, her angle should be in the [1] position.

Cutting Multiclips During Playback

Next, you'll cut the multiclip as it plays in the Timeline. To cut the multiclip you simply click the angle in the Viewer that you wish to cut to. You can also use the Cut Video to Angle buttons in the Button List window.

A temporary blue marker appears in the Timeline at each new angle cut point. Once you finish playback, the cuts appear in the multiclip.

1 Choose Open from the Playhead Sync pop-up menu on the Viewer.

2 Click the Shark_solos angle in the Viewer to make that the active angle.

> **TIP** ▶ While playback is paused, click the first angle on the Viewer that you'd like to use. That way your multiclip will already be set to the first angle before you begin playback and cutting.

3   Click the Timeline window to make it active, then move the playhead to the beginning of the Timeline.

4   Deselect the multiclip in the Timeline if it is selected.

5   Press the Space bar to begin playback.

6   Click different angles in the Viewer as the playhead moves to cut the scene.

     Hint: The Dive_Master angle includes a great biting close-up toward the beginning of the scene.

7   Pause playback once you've finished cutting the multiclip scene.

The multiclip in the Timeline shows cuts that correspond with each time you changed the active angle during playback.

8   Play the multiclip from the beginning and watch your edit in the Canvas.

     Don't worry if it's not perfect; you can always undo (Command-Z) the edit and try again, or change the cuts or angles that you don't like.

     To change an angle, double-click the part of the edited multiclip that you wish to change to open it in the Viewer, then click a different angle. Or, you can Control-click the clip and choosing a new active angle from the shortcut menu.

Congratulations! You just edited a multiclip montage with five angles. Next, you'll create a multiclip using four camera angles including audio from a multiple-camera shoot.

Working With Multicamera Footage

In this exercise you'll be cutting four camera angles all shot at the same time with matching timecode and audio.

1   Click the 2 Multi Camera hockey tab at the top of the Timeline to view that sequence.

2   On the Browser, close the Multi-Angle Montage bin.

3   Locate the 2 Multi-Camera footage bin on the Browser.

You can create multiclips from selected clips in the Browser or from an entire bin of clips. For this exercise you'll create a multiclip from the 2 Multi-Camera footage bin.

4   Control-click the 2 Multi-Camera footage bin and choose Make Multiclip from the shortcut menu.

The Make Multiclip window opens.

Notice that this time the clips are identical in length. Since they were shot using synchronized timecode, let's change the "Synchronize using" pop-up menu to Timecode.

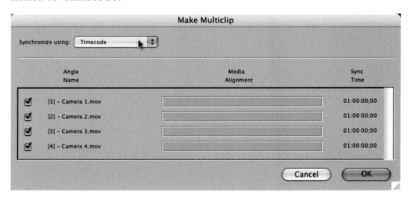

5   Click OK to create the multiclip.

6   On the Browser, open the Multi-Camera clips bin and locate the new multiclip.

NOTE ▶ Multiclips are numbered in the order that they are created within a project.

7   Double-click the new multiclip in the Browser to open it in the Viewer.

Since this multiclip contains only four angles, you can change the Viewer back to the multiclip 4-up view.

8   Choose Multiclip 4-Up view from the View pop-up menu.

The Viewer changes to the multiclip 4-up view. While you are at the View pop-up menu, you might as well turn off the Show Multiclip Overlays feature, since the overlays on these clips don't offer any useful information.

9   Deselect Show Multiclip Overlays on the View pop-up menu.

10   Click the Play button in the Viewer to watch the multiclip and hear the audio.

Angles 1, 2, and 4 have audio that was recorded at the same time, but from different camera locations.

If you cut between the camera angles and the different audio tracks you'll hear the abrupt changes in audio with each cut. Instead, you can choose the best audio track and use that for the entire scene.

Angle 4 is only sound of the cheering crowd, so that's not a good option for the commentary.

11 Click the Camera 1 angle to make it active, and play to listen to the audio.

12 Click the Camera 2 angle to make it active, and play to listen to the audio.

Camera 2 has appropriate audio, so it's a good choice for this scene.

Choosing Active Video and Audio

Once a multiclip has been created, you can choose whether to switch or cut audio and video, video only, or audio only.

1 Click the Camera 2 angle to make it the active angle if it is not already active.

NOTE ▶ The active video angle is highlighted with blue and the active audio angle is highlighted in green

2 Click the Playhead Sync pop-up menu to see the active audio and video options.

If Video + Audio is selected, you will change both elements whenever you change to a new active angle. If you select Video, only the video will change with the active angle.

4 Choose Video from the Playhead Sync pop-up menu.

NOTE ▶ You can also change the active angle by selecting a different angle from the bottom of the View pop-up menu.

Switching Multicamera Footage

Next you'll practice switching the angles, and then cut the scene. First, you'll need to edit the multiclip to the Timeline and set the playhead sync.

1 Click the Overwrite button on the Canvas to edit the multiclip to the Canvas.

2 Click the Timeline to make it active, and press Shift-Z to fit the multiclip to the Timeline window.

3 Double-click the multiclip in the Canvas to open it in the Viewer, then deselect the multiclip in the Timeline if it is selected.

4 Choose Open from the Playhead Sync pop-up menu on the Viewer.

5 Play the multiclip in the Timeline and switch between angles using Switch to Video Angle buttons.

> **TIP** ▶ Most sports are tricky to shoot and even harder to edit because everything happens so fast, and it's easy to switch to the wrong camera at the wrong time. Fortunately, this is a taped event rather than a live one, so you have the ability to stop and try again.

Cutting Multicamera Footage

Once you've practiced switching the scene, you can try cutting it. Remember, to cut the footage you click the angle of choice in the Viewer.

1 Make sure that the multiclip is deselected in the Timeline, and the Playhead Sync pop-up menu in the Viewer is set to Open.

2 Click the Timeline window to make it active if it isn't already.

3 Play the multiclip in the Timeline and click the different active video angles in the Viewer to cut the scene.

You can change any angle in the edited multiclip by double-clicking the part you want to change and selecting another angle. You can also change the timing of an edit with the Roll tool.

4   Double-click any edited angle within the multiclip in the Timeline to open it in the Viewer.

5   Click a different angle in the Viewer to change the active angle of the selected clip.

    NOTE ▶ If you see two red arrows pointing to each other on the edit point, that indicates a through edit, which means the clip to the left and right of the edit are from the same clip without any frames missing in between.

6   Press R to change from the Selection tool to the Roll tool.

    The Roll tool allows you to roll (move) an edit point between two clips to a different frame in the Timeline.

7   Click the Roll tool on any edit point (cut) within the multiclip.

8   Drag the edit point left or right to change where the edit occurs in time between the outgoing and incoming clips.

    The Roll tool can be very useful for syncing an edit point to music or action. With sports footage such as this, it's also useful to roll an edit forward or backward in the Timeline in case you cut too early or too late between angles.

9   Press A to return to the Selection (Arrow) tool.

    TIP ▶ You can also roll an edit point by clicking it with the Selection tool (A) and pressing], the right bracket key, to move the edit one frame to the right, or [, the left bracket key, to move the edit one frame to the left.

Collapsing and Expanding a Multiclip

As you can see, it's very easy to switch angles in a multiclip. To prevent accidentally switching angles by mistake, you can collapse the edited multiclip. This feature is also useful if others will be working with the sequence for color correction or effects and they want to focus only on the selected angles. Collapsing multiclips will also improve the performance of your computer. You can collapse or expand a multiclip as often as you'd like, even if you save and reopen the project.

To collapse a multiclip active angle, or an entire multiclip sequence, you select the items you wish to collapse, then Control-click and choose Collapse Multiclip(s) from the shortcut menu. To expand a collapsed multiclip, you Control-click the multiclip and choose Expand Multiclip(s) from the shortcut menu.

Advancing the Project

That concludes the multiclip portion of the Mastering Final Cut Pro tutorial. Before you continue, it's a good idea to close the previous sequences and remove the multiclip buttons from the Timeline button bar.

1   Control-click any button on the Timeline button bar and choose Remove > All / Restore Default from the shortcut menu.

2   Repeat step 1 with the buttons on the Canvas and Viewer windows and choose Remove > All from the shortcut menus.

1   Control-click the 2 Multi Camera hockey tab on the Timeline and choose Close Tab from the shortcut menu.

2   Repeat step 1 to close the 1 Multi Angle Montage Sharks tab.

When you close all of the sequences in the Timeline, you also close the Timeline window. To reopen the Timeline window, all you need to do is open another sequence.

3   On the Browser, scroll down to the 3 Sequences bin and click the disclosure triangle to view the contents.

4   Double-click the sequences numbered 3, 4, and 5 to open, respectively, the Starting, Mix, and Finished versions of the project in the Timeline.

5   Press Shift-Command-S to open the Save As window, and save your project to the My_Saved_Projects folder located in the Apple Pro Training Tutorials folder on your desktop.

Working With Advanced Final Cut Pro Features

In this part of the tutorial, you'll work with some of Final Cut Pro's advanced features, including opacity keyframes, time remapping, color correction, nested sequences, and audio mixing. First you'll take a look at the 5 Mastering Features Finished sequence in the Timeline to see the finished project.

1   Click the 5 Mastering Features Finished tab on the Timeline and play the finished sequence. (If you get a dropped frames alert, click Okay.)

Now that you've seen the finished sequence, you'll switch to the 3 Mastering Features Starting sequence and modify the clips in the Timeline to recreate and analyze some of the visual effects.

2   Click the 3 Mastering Features Starting tab at the top of the Timeline.

Notice that the 3 Mastering Features Starting sequence includes four video tracks and two audio tracks. You'll focus on the first part of the sequence for the next series of exercises, so it's a good idea to zoom in to the Timeline for a better view of the first third of the Timeline.

3   Press Home to move the playhead to the beginning of the Timeline.

4 Press Command-= two times to zoom in to The timeline by two levels.

You can also zoom out of the Timeline if needed by pressing Command- -(hyphen).

Animating Opacity in the Timeline

You can animate the opacity of a clip in the Motion tab of the Viewer or directly in the Timeline using clip overlays and the Pen tool. In this exercise you'll turn on clip overlays to see the opacity levels for the clips, then add and change opacity keyframes to create a customized transition from the clip on V1 to the clip on V2.

1 Press Option-W to turn on the clip overlays in the Timeline.

The black line at the top of each clip is the overlay that represents the clip opacity.

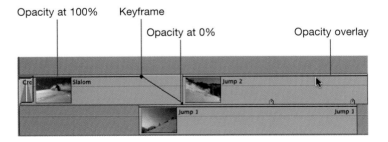

When the clip overlay is at the top of the clip, the clip is at 100 percent opacity with no transparency. If the overlay is at the bottom of the clip, the opacity level is 0 percent, which means the clip is fully transparent.

Your goal in this exercise is to animate the opacity for the second clip on V2 so that it fades up from 0 percent opacity to 50 percent and holds at 50 percent for 1 second, then fades up fully to 100 percent.

2   Move the playhead in the Timeline until it is over the second clip on track V2.

3   Press A to choose the Selection tool if its not already selected.

4   Drag the opacity overlay on the clip to change the opacity to 0 percent.

A small yellow help tag shows the current opacity value as you drag the overlay.

You can adjust the clip's opacity parameter over time by using the Pen tool to add two or more opacity keyframes in the different values. A keyframe lets you specify a parameter's value at a particular moment in time.

5   Press the Up Arrow to move the playhead to the first frame of the clip if it is not already on the first frame.

6   Press P to choose the Pen tool from the Tool palette.

7   Click the Pen tool once on the overlay toward the beginning of the clip to set a keyframe.

> **TIP** If you add a keyframe too close to the edge of the clip, it will be hard to select the keyframe later. Leave yourself a little wiggle room and click the keyframe near the beginning of the clip, without placing it exactly on the edge.

8   Press Shift–Right Arrow to move the playhead 1 second to the right.

9   Click the Pen tool on the overlay at the playhead position.

10 Drag the new keyframe upward to around the middle of the clip to change its value to about 50 percent opacity.

TIP If press the Command key while you drag the opacity keyframe on the overlay you'll be able to move it with finer incremental precision.

Notice that in the Canvas at 50 percent opacity you can see both the clip on V2, and the clip on V1 below.

11 Press Shift–Right Arrow once to move the playhead 1 second to the right.

12 Click the Pen tool on the Opacity overlay at the playhead position to set another keyframe at 50 percent.

13 Press Shift–Right Arrow one more time to move another second to the right.

14 Add an opacity keyframe at the playhead position, then drag it to the top of the clip (100 percent opacity).

15 Press the Home key to move the playhead to the beginning of the Timeline.

16 Play the beginning of the Timeline to view the animated opacity in the Canvas.

17 Press Option-W or click the Clip Overlays button to turn off clip overlays.

As you can see it's quite easy to animate a clip's opacity in the Timeline to create a custom dissolve from one track to another. The **Jump 1** clip on track V1 and the **Jump 2** clip on track V2 work well together. However, they will look even better if you reduce the speed of the **Jump 2** clip.

Modifying Clip Speed

Final Cut Pro includes both constant speed and variable speed features that enable you to change and view the speed of a clip in real time. In the next series of exercises you'll apply both types of speed changes to the **Jump 2** clip. Your goal is to first change the overall constant speed to 85 percent to slow down the action of the entire clip. Then you'll use the Time Remap tool to add variable speed changes to part of the clip.

> **NOTE ▶** Constant speed changes affect both audio and video, while variable speed changes affect only video.

You can modify a clip's constant speed by selecting the clip, then pressing Command-J, or Control-clicking the clip and choosing Speed from the shortcut menu.

1 Select the **Jump 2** clip in the Timeline.

2 Press Command-J to open the Speed window for the selected clip.

In the Speed window you can change the clip's speed using either the Duration field or Speed percent field. You can also reverse a clip by selecting the Reverse checkbox.

3 Type *85* in the Speed percent field, then click OK or press Return to change the clip's speed to 85 percent.

The **Jump 2** clip in the Timeline extends to accommodate the longer duration due to the reduced speed. The clip's speed is shown in parenthesis next to its name.

NOTE ▶ When a sequence clip changes duration because of a speed change, that affects the relative position of other clips in the Timeline. You can also change the constant speed of a clip in the Browser before you edit it to the Timeline.

4 Play the **Jump 2** clip in the Timeline to see how it looks at a constant speed of 85 percent.

Next, you'll create a variable speed change using the Time Remap tool. Time remapping allows you to make variable speed changes in a clip by moving a frame to another time in the clip. As you change a frame's position in time, it affects all of the other frames accordingly without changing the duration of the clip.

In this part of the exercise you'll use time remapping to slow part of the clip to 50 percent to make the skier hang in the air as he jumps for dramatic effect. The end of the clip when the skier lands will become faster to accommodate the remaining frames within the clip. The whole process may sound complicated, but the Time Remap tool makes it simple.

The **Jump 2** sequence clip includes two markers for you to use as a guide for using the Time Remap tool.

5 Press S three times to choose the Time Remap tool from the Tool palette. The Time Remap tool looks like a clock and is located in the center of the Tool palette along with the Slip and Slide tools.

6   Move the Time Remap tool over the **Jump 2** clip at the first marker in
    the clip.

When you click the Time Remap tool on a clip, you set a keyframe for that
specific frame at that specific position in the Timeline. If you continue
pressing the Time Remap tool you will see a help tag that shows the variable speed to the left and right of the selected frame.

7   Press the Time Remap tool on the clip at the first marker to set a keyframe
    and see the current clip time.

The help tag shows that the clip's speed to the left and right of the keyframe
is 85 percent. Do not change the time at this point. Only set the keyframe.

8   Click the Time Remap tool on the second marker on the clip and hold.

The help tag shows that the current speed is 85 percent on the right and
left of the clip.

NOTE ► If you changed the time to the right of the first time keyframe
your speed will not be exactly 85 percent.

9   Once the help tag appears, drag the mouse to the left to change the speed to the left of the current frame to around 50 percent. The speed to the right will increase accordingly.

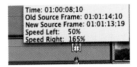

The clip will now start at 85 percent, then play at 50 percent between the two markers, then speed up at the end. When you're finished with the Time Remap tool, it's a good idea to change back to the Selection tool so that you don't accidentally remap time on any other clips.

10   Press A to return to the Selection tool.

11   Play the clip in the Timeline to see how the time remapping effect looks.

The skier jumps at 85 percent speed, hangs in the air at 50 percent speed then speeds up as he lands. The overall effect adds a little extra drama to the scene and fits well with the rest of the promo.

Working With the Color Corrector 3-Way Filter

Color correction can be applied to clips in the Timeline to balance or enhance the overall look of a scene. The Color Corrector 3-way filter gives you control of the color, midtones, blacks, and whites, as well as the saturation of a clip. In the next series of exercises you'll use the Color Corrector 3-way filter to white balance a clip. Then you'll apply two preset Color Corrector 3-way filters to demonstrate color tint and limited color effects.

The three clips you'll apply filters to are in the middle of the sequence in the Timeline and identified by sequence markers. You can move the playhead forward to a sequence marker by pressing Shift-M. Option-M moves the playhead to the previous marker.

1   Press Shift-M to move forward in the Timeline to the first marker.

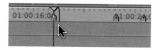

The playhead moves to the white balance marker. The Timeline marker and marker's name can also be seen in the Canvas.

The first clip is called Snowboard and Chopper Shadow and is located at the marker position on video track V1.

2   Locate the **Snowboard and Chopper Shadow** clip and select it in the Timeline.

Applying the Color Corrector 3-Way Filter

There are many methods for applying a filter to a sequence clip. One of the easiest ways is to select the clip, then choose the filter from the Effects > Video Filters menu.

1   Choose Effects > Video Filters > Color Correction > Color Corrector 3-way to apply the filter to the selected clip in the Timeline.

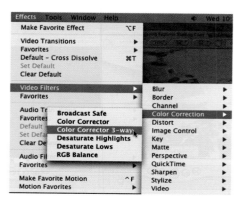

2   Double-click the **Snowboard and Chopper Shadow** clip in the Timeline to open it in the Viewer.

3   Click the Color Corrector 3-way tab at the top of the Viewer to show the graphical controls for the filter.

If you look at the image in the Canvas, you'll notice that the snow—which dominates the scene—has a bluish-gray tint. The bluish look is especially noticeable in the shadow of the helicopter. Snow is generally supposed to be white, so when it appears any other color there must be a reason. Perhaps it was natural lighting; perhaps the camera wasn't white balanced. Many things can alter the color of an image, and fortunately, there is one filter that can fix it.

White balancing an image with the Color Corrector 3-way filter is as easy as clicking the Whites Select Auto-balance Color button, then selecting a sample of white from the clip in the Canvas. The filter automatically adjusts the whites within the image so that the selected color is white.

4   Click the Whites Select Auto-balance Color button (the eyedropper) on the Color Corrector 3-way tab.

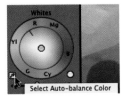

5   On the Canvas, click the white in the footsteps to auto-balance the white for the entire clip.

The color white in the scene become subtley less blue and the Whites Balance control has automatically shifted toward the reds to remove some of the bluish tint.

TIP ▶ When you sample a white value in the image, try to select a portion of the image that you think should be 100% white. Avoid shaded areas, hightlights, and areas with too much detail.

If you'd like to compare the clip before and after the color correction, you can use the Frame Viewer from the Tools menu.

6   Choose Tools > Frame Viewer to open the Tool Bench window with Frame Viewer.

The Tool Bench window appears above the Viewer window.

7   Change the pop-up menus at the bottom of the Frame Viewer to Current Frame, and Current w/o Filters.

If you look carefully you can see the difference between the image before and after the auto-balanced white in the Frame Viewer.

The Color Corrector 3-way filter can also be used to add a color tint to a clip, or remove all colors but one.

9 Press Shift-M to move the playhead to the next marker.

The clip on track V2 has the Color Corrector 3-way filter applied, but the effect has been limited so that the only color that appears is red. The rest of the colors have been romoved (desaturated) using the Limit Effect parameters of the Color Corrector 3-way filter.

You can double-click the clip to open it in the Viewer to analyze the filter settings.

10 Press Shift-M to move the playhead to the third Sequence marker.

The Color Corrector 3-way filter was applied to this image to add a light blue tint to the sky and surrounding snow.

11 Close the Tool Bench window.

As you can see, the Color Corrector 3-way filter is a powerful and versatile tool. Final Cut Pro includes Video Scopes in the Tool Bench window for precision color correction and image evaluation.

Working With a Nested Sequence

Sequences can be placed within other sequences, and then edited in the same way as clips. These are called nested sequences. Nested sequences allow you to apply filters, transitions, and effects to the nest rather than to individual clips.

You can create a nested sequence two ways: by selecting a group of clips within a sequence and then choosing Sequence > Nest Items, or by dragging an existing sequence from the Browser into the current sequence in the Timeline. In this exercise, you'll work with an existing nested sequence and change its background.

1 Move the playhead over the 4x4 Nest nested sequence in the Timeline.

The 4x4 Nest is a sequence with four video tracks and a solid background. Each of the video clips was scaled and cropped in the Motion tab of the Viewer.

NOTE ▶ Final Cut Pro 5 comes with improved scaling and motion algorithms for better-looking motion effects. You can also choose from three render qualities: Fastest, Normal, and Best. Earlier versions of Final Cut Pro were limited to the Fastest option.

2 Double-click the 4x4 Nest nested sequence in the Timeline to open the parent sequence.

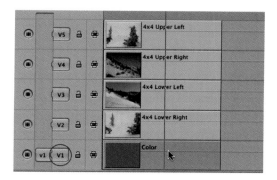

Any changes that you make to the 4x4 nest sequence will automatically update in the nested sequence within the project.

Let's change the solid blue background to a more exciting motion background created in Apple's Motion application. Motion and Final Cut Pro are fully integrated so that you can send a clip or group of clips to Motion to make changes. You can also bring a Motion project directly into a Final Cut Pro sequence.

3 Press the Home key to move the playhead to the beginning of the Timeline. Click the destination track V1 if it is not already selected.

4 On the Browser, open the Motion Projects and Clips bin and double-click the **BG from Motion.mov** file to open it in the Viewer.

7 Move the Pen tool to the right about 2 seconds and add a second keyframe.

8 Drag the second keyframe downward to lower it to −12 dB.

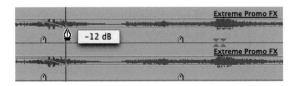

The help tag will indicate the new value of the keyframe as you drag it. Press the Command key for more refined incremental movement as you drag the keyframe.

Next you'll raise the volume level at the second marker to enhance the skier's landing at the end.

9 Add two more keyframes to the volume overlay, one at the second marker, and another placed one second after the marker.

10 Add two keyframes at the end and drag the last keyframe all the way to the lowest position to fade out the audio. You can use the keyframes at the end of the Extreme Promo Music clip as a guide to fade out the Extreme Promo FX track.

11 Play the ending of the project in the Timeline to hear the changes to the Volume levels.

You can also record keyframe automation in the timeline with the Audio Mixer. which is available from the Tools menu. Final Cut Pro 5 also allows you to audio level and pan settings using a supported Mackie or Logic control surface. Feel free to continue finessing the volume level overlays and don't forget to experiment with some of the color correction filters and effects in the project.

Learning More About Final Cut Pro

This Apple Pro Training tutorial includes only a sample of the features, tools, and techniques that Final Cut Pro has to offer. For detailed information about specific features, refer to the Final Cut Pro documentation that comes with the program, and explore the Apple Pro Training DVD tutorial (on the companion DVD).

To learn more, see page 302 for information on Apple certified training and the self-paced Apple Pro Training books, which use the same project-based learning style as this tutorial:

▶ *Apple Pro Training Series: Final Cut Pro 5*

▶ *Apple Pro Training Series: Advanced Editing Techniques in Final Cut Pro*

▶ *Apple Pro Training Series: Advanced Color Correction and Effects in Final Cut Pro*

▶ *Apple Pro Training Series: Optimizing Your Final Cut Pro System*

▶ *Apple Pro Training Series: Final Cut Pro for Avid Editors*

3

Lesson Files

Time

This lesson takes approximately 60 minutes to complete.

Goals

Begin a Motion project

Explore the Motion interface

Import a video clip to the project

Apply filters to the video file

Work with the Dashboard

Create text in the Canvas

Animate text with behaviors

Explore the Library

Apply particles to the project

Export the finished movie

Lesson 3
Introducing Motion

Welcome to the Apple Pro Training Motion tutorial. This step-by-step lesson will guide you through the process of creating a Motion project from start to finish. Over the next 60 minutes, you'll work with some of Motion's most exciting features, including filters, behaviors, and particles, as you build a ten-second promo for the fictitious eXtreme Living Channel.

If you want to learn more, check out the interactive Apple Pro Training DVD tutorial on the companion DVD, and the PDF Mastering Motion tutorial on this disk. See the About Apple Pro Training folder on this DVD for information on the self-paced *Apple Pro Training Series* books and the Apple Pro certified training program.

Preparing the Project

Before you start, you'll need to install the Motion software and content on your hard disk. You also need to drag the applicable Apple Pro Training Tutorial folder from the DVD to your computer's desktop.

NOTE ▸ Choose either the Apple Pro Training Tutorials NTSC folder (North America), or Apple Pro Training Tutorials PAL folder (Europe and some parts of Asia), depending on which broadcast standard you'll be using.

Once you have the Motion application and Apple Pro Training Tutorials Folder loaded on your computer, you're ready to begin this lesson.

MORE INFO ▸ You can find more specific installation instructions on the Read Me file included on the Apple Pro Tutorials DVD.

Opening Motion

There are three ways to open Motion:

▸ Double-click the Motion application icon on your hard disk.

▸ Click once on the Motion icon in the Dock (if you've placed it there).

▸ Double-click any Motion project file.

For this exercise, you'll open Motion by opening a project file.

1   Locate the Apple Pro Training Tutorials folder on your computer's desktop. Double-click the folder to open it.

The folder opens to reveal the Apple Pro Training Final Cut Studio tutorials.

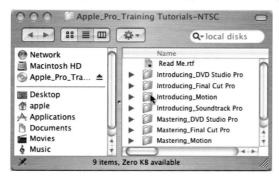

2   Open the Introducing_Motion folder.

3   Double-click the **1_Intro_Motion Starting file** to open Motion and open the project.

When Motion opens, you will see two windows displaying the project **1_Intro_Motion Starting**.

The long window at the left is the Utility window. The Utility window helps you organize and modify your project's elements. The larger window at the right is the Canvas, which is where you create and preview your project.

Let's start with the Utility window, since that is where you find and modify the content and media that you use to build your projects.

Exploring the Utility Window

The Utility window has three primary functions: You use it to browse for files, to preview content, and to modify content. The title bar at the top of the Utility window changes to reflect whichever tab is currently selected.

The Utility window separates its primary functions into three tabs:

▶ File Browser — Browse, select, and import media files.

▶ Library — Access Motion content to apply to your project.

▶ Inspector — Adjust the parameters for all objects and effects in your project.

We'll select the File Browser tab to locate the elements we need to create our project.

NOTE ▶ You'll work with the Library and Inspector panes in later exercises.

Working in the File Browser

The upper pane of the File Browser shows the Sidebar, which contains icons for different locations on your computer such as your Desktop Folder.

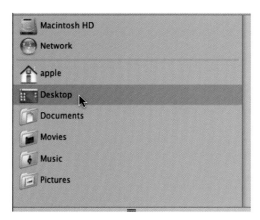

Upper pane / Sidebar

The lower pane displays the file stack of folders, files, and contents for whatever location you have selected in the upper pane.

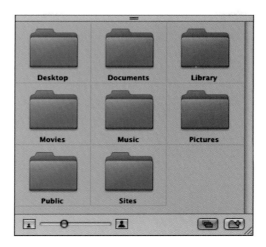

Lower pane / file stack

The Motion File Browser lets you view your files in either list or icon view. To change the way you view your files, you simply click the appropriate view button. For this lesson you'll use the list view.

Let's change the File Browser to list view, then navigate to the Introducing_Motion folder in the upper pane, and view the tutorial contents in the lower pane.

1   At the upper left of the Utility window, click the File Browser tab if it is not already selected.

2   At the middle right of the File Browser, click the List View button.

The files in the lower pane of the File Browser now appear in the list view.

3   In the upper pane of the File Browser window, click the Desktop icon to open your Desktop Folder in the lower pane.

4 In the lower pane, double-click the Apple Pro Training Tutorials folder, then double-click the Introducing_Motion folder.

The contents of the Introducing_Motion folder appear in the lower pane of the File Browser.

The **Backup_Projects** folder contains progressive versions of the project. If at any time you fall behind, or don't complete a step, you can open the appropriate backup project. Each backup project is lettered sequentially and is named for the last completed task in the project.

Previewing Files in the File Browser

With your files displayed in the lower pane, you can easily preview any of them in the Preview area at the top of the File Browser.

To preview a file in Motion, you simply click the file icon to select it. Let's preview a movie of the finished Introducing Motion tutorial project.

1 Locate the file called **Final Composite.mov** and click to select it.

The file opens in the Preview area of the File Browser.

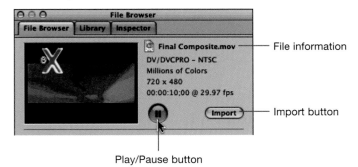

Play/Pause button

Moving the Playhead

If the playhead is moving, you will see each frame sequentially, which allows you to see movement over time. If the playhead is paused, as it is in your project, you will see only the current frame

There are many ways to move the playhead to view your project. One method is to drag the playhead in the scrubber area. You can also move the playhead one frame at a time forward or backward using the Left and Right Arrow keys. Let's try both methods to move the playhead.

1 Click the Canvas window and press the Space bar to pause playback in the Canvas, if it is not already paused.

2 Drag the playhead to the right or left to view different frames.

3 Press the Right or Left Arrow keys several times to move the playhead one frame at a time to the right or left.

When the playhead moves to the right, you are moving forward in time through your project. When the playhead moves to the left, you are moving backward in time (reverse) through your project.

4 Press the End key to move the playhead to the last frame in the project.

5 Press the Home key to move the playhead to the first frame in the project.

NOTE ▶ If you are working on a laptop computer, you will need to press and hold the Function (fn) key located at the lower-left corner of the keyboard to use the Home (Left Arrow) and End (Right Arrow) keys.

The Current Frame field is located at the lower left of the Canvas window and displays the playhead position in either frames or timecode.

Since your playhead is parked on the first frame of the project, the frame position is frame 1.

TIP You can view the frames as timecode by clicking the Stopwatch button at the left of the Current Frame field.

Saving a Project

Now that you've successfully imported a file into your project, it's a good idea to save.

1 Choose File > Save As, or press Shift-Command-S to open the Save As window.

2 Navigate to the Apple Pro Training Tutorials folder on your desktop, then double-click the My_Saved_Projects folder to open and select it.

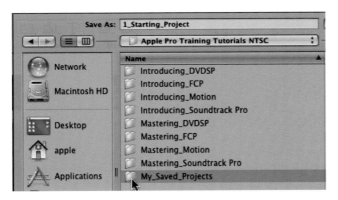

3 Click the Save button or press Return to save the project to the selected folder.

Working With Filters

Now that you've imported the movie file to the project, you'll add some filters to enhance the look of the movie. Filters can be used for practical and artistic reasons. In this case you'll add a Widescreen filter to the entire clip to serve both purposes. First, it will add a more artistic widescreen look, and second, it will cover up the timecode near the top of the underwater part of the clip.

Filters are located in the Library pane of the Utility window.

1   At the top of the Utility window, click the Library tab to view the Library pane.

The upper pane of the Library shows a Sidebar of categories for the different types of Motion content.

2   Click the Filters category in the Library to reveal the sub-categories of Motion filters.

3   Click the Border subcategory in the right column of the upper pane.

The border filters appear in the lower pane of the Library.

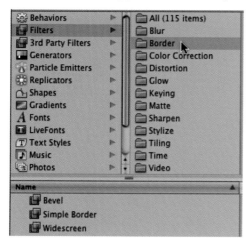

4   Click each of the border filters in the lower pane of the Library to preview
them in the Library's Preview area.

The Widescreen border adds black bars at the top and bottom of the image.

Applying a Filter to an Object

Now that you've selected and previewed the Widescreen border filter, let's
apply it to the video clip in the project. You can apply filters to any selected
object by either clicking the Apply button or dragging the filter from the
Library to the object in the Canvas. Let's use the second method and drag the
Widescreen filter to the video clip in the Canvas.

> **TIP**   Before you apply a filter, make sure that you select the object that
> you wish to apply the filter to. Otherwise, you may accidentally apply the
> filter to the wrong object.

1   On the Canvas, click the Video for Promo object to select it if it is not
already selected.

When an object is selected, a bounding box appears around the object in
the Canvas, and a region for the object appears in the mini-Timeline.

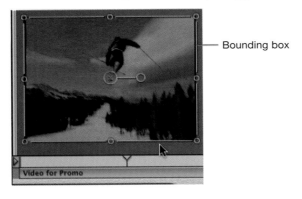

Bounding box

2 Drag the Widescreen filter from the Library to the selected object in the Canvas and release the mouse button.

Black bars appear at the top and bottom of the video clip, and a purple Widescreen region appears in the mini-Timeline.

NOTE ► Colored bars in the mini-Timeline are graphical representations of selected elements in the project. Media files and other objects such as shapes, text, and particle emitters, have blue bars. Effects have purple bars, and audio files have green bars.

3 Press the Space bar to view the video clip with the Widescreen filter.

As you can see, the widescreen bars created by the filter aren't quite large enough to cover up the timecode or to give the entire clip a balanced widescreen look.

Modifying a Filter in the Dashboard

Motion includes a handy floating window called the Dashboard, which can be used to modify objects and effects. To display the Dashboard you simply press the D or F7 key. You can use the Dashboard while the playhead is moving or static. For this exercise, you'll modify the filter while the playhead is moving.

1   Press D to open the Dashboard (if it's not already open).

A small gray Dashboard appears.

The title bar at the top of the Dashboard shows whatever is currently selected. In this case it shows Video for Promo: Widescreen.

NOTE ▸ If the title bar for your Dashboard says "Video for Promo," and the region in your mini-Timeline is blue, then press the D key to toggle the Dashboard from the object to the Widescreen filter applied to it. If your Dashboard shows "Nothing Selected" in the title bar, then you need to click the video clip in the Canvas to select it, then press D to toggle the Dashboard to the Widescreen filter.

2   Click the Aspect Ratio pop-up menu in the Dashboard and choose 3.00:1 for the widest Widescreen look.

The widescreen bars at the top and bottom of the video image become much wider, and they now cover up the timecode. Unfortunately, they also cover up the skier's head as he jumps, and the dancer's head and body as he flips over.

The Widescreen Dashboard controls also include an Offset slider to move the video image up or down to accommodate the widescreen look. Let's change the offset in the Dashboard to lower the image.

3   Drag the Offset slider on the Dashboard toward the left to a value of –0.41.

The video image moves downward for a better view of the skier and the dancer.

4   Press Command-S to save your progress.

TIP ▶ You can move the Dashboard by dragging the title bar or any empty space around the edges of the window.

Modifying Filters in the mini-Timeline

Let's add and modify two more filters to the video clip. This time you'll change the length and position of the new filters in the mini-Timeline so that they appear for only part of the video clip's overall duration. For this exercise you'll apply a Posterize filter to the beginning of the clip to stylize the look of the airborne skier. Then you'll apply a Trails filter to the end of clip to change the look of the dancer's movement.

1   Click the gray area around the image to deselect the filter, then select the Video for Promo object in the Canvas if it is not already selected.

2   At the left side of the Library click the Filters icon, then choose the Stylize folder.

The list of stylize filters appears in the lower pane of the Library.

3   Scroll downward through the list of stylize filters and locate the Posterize filter.

4   Select the Posterize filter in the lower pane of the Library.

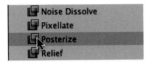

5   Click the Apply button at the top of the Library pane to apply the Posterize filter to the selected object.

The look of the video clip changes dramatically, a purple Posterize region appears in the mini-Timeline, and the Dashboard changes to the Posterize filter controls.

Notice that the Posterize filter affects the look of the video image and muddies the black bars from the Widescreen filter. Why? Because, when you apply a filter it affects the object and all the filters applied before it. You'll fix this later in the lesson.

6   Drag the Levels slider in the Dashboard toward the right and change the Posterize filter level to 11.

By default, any filter is the same duration as the object to which it is applied.

To change the duration you can drag the right edge of the purple bar in the mini-Timeline, or use the keyboard shortcut O to set a new Out point (ending).

First, let's use the playhead to find the frame where the Posterize filter should end.

NOTE ▸ Since the video clip includes a dissolve from the skier to the underwater shot, it's a good idea to end the filter toward the beginning of the dissolve rather than the end, where the sudden change would be more obvious.

7   Press the Space bar to pause playback.

8 Drag the playhead to frame 58, or type *58* in the Current Frame field and press Return to move the playhead (for PAL, frame 49).

9 Press O (for Out point) to change the Out point, or ending, of the Posterize filter to the current playhead position.

The Posterize filter now ends at frame 58 (for PAL, frame 49) in the mini-Timeline.

10 Click the "Play from start" button in the Transport controls, or press Home and then the Space bar to view the modified video clip.

11 Pause playback, and deselect the Posterize filter by clicking the gray area outside the image.

Now let's add a Trails filter from the Time category to the end of the clip.

12 Select the Time folder in the Library, then select the Trails filter and apply it to the clip in the Canvas.

13 Move the playhead to frame 136 (for PAL, frame 114), which is the beginning of the dissolve to the dancer part of the video clip.

14 Press I (for In point) to change the In point (beginning) for the Trails filter to the playhead position.

Before you preview the new filter, let's change the project's play range to view only the end of the video clip.

Changing the Project's Play Range

The project's play range is the portion of the Timeline you can preview when you press Play. By default, the play range is the same as the project's duration.

The play range In point indicates the beginning of the play range, and the play range Out point indicates the end of the play range. You can change the play range In and Out points by dragging the points on the scrubber area, choosing from the Mark menu, or using keyboard shortcuts.

Since the playhead is already at the beginning of the Trails filter, let's use the keyboard shortcut to change the play range In point to frame 136 (for PAL, frame 114).

1   Press Option-Command-I to change the play range In point to the play-head position (frame 136). (for PAL, 114).

You can also drag the play range In or Out points to a new position on the mini-Timeline.

2   Press the Space bar to preview the new play range and see the Trails filter at the end of the video clip.

3   In the Dashboard, change the Echoes parameter for the Trails filter to 1 to remove the echoes effect. Then change the Echoes parameter to 6 to add more visual echoes to the dancer's movement.

4   Stop playback and press Command-S to save your progress.

   TIP ▶ The best way to get to know how filters work is to experiment with them and try the different parameters to see what they do. You can experiment more with the Trails and Posterize filters after this lesson.

Exploring the Project Pane

Now that you've imported a movie clip into your project and applied three filters, let's take a look at how everything is organized in the Project pane of the Canvas.

The Project pane is used primarily for organizing your project's elements, and it contains three tabs: Layers, Media, and Audio. You can show the Project pane by using keyboard shortcuts, choosing from the Window menu, or dragging the resize handle on the middle left of the Canvas window. Let's use the keyboard shortcut Command-4 to show the Layers list in the Project pane.

1   Press Command-4 to show the Layers list.

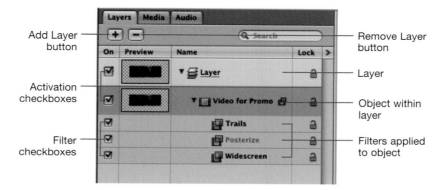

The Layers list appears with one layer, one object within that layer, and three filters applied to that object.

2   Press Command-5 or click the Media tab.

The Media list shows all of the media applied to the current project. At this time there is only one file in the project.

3   Press Command-6 or click the Audio tab.

The Audio list shows all of the audio files applied to the current project. At this time there are no audio files in the project.

4   Press Command-4 to return to the Layers list.

TIP ▶ The keyboard shortcuts for showing or hiding lists in the Utility window and Project pane are in the same numerical order that they appear in the interface: Command-1 = File Browser, Command-2 = Library, Command-3 = Inspector, Command-4 = Layers, Command-5 = Media, Command-6 = Audio.

Moving Elements in the Layers List

Every new Motion project includes one empty layer named simply "Layer." Each file that you import to the project goes into that layer. Files and effects are added to a layer in the order that they are added to the project, from the bottom up.

Notice that the three filters applied to the Video for Promo object are in the same order that they were applied, starting with the Widescreen filter in the lowest position. Sometimes you need to change the order of objects or effects. For example, the Posterize filter was applied after the Widescreen filter, so it modifies the look of both the video clip and the Widescreen filter. Moving the Widescreen filter to the highest filter position on the Layers list means it will be the last filter applied to the object, so the other filters won't alter the appearance of the widescreen bars.

To move objects or effects within the Layers list all you need to do is drag them to a new position.

Let's move the Widescreen to the highest filter position, above the Trails filter.

1   Press the Home key to move the playhead to the first frame of the project.

Notice that the black bars created by the Widescreen filter are slightly posterized along with the video image in the Canvas.

2 On the Project pane, click the Widescreen filter to select it, then drag the filter upward and release it above the Trails filter.

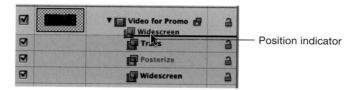 ——— Position indicator

A black position indicator appears to show you where you will be releasing the element that you are moving.

The black widescreen bars are no longer affected by the Posterize filter.

Naming and Adding Layers

It is a good idea to keep your project organized as you go. Naming a layer is as simple as double-clicking on the name field and typing a new name. You can also add or delete layers by clicking the Add button (+) or the Delete button (–). For this exercise you'll rename the original layer *Video*. Then you'll create a new layer and name it *Text*.

1 Double-click the layer's name ("Layer") to open the Text field.

2 Type *Video* in the layer's Text field, then press Return.

3 Click the Add Layer button to add a new layer to the project.

4   Change the name of the new layer to *Text*.

5   On the Layers list, click the new Text layer to make sure it is selected.

(The Text layer darkens on the Layers list to show that it has been selected.)

6   Press Command-4 or F5 to hide the Project pane.

NOTE ▶ Motion places new objects in the selected layer. If no layer is selected when you import a file, a new layer will be created for the object. You can also create sublayers within existing layers to organize your project's elements even further. You can move a file to a different layer once it has been imported to the project.

Resetting the Play Range

The project's play range is still set for the ending shot of the video clip. Let's reset the play range to the full duration of the project. You can reset the play range in the Mark menu, or with the keyboard shortcut Option-X.

1   Choose Mark > Reset Play Range, or press Option-X to reset the play range.

The play range In and Out points reset to the first and last frames of the project.

2   Press the Space bar to begin playback in the Canvas if it isn't already playing.

Now that you've added a Text layer and reset the play range, let's create some text.

Working With Text

To create a text object in Motion, you first need to select the Text tool. Once you create the text object, you can modify it in the Dashboard. Any object that you create in Motion, including text, is added to the project like an imported media file. Therefore, you need to consider *when* you want the text to appear in the project. Make sure the playhead is parked where you want the text to begin, or start the playhead moving if you want the text to begin on the first frame.

Over the next series of exercises you'll create the word *extreme* using two separate text objects. You'll create the X separate from the rest of the word *extreme* so that you can animate it with different behaviors and timing. First, you'll create, resize, and align both text objects in the Canvas; then you'll change their style and appearance.

Creating a Text Object

The toolbar at the top of the Canvas window includes a set of tools for creating shapes and text. To create text, you first select the Text tool, then click in the Canvas and type the desired text. For this exercise you'll create the letter X on the upper-left corner of the frame in the Canvas. Once you've finished typing, you'll need to change back to the default Select/Transform tool (arrow).

1   Press T, or click the Text tool on the toolbar.

The Text tool darkens on the toolbar to show it has been selected.

2   Move the Text tool over the upper-left corner of the frame in the Canvas.

3   Click once to create a text object.

A flashing white line (a cursor) appears on the Canvas.

4   Type *X* (capitalized).

A plain white X appears on the Canvas, followed by the flashing cursor, and a blue text object appears in the mini-Timeline.

OK, it's not art, but you accomplished your goal and created an X. To change the look of the text object, you first need to go back to the Select/Transform tool.

5   Press Escape or click the Select/Transform tool (the arrow), located on the far left of the toolbar.

Select/Transform tool

A bounding box appears around the X to show that it has been selected.

Modifying Text in the Dashboard

The Dashboard always shows parameters for the selected object or effect. Since you selected the X text object, the title bar of the Dashboard should now read Text: X. Let's use the Dashboard controls to modify the X's size and font. The default font setting for text objects is 48-point Geneva.

1   Press D to show the Dashboard if it is not already showing.

Make sure that the X is selected; if it isn't, click the X in the Canvas to select it.

2   On the Dashboard, drag the Size slider to a value of 200pt.

Not only is the X much bigger, but the top of it may be out of the visible frame area. Anytime an object is in the gray area surrounding the frame, it is no longer in the visible frame area.

3   Click the X object and drag it downward until you can see the entire letter within the frame.

You'll align it more precisely later.

In the middle left of the Text Dashboard you'll see a pop-up menu. The typeface is set to the default, Geneva.

To change the typeface, you simply click the arrow on the pop-up menu and choose a new typeface.

4   Click the pop-up menu and choose the Arial typeface.

The text object instantly updates to the new typeface.

NOTE ▶ The Typeface pop-up menu in the Text Dashboard is a terrific feature, especially if you're working with someone who changes type-faces often.

Creating Additional Text

Now it's your turn to apply your new text-creation skills on a second text object. This time you'll create the word extreme—without the X. Then, you'll change the size in the Dashboard and adjust the alignment.

1   Press T to select the Text tool.

2   Click the Text cursor in the empty space to the right of the X.

When you type the word *extreme*, you'll need to leave three spaces for the 200-point X to fit within the word.

3 Type *e treme* (with three spaces between e and t), then press Escape to change back to the Select/Transform tool.

4 In the Text Dashboard, change the Size value to 68pt.

Next you'll align the two text objects with each other.

Positioning Objects in the Canvas

You could now try to place the text visually, or you could use tools that Motion provides to help you work with more precision.

The Motion Canvas includes visual tools and overlays to help you move, crop, and align objects. These tools include a grid, rulers, guides, Dynamic Guides and Safe Zones, and they can be turned on and off in the View pop-up menu in the Canvas. You can use these tools one at a time or all together.

Working with Safe Zones and Dynamic Guides

When you create projects that will eventually be viewed on a television screen, it is very important to understand Safe Zones.

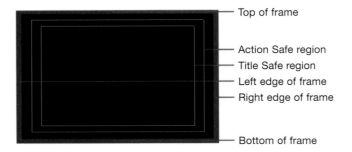

The *Title Safe region* is the inner blue rectangle. You should place all text within the Title Safe region. Objects inside the Safe Zone guides of the region will be visible on any television screen.

The *Action Safe region* lies within the outer blue rectangle. Objects inside its boundaries (its Safe Zone guides) will likely be seen on a television screen.

You can turn the display of Safe Zones on or off in the View pop-up menu at the upper right of the Canvas window.

Let's turn on the Safe Zones overlay in the Canvas.

1 From the View drop-down menu in the Canvas, choose Safe Zones to turn on the Safe Zone guides.

2 In the Canvas, click the X object to select it.

You'll see a bounding box around the X to show that it has been selected.

3 Drag the X object downward until the top of the X is inside the Action Safe region, and the left side of the X is within the Title Safe region.

Now that the X is in its final position, let's align the e treme object.

4   On the Canvas, select the e treme text object, then drag it left until the e is on the left side of the X object. Keep the entire e treme text object inside the Title Safe region.

Did you notice the yellow lines that appeared as you dragged the text objects in the Canvas? Those lines are called Dynamic Guides, and you can use them to help align your objects in the Canvas.

5   Drag the e treme text object up and down until you see the horizontal Dynamic Guide.

The horizontal Dynamic Guide shows you when the e treme text object is aligned with the center of the X.

6   Drag the e treme text object left and right until you see a vertical Dynamic Guide along the left edge of the text objects.

The vertical Dynamic Guide shows you when the left edges of the objects are aligned.

7   Press Command-S to save your progress.

Your project is coming together. You've already imported video, applied filters, and created two text objects.

Working With LiveFonts

Let's liven things up and bring your plain white text objects to life. LiveFonts are animated fonts that you can use to add excitement to the text in your projects. In this exercise, you'll preview the LiveFonts in the Library and then apply a LiveFont to both text objects in your project.

Previewing LiveFonts in the Library

The LiveFonts are located in the Library.

1   Click the Library tab if it is not already selected.

2   In the Library, click the LiveFonts category, and the All subcategory.

3   Select Salute LiveFont in the lower pane of the Library to see it in the Preview area.

    The Salute LiveFont looks like blue text with a glistening white outline and will work perfectly for the eXtreme text.

Selecting Multiple Objects in the Canvas

Before you apply the Salute LiveFont, let's select both text objects. With both objects selected, you'll be able to apply the LiveFont to the X and the e treme objects at the same time. To select additional objects in the Canvas you simply press the Shift key and click. Shift-clicking will also deselect objects once they have been selected.

1   Shift-click the X object on the canvas to select it in addition to the e treme object that is already selected.

    The Dashboard's title bar changes to Multiple Selection, to show that multiple objects have been selected.

2   On the Library, click the Apply button.

    Both text objects change to the Salute LiveFont.

    The font change also altered the alignment of the X object. To fix the alignment you'll first need to deselect the other object.

3   Shift-click the e treme object to deselect it.

    Let's move the X back into alignment with a keyboard shortcut. You can use the Command key plus the Up, Down, Left, or Right Arrow Keys to precisely align any selected object in the Motion Canvas.

4 Press and hold the Command key, then tap the appropriate arrow keys to realign the X with the other text.

5 Press Command-S to save your progress.

Working With Text Behaviors

Another really exciting feature of Motion is its ability to add behaviors to project elements. Behaviors allow you to animate objects using simple graphical controls. You'll be working with many behaviors throughout the course of this tutorial. Let's start with behaviors designed specifically for text.

Previewing a Behavior in the Library

Let's go to the Library and find the Text Sequence behaviors. Your goal is to add a Text-Zoom behavior to the X to make it fly onscreen and slam into position. Then, you'll apply a Text-Glow behavior to the e treme text for a more dramatic entrance.

1 Click the Behaviors category at the top of the Library.

Motion behaviors are organized into sub-categories.

2 Click the Text Sequence subcategory in the right column of the upper pane.

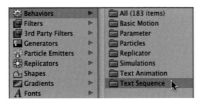

Six types of text behaviors appear in the lower pane.

3   In the lower pane, click the disclosure triangle for the Text-Zoom subcategory to reveal the different Text-Zoom behaviors.

4   Click the Behind Camera behavior to view it in the Preview area at the top of the Library window.

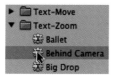

Applying Text Behaviors

You can apply behaviors to objects the same way that you apply filters: simply drag the behavior to the object, or select the behavior and click the Apply button.

1   On the Canvas, select the X text object if it is not already selected.

2   Click the Apply button on the Preview area of the Library.

The Behind Camera behavior is applied to the X, and a purple Behind Camera behaviors bar appears in the mini-Timeline.

3   Play the project in the Canvas to see the Behind Camera behavior on the X object.

NOTE ▶ The Behind Camera behavior is designed to make the text appear, so the Behind Camera region is only at the beginning of the object in the mini-Timeline.

The effect looks good, but for this project, it would be better if it happened faster. Remember the X is supposed to slam into position.

Changing the Timing of a Behavior

To speed up or slow down a Basic Motion behavior, you can change the length of the behavior's region in the mini-Timeline. The longer the behavior's region, the longer it takes to complete the effect. The shorter the behavior's region, the less time it takes to complete the effect.

1 Press the Space bar to pause the playhead if it is not already paused.

2 Press Shift-O to move the playhead to the last frame of the Behind Camera behavior.

> **NOTE ▶** If you deselected the X object and no longer see the Behind Camera behavior in the mini-Timeline, just select the X object, then press D to toggle the Dashboard and Timeline to the next element applied to the object.

> Shift-I always goes to the first frame of the selected object (the In point), and Shift-O goes to the last frame (the Out point).

> The current frame field indicates 60 frames, which is about 2 seconds (for PAL, about 10 frames).

> Let's change the project play range Out point to the current playhead position, then shorten the effect so it is only 15 frames in length.

3 Press Command-Option-O to change the play range Out point.

4 In the mini-Timeline, drag the right edge of the Behind Camera bar to the left until the yellow help tag window shows a new duration of 15 frames.

5 Press the Space bar to view the modified behavior in the Canvas.

> Now that the X slams onscreen, let's apply a Text-Glow behavior to the e treme object.

6 In the Canvas, select the e treme text object.

7 In the Library's lower pane, click the disclosure triangle for the Text-Glow subcategory to reveal the different Text-Glow behaviors.

8   Click the Fast Beam behavior to view it in the Preview area at the top of the Library window, then click the Apply button.

The Fast Beam behavior really enhances the introduction of the text. Let's slow it down a little, so the entire behavior lasts for 60 frames (for PAL, 50).

9   Press the Space bar to pause the playhead.

10 Move the playhead to frame 60 (for PAL, frame 50).

TIP You can move the playhead to the play range In point by pressing Shift-Home, and the play range Out point by pressing Shift-End.

11 Press O to extend the Out point of the selected behavior to the playhead, or drag the right edge of the Fast Beam bar to current frame position (60, or for PAL, 50).

12 Play the project to see the modified behaviors in action.

13 Press Command-S to save your progress.

Working With Basic Motion Behaviors

While text behaviors can be applied only to text objects, Basic Motion and Simulation behaviors can be applied to any object. Basic Motion behaviors include common animation effects for opacity, scale, and movement. Also, unlike text behaviors, Basic Motion behaviors are of the same duration as the object they are applied to. You can modify the duration once the behaviors are applied to the object.

In addition to clicking the Apply button, you can also drag behaviors to the selected object in the Canvas. Let's try the drag-and-drop method to apply a simple Fade In/Fade Out behavior to the video file and the e treme object.

1   Press Option-X to reset the project play range to the full project duration.

2   Click the video image on the Canvas to select the Video for Promo object.

3   Click to select the Basic Motion behaviors folder in the right column of the Library.

4   Drag the Fade In/Fade Out behavior from the lower pane to the Video for Promo object in the Canvas and release the mouse button.

   The Video for Promo object fades in at the beginning and out at the end.

   Notice the Fade In/Fade Out Dashboard includes a graphical control for the behavior. The default setting is a 20-frame fade-in, and a 20-frame fade-out. That works perfectly for the video clip.

5   Shift-click the video object in the Canvas to deselect it.

6   Select the e treme text object.

7   Drag the Fade In/Fade Out behavior from the lower pane to the e treme object.

   Since you have already applied the Fast Beam behavior to the e treme text, you don't need it to fade in.

8   On the Fade In/Fade Out Dashboard, drag the left edge of the Fade In control to the left until the Fade In value is 0 frames (no fade).

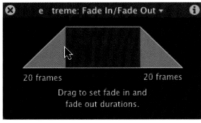   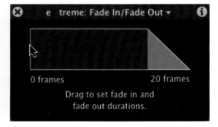

Default Fade In setting   Fade In changed to 0 frames

Working with the Spin Behavior

You've successfully animated the X object at the beginning of the project. Now let's add a Spin behavior to the X at the end of the project to mimic the movement of the dancer in the video clip.

Spin is another Basic Motion behavior.

1   Pause the playhead and move it to frame 180 (for PAL, frame 151).

2   Press Command-Option-I to change the play range In point to the play-head position.

3   Select the X object on the Canvas.

4   Drag the Spin behavior from the lower pane to the X object on the Canvas.

    The Spin behavior is applied to the entire X object.

5   Press I to change the In point of the Spin behavior to the playhead position.

6   Press the Space bar to begin playback.

7   On the Spin Dashboard, click the top of the circle in the graphical display and drag clockwise one full revolution.

An arrow appears on the circle to show the direction and length of the move.

To achieve the desired move, you'll need to drag the arrow for five full revolutions on the graphical display. Another option is to change the behavior in the Inspector.

Modifying a Behavior in the Inspector

The Inspector, the third pane on the Utility window, includes detailed parameter controls for whatever object is selected. Inside the Inspector are four tabs: Properties, Behaviors, Filters, and a contextual tab for the selected object. In this exercise you'll use the Inspector to modify the parameters for the Spin behavior.

1   Press Command-3 to view the Inspector in the Utility window.

   The Behaviors tab in the Inspector is automatically selected, because the Spin behavior is currently active in the Canvas.

2   Locate the Spin behavior parameters at the top of the Behaviors pane.

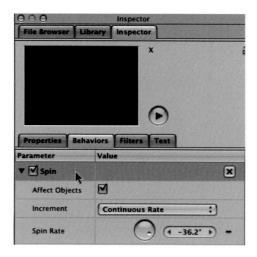

   The Spin Rate field allows you to set an exact amount for the Spin behavior. A negative number means the spin is clockwise. A positive number would be a counterclockwise spin.

3   Pause playback. Then press the End key.

   The playhead moves to the last frame of the project.

4   In the Behaviors pane of the Inspector, click the Spin Rate field and drag the mouse left to around –180, or type *–180* in the Spin Rate field and press Return.

The X object in the Canvas continues to spin as you modify the parameter.

5   Press the Space bar to see the modified Spin behavior.

6   Press Command-S to save your progress.

Working With Particles

Particles are used in Motion graphics to create smoke, fire, snow, explosions, and other visual effects that require many objects created from one primary object (a cell). The particle cell is multiplied through a particle emitter.

Motion includes over one hundred premade particle emitters, and you can also turn virtually any object into a particle emitter to create your own particle system. For this exercise let's work with some of the particle emitters that come with Motion.

First, you'll apply a Drop Impact emitter to the X to emphasize the moment it slams onto the screen. Then you'll apply one of the Sparkles emitters to the last frame of the X to make it appear to explode in a shower of sparks.

Since the particles need to appear at an exact moment, it's best to apply them with the playhead parked on the desired frame.

1   Pause the playhead if it is still moving.

2   Press Option-X to reset the play range.

3   Move the playhead to frame 12.

This should be the exact frame where the X stops on the Canvas.

4   Click the empty space in the Canvas to deselect all objects in the project.

5   Click the Library tab or press Command-2 to open the Library.

6   Locate the Particle Emitters category in the Library.

7   Click the Nature folder to narrow the selections to the Nature category.

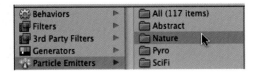

8   Select the Drop Impact emitter from the lower pane to preview it.

9   Drag the Drop Impact emitter from the lower pane to the Canvas and drop it on the center of the X object.

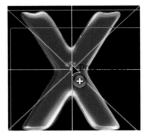

10   Play the project from the beginning to see the result of the Drop Impact emitter.

That was easy. You've successfully added the first particle emitter to your motion graphics project. You'll need to extend the project's duration before you add the second emitter.

Changing the Project Duration

You can view and change the project duration in timecode or frames, depending on your workflow. To change from frames to timecode, you can use the Stopwatch button to the left of the Project Duration field. For this exercise you'll use the default setting of frames.

1 Locate the Project Duration field at the lower right of the Canvas window.

2 Click the Stopwatch button to the left of the Project Duration field to change from frames to timecode.

The project is currently 7 seconds long.

NOTE ▶ The project frame rate is 30 frames per second (NTSC) or 25 frames per second (PAL).

3 Click the Project Duration field, then type *10.00* and press Return.

The project duration changes to 10 seconds.

4 Press Option-X to reset the play range to the new project duration.

5 Click the Stopwatch again to change the field back to frames.

TIP ▶ You can change the project duration by clicking the Project Duration field and typing a new duration, clicking the incremental arrows, or dragging in the field.

Now that the project has been extended, you can add the final particle emitter.

Applying a Second Particle Emitter

The next particle emitter that you'll add needs to start on the last frame of the X object. Let's move the playhead into position, then apply the emitter. The goal is to make the X object appear to explode in a burst of sparks.

1 Move the playhead to frame 210 (for PAL, frame 176).

2 Choose Edit > Deselect All to make sure all objects are deselected.

3 In the Library, click the Sparkles folder of Particle Emitters to narrow the selections to the Sparkles category.

4 Select the Pop Star emitter from the lower pane to preview it.

5 Drag the Pop Star emitter from the lower pane to the Canvas and drop it on the center of the X object.

6 Play the project from the beginning to see the result of the Pop Star emitter.

7 Stop playback, and press Command-S to save your progress.

Importing a Motion Project File

The first file that you imported into the project was a .mov file. For this exercise you'll import two Motion projects into the existing project. When you import a Motion project, all of the elements from the imported project are incorporated into the current project.

There are some text elements missing from this project. The missing text elements have already been created in separate Motion projects. For this exercise, you'll simply import the Motion projects from the Media folder in the File Browser to incorporate the text.

1 Move the playhead to the beginning of the timeline.

The eXtreme Living text begins at frame 200 (for PAL, frame 169).

2 Click the File Browser tab or press Command-1 to open the File Browser.

3   In the Media folder, click the eXtreme Living Text Motion project from the Media folder on the lower pane to see it in the Preview area.

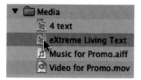

This is a simple Motion project containing two text objects with Text-Fade behaviors.

4   Click the Import button to import the selected file.

The eXtreme Living text is imported to the project, at the playhead position, and automatically centered in the frame.

5   Play the project in the Canvas to see the new imported text elements.

6   Pause the playhead and move it to the beginning of the timeline.

This is where the 4 text file will be imported. Instead of using the import button, which automatically centers the text, let's drag the file to the correct position on the frame.

7   Click the 4 text file in the lower pane to preview it.

This Motion project contains four text objects with Fade In/Fade Out behaviors. You'll place the file at the lower-left corner of the frame.

8   Drag the 4 text file from the lower pane to the lower-left corner of the frame in the Canvas.

9   Press Shift–Right Arrow to move the playhead ten frames to the right.

10 Drag the 4 text object so that it is centered with the e treme object.

Use the Dynamic Guides to show you when the objects are centered.

Applying a Throw Behavior

You can apply behaviors to objects or layers. In this case, the 4 text object is a group sublayer containing four text objects. Let's apply the Throw behavior to the 4 text group to move it across the Canvas. The Throw behavior is another one of the Basic Motion behaviors.

1 Press the Space bar to begin playback if your project is not already moving.

2 Click the Library tab or press Command-2 to open the Library.

3 Click the Behaviors icon, then click the Basic Motion behaviors folder in the right column of the upper pane.

4 Click the Throw behavior on the lower pane, then click the Apply button.

The Throw behavior is represented by a circle in the Dashboard.

The crosshairs in the center of the circle represent your object. Drag your pointer on the circle in the direction you want the object to go. An arrow appears in the direction that you drag the mouse. The longer the arrow, the farther and faster the object will be thrown.

5   Drag toward the right of the Throw display in the Dashboard to throw the object toward the right.

   TIP If you press the Shift key while you drag the arrow in the Throw display, the arrow will only move in exact 45-degree angles, or a straight line.

6   Modify the length of the arrow in the Throw Dashboard until the text moves smoothly from the left to the right and fades out before it reaches the right Title Safe region.

7   Choose Edit > Deselect all to deselect all objects in the project.

8   Press Command-S to save the finished project.

9   Press F7 to close the Dashboard.

10 Press F8 to view the project full screen.

11 Press F8 again to return to the Motion interface.

Importing an Audio file

You can import audio files to your Motion projects the same way that you import other media files. Let's import the **Music for Promo.aiff** file that was created in Soundtrack.

1   Press the Space bar to begin playback if it is not already playing.

2 Drag the **Music for Promo.aiff** audio file from the lower pane of the File Browser to the Canvas.

A green Music for Promo audio bar appears in the mini-Timeline.

If you wish to mute the audio at any time, you can click the Mute button in the transport controls.

NOTE ► By default, the audio that you import to a project takes precedence over the graphic elements. Motion will try to play the audio in sync and may stutter the video. You can change this default in the Project pane of the Motion Preferences window.

Exporting a Motion Project

There are many options for exporting your Motion project. For this exercise, you'll export a simple QuickTime file of the finished project.

1 Choose File > Export, or press Command-E to open the Export window.

2 Type *Finished Motion* in the Save As field.

3 Choose the Desktop Folder as the location for your exported file.

The default settings at the bottom of the Export window will automatically export a QuickTime movie that matches the project properties.

4 Click the Export button to export the finished project.

An Export progress indicator appears as the file is created and exported.

NOTE ► If you wish to change the default settings, you can choose different settings from the pop-up menus and Options dialog.

5 Press Command-H to hide Motion.

6 Locate the Finished Motion QuickTime movie on your desktop.

7 Click the Motion icon on the Dock to return to your finished project.

Congratulations! You completed the Introducing_Motion project and used many of Motion's features, including filters, behaviors, and particles.

Project Task

Take a moment to explore the Project pane and see the various layers, objects, and effects that make up your finished project. If you're feeling really ambitious, try adding two more Text-Glow behaviors to the e treme and X objects. Your goal is to add a Highlight Text-Glow behavior to the end of the e treme object. Then apply a Highlight Text-Glow behavior to the end of the X object right before it explodes into particles.

To see the finished project with the additional glows applied, you can open the **21.final glows** project from the Backup_Projects folder.

What's Next?

This Apple Pro Training tutorial was designed to teach you some fundamentals of working with Motion as you build a project. Clearly, it just scratches the surface of features, tools, and techniques that Motion offers.

If you want to learn more, the next tutorial, Mastering Motion, introduces you to some of Motion's more advanced features, such as working with replicators, creating an image mask, animating objects and filters with keyframes, and more.

For more complete training resources, see page 302 for information on Apple certified training and the self-paced Apple Pro Training books, *Apple Pro Training Series: Motion* and *Apple Pro Training Series: Getting Started with Motion*.

4

Lesson Files

Time

This lesson takes approximately 1 hour to complete.

Goals

Work with replicators

Create an image mask

Animate objects and filters with keyframes

Use the 3D filter

Work with the Caustics generator

Extending a Replicator in the mini-Timeline

Let's modify the duration of the Moving Curtains replicator so that it lasts the entire length of the project. You can change the duration of the replicator the same as you would any other element in the mini-Timeline.

1   Press the Space bar to pause playback if it is playing.

2   Locate the end of the Moving Curtains bar in the mini-Timeline at the bottom of the Canvas.

Notice that the Moving Curtains region is much shorter than the project's duration.

3   Press End to move the playhead to the last frame of the project.

4   Press O to change the Out point (end) of the selected object to the playhead position.

> **TIP** You can press I (In) to change the In point of any selected element to the playhead position. You can also drag the edge of the region in the mini-Timeline to change its duration.

5   Press the Space bar to see the extended Moving Curtains. Press the Space bar again to pause playback.

6   Press Command-S to save your project.

Modifying a Replicator in the Dashboard

Remember, your goal is to turn the curtains into the video image, or vice versa. Let's lower the number of curtains and slow them down a bit using the Dashboard.

1   Press D or F7 to open the Dashboard if it's not already showing.

2   On the Moving Curtains Dashboard, drag the Columns slider to the left and change the number of columns to 8.

To adjust the speed of the Moving Curtains replicator, you need to modify the behavior that causes the movement.

3   Press D to toggle the Dashboard from the Moving Curtains replicator to the Attractor behavior applied to it.

The Moving Curtains replicator is essentially seven columns of rectangles that are attracted to each other in the center of the frame. The Attractor behavior causes the rectangles to move toward each other with various momentums.

4   On the Moving Curtains: Attractor Dashboard, drag all four sliders to the far left.

The Moving Curtains cells no longer move at all.

5   Change the sliders on the Dashboard to the following settings: Strength to 18, Falloff Rate to 85, Influence to 169, and Drag to 0.00.

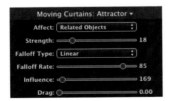

That's it. You've successfully added and modified the Moving Curtains replicator. Feel free to experiment with the settings after you finish this tutorial.

Adding an Image Mask

An image mask is like an image cookie cutter that allows you to create transparency in one object by taking the transparency information from another object.

Adding an image mask to the background video is a simple procedure. First you add the image mask to the video layer; then you assign the mask source. In this exercise you'll create an image mask on the Sequence from FCP layer and use the Moving Curtains replicator as the mask source.

1 Press Command-4 to open the Layers pane.

2 Click the Sequence from FCP layer to select it.

3 Choose Object > Add Image Mask, or press Shift-Command-M to add an image mask to the selected layer.

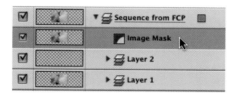

An image mask object appears in the Sequence from FCP layer.

Notice the Image Mask Dashboard includes a Mask Source well that you can use to assign the source.

4 Drag the Moving Curtains replicator from the Layers tab to the Mask Source well in the Dashboard.

5 Play the project in the Canvas to see the results of your image mask.

6 Press Command-S to save your progress for this version of the project.

Advancing the Project

Now that the background video curtains portion of the project is complete, it's time to fast-forward to the next section. If this tutorial were a cooking show, you would have just completed preparing the appetizer, so it's time to pop it in the oven and move on to the main course.

1 Choose File > Close, or press Command-W to close the current project.

2 Choose File > Open and navigate to project **2_Mstr_Motion_LowerThird** inside the Mastering_Motion folder.

   2_Mstr_Motion_LowerThird is a "baked" version of the project. Once you've completed an element for the project, such as a Motion background containing video, replicator, and image mask, you can export the project as a QuickTime movie. Playing a QuickTime movie in the Canvas requires a lot less processing, and it frees up the processor to create additional graphic elements.

   Building complex projects in stages and assembling the elements into a master project helps maximize your processor speed and real-time capabilities without limiting your creativity. This process is often referred to as baking because the separate elements (ingredients) are exported (baked) into a finished QuickTime file. Unlike a cake, however, you can always go back to the original project and make changes to the elements.

3 Press F5 to close the Project pane.

4 Press Command-7 to open the Timeline tab.

Working With Markers in the Timeline

This version of the project includes a Lower Third layer for organization, and three markers in the Timeline: Start Lower 3rd, Text and Caustics, and XL revealed. You'll use these markers as a guide for choreographing animated elements as you build the project. Let's zoom in to the Timeline for a closer look and then create another marker.

1   Drag the Timeline Zoom slider toward the left to zoom in to the Timeline until you can read the names of the markers.

You can add markers to the Timeline or to a selected object or layer. To add a marker to the Timeline, you first need to deselect all other objects. Then, move the playhead to the frame where you'd like to place the marker.

2   Choose Edit > Deselect All, or press Shift-Command-A to deselect all objects in the Timeline.

At the left of the Timeline ruler is a Current Frame field that displays the current playhead position and can be used for playhead navigation.

NOTE ▶ The Current Frame field and the ruler in the Timeline display either frames or timecode depending on the display mode of the Current Frame field next to the Transport controls.

3   Press the Space bar to pause playback if it is currently playing.

4   Click the Timeline Current Frame field and type 292, then press Return.

The playhead moves to frame 292.

5   Press M to set a project marker at the playhead position.

A green marker appears above the playhead.

6   Double-click the new green marker to open it in the Edit Marker window.

The Edit Marker window allows you to name and modify a marker.

7   Type *Throw and Glow* in the Name field.

8   Click the Color pop-up menu and change the color to purple.

9   Click OK or press Return and close the window.

To quickly zoom out of the Timeline to see the entire project play range, you simply click the Zoom to Fit button that looks like a magnifying glass at the upper-right corner of the Timeline.

10   Click the Zoom to Fit button to see the entire project and the markers in the Timeline.

Navigating between markers is as simple as pressing Option-Command and the Left or Right Arrow keys.

11   Press Option–Command–Left Arrow several times until your playhead is on the first marker (Start Lower 3rd).

Navigating to Layers and Objects

The current project includes two primary layers: Background Video and Lower Third. Let's take a moment to explore the Lower Third layer.

1   Click the Lower Third disclosure triangle to show the contents if it's not already open.

Inside the Lower Third you'll see Lower Third Text and Lower Third Bar sublayers. These layers are currently empty but were created to help organize the project as you build it.

2   Click the Lower Third layer to select it.

You can navigate between layers and elements within a layer by pressing the Up or Down Arrow keys.

3   Press the Down Arrow key twice to select the Lower Third Bar sublayer.

This is where you will create the first new project element.

4   Press Command-7 or F6 to close the Timeline tab.

Notice that you can see colored lines representing each of the Timeline markers in the mini-Timeline.

TIP ▶ The Up and Down Arrow keys can be used to navigate between objects and layers showing in either the Timeline or Layers pane even if the Timing and Project panes are closed.

Creating a Lower Third Bar

You could use a solid color, gradient generator or shape to create a bar for the lower third. Or you could use a replicator to make a more exciting lower third bar that builds itself a block at a time as it appears onscreen.

1   Click the Library tab or press Command-2 to open the Library in the Utility window if it's not already open.

2   Click the small circled x icon at the right of the Library Search field to delete the word *Curtain* from the previous search.

3   In the Sidebar, click the Replicators category. The right column shows four replicator categories.

4 Click the Transitions folder to show Transitions replicators in the lower pane of the Library.

5 Click the Blocks Left Down > IN replicator to view it in the Preview area at the top of the Library.

NOTE ▶ Most of the prebuilt replicators are named after their animated pattern, such as Blocks Left Down > IN, which animates from the left with the blocks moving down into position.

6 Press D or F7 to open the Dashboard if it is not already showing.

The Dashboard shows controls for the selected object, effect, or layer.

Before you apply the selected replicator project, make sure that the playhead is on the first marker and the Lower Third Bar layer has been selected.

If the Dashboard title bar shows Lower Third Bar, you have the correct layer selected. If not, use the Up and Down Arrow keys to navigate to the Lower Third Bar layer.

7 Click the Apply button to add the Blocks Left Down > IN replicator to the project.

8 Press the Home key to move the playhead to the first frame of the project.

9 Click the Canvas title bar to select it, then press the Space bar to play the project in the Canvas and see the replicator in action. Press the Space bar again to pause playback.

The Blocks Left Down > IN replicator builds a solid white pattern that covers the entire frame. With a little modification, you can transform that solid white pattern into a colorful lower third bar.

10 Press End to move the playhead to the last frame of the project.

11 Press O to change the Lower Third Bar Out point to the playhead position.

Extending the Lower Third Bar layer also extends the contents of that layer, including the Blocks Left Down > IN replicator.

Modifying Scale and Position

You can change the scale and position of the replicator pattern in the Inspector or directly in the Canvas. Drag the handles on the bounding box around the replicator to scale it in the Canvas. First, you'll need to zoom out of the Canvas for a better view of the replicator's bounding box.

1 Move the playhead to the second marker, frame 151 (for PAL, frame 147).

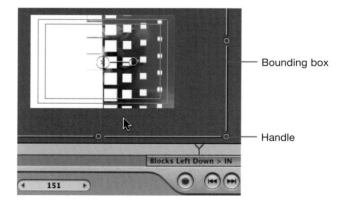

Bounding box

Handle

Now zoom out of the Canvas and resize the replicator.

2 Press Command--(minus) twice to zoom out of the Canvas enough to see the entire bounding box.

TIP ▶ Other handy Canvas keyboard shortcuts are Command-= to zoom in, Shift-Z to fit the frame to the Canvas window, Option-Z to make the image 100 percent of its native size, Command–Space bar–drag right or left to zoom in or out. Space bar–drag allows you to drag the entire frame to a different position in the Canvas.

Once you're zoomed out of the Canvas, you can see the bounding box and the replicator as it's building the pattern in the Canvas.

You can resize any selected object in the Canvas by dragging the handles (circles) around the bounding box with the Select/Transform tool. Shift-dragging the handles will constrain the proportions, and Option-Shift-dragging will constrain proportions and resize the object toward its center.

3   Option-Shift-drag the upper-right corner handle of the bounding box toward the center until the gray info box shows a new scale of 60% (for PAL, 76%).

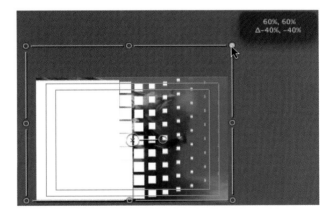

At 60 percent (for PAL, 76 percent) of the original scale, the Blocks Left Down > IN replicator fits better on the overall frame. Let's move it down to the lower third of the frame.

4 Drag the Blocks Left Down > IN replicator downward until the top of the white bar sits below the yellow water scooter on the image in the frame.

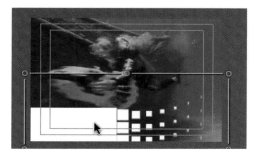

5 Press Command-Shift-S to open the Save As window.

6 Save the project into the My_Saved_Projects folder located in the Apple Pro Training Tutorials folder on your desktop.

Your lower third bar is in position, but it still needs a splash of color, a change of direction, and a lower opacity. Let's start with the color.

Changing the Replicator Color in the Inspector

Your goal in this exercise is to open your Blocks Left Down > IN replicator in the Inspector and modify the color to blend better with the underwater colors on the video clip.

1 Click the Inspector tab, or press Command-3 to open the Inspector in the Utility window. Click the properties tab in the Inspector.

The Inspector shows all available parameters for the selected object.

2 Click the Canvas title bar and press the Down Arrow key several times until the Blocks Left Down > IN object is selected.

The name of the selected object appears at the top of the Inspector and in the Dashboard title bar.

3 Click the Replicator tab to view the various replicator parameters.

Don't let the long list of controls and parameters scare you; they're really quite self-explanatory. For example, the Columns and Rows parameters allow you to choose the number of Columns and Rows that will be used in the replicator pattern.

MORE INFO ▶ You can learn more specific information about each of the replicator controls in the Motion User Manual (available from the Help menu).

4 Locate the Color Mode pop-up menu toward the bottom of the Inspector.

5 Click the Color Mode pop-up menu and choose Over Pattern.

The Over Pattern color setting allows you to choose the colors that will be used in the replicator pattern.

The default colors are a gradient from red to blue. It's colorful, all right, perhaps a bit too colorful for this project. Let's edit the color gradient and change the red to aqua to better fit the underwater color scheme.

6   Click the Gradient disclosure triangle to open the Gradient Editor in
    the Inspector.

7   At the lower left of the Gradient Editor, click the red color tag to select
    that color.

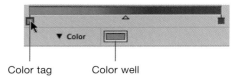

Color tag   Color well

8   Control-click the red color well below the Gradient Editor and choose an
    aqua color from the dynamic Colors window.

    As you can see, it's quite simple to modify color in the Inspector.

9   Press Shift-Z to fit the frame to the Canvas window.

Modifying the Origin and Opacity

You'll make the last two modifications to your replicator in the Dashboard while
the project is playing. First, let's change the play range in the mini-Timeline to
include only the first few seconds of the Blocks Left Down > IN object.

1   Press Shift-I to move the playhead to the first frame of the selected object.

    Make sure that the Blocks Left Down > IN replicator is selected.

2   Press Option-Command-I to change the play range In point to the play-
    head position, frame 111 (for PAL, frame 106).

3 Press Option–Command–Right Arrow twice to move the playhead to the third marker (frame 195, or for PAL, frame 184).

4 Press Option-Command-O to change the play range Out point.

5 Press the Space bar to play the project.

> **TIP** ▶ Setting a shorter play range allows you to focus on a small portion of the project, and it is also less demanding on your processor and graphics card.

6 On the Replicator: Blocks Left Down > IN Dashboard, drag the Opacity slider to 35%.

Now let's change the replicator's origin from the lower left to the lower right so that it follows the action onscreen.

7 Click the Origin pop-up menu on the Dashboard, and choose Lower Right.

8 Press Command-S to save your progress.

The lower third bar is complete. Now let's add some text and create a logo.

> **TIP** ▶ The first time you play your project, and with each modification, Motion caches each frame into video RAM on your computer's graphics card. The longer and more complicated the project, the more VRAM required for real-time playback. You can also render frames to your computer's RAM by creating a RAM preview. Choose Mark > RAM Preview > Play Range to render the current play range, or press the keyboard shortcut Command-R.

Adding Lower Third Text

You've created the lower third bar. The next step is to add the lower third text. You could create text elements from scratch, modify them, and add behaviors. However, since you covered those techniques in the Introducing Motion tutorial, let's simply import a Motion project with the lower third text already created.

1 Press Option-X to reset the project play range to the full duration of the project.

2 Move the playhead to the second marker (frame 151, or for PAL, frame 147).

3 Click the Canvas to make it active, then press the Up Arrow key until the Lower Third Text layer is selected.

The Dashboard title bar will indicate when the Layer: Lower Third Text has been selected.

4 Click the File Browser tab or press Command-1 to open the File Browser.

5 From the Media folder in the File Browser, click the Finished Text project to select it.

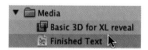

6 Click the Import button to import the Finished Text file to the selected layer and frame of your project.

7 Play the project in the Canvas to see the lower third with the text applied.

TIP ▶ Creating text in a separate project makes it easy to modify, update, or save as a template to reuse for other projects.

Creating a Logo

Now that the lower third bar is finished, let's create an animated logo for the eXtreme Living Channel. During the next series of exercises you'll use the **AquaBall.png** from the Motion Library content as the primary shape for the logo. First you'll add the **AquaBall.png** to the lower-left corner of the Canvas. Then you'll animate the AquaBall with keyframes for a more dramatic entrance. Finally, you'll create the logo text and apply the new 3D filter to animate the text.

1 Move the playhead to the second marker (frame 151, for PAL frame 147).

2 Click the Canvas to make it active, then press the Up Arrow key until the Lower Third layer is selected.

3 Click the Library tab.

4 Click the Content folder in the Library.

The Content folder includes over 240 items that are sorted into categories that match the Motion premade templates.

5 Press Command--(minus) to zoom out of the Canvas one level.

6 Click the **AquaBall.png** in the lower pane of the Library and drag it to the lower-left corner of the Canvas.

7 Align the AquaBall object in the Canvas so that the left and bottom edges are just inside the Action Safe boundary.

8 On the AquaBall Dashboard, drag the Opacity slider to 35%.

Working With Keyframes

Keyframes allow you to set a precise parameter value at a specific frame. There are many methods for setting keyframes. For this project, you'll first use the Record button in the transport controls to record keyframes for the position of the AquaBall object in the Canvas. Then you'll try a manual keyframe technique to animate the 3D filter in the Inspector.

The only parameter you'll work with in this first keyframing exercise is the position of the AquaBall. Your goal is to have the AquaBall enter from the right side of the Canvas and stop in the current position.

1   Press Shift-I to make sure the playhead is on the first frame of the AquaBall object.

2   Drag the AquaBall to the right and position it just outside the frame. This is the starting position for the AquaBall.

3   Click the Record button on the Transport controls, or press A to start recording animation.

Once the Record button is on, any changes that you make to the elements in the project will be recorded with keyframes. You can record keyframes with the playhead moving or paused. For this exercise, you'll manually move the playhead.

Next, you'll need to move the playhead 30 frames to the right. You can move the playhead 10 frames at a time left or right by pressing the Shift key as you press the Left or Right Arrow keys.

4   Press Shift–Right Arrow three times to move the playhead 30 frames to the right.

At this point in the Timeline, we want the AquaBall to be in its final position.

5   Drag the AquaBall to the left and place it back into the original left position.

The red line indicates the animation path of the AquaBall.

6   Click the Record button again or press A to turn off animation recording.

7   Play the project in the Canvas to see the animated AquaBall.

You'll use a Throw behavior to move the AquaBall object out of frame at the end of the project. For now, let's add the XL text to the logo.

TIP ▶ Motion 2 includes a new Record Animation settings feature that lets you choose to record keyframes only for animated parameters. This is very useful if you are recording keyframes while you manipulate objects in the Canvas. To open the Recording Options window, double-click the Record button.

Applying a Text Style

In this exercise you'll first create the text XL over the AquaBall. Then you'll apply a Chrome text style from the Library to color the text.

1   Move the playhead to the third marker (frame 195, for PAL frame 184).

2   Press Shift-Z to fit the frame to the Canvas.

3   Press T to select the Text tool.

4   Click the AquaBall with the text tool to create a text object.

5   Type *XL*, then press Escape to return to the Select/Transform tool.

6   On the Text Dashboard, drag the Size slider to 68pt.

7   Click the Font Family pop-up menu on the Dashboard and choose Helvetica Neue.

8   In the Library, click the Text Styles category.

NOTE ▶ Motion includes 13 preset text styles. You can also modify the styles and save them as favorites.

9   Select the Chrome Text style in the lower pane of the Library, then click the Apply button.

10   Drag the XL object to the center of the AquaBall. Use the Dynamic Guides to center the text inside the AquaBall.

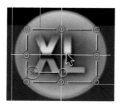

11   Press Command-S to save your progress.

Animating a Filter

Motion 2 has a host of new filters, including a Basic 3D filter that allows you to change or animate the X, Y, and Z coordinates of an object. For this exercise, you'll apply the Basic 3D filter to the XL object, then animate the Y coordinates so that the object revolves into position.

You can preview and apply filters in the Library or access them from the Add Filter pop-up menu in the toolbar.

1   Select the XL object if it is not already selected.

2   Click the Add Filter pop-up menu in the toolbar and choose Distortion > Basic 3D.

The Basic 3D filter has slider controls in the Dashboard and graphical controls around the object.

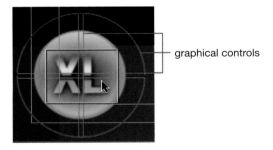

graphical controls

3   Drag the graphical controls (circles) around the XL object to modify the X, Y, and Z coordinates.

Now that you are familiar with the controls, let's reset the coordinates in the Inspector.

4   Click the Inspector button (i) at the upper right of the Dashboard to view the Basic 3D parameters in the Inspector.

The Inspector opens to the Filters tab. You can reset filters and behaviors in the Inspector by clicking the Reset button (x).

5   In the Inspector, click the Reset button for the Basic 3D filter.

You can change parameters in the Inspector by dragging the value field or by typing a new value in the field.

6   Click the Y Rotation field in the Inspector, then type –90 and press Return.

The object rotates –90 degrees on its Y-axis.

Now let's add a keyframe to the Y Rotation parameter in the Inspector. To add a keyframe, you click the Animation pop-up menu (–) located to the right of each parameter.

Make sure your playhead is on the first frame of the Basic 3D filter when you add the first keyframe.

7   Click the Y Rotation keyframe pop-up menu, and choose Add Keyframe.

A small black diamond appears on the pop-up menu to indicate a keyframe has been set for that parameter.

8   Click the title bar of the Canvas to make it active.

9   Press Shift–Right Arrow three times to move the playhead forward 30 frames.

10   Click the Record button to turn on Animation recording.

11   Change the Y Rotation parameter to 0 in the Inspector.

12   Press A to turn off keyframe recording.

13   Choose Edit > Deselect All.

14   Play the project from the beginning to see the animated logo.

15   Press Command-S to save your progress.

Grouping Objects

The last step to finish the animated logo is to apply a Throw behavior and a Glow filter to both items. Since you will be animating both objects at the same time, you can group the objects and modify the group as a single layer.

1   Press Command-4 to open the Layers tab of the Project pane.

2 In the Layers pane, click the AquaBall to select it, then Shift-click the XL object to select it as well.

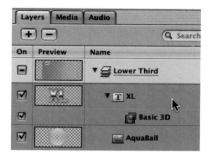

NOTE ▶ If your AquaBall and XL objects are not in the Lower Third layer at the top of the Layers pane, drag them into the Lower Third layer before you continue.

3 Control-click the selected objects in the Layers pane to open a shortcut menu.

4 Choose Group from the menu. A new layer is created that contains the XL and AquaBall objects.

TIP You can also group items from the Object menu or with the keyboard shortcut Shift-Command-G.

5 Change the name of the grouped layer to *Logo*.

Applying a Customized Effect

Now that you've created the Logo group layer, you can apply customized behavior to the logo. First, you'll apply a customized Throw behavior to move the logo out of the frame. Then, you'll create a customized Light Rays filter to create a unique glow effect as the logo exits the frame. Remember the Throw and Glow marker that you made earlier in the tutorial? It's time to put that marker to use for choreographing the Throw and Glow effects on the logo.

1 Select the Logo layer if it is not already selected.

2 Press Command-4 to close the Layers tab.

3 Move the playhead to the fourth marker (frame 292).

4 Press Command-1 to open the File Browser if it is not already showing.

The customized Throw behavior is located in the Media folder for the Mastering Motion tutorial.

5 Drag the Throw behavior from the lower pane of the File Browser to the group Logo object in the Canvas.

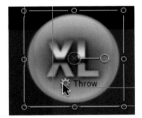

Behaviors always appear on the first frame of the object to which they are applied. You can easily move the entire Throw behavior in the mini-Timeline to the playhead position by dragging or using a keyboard shortcut.

6 Press Shift-[(left bracket) to move the Throw in the mini-Timeline to the playhead position.

NOTE ▶ Shift-[(left bracket) moves the first frame of the selected element to the playhead position. Shift-] (right bracket) moves the last frame of the selected element to the playhead position.

Next, you'll apply a Light Rays glow filter to the Logo object and animate it in the Canvas.

Make sure that the Logo is selected and the playhead is on the fourth marker in the Timeline.

7   From the Add Filter menu in the Toolbar, choose Glow > Light Rays.

8   Press I to change the In point of the Light Rays filter in the mini-Timeline.

9   On the Light Rays Dashboard, drag the Amount slider to 0 and the Glow slider to 0.81.

10   Click the Record button to begin animation recording.

11   Press Shift–Right Arrow twice to move the playhead 20 frames to the right. (For PAL, move the playhead 30 frames to the right. If you see an alert regarding rendering the object, click OK.)

12   Drag the Amount slider to 200 and the Glow slider to around 2.85.

13   Press A to turn off Animation recording.

These new animated effects might be taxing your computer's processor. Let's change the play range and create a RAM preview of the animated logo.

14   Press Option-Command-I to change the play range In point to the playhead position.

15   Press Shift–Right Arrow six times to move the playhead 60 frames to the right. Press Option-Command-O to set the play range Out point.

16   Press Command-R to render, then press the Space bar to play the rendered play range.

Since the Throw behavior was applied to the layer before the Light Rays filter, it throws both the object and the filter.

TIP▶ Experiment with different behavior and filter combinations to come up with unique animated effects.

17   Press Command-S to save your progress.

Advancing the Project

Once again, it's time to bake part of the project into a movie before finishing the last steps. You can export an entire project or just part of it. For this exercise, only the Lower Third layer was exported as a lossless movie (with an animation codec of millions of colors to preserve the alpha channels and quality).

1 Close the current project.

2 Open the file **3_Mstr_Motion_Generator**.

3 Play the project once in the Canvas to see all of the finished elements interacting.

Remember, you can always go back to the previous project if you decide to change any of the elements.

Applying a Caustics Generator

Let's polish off the project by adding a Caustics generator to the lower third bar. Motion 2 has several new generators, including Clouds and Caustics. Generators are elements that don't exist until they are generated by Motion for use in your project. You'll find the generators in the Motion Library.

1 Press Command-2 to open the Library pane.

2 Click the Generators category in the Library to view the different generators.

3 Click the Caustics generator to see it in the Preview area of the Library.

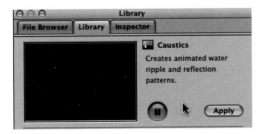

You can also apply effects and generators by dragging them from the Library directly to a layer in the Layers pane or Timeline. For this exercise you'll apply the Caustics generator by dragging it directly to the Lower Third Bar layer.

4   Move the playhead to frame 172.

5   Press Command-4 to open the Layers pane if it's not already open.

6   Drag the Caustics generator from the Library to the Lower Third layer.

Your goal with the Caustics generator is to add an interesting effect to the lower third bar without overpowering it. Before you modify the Caustics generator, it's a good idea to move it behind the lower third bar.

7   Select the Caustics generator in the Layers pane.

8   Choose Object > Send to Back to move it to the lowest position in the layer.

9   Close the Layers pane.

Modifying the Caustics Generator

You can modify the Caustics generator in the Inspector or the Dashboard. Since the modifications are simple, let's start in the Dashboard.

1   On the Caustics Dashboard, drag the Height slider to 135.

2   Drag the Caustics object in the Canvas down to the bottom of the frame.

3   Press the Space bar to pause playback if it is currently playing.

4   Press Shift-I to move the playhead to the first frame of the Caustics generator, then press Option-Command-I to set the play range In point.

5   Press the Space bar again to begin playback.

6   Change the Caustics parameters as follows: Size to 0.20, Speed to 0.15, Refraction to 75, and Brightness to 10.

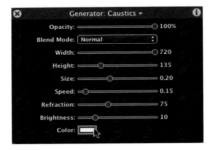

7   Click the color well on the Caustics Dashboard to open the Colors window.

8   Choose a dark aqua or blue color, then close the Colors window.

Feel free to modify the Caustics parameters to taste.

NOTE ▶ Motion 2 includes a MIDI Parameter behavior that allows you to edit and animate object parameters using standard MIDI devices, such as a musical keyboard or synthesizer. You can apply the MIDI behavior to parameters in the Inspector, then use the MIDI device to dial, play, and mix the parameters.

The Caustics look great, but they need a Fade In/Fade Out behavior to soften their debut.

9   From the Add Behavior menu in the toolbar, choose Basic Motion > Fade In/Fade Out.

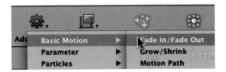

Previewing the Finished Project

The final step to completing your project is adding the music track and viewing it in Full Screen mode.

1   Press Option-X to reset the play range.

2   Play the project in the Canvas if it's not already playing.

3   Open the File Browser if it's not already open.

4   Drag the **XL Bumper music.aif** file from the Media folder in the File Browser to the Canvas.

5   Press F8 to preview the finished project in Full Screen mode.

6   Press Command-/ (forward slash) to turn off all overlays.

7   Press F8 again to return to the Motion interface.

8   Press Command-/ to turn on the overlays.

Nice work! In about an hour, you created a complex motion graphics composite using some advanced techniques. You can now export the finished movie or export the finished Motion project to Final Cut Pro or DVD Studio Pro.

Learning More About Motion

This Apple Pro Training tutorial just scratches the surface of the features, tools, and techniques that Motion has to offer. For detailed information about specific features, refer to the Motion documentation that comes with the program, and explore the Apple Pro Training DVD tutorial (on the companion DVD) and the tutorials that ship with Motion (accessible through the Motion Help menu).

To learn more, see page 302 for information on Apple certified training and the self-paced Apple Pro Training books, *Apple Pro Training Series: Motion* and *Apple Pro Training Series: Getting Started with Motion*.

5

Lesson Files   Apple_Pro_Training_Tutorials > Introducing_Soundtrack_Pro >
1_SoundtrackPro_starting; 2_panned; 3_automation; 4_fx; 5_reversecymbal.stmp;
6_VO edited.stmp; 7_recording; 8_mixing; 9_finished

Time   This lesson takes approximately 60 minutes to complete.

Goals   Explore the Soundtrack Pro interface

Create a crossfade

Add sound effects to the Timeline

Create track automation

Edit a voiceover file in the Timeline

Explore the Waveform Editor

Repair and modify audio files in the Waveform Editor

Work with a multiple take recording

Explore the Mixer

Mix and export the finished project

Lesson 5
Introducing Soundtrack Pro

This is a self-paced, hands-on tutorial designed to guide you through the Soundtrack Pro interface and features as you build and mix a project. Over the next hour, you'll work with many of Soundtrack Pro's professional sound design features to arrange audio clips on the Timeline, synchronize audio and video, automate volume and pan levels, edit audio files, reduce noise, normalize voiceover, add effects, and create a mix. Along the way you'll also learn some handy keyboard shortcuts and sound design tricks.

Preparing the Project

Before you start, you'll need to install the Soundtrack Pro program and Soundtrack Pro Loops on your hard disk. You also need to drag the applicable Apple Pro Training Tutorials folder from the DVD to your computer's desktop.

NOTE ▸ Choose either the Apple Pro Training Tutorials NTSC folder (North America), or Apple Pro Training Tutorials PAL folder (Europe and some parts of Asia), depending on which broadcast standard you'll be using.

Once you have the Soundtrack Pro program and Apple Pro Training Tutorials folder on your computer, you're ready to begin this lesson.

Opening Soundtrack Pro

You can work on two types of projects in Soundtrack Pro: *multitrack* projects and *audio file* projects. Multitrack projects involve arranging, editing, and mixing audio clips in the Timeline. Soundtrack Pro also includes a powerful Waveform Editor where you can modify, repair, analyze, and sound-design audio files. For this tutorial, you'll start with a multitrack project and then modify audio files in the Waveform Editor.

There are three ways to launch Soundtrack Pro:

▶ Double-click the Soundtrack Pro icon on your hard disk.

▶ Click once on the Soundtrack Pro icon in the Dock.

▶ Double-click any Soundtrack Pro project file.

For this exercise, you'll open Soundtrack Pro by opening a project file.

1 Locate the Apple Pro Training Tutorials folder on your computer's desktop, then double-click the folder to open it.

The folder opens revealing the different Apple Pro Training Final Cut Suite tutorials.

2 Open the Introducing_Soundtrack_Pro folder.

The Introducing Soundtrack Pro folder contains all of the projects and media that you'll need to complete this tutorial.

3 Double-click the **1_SoundtrackPro_starting** file to open Soundtrack Pro and open the project.

When Soundtrack Pro opens, you will see three windows displaying the project.

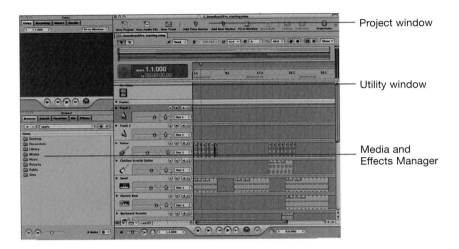

The largest window at the right is the Project window. It includes the Timeline, where you arrange audio clips for your project. The two smaller windows at the left are the Utility window and the Media and Effects Manager. You can use the Utility window to view a project's video, recording levels, master level meters, and details about individual clips within the project. The Media and Effects Manager is where you locate and preview files as well as add and modify effects.

Working With Backup Projects

You will be prompted throughout the tutorial to open progressive versions of the project. The Introducing_SoundtrackPro folder includes progressive versions of the project.

If at any time you don't complete a step, you can open the appropriate backup project. Each project is numbered sequentially and named for the last task that was completed in that project.

Exploring the Project Window

The Project window is your primary window, where you create your multi-track projects in the Timeline or edit audio files in the Waveform Editor. At the top of the Project window is a customizable Toolbar for easy access to common functions. At the bottom you'll find the transport controls as well as controls for the tracks. The title bar at the top of the Project window changes to reflect whichever project tab is currently selected. The Timeline is where you work with the elements of your multitrack project.

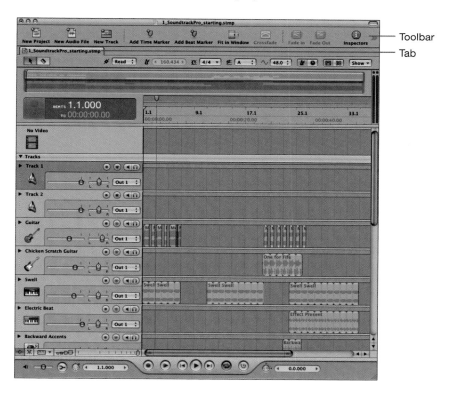

NOTE ► If you've worked with the Soundtrack program, you're already familiar with the Timeline portion of the Project window. You can upgrade from Soundtrack to Soundtrack Pro, which will enable you to open your Soundtrack projects as Soundtrack Pro multitrack projects.

Green audio clips appear in the Timeline including Apple Loops. Apple Loops are prerecorded pieces of music included with Soundtrack Pro, and they can be arranged in the Timeline to build a song. You can arrange audio clips on tracks to build music in much the same way that you arrange video clips on tracks in the Timeline of Final Cut Pro.

The current project includes eight music tracks, with two empty tracks at the top. You'll add sound effects to the empty tracks a few minutes after you finish working with basic Timeline navigation.

Playing a Project in the Timeline

As in the other Apple Pro applications, you can play the project by clicking the Play button in the transport controls or simply pressing the Space bar.

1   Press the Space bar to play the project in the Timeline.

   The playhead moves across the tracks as it moves forward in the Timeline and plays the project. Once the playhead reaches the end of the last clip in the Timeline, it automatically cycles back to play the song again from the beginning.

   NOTE ► You can stop the playhead from cycling by clicking the Cycle button in the transport controls.

2   Press the Space bar again to stop playback.

3   Press Return to move the playhead to the beginning of the project.

Navigating in the Timeline

Now that you've played the project, you'll learn to navigate as well as zoom in and out of the Timeline. The current playhead position is displayed in both timecode and beats in the Time display at the upper left of the Timeline. *Timecode* is generally used to reference video and displays four pairs of numbers: 00:00:00;00. From left to right, these represent hours, minutes, seconds, and frames. *Beats* represents musical time as 1.1.000; that is, in measures, beats, and fractions of a beat.

NOTE ▶ The timecode will match any video clip imported into the project.

There are many methods for positioning the playhead in the Timeline. For example, you can drag the handle at top of the playhead horizontally in the Time ruler, click anywhere in the Timeline, or change the value in the Playhead Position value slider.

1   Click the green handle at the top of the playhead and drag to the right in the Timeline.

You'll hear the sound of the clips as you drag the playhead. Dragging the playhead is called *scrubbing* because it scrubs the playhead across the clips in the Timeline.

2   Press the End key to move the playhead to the end of the song in the Timeline.

You can also navigate in the Timeline using the keyboard.

The Left and Right Arrow keys move the playhead right or left one grid line at a time. Grid lines are the vertical gray lines within the tracks.

3   Press the Left Arrow key several times to move the playhead to the left one grid line at a time.

There are also many ways to zoom in and out of the Timeline. One of the easiest ways to zoom in and out is to use the Up and Down Arrow keys. The Up Arrow zooms in, and the Down Arrow zooms out.

4   Press and hold the Up Arrow to zoom all the way in to the Timeline.

Once you are zoomed in to or out of the Timeline, you can easily fit the entire project to the Timeline window by clicking the Fit in Window button in the Toolbar, or using the keyboard shortcut Shift-Z.

5   Click the Fit in Window button on the Toolbar.

The Timeline scale changes to show the project from the beginning to the last clip at the end.

Working With Video

Which comes first, the picture or the sound? If you're editing a project dependent on the music, it's much easier to have the music *before* you begin editing the picture. If you're creating music that goes with video, it's much easier to score if you have the finished video. Fortunately, Final Cut Pro and Soundtrack Pro work well together so that you can create a temporary score in Soundtrack Pro, export it to Final Cut Pro, and then once the picture is complete, export the finished video for Soundtrack Pro to complete the sound design.

The music tracks in this project were arranged and exported as a stereo mix to Final Cut Pro to be a temporary score for the show *Capturing the eXtreme*. Now that the video has been edited, you can import the finished video clip into the Soundtrack Pro project to add sound effects and complete the sound design.

Soundtrack Pro supports standard QuickTime-compatible file formats up to four hours in length. The music tracks in this project were originally created as a score for a Final Cut Pro project. Your goal in this tutorial is to import the finished video clip, add sound effects and voiceover, and complete the sound design for the project.

Importing a Video Clip

To import a video clip, you'll first need to locate the clip in the Browser. Like the other Apple Pro applications, Soundtrack Pro includes a Browser where you can access files. The Browser is located in the Media and Effects Manager at the left of the interface.

1   In the Browser tab, navigate to the Introducing_Soundtrack Pro folder in the Apple Pro Training Tutorials folder on the desktop.

2   Double-click the Introducing_Soundtrack Pro folder to open it in the Browser.

    You can preview audio and video files in the Browser by selecting the file, or you can click the Play button at the lower left of the Media and Effects Manager.

3   Click the **1 Capturing Extreme Promo** clip in the Browser to select the clip.

4 Click the Play button at the bottom of the Media and Effects Manager to preview the file in the Details tab of the Utility window.

The Details tab includes a thumbnail of the clip and information about the selected file.

5 Click the Video tab, or press Command-1 to open the Video tab in the Utility window.

The Video tab is where you can import and view the project's video.

6 Drag the file **1 Capturing Extreme Promo** from the Browser to the empty viewer on the Video tab and release the mouse button.

The green circle with a plus (+) sign indicates that you are adding a file to the project.

The video clip appears in the Viewer and in the video track at the top of the Timeline along with orange scoring markers that were added to the project in Final Cut Pro. Scoring markers can be used as cues for sound effects and music.

7 In the Video tab, click the Play button in the Video transport controls to play the project.

Resizing the Video Tab

You can detach and resize any of the tabs in the Utility window or Media and Effects Manager, including the Video tab. To detach a tab you simply drag it to a new location on the screen.

Let's drag the Video tab from the Utility window, then resize the window for a larger view of the video.

1 Click the Video tab and drag down and toward the right to remove it from the Utility window.

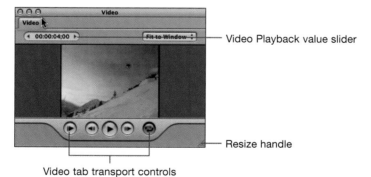

Video Playback value slider

Resize handle

Video tab transport controls

The Video tab is now a separate Video window on the interface. You can resize the window by dragging the resize handle on the lower-right corner of the window. The resize handle looks like three diagonal lines.

2 Drag the resize handle to increase the size of the Video window.

NOTE ▶ With Soundtrack Pro you can connect an external video output to your computer to play the project on your external monitor or Digital Cinema display.

3 Press F1 to return the interface to the standard window layout.

The Video tab returns to the default position in the Utility window.

Exploring the Search Tab

In addition to the Browser, the Media and Effects Manager includes Search, Favorites, and Bin to give you different ways to find media files. The Bin tab lists media files for the current project, and Favorites allows you to access your favorite loops to use in any project. The entire loops library is accessible through Search. Soundtrack Pro comes with 5,000 prerecorded royalty-free audio loops ranging from musical parts to sound effects. Let's use Search to locate the Sound Effects files and then add a sound effect to the project. Specifically, you're looking for the sound of skiing to go with the various skiers and snowboarders in the video clip.

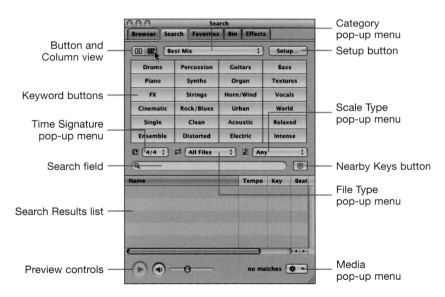

1   Click the Search tab on the Media and Effects Manager to open the Search tab.

You can view Search in either Button view or Column view. For this exercise, you'll use the Button view.

2   Click the Button View button if the Search tab is not already in Button view.

The keyword buttons allow you to narrow the search using keywords for the default category Best Mix. Best Mix includes an assortment of commonly used keyword buttons for Instruments, Genres, and Descriptors. Next, you'll change the Category pop-up to Sound Effects for easy access to the Sound Effects keyword buttons.

3   Click the Category pop-up menu and choose Sound Effects if it's not already selected.

Soundtrack Pro includes 14 categories of Sound Effects, from Ambience to Weapons. Since you're looking for sound effects to go with sports footage, the Sports and Leisure category is a good place to start.

4   Click the Sports and Leisure keyword button to narrow the Sound Effects to files that relate to Sports and Leisure.

5   Scroll through the results list to locate the Ski sound effects.

TIP ▶ Typing the first letter of the file you are looking for will automatically select the first file in the list starting with that letter. You can also use the Up and Down Arrow keys to move through the list, or the scroll button on a three-button mouse.

6 Click the **Ski 1.aiff** file to preview it.

7 Press the Down Arrow to preview each of the Ski files in the list.

They're all good, but Ski 3 shows great promise for the end of the video. You're not quite ready for that part of the project, so let's just add it to Favorites, so it will be handy when you need it.

8 Select the **Ski 3.aiff** file, then choose Add to Favorites from the Media pop-up menu on the lower right of the Search tab.

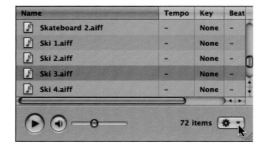

Media pop-up menu

Adding a File to the Timeline

To add a file to the Timeline you simply drag the file from the Media and Effects Manager to the desired track on the Timeline. The file will appear on the track wherever you release the mouse button. For this exercise you'll add the **Snow Skiing FX.aiff** to the beginning of track 1 on the Timeline.

1 Select the **Snow Skiing FX.aiff** file and drag it to the beginning of track 1 in the Timeline and release the mouse button.

Soundtrack Pro includes three modes for recording automation: Read, Touch, and Latch. Read only reads the automation data and does not record new data while you play the project. Touch and Latch both record new data when you change the controls while playing the project. Both overwrite any current data with changes to the controls while the project is played. The difference between Touch and Latch is when you release the controls. Releasing the controls in Touch mode returns to the value it previously had at the point of release. Latch on the other hand maintains the same value at which you released it.

For this exercise you'll use the Touch automation mode to record volume envelope automation on the Skiing track. First, you'll extend the playback region to the third scoring marker (28;03). Also, before you record automation it's a good idea to watch the playback region so you'll know the action in the scene.

1   Press the Down Arrow to zoom out of the Timeline a few times until you can clearly see the first four markers in the Timeline.

2   Drag the right edge of the playback region to the fourth marker in the Timeline.

3   Press the Space bar to view the new playback region.

Watch the video clip to see when the skier or snowboarder is actually making contact with the snow.

4   Drag the volume slider on the Skiing track to raise the volume to match the action on the video.

Practice changing the volume level a few times before moving on to the next step.

5   Press the Space bar to pause playback, then double-click the volume slider to reset it to the default level.

This will be the starting level for the track.

6   Choose Latch from the Automation pop-up menu to change the Timeline automation mode.

7   Press Shift-Return to start playback from the beginning of the Timeline.

8   As the project plays, drag the volume slider to change the levels and record the data on the volume envelope.

9   Press the Space bar to stop playback once you finish recording.

Notice the envelope points that have been recorded to the track.

Recording automation takes practice and patience. If you'd like to try again you can press Command-Z to undo your recorded data, or simply overwrite the automation data as you record again. Don't worry about getting it perfect. For this tutorial your goal is to learn how to use some of the Soundtrack Pro features. You can always practice after you finish the tutorial.

10   Click the Solo button on the Skiing track to unsolo the track.

11   Press Shift-Return to hear the play range with the music and automated Skiing track.

12   Click the lower half of the Time ruler to the right of the play range Out point to clear the play range.

NOTE ▶ You can also record automation in the Mixer, which you'll work with later in the lesson. Soundtrack Pro includes a control surfaces feature that allows you to record automation using external hardware controls such as a mixing board.

Advancing the Project

Now that you've added a sound effects file and automated its levels, let's open a different version of the project with the remaining sound effects already added.

1   Choose File > Close Window to close the current project.

2   Click Don't Save when prompted as you close the project.

3   Choose File > Open, then navigate to the **4_fx project** in the Introducing_ SoundtrackPro tutorial folder.

4   Click the Open button to open that version of the project.

5   Play the **4_fx** project and listen to the music and sound effects (fx).

Moving Clips in the Timeline

You can manually drag clips in the Timeline to arrange dialogue, music, and sound effects, or you can use keyboard shortcuts for fine-tuning a clip's position on the track. In this exercise you'll add the **Ski 3.aiff** sound effect file to the end of the project, then nudge its placement to sync it to the video.

1   Locate the FX – Hits track in the Timeline. It's the third audio track from the top.

You'll add the **Ski 3.aiff** file to the last scoring marker (last ski landing) on the FX – Hits track.

2   Click the Favorites tab on the Media and Effects Manager.

You should see the **Ski 3.aiff** sound effect that you added to Favorites earlier in this lesson.

NOTE ▶ If you don't see the *Ski 3.aiff* file in the Favorites tab, click the Search tab and locate the file under the Sports and Leisure sound effects category.

3   Drag the **Ski 3.aiff** file from the Favorites tab to the last landing marker on the FX – Hits track.

Last landing marker

4   Solo the FX – Hits track to isolate the sound of that track.

5   Press Shift-M to move the playhead to the last landing marker.

6   Play the Timeline from the last marker to hear the Ski 3 sound effect.

It's a great sound effect, but definitely not in sync with the picture.

Nudging Clips

Now that the clip is in the Timeline, you can work on nudging it into position. First, you'll need to create a playback region so that you can focus on the ending of the Timeline. It's also a good idea to make the tracks a little bit larger and zoom in for a better view of the clip.

The play range should start about one grid line before the last landing marker, and end a grid line after the end of the video track.

1   Click, then drag the mouse on the lower half of the Time ruler to create a playback region at the end of the project in the Timeline.

2   At the bottom left of the Timeline, click the largest Track Height button.

3   Press the Up Arrow several times to zoom in until you have a clear view of the Ski 3 clip, the last landing marker, and the playback region.

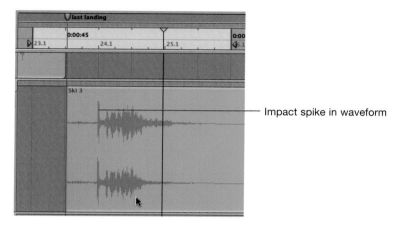

Impact spike in waveform

You may need to drag the Timeline scrollers to center the Ski 3 file in the Timeline.

4   Click the Ski 3 clip in the Timeline to select it.

If you look carefully you'll see the spike in the waveform near the beginning of the Ski 3 clip. That is the impact portion of the waveform, which you will align to the last landing marker. The last landing marker is on the frame where the skier lands on the snow. Your goal is to align the impact portion of the waveform with the scoring marker.

You could turn off snap and try to drag it manually, or use the keyboard shortcut Option–Left Arrow or Option–Right Arrow to nudge the clip. Shift–Option–Left or Right Arrow moves the selected clip one full gridline left or right.

5   Press Shift–Option–Left Arrow to move the clip one grid line to the left.

It's closer, but it needs a little nudge into position.

6   Press Option–Right Arrow, or Option–Left Arrow several times to nudge the clip into position.

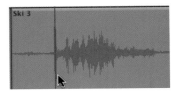

7   Press the Space bar to see and hear the playback region.

You can nudge the clip while the playhead is moving to fine-tune the sound effects placement.

8   Unsolo the FX – Hits track.

As you can see, it's quite easy to nudge clips into position once they are in the Timeline.

Reversing an Audio Waveform

Now that you've added sound effects to the project, let's work on some additional sound design to the project. An easy sound design trick is to simply reverse the waveform of a clip to create a different sound. In this case, you'll reverse the sound of the Cymbal Crash clip at the end of the project to enhance the ending of the project.

Up to this point you have been working on a multitrack project. To reverse a clips waveform, you'll need to edit the audio file in the Waveform Editor.

First, you'll need to scroll down two tracks in the Timeline to find the Cymbal Crash file.

1   Locate the FX – Additional track, which is four tracks below the FX – Hits track.

2   Click the Solo button on the FX – Additional track.

3   Press Home to move the playhead to the beginning of the play range.

4   Listen to the playback region to hear the Cymbal Crash clip at the end of the song.

The placement and sound of the cymbal crash are OK, but why settle for OK when you can make it really great?

Opening a File in the Waveform Editor

You can open files into the Soundtrack Pro Waveform Editor directly from the hard disk, or from within the Soundtrack Pro or Final Cut Pro Timelines. For this exercise, you will open the Cymbal Crash file in the Waveform Editor and reverse the waveform. You can either edit the existing audio file, or create an audio project that allows nondestructive editing of an audio file. For this exercise you'll open the file as a project.

1   Control-click the Cymbal Crash file in the Timeline to open a shortcut menu.

2   Choose Open as Project from the shortcut menu.

The Create Audio Project dialog opens so that you can name and save the audio project.

3   Type *Reverse Cymbal Crash* in the Save As field; then click Save. If the file already exists, just save over the previous version.

The Reverse Cymbal Crash project opens in the Waveform Editor.

Waveform
editing tools

Previous and Next
Selection buttons

Automation Mode
pop-up menu

Global Waveform view

Waveform View and
Spectrum View buttons

Time display

Level meters

Actions list

Waveform display

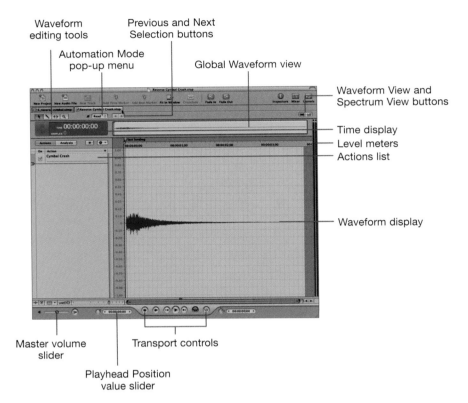

Master volume
slider

Transport controls

Playhead Position
value slider

Exploring the Waveform Editor

The Waveform Editor has many of the same features as the Timeline, such as
a playhead, a ruler, track controls, transport controls, and Time display. In this
exercise you'll explore some of the features unique to the Waveform Editor, such
as Waveform view and Spectrum view. Rather than explain each feature, this section will be more of a guided tour that focuses on some of the highlights.

The Waveform Editor includes graphical waveform editing tools, including the
Selection, Sample Edit, Audio Stretching, and Zoom tools.

Selection tool
Sample Edit tool

Audio Stretching tool
Zoom tool

The default tool is the Selection tool (Arrow), which you use to select part of a waveform in the editor. Let's use the Selection tool to select the waveform in the Cymbal Crash file.

1   Click the end of the Cymbal Crash waveform (3;00) and drag left to the beginning of the waveform to select it.

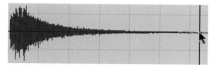 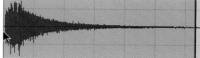

The selected part of the file is highlighted in blue.

2   Press the Space bar to play the selection, then pause playback.

Selections are used for isolating part of a file to edit, repair, analyze, or process.

3   Click the Zoom tool and then click the waveform several times to zoom in to the waveform until you see small dots on the waveform.

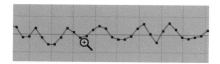

Those dots are the actual samples for the waveform, and they can be edited and redrawn using the Sample Edit tool.

4   Option-click the waveform with the Zoom tool to zoom out of the waveform.

TIP ▶ Press Z to instantly zoom in to the sample level at the playhead position. Press Z again to return to the normal view.

Next you'll use the Audio Stretching tool to decrease the size of the waveform from 3 seconds to around 2 seconds.

5   Click the Audio Stretching tool, then grab the right edge of the selection and drag about one-third of the length of the waveform to the left.

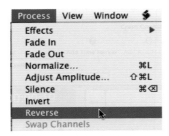

The waveform compresses to fit the reduced selection area.

6   Click the Selection tool to return to the normal selection functions.

The last step of this tour is to process the selection and reverse the waveform.

The Process menu includes many options for enhancing, designing, and repairing your audio file.

7   Choose Process > Reverse.

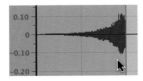

The selected waveform reverses.

8   Play the reversed cymbal crash to hear how it sounds.

Mission accomplished, with two simple actions. First you decreased the length of the waveform; then you reversed it.

At the left of the Waveform Editor is the Actions list that shows each action in the order that it was applied to the waveform.

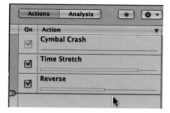

Actions can be turned on or off, reordered, or deleted.

The Waveform Editor also includes the Analysis list that can quickly analyze and fix common audio problems.

9 Click the Analysis button to view the different options.

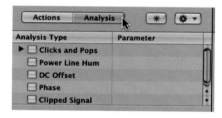

10 Click the Actions button to return to the Actions list.

Saving the Audio File Project

Now that you've edited the audio project, you'll need to save the changes.

1 Press Command-S to save the changes to the Reverse Cymbal Crash audio project.

The new Reverse Cymbal file will be saved with the other audio files for this project.

Once you've edited a file in the Waveform Editor, you can return to the project by clicking the tab at the top of the window. Notice that the name of the audio in the Waveform Editor has changed to Reverse Cymbal Crash.

2   Click the 4_fx.stmp tab at the top of the window to return to the project in the Timeline.

Creating a Crossfade in the Timeline

If you look closely at Cymbal Crash in the Timeline, you'll see that the original Cymbal Crash file has been replaced with the Reverse Cymbal Crash audio project. You can reopen the audio project in the Waveform Editor anytime by double-clicking it in the Timeline.

Once audio files or projects have been added to the tracks, they can be moved, edited, resized, and overlapped. In this exercise you'll move the Reverse Cymbal Crash audio project upward and overlap it with the Crash Metal 2 file on the track above. When you overlap audio clips in the Timeline, you can either truncate the overlapping clips or create a crossfade. The default setting is to create a crossfade where the clips overlap. The crossfade fades out the audio of the outgoing clip while it fades in the audio of the incoming clip.

First you'll play the edited clip in the Timeline. Then you'll combine it with the Crash Metal 2 loop on the track above to create a different effect.

1   Press Home to move the playhead to the beginning of the playback region.

2   Press Space bar and watch the play range.

Interesting effect, but let's hear how it sounds combined with the Crash Metal 2 file on the track above.

3   Solo the Crash Metal 2 track (above the FX – Additional track) to isolate it along with the FX – Additional track.

Next, let's trim the excess from the right edge of the Reverse Cymbal Crash project in the Timeline.

4 Drag the right edge of the Reverse Cymbal Crash in the Timeline to remove the empty waveform after the reverse crash sound.

5 Drag the Reverse Cymbal Crash toward the left until the waveform ends at the "last landing" scoring marker.

6 Listen to the playback region to hear the Reverse Cymbal Crash followed by the Crash Metal 2 sound.

The two sounds work pretty well, but would sound even better if they were combined with a crossfade.

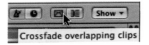

7 Click the Crossfade button at the top of the Timeline if it's not already selected to make sure the overlapping clips will crossfade.

8 Drag the Reverse Cymbal Crash upward to the track above and overlap it with the beginning of the Crash Metal 2 file.

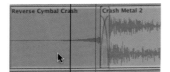

A crossfade appears where the clips overlap in the track.

9   Experiment with the position of the Reverse Cymbal Crash and the size of the crossfade until you are satisfied with the overall effect.

> **NOTE** ▶ You can resize the crossfade by dragging the edges or reposition the crossfade by dragging it from the center.

10   Click the lower half of the Time ruler outside the play range to close the playback region.

11   Press Shift-Z or click the Fit in Window button to fit the project to the window.

You may wish to scroll up to see the higher tracks in the Timeline.

12   Unsolo the Crash Metal 2 and FX – Additional tracks. Then, press Shift-Return to play the project from the beginning.

Editing Voiceover Files

Over the next series of exercises you'll edit two voiceover tracks. The first is a standard voiceover that needs a little finessing in the Waveform Editor. The second is a vocal track that needs to be processed with effects to sound as if it's coming over a helicopter radio. You'll start by adding a new track at the top of the project and importing the voiceover file. To add a new track, you simply Control-click the drag handle on the left edge of an existing track and choose Insert Track from the shortcut menu.

1   Control-click the drag handle (dots) on the left edge of the Skiing track and choose Insert Track Before from the shortcut menu.

A new numbered track appears above the Skiing track in the Timeline. The track number corresponds to the number of tracks already in the project.

2   Click the Browser tab on the Media and Effects Manager.

3   Navigate to the Introducing_Soundtrack Pro folder.

4   Select the **1 Producer VO.aif** file to preview it in the Browser.

You'll add this voiceover file to the new track so that it starts at the board hits snow marker.

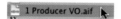

5   Drag the **1 Producer VO.aif** file from the Browser to the "board hits snow" marker on the top track in the Timeline.

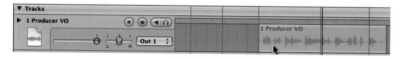

The track name changes to 1 Producer VO, and the track icon looks like an audio file.

6   Play the project from the second marker to hear the voiceover with the music.

The voice is quite low compared to the music. You can fix that when you mix the project; however, let's open it in the Waveform Editor to make a few common enhancements.

7   Double-click the 1 Producer VO file and click "Create audio file project (edit non-destructively)" from the dialog if it's not already selected and click OK.

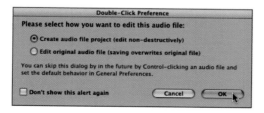

8   Save the new audio project as *Producer VO edited* into the Introducing_
SoundtrackPro folder.

> **NOTE ▸** Soundtrack multitrack projects have the extension .stmp.
> Soundtrack audio file projects have the file extension .stap.

Normalizing the Audio Waveform

Normalizing an audio file is the process of raising the overall level until the
highest or lowest peak is just below a set amount, usually 0 dB. In digital
audio, 0 dB is the maximum level you can set without causing distortion.
When you normalize a waveform to 0 dB, you're increasing the amplitude of
the entire waveform to the maximum level without causing digital distortion
(also known as *clipping*). To normalize a file in the Waveform Editor you simply choose Normalize from the Process menu. You can normalize all or just a
selection of the waveform.

1   Choose Process > Normalize.

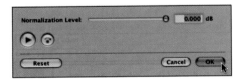

The Normalize dialog opens. For this exercise, you'll use the default level,
0.000 dB.

2   Click OK to normalize the waveform.

The amplitude (height) of the waveform increases until the highest or
lowest peaks reach 0 dB.

You can change the sample units in the waveform display to Sample Value,
Normalized, Percent, or Decibels. Let's change the sample units to Decibels
to see the overall effect of the Normalize action.

3   Control-click the numbered scale on the left edge of the Waveform Editor,
then choose Decibels from the shortcut menu.

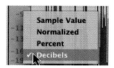

The Sample display changes to show the Decibel values of the waveform. Notice that the lowest and highest peaks are just below 0 dB.

Reducing Noise in the Waveform Editor

You can remove noise from an audio file in the Soundtrack Pro Waveform Editor in very much the same way as you remove color when keying a video image. First you choose the sound to remove, then you remove it. When you normalized the waveform, you also raised the underlying noise level. For this exercise, you'll start by making a noise print and then reduce the noise.

1   Press the Up Arrow key to zoom in to the waveform one level.

2   Press the Home key to move the playhead to the beginning of the waveform.

3   Drag the Selection tool over the beginning of the waveform, before the dialogue starts, to select the noise.

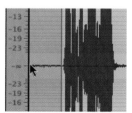

4   Press the Space bar to play the selection.

   If there is any dialogue in the selection, click outside the selection, and try again.

5   Choose Process > Set Noise Print.

   The selected noise is saved in memory and will be used to reduce the noise in the next step.

NOTE ▶ If this were an image and you were trying to remove the blue screen, you would first select the blue color, then remove it.

6   Click anywhere outside the selection to remove the selection.

7   Play the waveform. It will automatically repeat.

8   Choose Process > Reduce Noise.

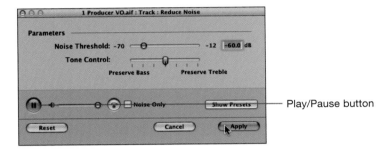 ———— Play/Pause button

The Reduce Noise dialog opens.

9   Select the Noise Only checkbox.

When Noise Only is selected, you hear only the part of the waveform that will be reduced. Your goal is to raise the Noise Threshold level as much as you can without damaging the vocals.

NOTE ▶ The Noise Only control is similar to viewing "matte only" while keying a video image.

10 Drag the Noise Threshold slider all the way to the right (to −12).

You can clearly hear the voice along with the noise.

11 Drag the Noise Threshold slider toward the left until you no longer hear any voice with the noise (around −55).

12 Deselect the Noise Only control to hear what the result will sound like.

> **NOTE ▶** When the Noise Only feature control is deselected, it is similar to viewing the final version of a keying filter in video.

13 Click the Apply button to apply the Noise Reduce process to the vocals.

Before Noise Reduction   After Noise Reduction

The waveform changes and most of the noise between the vocals has been eliminated.

Adding Effects in the Waveform Editor

Next you'll add a Pitch Shifter II filter to the waveform and slightly lower the sound of the vocal pitch. This is an example of adding a filter to a file in the Waveform Editor. You can learn more details about the specific controls in the Soundtrack Pro documentation available through the Help menu.

1 Play the project in the Waveform Editor.

2 Choose > Process > Effects > Miscellaneous > Pitch Shifter II.

The Pitch Shifter II graphical controls dialog opens.

3 Drag the Mix slider to the highest position (100%).

4 Drag the Semi Tones slider to –1.

It's not a big change, just enough to deepen his voice slightly.

5 Click Apply and listen to the results.

6 Press Command-S to save the edited audio file project.

> **NOTE ▶** Processes and effects will be applied to the entire audio file unless you create a selection before applying the effect.

7   Click the 4_fx.stmp tab to return to the project in the Timeline.

8   Click the Solo button on the 1 Producer VO track and play the Timeline starting at the "board hits snow" marker to hear the changes to the file.

Splitting a Clip in the Timeline

The last step to completing this voiceover section is to edit the file in the Timeline so that it fits better with the timing of the video clips. Once you've added files to the Timeline you can edit them with the Split tool the same way that you edit a video clip in Final Cut Pro. You can also split a selected file at the playhead position by pressing S, for split.

1   Press B (for blade) to change from the Selection tool to the Split (razor) tool.

2   Play the voiceover clip and stop the playhead after the narrator says ". . . In their element" (at approximately 00:30.45).

    The Split tool splits a file on the nearest grid line while the snap feature is on.

3   Press N to turn off snap if snap is turned on.

4   Press the Up Arrow to zoom in to the track for a better view of the clip.

5   Click the Split tool on the clip at the playhead position.

    The Producer VO edited clip splits into two pieces.

6   Press A to change from the Split tool to the Selection (Arrow) tool.

7   Drag the second Producer VO edited clip toward the right so that it begins at 00;32.00.

    The timing of the second half should now work much better with the action on the screen.

Advancing the Project

Before you move on to mixing the project, let's take a quick look at recording and editing recordings in the Timeline.

1   Choose File > Close Window to close the current project, and save the changes.

2   Choose File > Open, then navigate to the **7_recording.stmp** project in the Introducing_SoundtrackPro tutorial folder.

3   Click the Open button to open the project **7_recording.stmp**.

Working With Multiple Take Recordings

You can record files directly into your multitrack projects in either the Timeline or the mixing windows. Each track includes a record enable button that allows recording to that track. You can record a single take starting at the playhead position, or multiple takes if you record using a playback region. In this exercise you will work with a multiple take recording and then modify it in the Waveform Editor.

The recording is located on the Chopper Radio track near the top of the Timeline.

The recorded clip is titled Chopper Voice 1. At the lower right of the recorded clip is the numbered take. The recording session begins when you click the Record button and ends when you click Record again to stop recording. During the recording session the playhead continually cycles through the play range. Each cycle creates a new take.

Let's take a look at the ways to see the different takes from the recording. One of the easiest ways to view takes is via the shortcut menu.

1   Press the Space bar to begin playback of the current play range.

2   Control-click the clip on the Chopper Radio track and choose 1 from the Take submenu.

The take in the Timeline changes to Take 1.

3   Press the Space bar to pause playback.

Another way to view and edit the different takes is to extend the clip in the Timeline.

4   Drag the right edge of the clip to the right to reveal all four takes.

The dotted lines on the clip separate each recorded take.

NOTE ▶ Take 4 is incomplete because the recording session was stopped in the fourth cycle of the recording play range.

5   Drag the right edge of the clip to the left until it ends at the playback region Out point.

The playback region now shows only Take 1 of the recording session.

6   Select the recording in the Timeline.

7   Play Take 1 and pause the playhead after the voice says "Roll B-camera on my mark" (at approximately 13:25).

8   Press S to split the selected clip at the playhead position.

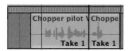

The recording splits into two clips.

NOTE ► This feature works the same as the Split tool, except the split feature requires the clip to be selected and it is not affected by snap. The Split feature will split all selected tracks.

9   Control-click the first section of the recording in the Timeline and choose Take > 2 from the shortcut menu.

10   Press the space bar to listen to the edited takes.

Adding Effects in the Waveform Editor

You probably noticed that the recording on the Chopper Radio track doesn't sound like a radio. Your goal in this exercise is to add two effects to the recording to modify the sound. You could add the effects to the track or you could add them to the recording itself in the Waveform Editor. Let's use the Waveform Editor and add effects to the entire recording.

1   Control-click the Take 2 segment of the recording in the Timeline and choose > Open in Editor from the shortcut menu.

The recording opens in the Waveform Editor. You can use the Global view at the top of the Waveform Editor window to see a scaled version of the entire recording.

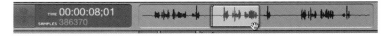

The highlighted rectangle in the Global view is the area of the recording that is visible below in the Waveform Editor.

First, you'll apply a Graphic Equalizer effect from the Mac OS filters, then you'll apply a Bitcrusher effect to distort the sound.

To add the effects to the recording you'll apply Effects from the Process menu.

2   Press the Space bar to begin playback.

3   Choose Process > Effects > Mac OS > GraphicEQ.

The GraphicEQ parameter controls window opens.

4   Change the Bands pop-up menu at the top of the window to 10 Bands.

5   Drag the first five sliders from the left to the lowest position.

6   Drag the last two sliders to the lowest position.

7 Leave the 1k, 2, and 24.1 kHz sliders at 0 dB.

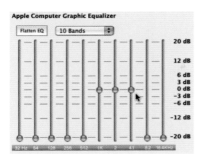

8 Click Apply.

AUGraphicEQ appears in the Actions list to show that the Audio Units Graphic EQ has been applied. The recording sounds more like a voice on the radio. Next you'll add some distortion.

9 With the playhead moving, choose Process > Effects > Distortion > Bitcrusher.

The Bitcrusher graphical control window opens. You can add a light effect for slight distortion or a dramatic effect with heavy distortion.

10 Drag the Drive slider up to increase the distortion to around 28.0 dB, then click Apply.

The Actions pop-up menu allows you to listen to the file with or without the actions applied.

11 Choose "Play without actions" from the Actions pop-up menu to hear the file without actions.

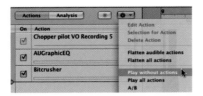

12 Choose "Play all actions" from the Actions pop-up menu to hear the file with all actions.

13 Press Command-S to save the changes to the Chopper Voice 1 project.

14 Click the 7_Recording.stmp tab to return to the multitrack project in the Timeline.

Playing the Edited Recording in the Timeline

Now that you've added effects to the recording, let's listen to it with the rest of the tracks in the Timeline.

1 Click the Solo button on the Chopper Radio track to unsolo the track.

2 Drag the volume slider on the Chopper Radio track to the middle position to lower the volume of the track.

3 Clear the play range so you can listen to the entire project.

4 Press Shift-Return to play the project from the beginning.

The Chopper Radio track works pretty well with the beginning of the project; however, the producer's voiceover is hard to hear because the music tracks are too loud. You'll fix the levels in the next exercise.

Before you move to the next exercise, notice that each track is currently assigned to Output 1, the default output.

Advancing the Project

It's time to mix and output your project. First, you'll need to open the mixing version of the project.

1   Choose File > Close Window to close the current project, and don't save the changes that you made to the files.

2   Choose File > Open, then navigate to the **8_mixing.stmp** project in the Introducing_SoundtrackPro tutorial folder.

3   Click the Open button for the project **8_mixing.stmp.**

4   Choose File > Save As to open the Save As dialog.

5   Type *TEST MIX* in the name field, then click Save to save the project into the Introducting_SoundtrackPro folder.

> **TIP** It's a good idea to save different versions of the project for each mix or submix so you'll have the ability to go back and adjust the different versions without needing to create a mix from scratch.

Mixing the Project

The last step in completing your project is creating a final mix. *Mixing* is the art of balancing the levels of the different tracks. First you adjust the level of each track individually using volume and pan sliders in the track controls. Once you're happy with the individual track levels, you can create busses to add effects to groups of tracks. Then you can use one output for all of the combined tracks, or you can create multiple outputs for mixing the output levels of different groups of tracks such as music, dialogue, effects, background, Foley, and ADR.

In the next series of exercises you'll create a Dialogue output in the Timeline and assign the 1 Producer VO and Chopper VO tracks to the Dialogue output. Finally, you'll open the mixer and create a final mix of the project.

Creating Outputs

For this final version of the project a few additional sound effects have been added. You'll also notice that the track headers are assigned to new outputs, either FX, Music, or None. If a track is not assigned to an output, you will not be able to hear the track when you play the project. In the current project, both of the dialogue tracks at the top of the Timeline need to be assigned to an output.

Outputs are also useful in creating submixes of a project. There are currently 19 audio tracks in your tutorial project. Busses and Outputs are located near the bottom of the Timeline.

1   Scroll to the bottom of the Timeline.

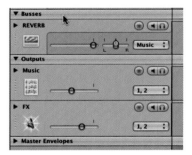

Notice the Busses, Outputs, and Master Envelopes areas of the Timeline.

You can use the disclosure triangles to view or close the Busses and Outputs in the Timeline.

The project includes one bus: REVERB, which adds reverb to the tracks sent to that bus. The project also includes two outputs: Music and FX. Each output or bus includes envelopes for automation.

Let's create a new output for the dialogue tracks.

2   Control-click the drag handle of the Music output, and choose Insert Output Before from the shortcut menu.

3   Click the new output track, and type *Dialog* in the text field.

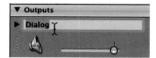

4   Scroll up to the top of the Timeline to the 1 Producer VO track.

5   Choose Dialog from the 1 Producer VO Track Output menu.

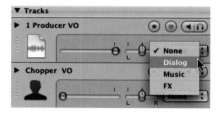

6   Choose Dialog from the Chopper VO Output menu.

Both of the tracks containing dialogue files are now assigned to the Dialog output.

Once you've assigned the tracks to outputs you're ready to create a mix.

> **NOTE** ▶ You do not have to assign tracks to new outputs in order to mix the project. You can use the default Output 1, as long as the tracks are assigned to at least one output.

Exploring the Mixing Layout

The Mixer looks and responds just like a real-world mixing board and includes
a channel strip with controls for each track in the Timeline. You can open the
Mixer from the Window menu or use a simple keyboard shortcut.

1   Choose Window > Mixer, or press Command-2 to open the Mixer.

You can resize any of the windows in the interface and create custom lay-
outs. Soundtrack Pro comes with three preset interfaces, including a handy
mixing layout.

2   Press F2 to change to the mixing layout.

This layout gives you easy access to the Timeline while you work with
the Mixer.

3   Press F1 to return to the standard layout, then Command-2 to show the full-size Mixer.

> **NOTE** ▸ Recording automation works the same in the Mixer as the track controls in the Timeline. In the Read automation mode the faders will read the levels only from the Timeline. In the Latch and Touch modes, you will be able to record new data for tracks, busses, and outputs.

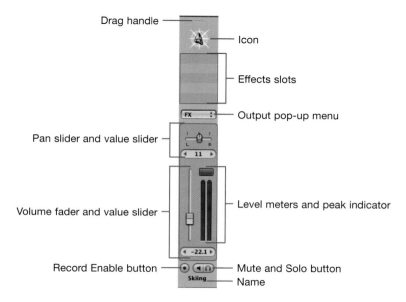

Each track, bus, and output channel strip includes a level meter to show the volume levels.

The peak indicator shows the highest level of the track or bus. If the level exceeds 0 dB, the indicator turns red. You can reset the peak indicator by clicking it.

Creating a Mix

As you create a mix, you want to make sure that the output level remains below 0 dB. First, you'll practice adjusting the faders to get the right levels; then you'll create a mix using the Touch automation mode.

1   Scroll to the right side of the Mixer to see the output level meter.

    Notice that all of the outputs are on the far right of the Mixer.

2   Play the project from the beginning.

3   While the project is playing, adjust the faders on the Dialog, Music and FX outputs to get a good mix of the levels.

    You may wish to start with the FX output at a higher level and the Music output at a lower level to emphasize the skiing sound effects at the beginning of the Timeline. Then raise the music after the first skier exits the frame at the beginning. Lower the music again when the Chopper Voice starts. You can raise the Music output fader toward the end after the voiceover finishes.

4   Pause playback, and then choose Latch from the Automation pop-up menu at the top of the Mixer.

5   Press Shift-Return to start playback from the beginning of the Timeline.

6   Mix the bus faders as needed to create a mix.

7   Once you're happy with the mix, pause playback.

8   Press Command-S to save your mixed project.

9   Press Command-W to close the Mixer.

10 On the Timeline, scroll down to the Outputs section.

11 Click the disclosure triangle for the Music output to see the automation levels that you recorded from the Mixer.

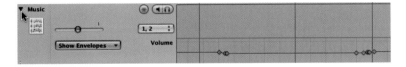

NOTE ► You can also show and automate envelopes for effects parameters that are applied to tracks, busses, or outputs. The Music output includes envelopes for the limiter effects applied to that output.

TIP ► When exporting audio for film or television, it's common to export submixes, including a music and effects submix and a dialogue-only submix. Exporting music and effects without the dialogue is necessary to add dialogue or overdubs in other languages. To export the project without dialogue, you can simply mute the dialogue tracks and busses.

Exporting Multitrack Projects

Once you have mixed your multitrack project, you can export the mix or individual tracks, busses, or outputs. You can also export a multitrack project using Compressor. The export options are available from the File > Export menu. For detailed information about how to export your project, please see the user manual, available through the Help Menu.

What's Next?

Congratulations! You have completed the tutorial. This Apple Pro Training tutorial was designed to give you a basic working knowledge of Soundtrack Pro.

To learn more, explore the interactive Apple Pro Training DVD Tutorial, located on the companion DVD. For more detailed information about Soundtrack Pro features and capabilities, please see the user manual, available through the Help Menu.

For more complete training, see page 302 for information on Apple certified training and the self-paced training book, *Apple Pro Training Series: Soundtrack Pro*, which uses the same project-based learning style as this tutorial.

6

Lesson Files   Apple_Pro_Training_Tutorials > Introducing_DVD_Studio_Pro > 1_Intro_DVDSP_Starting

Apple_Pro_Training_Tutorials > Introducing_DVD_Studio_Pro > 2_Intro_DVDSP_Finished

Time   This lesson takes approximately 45 minutes to complete.

Goals   Explore the DVD Studio Pro interface

Explore the Project window, Palette, and Inspector

Add a template to the Menu Editor

Modify and work with buttons

Work with drop zones

Add a shape from the Palette

Create a track and connect it to a button

Add a slideshow and connect it to a button

Modify the slideshow and add audio

Create a title

Build and burn your DVD project

Lesson **6**
Introducing DVD Studio Pro

In this Apple Pro Training tutorial, your will use DVD Studio Pro's Basic configuration to author a simple DVD containing one track, a slideshow, and one menu. You'll learn how to modify an existing menu template to your own design, create custom buttons, and connect your assets for a DVD. By working through a few of the basics, you'll have a solid foundation and be ready to tackle your next project.

If you want to learn more, check out the PDF Mastering Motion tutorial on this disk, and see the About Apple Pro Training folder on this DVD for information on the self-paced *Apple Pro Training Series* books and the Apple Pro certified training program.

Preparing the Project

Before you start, you'll need to install the DVD Studio Pro software and content on your hard disk. You also need to drag the applicable Apple Pro Training Tutorials folder from the DVD to your computer's desktop.

NOTE ▶ Choose from either the Apple Pro Training Tutorials NTSC folder (North America) or the Apple Pro Training Tutorials PAL folder (Europe and some parts of Asia), depending on which broadcast standard you'll be using.

Once you have the DVD Studio Pro application and Apple Pro Training Tutorials folder on your computer, you're ready to begin this lesson.

MORE INFO ▶ You can find more specific installation instructions on the Final Cut Studio Tutorials Read Me file included on the DVD.

Opening DVD Studio Pro

There are three ways to open DVD Studio Pro:

▶ Double-click the DVD Studio Pro application icon on your hard disk.

▶ Click once on the DVD Studio Pro icon in the Dock (if you dragged it during installation).

▶ Double-click any DVD Studio Pro project file.

For this exercise, you'll open a project file.

1 Locate the Apple Pro Training Tutorials folder on your computer's desktop, then double-click the folder to open it.

The folder opens, revealing the Apple Pro Training Final Cut Studio tutorials.

2 Open the Introducing_DVD_Studio_Pro folder by double-clicking on
the folder.

3 Double-click the 1_Intro_DVDSP_Starting file to open DVD and the project.

When DVD Studio Pro opens, you will see the Basic configuration displaying the project 1_Intro_DVDSP_Starting.

The interface displays three windows. The large window at the left side is the
project window. The two windows on the right are the Palette and Inspector.

4 Press F1 to set the Basic configuration if it's not already selected.

Let's start with the project window, since that is where you create and modify
your projects.

NOTE ▶ If the Choose Application Configuration dialog appears when you open the program for the first time, choose Basic as your configuration under step 1 and the video standard for your project, NTSC or PAL, under step 2. Then click OK and the program will open in the Basic configuration.

Working With the Interface

Before you start to build this project, a quick tour of the interface will help give you a good foundation. Choosing the Basic configuration displays the project window, Palette, and Inspector. The project window contains the Menu, Slideshow, Viewer, and Graphical tabs at the top left.

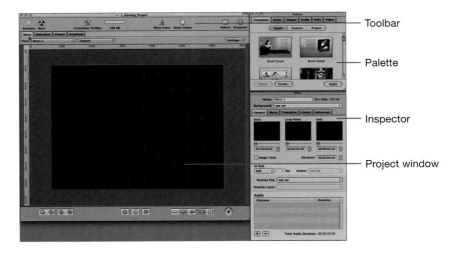

Exploring the Project window

The Project window is where you can make menus, view project assets, create slideshows, and see their relationship to each other in the Graphical tab.

The four tabs in the Project window are:

▶   Menu tab — enables you to put together the assets you want to use in creating and designing your menus.

▶ Slideshow tab —allows you to arrange slides and add audio, transitions, and timing for your slideshow.

▶ Viewer tab — offers a view of assets, such as a moving image in a track, that you want to add to your project or have already added.

▶ Graphical tab — shows graphic representations of your project and the way the items are linked together.

The toolbar at the top of the Project window allows you to easily select frequently used tools for working with your project. It can be customized to your specific needs.

The Palette

The Palette is a free-floating window at the upper-right corner of the interface. It is made up of six tabs with a number of options under each tab.

Consider the Palette as if it were an artist's palette. This is where you work with your paints—or in DVD Studio Pro, your assets. Nothing is added to your DVD until you dip into your assets in the Palette and add it to your project. This is where you will put all the still images, moving images, and shapes for your project. Let's take a moment to get familiar with the Palette.

1 Click the title bar at the top of the Palette and drag the window to the middle of your screen, on top of the Project window.

   You are in the Templates tab and can scroll through the many templates included with DVD Studio Pro. Templates are used to create a menu.

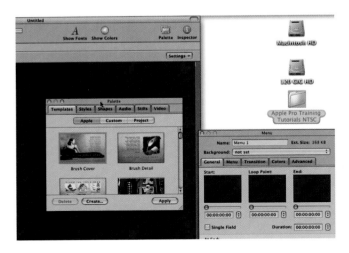

2 Click the Styles tab.

3 In the Styles tab click the Apple button, then the Drop Zones button.

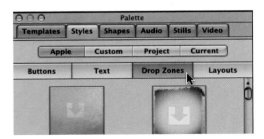

Scroll down to see drop zones that can hold a still or moving image as an element of your project.

4 Click the Shapes tab, then the Apple button.

Here you will find prebuilt shapes to enhance your project.

5 Press F1 to return the interface to the Basic configuration.

Audio, Stills, and Video are the last three tabs. You will be adding project assets under these tabs.

The Inspector

Also a free-floating window, the Inspector is directly below the Palette. The Inspector is where you can modify just about anything in your DVD project. It updates to show you the properties of the currently selected item. Let's select Menu 1 to see how the Inspector works.

1   Click the Graphical tab in the Project window.

If you don't see the two icons, click the Zoom to Fit button in the upper right of the Graphical tab.

2   Click the Menu 1 icon in the Graphical tab.

The Inspector updates to display the properties of Menu 1, and the title bar of the Inspector changes to *Menu,* showing what element is currently selected.

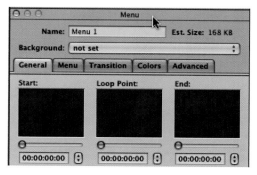

3 Click the green Track 1 icon in the Graphical tab.

The Inspector updates to display *Track* in the title bar of the window and shows the properties of Track 1.

TIP ▶ Remember, you first need to select an item; then it will appear in the Inspector for your review.

Importing Assets Into the Palette

The Palette displays imported assets that are ready to use.

1 Go to the Palette and click the Audio tab.

NOTE ▶ DVD Studio Pro will integrate your iTunes Library music files in the Audio tab, movies from your Movies folder in the Video tab, and iPhoto pictures in the Stills tab of the Palette.

2 Click the Add (+) button in the upper-left corner of the Audio tab.

3 Navigate to the Apple Pro Training Tutorials/Introducing_DVD_Studio_ Pro > X_Assets > X_Audio folder, then click Add in the lower-right corner of the window.

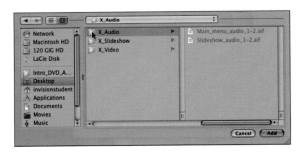

The X_Audio folder is added to the Palette with two audio files in the Name column.

4 Click the Stills tab.

5 Click the Add (+) button in the upper-left corner of the Stills tab.

6 Navigate to the Introducing_DVD_Studio_Pro > X_Assets > X_Slideshow folder, then click Add.

With the Slideshow folder added to the Stills tab, you will be able to see a thumbnail of each still that is an asset in your Palette.

7 Click the Video tab.

8 Click the Add (+) button in the upper-left corner of the Video tab.

9 Navigate to the Introducing_DVD_Studio_Pro > X_Assets > X_Video folder, then click Add.

10 Select the thumbnail of the video asset **eXtreme_snow.m2v,** then click the Play button to preview the video. (If your thumbnails are smaller than those shown here, go to Preferences > General and choose Large Thumbnail Size for the Palette.)

TIP You can resize the Palette by dragging the resize handle on the lower-right corner of the window. F1 will take you back to the Basic configuration at any time.

Creating a Menu

Using menus to navigate through a DVD is an easy interactive feature for the viewer. When creating menus you can use graphics that you have prepared, the provided templates, or a combination of both.

Applying a Template

Let's start with a template that you can modify for this specific project. The supplied templates can define a style for your project. They are made up of elements that give a consistent look to your menus in the DVD.

1 Click the Menu tab in the Project window to display the Menu Editor.

2 Go to the Palette and click the Templates tab.

3 In the Templates tab, click the Apple button and, using your scroller on the right side of the window, scroll down to the template named Portfolio Cover.

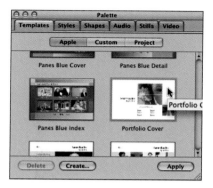

4   Click to select the Portfolio Cover from the templates and drag it to the Menu Editor. Don't release the mouse button until you see the Drop Palette appear with your options.

> **NOTE ▶** The Drop Palette will appear and give you options when you drag an asset to the Menu Editor. The options you have will depend on the type of asset or element you are using, where you are dragging the element to, and how it may be used.

5   Place the mouse pointer over Apply to Menu. Release the mouse to choose Apply to Menu from the Drop Palette.

> **NOTE ▶** If you get a result you didn't want during this tutorial, you can undo the last change to your project by pressing Command-Z.

6   Click on the white portion of the menu background.

Menu 1 will now be selected and appear in the Inspector. Next you'll rename your menu to help find it later and stay organized as you build the project.

7   In the Name field of the Inspector, type *Main_menu*, then press Return.

Using the Simulator

The Simulator lets you test your project as you build the elements. You will see a real-time preview of your DVD and be able to check your work before burning your disc. Use the Simulator often to check on how your DVD is progressing.

1   Click the Simulate icon at the upper-left corner of the toolbar.

The Simulator provides you with the functions of a DVD player's remote control.

The Log tab will also open behind the Simulator to display the details of your simulation.

2   Click the remote buttons in the Simulator and test the buttons on your menu.

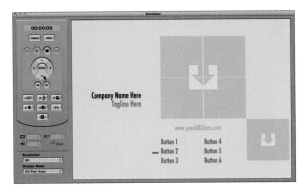

3   Roll over the buttons with your mouse to see the highlights.

Button highlight colors show the selected state of the button and the activated state when you click the button. This is important for viewer interaction and lets the viewer know when a selection is made.

4   Click the close button at the upper-left corner of the Simulator window, or press Command-W to close the window.

The Log remains open. For now just click on the background of your menu to hide the Log. It will go behind your Project window until you want to access details again.

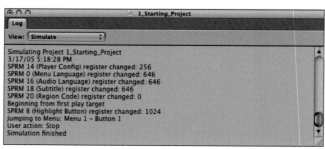

NOTE ▶ Use the Log tab to see information about your project when you simulate, build, and encode. Reviewing the Log can help you find details, such as errors, in your project.

Saving a Project

You've successfully applied a template to your project, so it's a good idea to save.

1   Choose File > Save As, or press Shift-Command -S to open the Save As window.

2   Navigate to the Apple Pro Training Tutorials folder on your desktop, then double-click the My_Saved_Projects folder to open it.

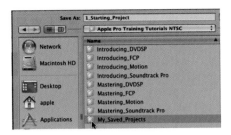

3   Click the Save button, or press Return to save the project to the selected folder.

Modifying a Template

The best part of working with templates is that most of the work is already done. You can choose to use all or part of any template you apply to a menu. This template will work well with just a few modifications.

Selecting Buttons

Setting up the buttons on your menu involves deciding where they will be located, what happens when they are selected, and what the highlight colors will be for the button states of normal, selected, and activated.

You will learn how to move, resize, batch-select, and delete buttons in the next few steps. The first step is to delete the default buttons from the template and create your own custom buttons.

1   Make sure your button outlines are turned on (you'll see dotted outlines around your buttons) by clicking the Button Outlines button at the bottom of the Menu Editor.

Buttons are outlined with a bounding box when the button outlines are active. Small circles or handles appear on the bounding box when a button is selected.

NOTE ▶ If your guides are being displayed, you can hide them by clicking the Show/Hide Guides button next to Show/Hide Button Outlines button on the bottom of the Menu Editor.

2   Click Button 6 to select it and press Delete.

3   Hold down the Command key and drag a selection box around the remaining buttons 1, 2, 3, 4, and 5.

TIP ▶ If you don't press the Command key you will be drawing a button instead of selecting the buttons on the menu.

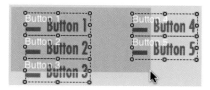

4   Press Delete to remove all of the highlighted buttons from the main menu.

Now that you have deleted the template buttons, you can make your own buttons for this menu.

Adding an Asset to a Drop Zone

Drop zones are elements of your project that can hold still or moving images. Drop zones can be moved and be modified in the same manner in which you modified buttons or shapes on your menu. In this exercise you will add a still image and a moving image to a drop zone.

1   Click the Stills tab in the Palette.

2   Scroll through the thumbnails of your X_Slideshow folder to **xslide_01**.

3   Drag **xslide_01** to the large drop zone named Content Here 1 toward the middle of your menu. Do not release the mouse button until the drop zone is outlined. A Drop Palette will appear.

4   Choose Set Asset from the Drop Palette.

The still image of the skier will become part of the menu background when you build the project.

5   Click the Video tab in the Palette.

6   Scroll through the video thumbnails in your Video tab until you see the video called **Chopper_1.m2v**.

7   Drag the video **Chopper_1.m2v** to the small drop zone named Content Here 2 at the lower-right corner of your menu. Do not release the mouse button.

When the drop zone is outlined and the Drop Palette appears, choose Set Asset.

8   Click the Motion button at the lower right of your Project window (or press Command-J).

The video will play and loop at the end as part of the menu.

TIP ▶ The Motion button will let you start and stop the playback of audio and video assets you have added to your menu.

9   Click on the white portion of the menu background to open the Menu Inspector.

The Duration field under the General tab of the Menu Inspector displays the length of the motion playback for the menu.

NOTE ▶ The default motion duration for the menu is 30 seconds. If your duration is not 30 seconds, you can change it in the Duration field in the Menu Inspector.

Customizing Text

Now let's create a custom title for our main menu.

1   Click once on the placeholder title *Company Name Here* to select the title.

2   Click again to highlight the text so you can customize the font and color.

3   Type *eXtreme Living Channel.*

TIP ▶ If you press the Return key when typing in the title, it will add another line to your text. If you press the Enter key or click on the background, it will accept the text change.

4   Deselect the text by clicking on the background of the menu.

5 Double-click the text *Tagline Here* to highlight the text.

6 Click the Show Colors icon in the toolbar to open the Colors window.

7 Click the Crayons icon on the upper right of the Colors window.

8 Click the Blueberry crayon toward the middle of the crayons.

9 Close the Colors window.

The *Tagline Here* text is now customized to the blueberry color.

10 Click the Show Fonts icon in the toolbar to open the Font panel.

11 Click the Size field and make sure the numbers are highlighted.

12 Type *18* in the Size field for our font size and press Return.

The font on the menu updates for you to see the new size without having to close the Font panel. Size 18 is a bit too small for our menu.

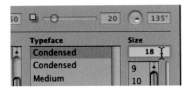

13 Type 22 in the Size field and press Return.

14 Close the Font panel.

15 With your text still highlighted, type *Capturing the eXtreme.*

16 Click outside the text on the menu background to deselect the text, or press the Enter key.

Copying Text

Now you have the type sizes and fonts you like for your project. Let's make a copy of it for our web address, by using the Option-drag method. To Option-drag, you press the Option key while you drag the object.

1 Click the text *www.yourURLhere.com* to select it, then press Delete.

2 Option-drag the text *Capturing the eXtreme* down and to the right, below the large drop zone, to the area where the old web address was positioned.

3 Click the new *Capturing the eXtreme* text copy you created to highlight the text.

4 Type *www.extremelivingchannel.com*.

Deselect the text by clicking on the menu background.

Positioning Text

Now would be a good time to check the title safe area of our menu to make sure the text is visible on a television when viewed. Placing text within the title safe area will make sure it is visible when viewed on a television and not lost off the edge of the screen.

1 In the Settings pop-up menu in the Project window, choose Title Safe Area.

NOTE ▶ The title safe area is the inner rectangle outlined by the gray border. You should place all text within the title safe area. Objects inside the boundaries of the zone will be visible on any television screen.

2   Drag the title *eXtreme Living Channel* to the right, inside the title safe area.

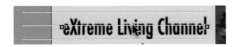

3   Drag the tagline *Capturing the eXtreme* to the right, inside our title safe area, and align it with the right side of the title by using the Dynamic Guides.

NOTE ▶ Use your alignment guides or press the Shift key to make sure you drag in a straight line.

4   In the Settings pop-up menu in the Project window, choose Title Safe Area to turn title safe off.

You will be able to see the full design of your menu as you finish adding elements.

5   Simulate your project, then press Command-S to save your work.

Adding a Shape

The design looks good with the new custom text, but you can still add your own touch to the template by creating shapes.

1   In the Palette, click the Shapes tab.

2   In the Shapes tab, click the Apple button.

3   Scroll down the thumbnails of shapes until you get to Square Navy 50p.

If you pause the mouse over the Square Navy 50p shape, a tooltip displays the full name of the shape for you.

4   Drag the shape Square Navy 50p to the white area of the main menu, but don't release the mouse button.

Make sure the entire menu is outlined and that you are not selecting a button, text, or drop zone. The Drop Palette will appear.

5   Choose Create Drop Zone, Set Shape from the Drop Palette.

6   Click the new drop zone to inspect the properties, then name it *Text_Highlight* in the Inspector.

7   Press Return, and the outline on the menu updates with the new name of the drop zone.

Aligning a Shape

The next step is to reposition the Text Highlight drop zone to enhance the menu design. You can watch the shape's coordinates and size change in the Inspector as you move the Text Highlight drop zone.

1   Drag the Text Highlight drop zone on top of the text *www.extremelivingchannel.com.*

2   In the Inspector, click the Coordinates & Size field named Top.

3 With the Top coordinate number highlighted, type *207* (for PAL, *249*) and press Return.

4 Change the coordinates and size of the remaining fields in the Inspector as follows: Left to 0, Width to 720, Bottom to 349 (for PAL, 415), Right to 720, and Height to 142 (for PAL, 166).

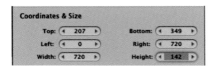

5 Create a second shape (Palette > Shapes > Apple) using the Square Black 40p shape from the Palette. Drag the shape to the white area of the Main menu. (Follow the steps for Adding a Shape, which you just completed.)

Remember to select the element you want to inspect—*your new shape*—before changing any settings in the Inspector.

6 Change the coordinates and size in the Inspector as follows: Top to 0, Left to 51, Width to 20, Bottom to 480, Right to 71, and Height to 480 (for PAL, Bottom is 576, Right is 81, and Height is 576).

7 Name the second shape you created *Grey_Highlight* in the Inspector.

The shapes look good, but they are covering your text and some of your images. Let's move the shapes to the background to place them behind the other elements in your design.

15 In the Inspector's Selected Highlight pop-up menu, choose the color blue.

> **NOTE ▸** You can use the W key to toggle through the states of a selected button: normal, selected, and activated.

16 Simulate your project.

Your menu design is finished, but you still have to target a few assets to make this DVD work.

Connecting Assets to the Menu

There are several ways to connect assets, and you already know that using the Inspector would probably do the job. Some methods can be quicker than others and even make the connections automatic.

Lets start with adding audio to our menu.

1 In the Palette click the Audio tab.

2 Drag the **Main_menu_audio** file to the main menu background and choose Set Audio from the Drop Palette.

3 Click the Motion button at the lower right of your Project window.

You will hear your audio and preview the menu you built.

4 Press F2 for the Extended configuration in DVD Studio Pro.

You are viewing the project interface at an extended level, to access more features. Even though it looks very involved, you already know much of this layout and will feel comfortable after completing the next few steps.

The interface is laid out in three sections that are called quadrants, plus the Palette and Inspector. The assets you have added to your project are displayed in the first quadrant in the Assets tab. Now it's time to link the buttons and put the assets to work.

NOTE ▶ DVD Studio Pro includes Basic, Extended, and Advanced window configurations. There are benefits with each configuration, such as the ease of dragging with Basic, more available features with Extended, and access to all features with Advanced. You can also customize the interface and save your own configuration to meet your needs.

Creating a Slideshow

Slideshows can be a powerful tool by bringing together a series of stills to convey information to viewers or just entertain them. You can control the length of the slideshow, add audio, and even add audio to individual slides.

With drag-and-drop simplicity you can create a slideshow, link it to a button, and have it jump back to the main menu after playing. All of these connections will be made for you using the Drop Palette, saving you time in authoring your DVD.

1   Go to the Palette and click the Stills tab.

2   Drag the X_Slideshow folder to the Slideshow button in the Menu Editor. An outline appears around the button when you drag the folder onto it.

3   From the Drop Palette that appears, choose Create Slideshow, Connect to Slideshow.

The button is named Slideshow1 automatically.

4   Click the Slideshow tab in the lower quadrant to see the Slideshow Editor.

You can modify your slideshow in the Slideshow Editor by rearranging, adding, or deleting slides and audio.

5   Select **xslide_04** and drag it up toward the top of your slideshow until
you see the black position indicator above the first slide, then release the
mouse button.

Xslide_04 is now the first image that will be seen when you play your
slideshow.

6   Click the Audio tab in the Palette and select the **Slideshow_audio** file.

7   Drag the **Slideshow_audio** file to the Audio well in the Slideshow Editor.

8   In the Transition pop-up menu in the Slideshow Editor, choose Dissolve.

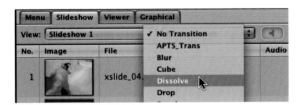

TIP You can set a transition to be used on all the slides in your slideshow or set a transition for each individual slide by using the Transitions
tab in the Slideshow Inspector.

Setting a Button Transition

You can set a transition from individual buttons to another element in your
project, or use a default transition for all the buttons on your menu. You already
connected your Slideshow button when you created the slideshow. Next you will
add a transition between the Slideshow button and your slideshow.

1   Click the Slideshow button on your menu in the Menu Editor to select the button.

The Button Inspector opens to view the parameters of the button.

2   Click the Transition tab in the Button Inspector and select Mosaic from the Transition pop-up menu.

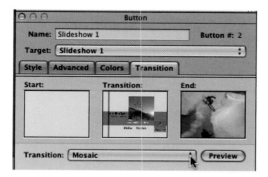

Preview the transition by clicking the Preview button in the Transition tab. The preview displays what the transition will look like when you click the Slideshow button.

NOTE ▶ You can modify the parameters of a button transition in the Button Inspector.

The slideshow is now part of your DVD. Use the Simulator (in the middle of your Toolbar) to view your new slideshow with the audio and transitions added.

Creating a Track

Tracks contain a combination of video streams, audio streams, subtitle streams, chapter markers, and stories. In the next tutorial you will learn more about chapter markers, subtitles, and stories. For this project you will create a track with a video stream and an audio stream.

1   Click the Menu tab in the Project window to return to the Menu Editor.

2   Go to the Palette and click the Video tab.

3   Drag the video file **eXtreme_snow** to the Play Movie Button and keep your mouse button depressed.

4   Wait for the Drop Palette to appear, then make sure Create Track, Connect to Track is highlighted, and release the mouse button.

The Play Movie button is now connected to a newly created track and will jump back to the main menu when it has finished playing.

5   Click the Graphical tab to see an icon view of all the elements in your project and how they are connected to each other.

TIP   You can arrange the icons and print the graphical view to help in designing your projects.

6   Choose File > Save, then simulate your project.

Build and Burn

Build is where DVD Studio Pro combines all of the elements and assets you have put together and creates a series of files. This is useful for testing. This feature is covered in more detail in the next tutorial. *Burn* writes these files to your DVD burner and places them on a disc, so you can watch the DVD in a player.

For this exercise, you will burn this project and try it in a DVD player. Before you burn a disc, test, test, and retest your project to make sure it works correctly and that you are pleased with what you have made.

1 Click the Burn icon in the toolbar.

A dialog will ask you to insert an acceptable disc into your burner.

2 Insert the disc in your DVD burner.

You can see the progress of the build and burn as DVD Studio Pro creates your DVD.

Terrific! You have just authored a professional DVD and learned a solid working foundation of DVD Studio Pro.

What's Next?

The Introducing DVD Studio Pro tutorial was designed to teach you some of the fundamentals as you build a project. Once you're comfortable with these features, you can move on to the Mastering DVD Studio Pro tutorial or the interactive Apple Pro Training DVD tutorial (on the companion DVD), both of which show more advanced DVD Studio Pro features and features new to the upgrade. For detailed information about specific features, see the documentation that comes with DVD Studio Pro.

To learn more, see page 302 for information on Apple certified training and the self-paced Apple Pro Training book, *Apple Pro Training Series: DVD Studio Pro*.

7

Lesson Files   Apple_Pro_Training_Tutorials>Mastering_DVD_Studio_Pro>1_Mst_DVDSP_Starting

Apple_Pro_Training_Tutorials>Mastering_DVD_Studio_Pro>2_Mst_DVDSP_Finished

Time   This lesson takes approximately 60 minutes to complete.

Goals   Import and organize menu assets

Add a still background to a menu

Add a motion background to a menu

Apply overlays and create custom buttons

Work with drop zones

Add a transition track and modify tracks in the Track Editor

Use advanced menu design

Use chapter markers and create a chapter index menu

Use alternate angles in a track

Create subtitles

Build and burn a DVD project

Lesson 7

Mastering
DVD Studio Pro

In this Apple Pro Training tutorial, you will learn techniques for designing more advanced menus in DVD Studio Pro, including how to create motion menus, transitions, subtitles, and more.

You'll be authoring a DVD to promote a fictitious show *Shark Encounter* on the eXtreme Living Channel. The project will include a slideshow of the production, a movie track, chapter index menus, and alternate angles.

To learn more, explore the Apple Pro Training DVD tutorial (on the companion DVD). For more comprehensive training, see the About Apple Pro Training folder on this DVD for information on the self-paced *Apple Pro Training Series* books and the Apple Pro certified training program.

Preparing the Project

If you are unfamiliar with DVD Studio Pro, complete the Introducing DVD Studio Pro tutorial before beginning this lesson. Once you have the basics down, you're ready to begin.

You should have the DVD Studio Pro application and the Mastering DVD Studio Pro tutorial files already installed on your computer. (See previous lesson for how to copy these files to your computer.)

1   Locate the Apple Pro Training Tutorials folder on your computer's desktop, and then double-click the folder to open it.

2   Open the Mastering_DVD_Studio_Pro folder.

3   Double-click the **1_Mstr_DVDSP_Starting** file to open the project in DVD Studio Pro.

When DVD Studio Pro opens, you will see the the project **1_Mstr_DVDSP_Starting** displayed in the Extended configuration. Press F2 to make sure you are in the extended configuration before you start the tutorial.

Let's get comfortable with the extended configuration before building our DVD.

Working With the Interface

The DVD Studio Pro project window can display up to four quadrants, each made up of various tabs or controls. The extended configuration displays three quadrants plus the Palette and the Inspector. In the Introducing DVD Studio Pro tutorial, you were working in the Basic configuration, which displays only one quadrant. Familiarize yourself with the quadrants in the picture below. You will get to know the function of each quadrant as you build the project.

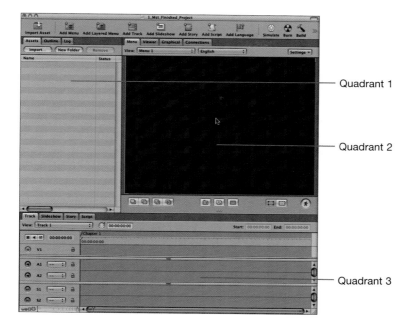

Quadrant 1

Quadrant 2

Quadrant 3

Importing Assets

For this project you will import your assets by using the Assets tab in quadrant 1. There are different ways to import graphics, video, and audio into your project, including dragging them to the Assets tab or directly to an element of your DVD.

1   Click the Import button in the Assets tab, located in quadrant 1.

An Import Assets dialog opens to let you locate assets.

2   Choose Apple_Pro_Training_Tutorials > Mastering_DVD Studio Pro > Encounter_ Assets, then click the Import button.

The folders you choose are imported and opened, and the files are high-lighted to let you know what has been added into your project.

NOTE ▶ The Assets tab is similar to the Browser in Final Cut Pro, as it is made up of a number of columns providing you with information on the assets. Shift–Space bar will maximize the quadrant for you to see information that includes the status, type, and size of your assets. Pressing Shift-Space bar again will return the quadrant to its normal size.

3 Click the disclosure triangle next to each folder to close the folders.

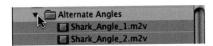

You can stay organized and navigate through the large number of assets by opening the folders as you need to see the assets.

TIP ▶ Folders are a great tool for keeping things organized. You can create subfolders, move assets between folders, and move folders within the Assets tab.

Creating a Motion Menu

Using a video clip as a moving background can add greatly to any menu by being visually pleasing and conveying additional information to the viewer. Next you will create a motion menu that will use a video background to publicize the new show and promote the overall look of the cable channel.

Applying a Motion Background

The motion menu movie you will use was created entirely in Apple Motion software.

1 Click the Menu tab in quadrant 2 to display the Menu Editor if it is not already displayed.

2   In the Assets tab, click the Menu Assets disclosure triangle to reveal the contents.

All of the assets you'll need to build your project menus are organized in this folder.

3   Drag **Main_Menu_Movie.m2v** to the Menu Editor and choose Set Background from the Drop Palette.

4   Click the menu background to load its parameters into the Inspector.

The At End pop-up menu is set to Loop in the General tab. Your motion menu will loop, or play again from the start, after playing.

> **TIP** Remember, you must select the element you want to inspect before it will show in the Inspector.

5   Click the Motion button at the lower right of your Project window to view the motion menu background.

Text has already been added to the menu for the buttons you will create, but it doesn't appear for a few seconds after the beginning of the menu. You will loop the menu at a certain point in the video clip over the next few steps. Let your menu run as we add audio.

6   In the Inspector, type *Main Menu* in the Name field.

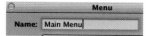

In the General tab of the Inspector you can see that the duration of this motion menu is 29 seconds.

Adding Audio to a Motion Menu

One of the features of DVD Studio Pro is the ability to concatenate, or add together, audio in a menu or even a slideshow. The first audio file you will use is designed for the beginning of the main menu, before the text appears. The second audio file will be used for the looping area of the menu. As a result you will need to add, or concatenate, two audio files for the main menu.

1   Drag **Main_Menu_Audio_1.aif from the Assets tab** to the Menu Editor and choose Set Audio from the Drop Palette.

The file name appears in the Inspector in the Audio column of the General tab. (If your Inspector is showing an audio asset, you clicked the audio file and selected it before dragging it to the menu. Simply click the background of the menu to select the menu and inspect the menu parameters.) The audio is only 10 seconds long and just the right length for the beginning of your menu before the text appears.

2   In the Assets tab drag **Main_Menu_Audio_2.aif** to the menu and choose Add to Existing Audio from the Drop Palette.

The combined audio is now the same length as your entire motion menu. Next you will use a new feature of DVD Studio Pro 4 that automatically sets the menu loop point: the point to which the menu jumps back once it has played through the first time.

In the Inspector's General tab the Loop Point field has a timecode set for 10 seconds, which fits exactly with the first audio file you added to the menu. A MenuLoopPoint chapter marker was set in Motion when this motion background was created.

The menu starts playing at 0, plays through once, and then loops from 10 seconds to the end. Your text stays onscreen. You can set the loop point manually or let DVD Studio Pro recognize a MenuLoopPoint chapter marker created in Motion or Final Cut Pro.

TIP ▶ In Final Cut Pro you add a chapter marker and name it MenuLoopPoint for it to be recognized as a loop point in DVD Studio Pro. In Motion you choose the Menu Loop Point option when adding a marker.

3   Simulate your project (Command-Option-O, or click the Simulator icon in the Toolbar) to view the looping of your menu, and then close the simulator.

4   Choose File > Save As, or press Shift-Command-S to open the Save As window.

5   Save your project in the My_Saved_Projects folder located in the Apple Pro Training Tutorials folder on your desktop.

You have made an exciting motion menu for the viewer, which will be complete once you add your buttons.

Creating Buttons

One of the advantages of creating your own motion background is that you can design and use custom fonts for your buttons. In this exercise you will create buttons, add an overlay, and select the highlight colors.

1 In the main menu, drag the mouse over the *Shark Encounter* text to draw a button.

The new button shows up in the Inspector as Button 1.

TIP To make the Button Outlines active you can choose Menu > View > Show Button Outline and Name, or click the Button Outlines button at the bottom of the Menu Editor.

2 Name this button *Shark Encounter* in the Inspector.

3 Option-drag the Shark Encounter button down to make a copy of the button for the chapters text, then name your button *Chapters* in the Inspector.

4 Option-drag the Chapters button to make a copy of the button for the slideshow text, then name your button *Slideshow* in the Inspector.

5 Position your buttons to make sure they don't overlap. Don't worry about the exact placement, we're about to align them.

Aligning the Buttons

You previously learned that Dynamic Guides are useful in aligning elements of your project. By batch-selecting your buttons you can align them all at the same time instead of individually.

1 Batch-select the three buttons you created by pressing the Command key and clicking them one at a time.

They will each be outlined with a bounding box to let you know they are selected.

2 Control-click one of the selected buttons to view a pop-up menu.

3 Choose Align Objects > Left.

The left side of your buttons will be aligned.

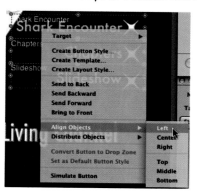

4 Control-click one of the selected buttons again, then choose Distribute Objects > Vertically.

The vertical distance between each button is now the same.

TIP ▶ Make sure your buttons do not overlap on your menu, or they will not work properly. You can move all of the selected items at once by dragging them or by nudging them with your arrow keys.

Setting a Simple Overlay

An overlay is a graphic used to show the different states of the buttons on your menu. The main menu background already has text that shows the normal state of your buttons. By adding an overlay you can show button states with multiple colors.

In these next few steps you will apply a simple overlay to the main menu and also learn a couple of navigation tricks for getting around DVD Studio Pro.

1   In the Assets tab double-click **Main_Menu_ol.jpg** to view the graphic in the Viewer tab.

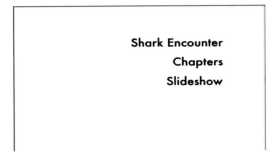

This file is a simple overlay where you will substitute a color value for the black and white.

2   From the Assets tab drag the **Main_Menu_ol.jpg** file to the Menu tab. Don't release the mouse button as the Menu Editor opens. Continue to drag the file down to the menu. The Drop Palette appears. Choose Set Overlay from the Drop Palette.

NOTE ▶ When applying an overlay, you won't see any change to the menu unless you have a button selected. You have to inspect the menu to see that the overlay file has been added.

Selecting Highlight Colors for a Simple Overlay

Now you can assign colors to the black and white values of your overlay. The text is black, so you will be able to assign a color that black equals for the normal, selected, and activated states of your buttons.

1   Click the menu background in the Menu Editor to open the Menu Inspector.

2   In the Inspector for the main menu click the Colors tab.

3   Set Overlay Colors to Simple by clicking the Simple button.

Advanced choices will be grayed out. Later in this lesson you will learn about advanced overlays. The Key and Color selections change in the Colors tab for a simple overlay.

4   Set the Opacity slider for the Normal button state to 0.

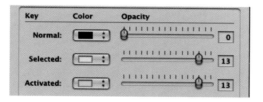

By setting the Opacity to 0, your motion menu graphics are visible in the normal state and the overlay is transparent.

5   Choose white from the Selected pop-up menu and set the Opacity to 13.

6   Choose yellow from the Activated pop-up menu and set the Opacity to 13.

The activated state is only briefly seen before the selection appears. It is important because the flashing lets the viewer knows a selection has been made.

TIP The Opacity slider ranges from 0 to 15. Consider 15 to be 100 percent opaque and 0 to be transparent. A setting of 10 would be the same as 66 percent opacity. You can cycle through the button states by pressing the W key to see the highlights of a selected button.

7 Control-click the menu background and choose Simulate Menu from the pop-up menu.

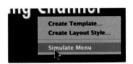

You can check the normal, selected, and activated states of the menu buttons in the Simulator.

8 Close the Simulator window.

Creating a Submenu

Now that you've created the main menu, let's create a submenu. By now you have learned that there are a number of ways to accomplish a task in DVD Studio Pro. It's the same with creating a submenu. By dragging a still image, you will create a submenu, connect a button to the submenu, and set the background of the submenu.

1 Go to the Assets tab and drag the **Menu_2_background.jpg** file to the Shark Encounter button. Choose Create Submenu from the Drop Palette.

Dragging an asset to a button will change the name of the button and make a connection to the submenu.

TIP ▸ Once you learn the tools and tips of DVD Studio Pro you can plan ahead how you will author the project to save time. For example, a button on the menu is automatically named when you drag assets to it that are the target of the button.

2 Double-click the newly named Menu 1 button.

The Menu Editor opens the new submenu and you can see the still image background that was applied.

3 Name the submenu you created *Menu 2* in the Menu Inspector.

4 In the View pop-up menu at the top of the Menu Editor, choose Main Menu.

The main menu is displayed in the Menu Editor. Next you will use a shortcut to copy your aligned custom buttons to Menu 2.

5 Batch-select the first two buttons of the main menu.

6 Copy the two buttons by choosing Edit > Copy, or press Command-C.

7 Double-click the Shark Encounter button to return to the submenu.

8 Paste the two buttons to Menu 2 by choosing Edit > Paste, or press Command-V.

9 You can now drag the two buttons and align them over the text on the menu background.

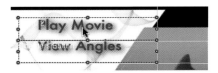

The menu buttons are aligned with the text on your graphic background. They still have to be named, which is done automatically when you connect them to their target tracks later in this tutorial.

The submenu at this point leaves no way for the viewer to return to the main menu. To complete the menu buttons you will create a custom button to return the viewer to the main menu.

10 Draw a button by dragging your pointer over the *Main Menu* text.

The new button shows up in the Inspector and is by default named Button 1.

11 In the Button Inspector name the button *Main Menu.*

To make these buttons work with highlights you need to set an advanced chroma overlay, which will give you more options for the normal, selected, and activated states of these buttons.

Setting an Advanced Overlay

You can set an advanced overlay by dragging the file to the menu or through the Inspector. Let's use the Inspector this time.

1 Click the **Menu_2_aol.tif** file in the Assets tab to select the file.

A thumbnail of the advanced overlay appears in the bottom of the Picture Asset Inspector. This overlay is a four-color graphic, or chroma overlay.

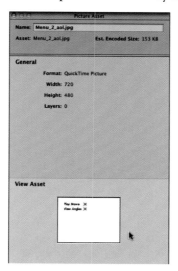

2   Make sure Menu 2 is in the Menu Inspector by clicking the menu background.

3   Click the General tab in the Inspector. In the Overlay File pop-up menu choose Encounter_Assets > Menu Assets > **menu_2_aol.tif.**

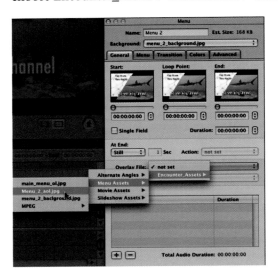

Selecting Highlight Colors for an Advanced Overlay

The advanced overlay has the advantage of using four colors: black, red, blue, and white. When you assign a color value to each, such as black equals blue, your overlays can have multiple colors. You will assign colors to your advanced overlay for the normal, selected, and activated states of a button.

1   Click the menu background in the Menu Editor to open the Menu Inspector if it's not already open.

2   In the Inspector for Menu 2 click the Colors tab.

3   Set Overlay Colors to Advanced by clicking the Advanced button.

4   Click the Chroma button for Mapping Type.

Now you can select the colors and opacity of the normal, selected, and activated states of the buttons.

5   Click the Selection State Normal button and set the Opacity slider to 0 for each key color. You will assign another color value to each of the four key colors on your chroma overlay.

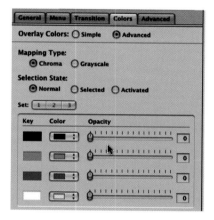

6   Click the Selection State Selected button to set the Opacity slider values and colors.

7   Choose Yellow for the black key, with an Opacity of 5.

8   Choose Black for the red key, with an Opacity of 3.

9   Choose Purple for the blue key, with an Opacity of 10.

10 Choose 0 for the Opacity of the white key.

11 Click the Selection State Activated button to set the Opacity slider values and colors.

12 Choose Yellow for the black key, with an Opacity of 5.

13 Choose Yellow for the red key, with an Opacity of 8.

14 Choose Blue for the blue key, with an Opacity of 11.

15 Choose 0 for the Opacity of the white key.

16 Control-click Menu 2 and choose Simulate Menu to test the buttons with the advanced overlay settings, then close the Simulator.

> **TIP** ▶ A common practice is to invert colors between the selected and activated states.

Creating Tracks

By default every new project contains one menu and one track. You will use different methods to create additional tracks for a transition, the main movie, and alternate angles. Ready to get started?

Configuring an Intro Track

The default track will work well for creating and configuring an introduction to your DVD.

1 Click the Graphical tab in the quadrant 2.

2 Click the Zoom to Fit button in the upper right of the Graphical tab to make sure you can see all of your project elements, also called *tiles*.

The Graphical tab icons show the project you have built to this point. You can drag the icons and arrange them to see all of the elements of your project.

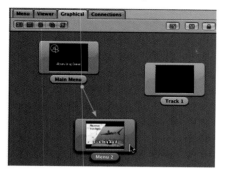

3   From your Assets tab drag the **Encounter_Intro.m2v** video file to the green Track 1 icon until it becomes outlined, then release the mouse button.

The track has been named the same as the asset, and both a video and an audio stream appear in the Track Editor in quadrant 3.

TIP ▸ If you choose Preferences > Track > Find matching audio when dragging, DVD Studio Pro will automatically look for audio with the same name and add it to the element you are working with.

4   Select the Encounter_Intro track in the Graphical tab to view its properties in the Track Inspector.

5 In the End Jump pop-up menu choose Menu > Main Menu > [Menu].

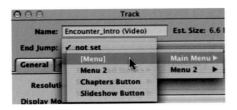

In the Graphical tab a one-way arrow points from the Encounter_Intro track to the main menu showing the end jump. (If you see a straight line instead of an arrow, move the tiles apart.) The Introduction track (Encounter_Intro) will jump to the main menu's root level after playing.

To make the Encounter_Intro track the first item a viewer sees when playing the DVD, it will need to be set as the First Play element.

NOTE ▶ Each project must have a First Play element, which appears when the viewer starts playing the DVD. Menu 1 is designated by default to be the First Play element when you create a new project.

6 Control-click the Encounter_Intro icon on the Graphical tab, and choose First Play from the pop-up menu.

The track tile displays the First Play icon in the upper-left corner.

7 Simulate and save your project.

Adding a Main Movie Track

With your menus complete you want to add a track and link it to the Play Movie button on Menu 2. Finding the most efficient way always saves you time in building your project.

1   Click the Menu tab and choose Menu 2 in the View pop-up menu in the Menu Editor.

2   From the Assets tab open the Movie Assets folder by clicking the disclosure triangle.

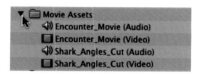

The assets for two of the tracks you will add are displayed.

3   Drag the **Encounter_Movie.m2v** file to the Play Movie button and choose Create Track, Connect to Track from the Drop Palette.

4   Click the Graphical tab to see the structure of your DVD.

The Encounter_Movie track is linked to Menu 2 with an arrow pointing in both directions, which tells you it has an end jump set to Menu 2 after playing.

TIP   When you are working on a large project, you can click the Macro View button at the top right of the Graphical tab to see a display of the entire tile area.

Setting Up a Multi-angle Track

DVD Studio Pro has the ability to create multi-angle tracks. A multi-angle track lets the viewer switch between different, or alternate, angles when viewing the track. This feature is often used to show different camera angles of the same shot or to place another video stream, such as storyboards, on an alternate angle.

Next you will create a multi-angle track that will use five video streams within the track. One stream will be the edited version of the shark dive, and four streams will have different perspectives. The viewer will be able to jump between streams when watching the DVD.

1 Click the Menu tab and choose Menu 2 in the View pop-up menu in the Menu Editor if it is not already selected.

2 From the Movie Assets folder in the Assets tab drag the **Shark_Angles_Cut.m2v** video file to the View Angles button and choose Create Track, Connect to Track from the Drop Palette.

The **Shark_Angles_Cut.m2v** video and audio streams are displayed in the Track tab in the lower quadrant (quadrant 3).

3 Click the Show Multiple Video Streams button at the upper left of the Track tab.

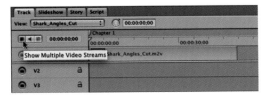

The Track Editor will display only the video streams to make it easier to add additional video streams to the Shark_Angles_Cut track.

4   In the Assets tab open the Alternate Angles folder by clicking the disclosure triangle.

5   Drag the **Shark_Angle_1.m2v** video file to the V2 stream in the Shark_ Angles_Cut track to add it to the track.

6   Drag the remaining alternate angles—the **Shark_Angle_2.m2v, Shark_ Angle_3.m2v,** and **Shark_Angle_4.m2v** video files—to the V3, V4, and V5 streams, respectively, in the Shark_Angles_Cut track.

The track now contains an edited cut of the shark encounter and the four different angles that were used to edit the piece in Final Cut Pro. The viewer can switch between angles by using the remote or viewer controls while playing the DVD.

7   Simulate your project and test the alternate angles by choosing various commands in the Angle Select pop-up menu in the Simulator's remote control.

The Simulator changes between each video stream as you select an angle. Close the Simulator.

Using a Button Transition

Transitions from element to element in your project are easy to create and can enhance the viewing experience. With Menu 2 you will add a transition track and configure it to work between the View Angles button and the Shark_ Angles_Cut track of your project.

1   Click the View Angles button on Menu 2 to open the Button Inspector.

The name of the button was automatically changed to Shark_Angles_Cut when you dragged the video file asset to the button and then chose Create Track, Connect to Track from the Drop Palette.

Next you will change the settings for the button to target the **Encounter_ Transition.m2v file** to use as a transition video.

2   In the Button Inspector click the Transition tab.

3   Choose Video Transition from the Transition pop-up menu.

4   Choose Encounter_Assets > Menu Assets > Encounter_Transition.m2v from the Asset pop-up menu.

The Shark_Angles_Cut button will now play the **Encounter_Transition.m2v** video before it takes the viewer to the targeted track.

Adding a Slideshow

Slideshows have a number of options. You can set how long a slide is displayed, add separate audio files to each slide, and have the viewer control when to jump to the next slide in the show. You will now build a slideshow of the Shark Encounter dive, set transitions, and fit the slides to the length of an audio file.

1   Click the Menu tab and choose Main_Menu from the View pop-up menu.

2   From the Assets tab drag the Slideshow_Assets folder to the Slideshow button. When the Drop Palette appears, choose Create Slideshow, Connect to Slideshow.

The Slideshow is named Slideshow 1 by default, and the Slideshow Inspector opens.

3   Click the Slideshow tab in quadrant 3.

Thumbnails of the slides are added to the Slideshow Editor.

4   On the Assets tab, click the Slideshow Assets disclosure triangle to view the contents of the folder.

The audio file for the slideshow is in the folder.

5   Drag the Slideshow_Audio file to the Audio Filename column in the Inspector and release the mouse button.

The audio file appears in the column and has a duration of 20 seconds.

6   Click the Slideshow tab to activate the window, then press Shift–Space bar to make quadrant 3 a full window and hide the other quadrants.

The length of each slide is set to 5 seconds in the Duration column of the Slideshow Editor. With a total of eight slides, your slideshow will continue to play after your audio is finished.

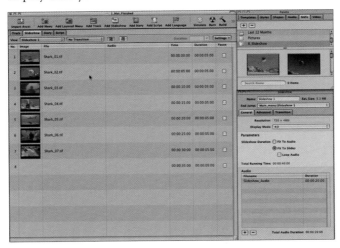

TIP ▶ To return the quadrant to the smaller size press Shift–Space bar again, and you will see all three quadrants of the extended configuration.

7   In the Slideshow Inspector click the Fit To Audio button.

The Duration column in the Slideshow Editor displays the time for each slide as 2 seconds and 15 frames to fit all the slides to the length of the audio file. (For PAL, 2 seconds, 12/13 frames. This fluctuation accommodates the odd number frame-per-second count of 25.)

8   Click the Transition tab in the Slideshow Inspector.

9   From the Transition pop-up menu choose the alpha transition Lens Flare.

> **NOTE ▶** Alpha transitions have transparency that allow you to see through the transparent area to view the outgoing and incoming video clips. DVD Studio Pro indicates an alpha transition by placing the α symbol in front of the name.

10 Press F2 to return to the extended configuration, and then simulate your slide show.

Using Chapter Markers

Chapter markers, which allow you to navigate through a movie to certain points, are a big part of the viewer interaction of DVDs. DVD Studio Pro recognizes markers created in Final Cut Pro, Compressor, Final Cut Express, Motion, and iMovie.

You can also create markers manually or import a text document to set chapter markers for your track. In this exercise you will learn different ways to add markers and then create a chapter index menu using the markers you set.

1   Click the Track tab in the lower quadrant (quadrant 3).

2   Choose Encounter_Movie from the View pop-up menu.

You will see the video and audio streams in the track along with three
purple chapter markers. These markers were created in Final Cut Pro and
were recognized by DVD Studio Pro when you imported the movie asset.

TIP ▶ If you don't see the markers, press Shift-Z to fit to window and
your markers will be visible.

3   Triple-click the timecode in the track's Duration field above the markers,
then type 25309 (for PAL, 25213) and press Return.

The playhead jumps to the timecode you entered and displays that frame
in the Viewer tab.

4   Press M (for marker).

A chapter marker appears on the Timeline ruler and the Marker Inspector
opens.

5   Name the chapter marker *Dive Master* in the Inspector's Name field.

The name of the marker updates in the Track tab to Dive Master. Import
the remaining markers from a text document, and you will be ready to
make your chapter index menus.

6   Control-click the gray marker area of the Track Editor and choose Import
Marker List from the pop-up menu.

7   Navigate to the Encounter_Docs folder in the Mastering_DVD_Studio_
Pro folder and select the **Encounter_Markers** file; then click Import.

A dialog lets you know how many markers were imported, and the markers are displayed automatically in the Timeline.

8   Click OK to close the dialog, and then save your project.

TIP ▶ When you make a chapter marker list you can use the Apple TextEdit
application. Enter the timecode, set a tab as a delimiter, then type the name of
the chapter marker. Save as a plain ASCII text file to be able to import it.

Creating a Chapter Index Menu

Chapter index menus are common in professional DVDs to provide viewers an easy
way to navigate through a movie. The chapter markers you set earlier provide the
ability to jump directly to a specific scene in the track with the press of a button.

In this lesson you will create two chapter index menus by using the markers
in your Encounter_Movie track. DVD Studio Pro templates include chapter
index menus that will make building the menus easy and help keep the same
overall design for your project.

1   Press F3 for the advanced configuration.

2   In the Graphical tab double-click the Main Menu icon. Use the Zoom to
Fit button if you need to see all of the icons.

The main menu opens in the Menu Editor.

3   Option-drag the Encounter_Movie track icon to the Chapters button on
the main menu. Do not release the mouse button. Choose Create Chapter
Index, Make Connections from the Drop Palette when it appears

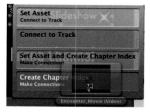

The Choose Template or Layout Style window appears. You can select an existing template or a custom template if you have created one.

4   Click the Templates tab, then the Apple button, and choose Panes Blue Index from the templates. Click OK.

This index menu template will be the third menu in the Panes Blue series of templates. You can move and resize the Choose Template or Layout Style window to view the templates better.

Two chapter index menus are added to the project and the buttons linked to the track's chapter markers.

5   Click the Outline tab to open the list of your DVD elements.

The new menus are listed in the Menus folder.

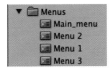

6   Click the Menu 1 icon and press Enter.

The text is highlighted and can be changed.

7   Type *Chapter Menu 1* and press Enter.

The name of the menu updates to *Chapter Menu 1*.

8   Rename Menu 3 *Chapter Menu 2* in the Outline tab, and press Enter.

9   Press F1 for the basic configuration.

The Menu Editor is the only quadrant on the interface. It will be easier to put the finishing touches on your chapter index menus in this configuration.

10   Double-click the menu title *Company Name Here* and type *Chapter Index Menu Two*.

11   From the View pop-up menu in the Menu Editor choose Chapter Menu 1.

12   Double-click the menu title *Company Name Here* and type *Chapter Index Menu One*.

Your menus are complete, and they give the viewer a convenient visual menu to jump to any chapter in your movie.

13   Save, then simulate your project.

Working With Subtitles

DVD Studio Pro allows you to create subtitles directly in the Track Editor. Subtitles are commonly used to overlay dialogue text on a video stream to communicate to the audience in different languages. They can also be used to overlay a simple graphic on a video stream to create a button.

Creating a Subtitle

For this project you will create a simple subtitle in the Timeline window of the Track Editor.

1   Press F2 for the extended configuration.

2   Make sure the Track tab is open and you are viewing the Encounter_ Movie track in the lower quadrant (quadrant 3).

3   Type *326* (for PAL, 401) in the Current Frame field and press Enter.

The playhead moves to 00:00:03:26 (for PAL, 00.00.04.01). This is where you will add a subtitle.

TIP ▶ To zoom in or out in the Track Editor press Command-– (hyphen) or Command-= (equals).

4   Control-click in the S1 subtitle stream and choose Add Subtitle at Playhead.

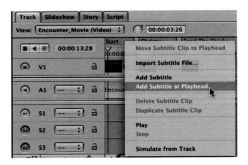

5   Type *Nassau Bahamas,* then click outside the text area to deselect the text.

The subtitle appears in your viewer as part of the track. DVD Studio Pro's subtitling feature allows you to modify the subtitles you create. For this track the default settings will work well.

TIP ▶ Subtitles can be modified in the same manner as the text you created. You can change their color, size, and font to make sure they are visible against the background image

6   Play the track, and then save your project.

Previewing Subtitles in the Simulator

After you have positioned and modified your subtitles it's always a good idea to preview them for alignment and timing.

1 Control-click in the Track Editor and choose Simulate from Track from the pop-up menu.

The Simulator opens and plays the track.

2 Click the View box just below the Subtitle Select pop-up menu.

The subtitle will now be visible in the Simulator. Your track has probably played past the subtitle you created and you'll have to navigate back to the beginning of your track.

3 Click the Chapter Skip Reverse button until you reach the first chapter marker at the beginning of your project.

The subtitle will now appear in the Simulator.

TIP Subtitles can be repositioned in a track and adjusted in length. They can also be imported from a text file.

Build and Format

The Build command tells DVD Studio Pro to combine all of the elements of your project and to create a VIDEO_TS or HVDVD_TS folder, depending on the type of project you have created. The *Format* command writes the file to a recordable DVD, a hard disk, or a digital linear tape (DLT). It gives you more formatting options than *Burn*, which is the simplest way to burn a DVD on your own system.

Once you have finished your project, it's important to test it thoroughly before you burn a disc. You should use the Simulator often, and you can also emulate the project with the Apple DVD Player on your computer. If you want to burn this project, then follow the next few steps.

> **MORE INFO** ▶ You can learn more specific information about testing your project in the Help documentation that comes with DVD Studio Pro and the Apple Pro Training Series books.

1 Choose File > Burn or press Option-Command-B to burn.

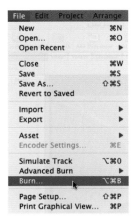

A dialog window asks you to insert an acceptable disc into your burner.

2 Insert the disc in your DVD burner.

You can see the progress of the build and burn as DVD Studio Pro creates your DVD.

What's Next?

Congratulations! You have just authored a professional DVD with advanced features.

This Apple Pro Training tutorial just scratches the surface of the features, tools, and techniques that DVD Studio Pro has to offer. For detailed information about specific features, refer to the DVD Studio Pro User Manual (accessible through the Help menu), and explore the Apple Pro Training DVD tutorial (on the companion DVD).

To learn more, see page 302 for information on Apple certified training and the self-paced Apple Pro Training book, *Apple Pro Training Series: DVD Studio Pro*.

The Apple Pro Training Program

The Apple Pro Training Program can give you a competitive edge in the digital production industry. Whether you're an editor, composer, special effects artist, sound designer, web developer or someone who teaches these skills, Apple-certified training will help you expand your knowledge and skills.

Become an Apple Certified Pro

 Certified Pro

The Apple Certified Pro program creates a benchmark for assessing an end-user's proficiency in Final Cut Pro, Motion, DVD Studio Pro, Shake, and Logic. By taking and passing the online Apple Certified Pro exam, you can become an Apple Certified Pro. Certification is an official recognition of your knowledge of Apple's professional applications, and allows you to distinguish yourself to colleagues, employers, and prospective clients as a skilled, pro-level user of the chosen software application.

The program offers both instructor-led and self-paced training. You can take a certification course taught by an Apple Certified Trainer at any Authorized Training Center worldwide. If you prefer to learn at your own pace, you can purchase the Apple Pro Training Series courseware and pursue it on your own (see catalog on following pages), and then take the online certification exam.

For more information please visit www.apple.com/software/pro/training.

The Apple Pro Training Series

The official curriculum of the Apple Pro Training and Certification Program, the Apple Pro Training books are a comprehensive, self-paced courses written by acknowledged experts in the field.

- Focused lessons take you step-by-step through the process of creating real-world digital video or audio projects.
- All media and project files are included on the companion DVD.
- Ample illustrations help you master techniques fast.
- Lesson goals and time estimates help you plan your time.
- Chapter review questions summarize what you've learned.

Apple Pro Training Series: Final Cut Pro 5
0-321-33481-7

In this best-selling guide, Diana Weynand starts with basic video editing techniques and takes you all the way through Final Cut Pro's powerful advanced features. Using world-class documentary footage, you'll learn to mark and edit clips, color correct sequences, create transitions, apply filters and effects, add titles, work with audio, and more.

Apple Pro Training Series: Advanced Editing Techniques in Final Cut Pro 5
0-321-33549-X

Director and editor Michael Wohl shares must-know professional techniques for cutting dialogue scenes, action scenes, fight and chase scenes, documentaries, comedy, music videos, multi-camera projects, and more. Also covers Soundtrack Pro, audio finishing, managing clips and media, and working with film.

Apple Pro Training Series: Color Correction and Effects in Final Cut Pro 5
0-321-33548-1

This Apple-authorized guide delivers hard-to-find training in real-world color correction and effects techniques, including motion effects, keying and compositing, titling, scene-to-scene color matching, and correcting for broadcast specifications.

Apple Pro Training Series: Optimizing Your Final Cut Pro System
0-321-26871-7

Written and field-tested by industry pros Sean Cullen, Matthew Geller, Charles Roberts, and Adam Wilt, this is the ultimate guide for installing, configuring, optimizing, and trouble-shooting Final Cut Pro in real-world post-production environments.

Apple Pro Training Series: Final Cut Pro for Avid Editors
0-321-24577-6

Master trainer Diana Weynand takes you through a comprehensive "translation course" designed for professional video and film editors who already know their way around Avid nonlinear systems.

The Apple Training Series:

Apple Training Series: iLife '05
0-321-33020-X

Apple Training Series: GarageBand 2
0-321-33019-6

Apple Training Series: Mac OS X Support Essentials
0-321-33547-3

Apple Training Series: Desktop and Portable Systems, Second Edition
0-321-33546-5

Apple Training Series: Mac OS X Server Essentials
0-321-36984-X

To order books or find out about the Apple Pro Training Series, visit: **www.peachpit.com/appleprotraining**

Apple Pro Training Series: Soundtrack Pro
0-321-35757-4

Create original soundtracks with Apple's exciting new sound design software. Author Mary Plummer guides you through the secrets of editing, repairing, mixing, and and arranging multi-track audio files.

Apple Pro Training Series: Shake 4
0-321-25609-3

The leading compositing choice for cutting-edge visual effects in feature films, Shake is pure magic. This Apple-certified guide uses stunning real-world sequences to reveal the wizardry of keying, matting, painting, rotoscoping, and more.

Apple Pro Training Series: Shake 4 Quick Reference Guide
0-321-38246-3

This compact reference guide includes cheat sheets, quick-glance tables, and a concise explanation of the Shake interface, work-space, views, and tools.

Apple Pro Training Series: Getting Started with Motion
0-321-30533-7

This Apple-certified guide is designed to make Motion's sophisticated visual effects accessible to newcomers. Author Mary Plummer starts with the fundamentals and takes you through more than a dozen real-world projects. Fully compatible with Motion 2.

Apple Pro Training Series: Motion
0-321-27826-7

In this guide to Apple's revolutionary motion graphics software, commercial artist Damian Allen shows you how to harness Motion's behavior-based animations, particles, filters, and effects to create professional TV promos and other projects. Fully compatible with Motion 2.

Encyclopedia of Visual Effects
0-321-30334-2

The ultimate recipe book for visual effects artists working in Shake, Motion, and Adobe After Effects, this is a compendium of the coolest and most useful effects from A to Z ("Adding Clouds" to "Zapping Wires"). Written by Hollywood and independent pros, it covers everything from rotoscoping and painting to advanced greenscreen techniques.

Apple Pro Training Series: Logic Pro 7 and Logic Express 7
0-321-25614-X

Audio producer Martin Sitter shows you how to create, mix, produce, and polish your musical creations using Apple's professional audio software; the DVD includes a 30-day trial version of Logic Express 7.

Apple Pro Training Series: Advanced Logic Pro 7
0-321-25607-7

Composer David Dvorin takes you through Logic's powerful advanced features, covering everything from production, editing, and mixing to notation and scoring to picture.

Apple Pro Training Series: DVD Studio Pro 3
0-321-25610-7

Learn to author professional, interactive DVDs with this best-selling guide, fully compatible with DVD Studio Pro 4. You'll master everything from motion menus to advanced scripting as you design and create four complete DVDs.

Apple Pro Training Series: Final Cut Express 2
0-321-25615-8

The only Apple-authorized guide to Final Cut Express 2, this book delivers the techniques you need to make movie magic from the comfort of your Mac. Fully compatible with Final Cut Express HD.

Apple Pro Training Series: Color Management with Mac OS X
0-321-24576-8

Graphics profession-als will welcome this unique project-based guide that shows, step by step, how to set up a real-world Mac OS X-based color management workflow.

Apple Pro Training Series: Xsan Quick Reference Guide
0-321-36900-9

Apple's exciting new enterprise-class file system offers high-speed access to centralized shared data. This handy booklet provides invaluable setup, configuration, and troubleshooting tips.

an askew view

an askew view

THE FILMS of KEVIN SMITH

John Kenneth Muir

An Askew View
By John Kenneth Muir
Copyright © 2002 by John Kenneth Muir
All rights reserved

ISBN: 1-55783-586-1

Library of Congress Cataloging in Publication Data

Muir, John Kenneth, 1969-
  An askew view : the films of Kevin Smith / by John Kenneth Muir.
      p. cm.
   ISBN 1-55783-586-1
   1. Smith, Kevin, 1970- I. Title.
   PN1998.3.S5864 M85 2002
   791.43'0233'092--dc21
                        2002008858

British Library Cataloging in Publication Data
A catalogue record for this book is available from the British Library.

Photo Credits

Unless otherwise noted, all photos courtesy Photofest

APPLAUSE THEATRE & CINEMA
151 West 46th Street, 8th floor
New York, NY 10036
Phone: 212-575-9265
Fax: 646-562-5852
Email: info@applausepub.com

SALES AND DISTRIBUTION:

NORTH AMERICA:

HAL LEONARD CORP.
7777 West Bluemound Road
P.O. Box 13819
Milwaukee, WI 53213
Phone: 1-414-774-3630
Fax: 1-414-774-3259
Email: halinfo@halleonard.com
Internet: www.halleonard.com

UNITED KINGDOM:

COMBINED BOOK SERVICES LTD.
Units I/K, Paddock Wood Distribution Centre
Paddock Wood, Tonbridge, Kent TN12 6UU
Phone: (44) 01892 837171
Fax: (44) 01892 837272
United Kingdom

Printed in Canada

This book is dedicated to my infinitely supportive wife, Kathryn — not only because she loves me, but because she has the world's biggest crush on Jason Mewes.

CONTENTS

Acknowledgements

This book would not have been possible without the assistance and support of many friends, supporters, and colleagues. Special thanks to June Clark, who got the ball rolling, and to Amy at View Askew Productions, who must have gotten tired of my daily calls.

And special thanks to the efficient Gail Stanley, Kevin Smith's assistant, who was not only helpful and commmunicative, but a constant source of information, support, and kindness.

Then there are the interviewees, whose recollections inform so much of this project. Much gratitude and respect to Jeff Anderson, Dwight Ewell, Walt Flanagan, Vincent Guastini, Bryan Johnson, Jason Mewes, Scott Mosier, Brian O'Halloran, Vincent Pereira, John Pierson, Jennifer Schwalbach, and Ethan Suplee, who spent hours recounting their experiences, perceptions, and memories of these interesting films. Thank you for being so candid, so funny, and so open.

And then there's the man himself, Kevin Smith. Thanks, Mr. Smith, for creating a universe that has meant so much to so many, and for granting me access to it for this project.

The Planet of the Apes Threshold

AN INTRODUCTION TO THE FILMS OF KEVIN SMITH

I remember precisely when and where I got hooked on the films of Kevin Smith and View Askew Productions. It was May 13, 1997, at a 7:30 p.m. showing of *Chasing Amy* at the now defunct Matthews Festival in Charlotte, North Carolina. I was there with my wife, Kathryn, to celebrate our two-year wedding anniversary, but very soon after we were seated, the characters on the screen—so passionate in expression, words and deeds—demanded our full attention.

The film was Kevin Smith's third opus, concerning twenty-something comic book artist Ben Affleck falling hard for Joey Lauren Adam's funny, experienced, and deeply affecting lesbian, Alyssa Jones. So raunchy and riotous one moment, so touching and raw the next, the movie was one of the most piercing and emotional viewing experiences of the 1990s; *Annie Hall* for the slacker set.

As *Chasing Amy* faded to melancholy black, my head was spinning. Here was a movie that joked about the nitty-gritty of oral sex in one scene, and then turned around and broke your heart in another. The balance was so deft, so accomplished, that it felt revelatory—the work of a major talent.

I knew then that many books would be written about *Chasing Amy*'s director. More to the point, I knew that I wanted to take a stab at one. Even then, as early as 1997, Smith's story had an irresistible hook. There was a self-financed, freshman home run (*Clerks*), a sophomore (or, as some reviewers insisted, sophomoric) fall from critical grace (*Mallrats*), and then *Chasing Amy*'s glorious ascension to top form. That's more than enough plot for any book.

Or so I thought.

As one of my film junkie friends promptly informed me, Kevin Smith had not yet surpassed the benchmark he dubbed "the *Planet of the Apes* threshold." According to this buddy (Randal Graves to my Dante Hicks), there would never be a book about Kevin Smith until he directed five films and produced a TV series. *Planet of the Apes* was the paradigm because that franchise included four cinematic sequels, a TV series, and a cartoon, yet apparently didn't merit one of those glossy film guide books until 2001 when the picture was "re-imagined" by Tim Burton.

How could I have the audacity to write a Kevin Smith book, my friend wanted to know, when there were just three films to his name and his future in Hollywood still seemed up in the air? Reluctantly accepting my friend's postulate, bide my time I did, like Yoda on Dagobah.

But now, some five years after *Chasing Amy*'s release, Kevin Smith has gotten the monkey off his back and crossed that damned simian hurdle. Two new films (the hugely controversial *Dogma* and *Jay & Silent Bob Strike Back*) have arrived in theaters, a TV series (*Clerks: The Animated Series*) bears Smith's unique stamp, and—lo and behold—this book is in your hands. Incidentally, my friend's faith in the *Apes* threshold is forever confirmed.

But leaving the pop-culture references behind for a moment, Kevin Smith's View Askew movies merit a book now more than ever, particularly as film historians are beginning to paint in broadstrokes a picture of the 1990s independent film movement. New Jersey born-and-bred, Smith may seem an unlikely torchbearer for the revolution: an Irish-Catholic kid from the 'burbs who spent the early years of his twenties learning not about *mise-en-scène,* but jockeying a cash register at a Quick Stop in Leonardo.

Yet this fledgling writer-director, along with a talented cadre of artists (most notably, producer Scott Mosier), masterminded his own calling card to Hollywood. More to the point, Smith did so in the midst of a decade when interest in film—and accessibility to film technology—was at its greatest in history. Had his initial effort, *Clerks,* not been so good, so funny, and so accomplished, Smith might easily have drowned in an indie tidal wave, just another Rob Weiss sinking in a sea of promising, would-be "auteurs."

But Smith has not disappeared in the years since *Clerks*. Instead, he is arguably the most high profile writer-director of his generation. His visibility is a result not only of his appearances in his own films as stoner Silent Bob, but his uncanny knack for effective promotion. He's been a frequent guest on *The Tonight Show*, appeared on late-night TV fare like *Loveline*, and hosted a slew of *Star Wars*-related specials such as *Exposure* and *The Official Star Wars Fan Film Awards* on the Sci-Fi Channel. Can a guest role on ABC's *Alias* be far behind?

But opportunity and visibility only carry one so far in Hollywood. Or, as Kevin Smith has noted:

> I always felt lucky enough to get my foot in the door...Getting in is luck. Staying in is talent. I don't profess to be the most talented individual working in films today. But obviously I'm doing something right because I'm still here and we have a fan base.[1]

So the question becomes this: What is Kevin Smith doing right, nearly a decade after breaking through with *Clerks*?

John Pierson, an executive producer of *Chasing Amy* and host of Independent Film Channel's *Split Screen,* offers a thought on the matter of Smith's continued success: "It's the quality of his humor, which is both hilariously down and dirty, but also unbelievably emotionally honest. That's the crux of the matter."

But where does that honesty, that understanding of the human condition, come from, especially in an artist still so young?

"He lives very quietly," Kevin Smith's wife, Jennifer Schwalbach, told me. "He doesn't drink. He doesn't do drugs. He doesn't even like to take Nyquil. He looks at life very straight, and his eyes are wide open. His movies—every single one of them—are a direct reflection of something he's experienced in his life. And because he lives life so openly, he listens to what people say.

"He digs," Schwalbach emphasizes. "Some of my friends can take it, and some can't. He'll have a conversation where he just wants to know. He doesn't want to talk about a new couch. He wants to talk about what someone's boyfriend said in bed when they broke up. He will dig, because he is genuinely interested in how other people live, how their emotions run, how they react, and the strange things that people do. Kevin doesn't go out to bars to drink. I've wasted years, just kind of living a twenty-something life. And instead, Kevin thought about things. He thought about his life; his relationships. And he's written about them. He doesn't write about fictional characters; he writes about himself and his friends. The movies he makes are a reflection of himself."

With one important caveat, as Pierson adds, "They're transcendent."

"He takes his own real life experiences, but just like Janet Maslin wrote in that *Clerks* review from *New Directors*, he spins straw into gold. To me, the essence of him spinning straw into gold is taking actual experience that he knows oh so well, and somehow, both on the comedic side and on the emotional, heartfelt side, making it transcendent."

Just like *Chasing Amy*.

And that's one reason why, when searching for historical antecedents, it's a no–brainer to compare Kevin Smith to Woody Allen (hence the *Annie Hall* reference). As Pierson considers, "they're both writers first," movie directors second, and both use life experiences as a platform to reveal stories about human nature.

Sure, Smith's films routinely reference Superman, Lucas, and Spielberg rather than Fassbinder, Bergman, or Wagner, but that's merely a generational quirk. In common, Allen and Smith share a common "style of slightly exaggerated comedy"[2] and the propensity to resort to slapstick antics and crude humor amidst their witty comedic word play. But that's the universality of the human condition too, as Smith has often remarked, "We all have sex, and we all take dumps."[3]

Smith is the Woody Allen for Generation X in the sense that he seems to be the only young writer-director working today who asks the deeper questions about love, religion, and sex in a way that makes audiences laugh. The countless *Scooby Doo, Planet of the Apes, The X-Files, Jaws,* and *B.J. and The Bear* references in his films are merely touchstones for viewers to understand that, when all is said and done, Smith is one of us and speaks our language. Those TV shows and films represent a short hand not only to coolness, but a shared heritage growing up in the 1970s. Smith is a director who, impressively, writes A-style personal material yet utilizes allusions to B-style productions as a hook to grab an audience weaned on television.

That's my generation, and Smith is undeniably a role model. Not coincidentally, his films have shadowed the progress of Gen Xers every step of the way during our maturation process: through our post-college career slump and ambivalence (*Clerks*), our professional blossoming and relationship blues (*Chasing Amy*), and even our skeptical but seemingly optimistic stance about religion (*Dogma*). Now he's perched to broach another turning point in Gen Xers—parenthood—with his sixth feature, *Jersey Girl*. At this point, it isn't hard to imagine a decade in which Kevin Smith makes films about the mid-life crisis, raising teenagers, or other vexing problems of thirty and forty-somethings.

Puritans may rail against the ubiquitous potty mouth or the predilection for body-function humor in his work, but Kevin Smith's View Askew movies always feature a distinct voice and his characters always speak in dialogue of unique cadences, loaded with startling wit, irony and intelligence. The writer has frequently been compared with Shakespeare, both by reviewers and the actors who vet his dialogue. Who would have expected such brilliance (let alone such vocabulary) from *The Brady Bunch* generation?

Accordingly, *Rolling Stone*'s Peter Travers has dubbed Smith "a fearless satirist"[4] and *Newsweek* has anointed him "cinema's funniest writer about sex...certainly its most candid."[5] He's even been termed "the William Faulkner of '90s cinema"[6] by some enthusiasts.

Not bad for a guy just over thirty.

That Smith's films invariably stir the pot of cultural controversy (irking the M.P.A.A., the Catholic League, and the Gay and Lesbian Alliance Against Defamation in less than a ten-year period), is not only some kind of anti-PC record, it's further evidence that Smith is doing something right. After all, nobody (besides bored movie critics) goes after a stupid little comedy that misses the mark by a mile. People only attack that which is threatening, or new, or daring. Like *Dogma*. Like *Clerks*. Like *Chasing Amy*.

And now, as this book is being written, Kevin Smith is at a crossroads in his moviemaking career. Jay and Silent Bob have been put out to pasture—or at least frozen in carbonite—and the artist is planning to delve into new frontiers. But before Smith blazes those trails, this is the perfect opportunity to look back at the specifics of his existing film universe, the one he created in his twenties: "The New Jersey Chronicles."

Consider this book a guided tour of the View Askew universe, one conducted by many of the individuals who conspired with Smith to make these films the stuff of legend. Scott Mosier, Smith's producer and partner in crime on every project, Jennifer Schwalbach, his outspoken and delightful lady love, and a host of other talents have all contributed their behind-the-scenes remembrances to this text. Jason Mewes, Jeff Anderson, Brian O'Halloran, View Askew Historian Vincent Pereira, John Pierson, Vincent Guastini, Ethan Suplee and Dwight Ewell have all helped put Kevin Smith's works into context, sharing how it was done, why it was funny, and what the experiences meant to each of them. The result is a kind of free flowing history of one artist's escalating success in Hollywood, from independent filmmaker to blockbuster celebrity.

So let's take a stroll down the turnpike...

NOTES

1. Teresa Wiltz, "Silent Bob's Last Words; Director Kevin Smith Takes the Scenic Route for his Final Jersey Chronicle." *The Washington Post,* August 23, 2001, p. C01.

2. Frank N. Magill (Ed.), *Magill's Cinema Annual 1995: A Survey of the Films of 1994* (14th Edition), "Clerks" (Farmington Hills, MI: Gale Group, 1995), p. 117.

3. Andy Seiler, "Kevin Smith is seldom 'Silent,'" *USA Today*, August 24, 2001, p. 1, http://www.usatoday.com/life/enter/movies/2001-08-24-kevin-smith.html

4. Peter Travers, "Jay & Silent Bob Strike Back," *Rolling Stone*, September 13, 2001, p. 115.

5. Devin Gordon, "A Phatty Boom Batty Flick," *Newsweek*, August 27, 2001, p. 55.

6. Tanya D. Marsh, "*Dogma*: Episode I—The Catholic Menace," *The Buzz*, October 1999, p. 2, http://www.the-buzz.com/dogma1.html

Coming of Age in New Jersey

Of all the comic book stories ever printed, the origin story remains the most popular. It's an irresistible tale, as the success of the WB's series *Smallville* no doubt testifies. How did Superman come to arrive on Earth and grow into the Man of Steel? How did Peter Parker acquire his spider powers? What were the events that led a brooding Bruce Wayne to take up the life of a crime fighter? These questions are so compelling because everybody desires to understand how heroes came to be special, how they got to be who they are today.

Like any superhero — or celebrity for that matter — filmmaker Kevin Smith has his own beginnings too, his own origin story. These are the events that led him first to Vancouver Film School, and then, eventually, to the world of independent filmmaking. These are the influences that made him so keen an observer of human behavior, and this is where you'll meet the Lois Lanes and the Jimmy Olsens. Or in this case, Walt Flanagan, Bryan Johnson, Jason Mewes, and the other friends who helped to spark Kevin Smith's creative impulse.

And, like the best of the origin stories, Kevin Smith's adventure commences in a strange and wondrous land. Not far away Krypton, but New Jersey. The 'burbs.

The son of a postal clerk, Donald, and his wife, Grace, Kevin Patrick Smith was born in the little town of Red Bank shortly after the commencement of the disco decade, on August 2, 1970. He arrived into a lower-middle class family with two older siblings, Virginia and Donald, Jr., and was raised in the Borough of Highlands in Monmouth County, just outside of Leonardo (population: 5,500), some 12 miles from the larger city of Long Branch.

Just a hop, skip, and a jump from New York City by land or sea (under thirty miles, actually), the Borough of Highlands is very nearly located on top of Sandy Hook and the Atlantic Ocean. Its most notable construction is the Twin Lights, two lighthouses constructed in 1862.

Bryan Johnson, the director of *Vulgar* and the actor who portrays comic book snob Steve-Dave in the View Askew universe, was born in Highlands, and later attended Highlands Elementary and Henry Hudson Regional High School (the latter named after the sea captain who first explored the region in 1609). He describes the borough as a "really small town, kind of blue collar," where expectations for children and teens were "fairly limited."

Years after his success in films, Smith would affectionately describe Highlands in another manner:

"It was the asshole end of the movie universe."[1]

It was in this environment that young Kevin Smith, like virtually all children of the 1970s, began gathering his inspirations, predominantly from TV series and movies. Because he was not particularly athletic, and self-conscious about his weight,[2] Smith escaped to the worlds of *Gilligan's Island*, *The Brady Bunch*, *Batman*, and other rerun staples of the era.

Though it is difficult to imagine today, the early-to-mid 1970s represented a world without cable television, where syndicated series (reruns), once broadcast on the big three networks (ABC, CBS, NBC), dominated the programming schedules of local affiliates. *All in the Family*, *M*A*S*H*, *Star Trek*, *The Twilight Zone*, and *Green Acres* formed the intellectual and entertainment gestalt of the decade's youth. This tends not to happen anymore, what with the WB, Fox, UPN, and basic and premium cable channels offering more programming choices. But for Kevin Smith's generation, these TV series are something akin to the Greek myths: a tradition, a bond, a shorthand; even ice-breakers at bars. Many people who grew up in the 1970s watched *Happy Days*, loved the Fonz, and remember "sit on it" as the ultimate insult.

Donald Smith, Kevin's father, often took Kevin out on Wednesday afternoons, following half days at school (another wonderful tradition of the 1970s and N.J. school systems), to see matinees at the local theater. When Kevin was five, his father brought him to see Steven Spielberg's 1975 horror blockbuster, *Jaws*.[3] When Smith was seven, he saw another movie that would impact his life and work, the George Lucas space opera, *Star Wars*. Depicting an exciting universe of space battles, daring rescues, and colorful alien creatures, *Star Wars* offered Smith the ultimate escape from humdrum life in the Highlands.[4]

Growing up in a predominantly Irish-Catholic community, Smith attended parochial school, Our Lady of Perpetual Help, on Navesink Avenue. During his adulthood, Smith remembered one particular instructor, Sister Theresa, who had a great impact on him. A fan of Thomas More, she exposed her class, including Smith, to one of his now-favorite films, and one he reportedly watched some fifty times: *A Man for All Seasons*.[5]

Released in 1966, *A Man for All Seasons* was directed by Fred Zinnemann and based on the play of the same name by Robert Bolt. Telling the story of Thomas More's conflict with King Henry VIII (who wanted to reject Catholic doctrine so he could acquire a divorce and a new wife), the Academy Award-winning film starred Paul Scofield as More, Robert Shaw as King Henry, Leo McKern, Orson Welles, John Hurt, Susannah York, and Nigel Davenport.

But the quality that impressed Kevin Smith most was the rich dialogue, the language of the film. So in many ways, *A Man for All Seasons*, like Richard Linklater's *Slacker*, forms the foundation of Kevin's Smith cinema: it is wordy, witty, and unremittingly smart. Like Smith's own *Dogma*, it debates the law of man and God in a barrage of delicious dialogue, all of it delivered with great flair.

By the time Smith was attending Henry Hudson Regional High School in the mid-1980s, he had turned his affection for film and television into something more than a hobby. Jeff Anderson, a Connecticut native who moved to Jersey when he was nine years old and grew up to be *Clerks*'s slacker philosopher, Randal, sets the scene:

"Henry Hudson was such a small school [it encompassed grades 7 through 12], and that's where I first met Kevin. Our graduating class had about 72 kids in it. Everybody knew everybody, and there were 600 kids in the whole school."

Those 600 students formed the basis of Kevin Smith's first audience. "He would always do these skits in the talent show, like *Saturday Night Live*-type things." Anderson remembers. "That was always the big thing for the talent show. There was the kid at school who could play guitar really kick-ass, and then there were Kevin's sketch comedy acts. That was why you went to the talent show."

And sometimes, as Anderson recalls, the skits were...avant-garde. "I remember going to the talent show one year, and we are all curious to see what Kevin was going to do, because it was always something crazy."

Anderson didn't go home disappointed. "Kevin and Ernie O'Donnell [*Clerks*'s Rick Derris] did this skit where Kevin was playing Ronald McDonald and Ernie was the Hamburgler. I don't quite remember why, because I was hyped up on a pint of peppermint schnapps in the audience; I just recall Kevin coming out on stage as Ronald McDonald. I can still picture it: Ronald tying up the Hamburgler and Kevin shoving a hamburger in Ernie's mouth. Somewhere, photographs of this still exist."

But if the subject matter of the skit was odd, it nonetheless forecasted Kevin Smith's later efforts. Some of the McDonald's Land characters (Mayor McCheese and Police Chief Big Mac, specifically) figure prominently in the third episode of the *Clerks* animated series — as Leonardo's city officials, no less!

If the Henry Hudson talent shows proved anything, it was, as Anderson reports dramatically, that "early on, yes, we can say Kevin knew what he wanted to do."

In 1989, Kevin Smith graduated from high school and his desire to break into comedy writing took him from New Jersey to Eugene Lang College, a division of the New School for Social Research in Manhattan, where he studied creative writing. While he was there for one semester, Smith would frequently spend time "hanging out" at Rockefeller Center, hoping to be discovered by the talents managing *Saturday Night Live*.

When that dream didn't materialize, a disillusioned Smith retreated to New Jersey and began working a series of low-paying counter jobs at convenience stores. But it was a job at the Highlands Community Center, a recreation center for high school students with no where to stay after school, where Smith first began to assemble a special group of friends, the troop that would later become the inspiration for so many of his movie adventures.

Walt Flanagan is one of those friends. A dark-haired, shy type with an open and friendly face, this future "Fanboy" of the View Askewniverse was born in Perth Amboy, New Jersey, a town north of Highlands and south of Metuchen. Two years older than Smith, Flanagan attended high school with Smith at Henry Hudson for a time. "I knew him, but I wasn't friends with him," Flanagan reports.

Instead, that friendship would blossom at the community center. Though they didn't really talk to each other for the better part of the year, one day the subject of comic books came up.

"I think Kevin saw I had on a shirt with Batman on it," Flanagan recollects, "and he made a comment that he used to watch the *Batman* TV show. I mentioned there was a really good *Batman* book, *The Dark Knight Returns*, the Frank Miller book, and he'd never heard of it. So the next day, I let him borrow my copy. And he loved it. He said, 'There's more stuff like this out there?' And I said 'Yeah,' and he wanted to go right out to the stores and have me show him what was good. We became friends through comics."

It probably isn't an exaggeration, then, to report that fans the world over who have enjoyed Smith's superhero chronicles in *Green Arrow, Daredevil,* and other books may have Flanagan to thank for fanning the artist's interest in the medium.

"I only *re*-introduced him to comics," Flanagan points out with modesty. "He had purchased comics growing up, but had fallen out of it, and didn't really follow them closely."

Smith also made another friend at the community center, a fellow by the name of Bryan Johnson. Like Flanagan, Johnson also knew Kevin from Henry Hudson, but never really talked to him until their tenure together at the recreation center.

"The first time I ever spoke to Kevin was the day I broke up with my girlfriend, a girl I'd been going out with for two years," Johnson details. "It was one of those high school romances where you just know you're going to get married. But we broke up. I was really down that day, and I was talking to a friend of mine about it, and Kevin was sitting there and said, 'Oh, you broke up with your girlfriend?' That was the first thing this guy had ever said to me, and I just said, 'Yeah.' So he said, 'Really? Can I have her?'

"I thought, 'This impudent dog! This insolent prick!' But actually, Kevin made me laugh and feel a little bit better."

Before long, Kevin, Walt, and Bryan were the best of friends, hanging out together, attending comic book shows in the city, and having a great time. And, then, on one fateful day, someone else walked into their lives, a rambunctious teenage kid who—some day—would star in every one of Kevin Smith's movies as the motor-mouthed stoner, Jay.

"Jason Mewes started coming down to the rec as a kid," Bryan Johnson calls to mind. "I think he was fourteen at the time. He was a participant in the after school program, and Kevin, Walter, and I were sort of overseeing him."

And what was the irrepressible Jason Mewes like at age fourteen? "He was pretty energetic, to say the least," Johnson remembers. "He had the skinniest mohawk I've ever seen on a person. He was very wild, just all over the place, like a pinball, bouncing from here to there. But he was also a lot of fun. He was the kind of kid you could just tease, and he'd give it back."

Years later, Smith described Mewes as "the kid that everybody knows in town; the kid that belongs to that town; the kid of urban legend."[6]

Jason Mewes also recalls those early days, when he first met Kevin Smith. "I used to go [to the community center] after school, and during the summer there was a program too. Walter and Bryan and Kevin used to collect comics, and I remember the first time we all hung out. They were going to a comic book show in New York, and Bryan asked me if I wanted to go. I wasn't there, but this is how Kevin tells it. They told Kevin I was going, and he was like, 'I don't want that kid going!' In his eyes, he saw me as one of those kids in town who everybody knew. 'Oh, that kid Jason Mewes, he busted a window. Or, he got caught making out with a girl behind the church.' All these silly things he heard about me; that I was a foul mouthed kid and stuff.

"So he told Walter and Bryan that I was underage and he didn't want to take me. And he wouldn't drive me to New York in his car, so Bryan offered to drive.

"We all went to New York, and it was a good time, but Kevin said that I was being obnoxious making my jokes the whole time. Walter and Bryan thought I was funny, but Kevin didn't. They were laughing, and Kevin told me later that he was always the funny guy in the group, and now someone else was coming in and being funny, stepping on his territory."

Then, one fine day, Jason Mewes arrived at the community center and finally did something Kevin Smith found amusing. Allegedly, he mock-fellated every phallic-shaped object in the room—flag-poles, doorknobs, you name it. "He didn't care who was there, who was watching. He had an agenda,"[7] Smith later recalled.

"He said that the day he found me funny I ran into the rec and started sucking everything off," Mewes reports with bemusement and a hint of skepticism. "I don't really remember that…"

It was the beginning of a beautiful friendship between the men who would be Jay and Silent Bob. When Johnson went away to school at the University of Massachusetts and Flanagan got married, the friendship between Smith and Mewes deepened. On days when Mewes wouldn't have anything to do, he'd visit Smith's house after work to watch movies and read comics with him.

Then, in the late spring of 1990, Kevin Smith took a job working at two adjacent shops in nearby Leonardo: the R.S.T. Video store and Quick Stop Groceries. "That's when we really started getting to know each other," Mewes confides. "We used to sit at the convenience store every Sunday, and I helped him make the [news]papers and stuff."

It was also at the Quick Stop in Leonardo where Kevin made the acquaintance of one more important friend, this one a few years younger than the future director: Vincent Pereira, now the officially noted View Askew historian.

"I got a job working at the Quick Stop a few months before Kevin got his job there," details Pereira, a well-spoken native of Monmouth County, whose photographic memory regarding the details of the scripts, production, and marketing of Kevin Smith's movies is nothing less than remarkable.

"It was funny, because for the first couple of weeks we didn't really talk much. Then one night I was hanging out and I asked him if he was a *Twin Peaks* fan. He said yes, and that kind of sparked the whole thing, because I was a total *Peaks* fan. So we started to talk about *Twin Peaks*, and I started to talk to him about filmmaking."

It was a subject that the knowledgeable and intense Pereira was well versed in, having been a movie buff all his life. A voracious reader and student of film, it was Pereira, with his excellent memory and encyclopedic knowledge of the medium, who really turned Smith on to the nuts and bolts of the filmmaking process (as well as the glories of the laserdisc home viewing format).

Smith's friendship with Pereira eventually resulted in late night pilgrimages to New York City, where the duo would go see offbeat, non-commercial films. Smith would often note the strange titles in the ads of *The Village Voice*, read reviews by Amy Taubin, and suggest to Vinnie that they give a movie a try.

"After we closed up on Friday nights," Pereira remembers, "we would go out to the night shows at the Angelika in New York. The first movie we ever saw there was *The Dark Backward*, this bizarre movie with Bill Paxton as a guy with a third arm [written/directed by Adam Rifkin]."

And then, of course, there was the trip that changed the course of Smith's adulthood. On his twenty-first birthday, he and Pereira went to the Angelika Film Center to see Richard Linklater's low-budget independent film, *Slacker*.

Produced for under $25,000 by the Texan, Richard Linklater (future director of *Dazed and Confused* [1993], *Before Sunrise* [1995], *The Newton Boys* [1998], and *Waking Life* [2001]), *Slacker* was a strange, almost stream-of-consciousness odyssey through the daytime and nightlife of a quirky college town, Austin.

A film about everything from parallel realities, chaos theory, and the patriarchal aspects of the *Smurfs* cartoon, to new conspiracy theories about the J.F.K. assassination, *Slacker* followed young, twenty-something characters seemingly at random. In the process, the movie exposed a well-educated but ultimately aimless and disaffected generation. Making it even more noteworthy, *Slacker* had no protagonist, no climax, and no big name actors to provide the audience a lifeline to the always-transforming material.

In an interview conducted in 1994, Kevin Smith told journalist Kenneth Chanko and *The New York Times* how *Slacker* both stunned and empowered him:

> I was a *Star Wars* generation kid. But here was a movie,
> *Slacker*, that had no plot, no car chases, no villain, and
> no three acts, and yet it was really engaging because of
> the dialogue. And dialogue is the thing I did best.[8]

John Pierson, author of the Hyperion/Miramax best seller, *Spike, Mike, Slackers & Dykes: A Guided Tour Across a Decade of American Independent Cinema,* also represented Spike Lee's first film *She's Gotta Have It*, Michael Moore's documentary *Roger & Me*, and *Slacker*. He puts into context for us the reasons why *Slacker* was a revelation to Kevin Smith.

"Here's a guy from some part of New Jersey that is within easy striking range of Manhattan, the art film capital of North America," Pierson begins. "It's right there; within an hour of where he lives. But it's not like he's ever going there to see movies. Instead, he's seeing things that are playing in the malls. So, when he does go to the Angelika Film Center in big, old Manhattan, — legendarily on his twenty-first birthday — he sees a film called *Slacker*, urged on by his friend Vinnie. And he sees this quasi-non-narrative film.

"He sees something unlike any experience he's had before. Essentially, the *Slacker* viewing experience is one of taking great joy, and sometimes laughing out loud at the stuff that is funny. Because Kevin is watching a film like that, which is playing with an audience, he thinks, 'This is funny, and it doesn't really have anything resembling the three-act story line a studio movie would have.' So he thinks, 'Shoot, I can write something funnier than this, something that has a little more story and a little more structure.' I think Kevin knew he could do a movie like that and make people laugh."

And, unbeknownst to Smith during the drive home from New York City that night, he had selected the absolute best time to emulate the *Slacker* formula, right down to the low, low budget.

"Several films came out around the same time as *Slacker*," Pierson reports. "*The Living End* was one, and *El Mariachi* was another movie in that under-$30,000 budget range which made its mark in the world with critics and, to a certain degree, with audiences.

"And, to give Peter Broderick his due, he wrote that story in *Filmmaker Magazine* where he broke down the budgets for those films. I guess *Laws of Gravity* fits into the under $50,000-type movie too. So there was an available illustration of how it is that you can shoot a 16mm film for this little. I think people were inspired by the aesthetic [of *Slacker*], but were also given practical information that became a blueprint or a guidebook to how this was done."

"We went to see *Slacker* in 1991, in the late summer," Pereira explains, "and I guess I could see it in Kevin's eyes driving home. 'Wow, I can make something like that.' You could just see it in his face."

Smith's interest "made sense," according to Pereira, "because Kevin is such a good writer." In fact, Smith was so inspired by *Slacker* that on the drive back from the showing, he had already begun contemplating the preliminaries of his first feature.

"We actually discussed ideas for films on the way home," reveals Pereira, "and talked about this bizarre David Lynchian thing he thought about doing for a time."

It wasn't long after his screening of *Slacker* that 21 year-old Kevin Smith made another decision. It was time to gain access to the knowledge and technical tools that would get him closer to his dream of making a movie.

"Kevin started looking around to see where he could go learn film-making real quick," notes Pereira, "and I think there were ads for Vancouver Film School in the back of *The Village Voice*."

That private trade school, which had opened its doors in 1987 to a class of only a dozen students, promised superior technical training. Located on the western coast of Canada, with mountains to the east and the Pacific Ocean to the west, the film school is located in a city often voted one of the most desirable places to live. But the cost of admission for the program was considerable: $9,000 for an eight-month curriculum.

British Columbia was a long way from Jersey, and some of Smith's friends were troubled when they first learned that their good friend would be moving away from the Garden State for nearly a year.

"Kevin, Walter, and I went to this pizza place, and Kevin told us he was going to film school to become a filmmaker," Bryan Johnson recalls. "We all thought it was a little weird, and there was a part of me that was upset he would be moving to Canada. We were good friends, and I thought,

'Don't go! We have so much hanging out to do. So many comic book shows to go to. So many beers to drink.' I suppose it didn't really dawn on me at the time that he was going to be a real filmmaker. To me, it was just like he was going away to school."

ÜBER PRODUCER

With the first half of his tuition ($4,000) paid, Kevin Smith attended Vancouver Film School in British Columbia in early 1992. One of his class-mates was Scott Mosier, the man who would partner with Kevin Smith as producer and editor on all of his films, and a driving force behind View Askew Productions.

Born in Vancouver, Washington, Scott Mosier spent the early part of his life moving with his family up and down the west coast, from Washington State to Los Angeles, and finally to Vancouver, Canada, when he was ten. From an early age, Mosier, like Smith, fostered a love of film.

"I always liked movies, but probably when I was in high school, I started to formulate an idea that I'd like to try it as a career," Mosier recounts. "When I went to college, I exposed myself to a lot of different kinds of movies. Once I started to watch some Fellini films and *Brazil*, I started thinking I wanted to make movies."

To make that leap, Mosier knew he needed to understand more about the medium, and immersed himself in the details of film study while enrolled in the Orange County College film program, which he describes as being "pretty dinky."

"I took a course in the history of film that started with the silent era and I read books. Once I left the classroom, I continued reading and watching as much as I could. Even if you don't like certain movies, if you watch them from an historical standpoint you can see the development of an art form. To understand Scorsese, you have to see that he didn't come out of nowhere, that he was influenced by someone else before him."

Mosier still remembers his first attempt to shoot a movie of his own. "As opposed to achieving anything on a scholastic level, I just kept reading, and made this short video with this girl. It was just terrible, because we were neophytes. When I watch it now, I go, 'Oh my god! It's so scattered!' There's no concept of eye lines, or what have you.

"Then, after two years, I transferred up to UCLA extension and went to night school. I couldn't transfer in because my grades were terrible and I didn't have enough credits. So I took the extension classes and all of these screenwriting classes. One was a lecture series where you go in a room and see Joe Eszterhas and Steven De Souza. One of my teachers co-wrote *Rock' n' Roll High School*, which was pretty killer for me—I think I was twenty at the time. And the other teacher wrote *Death Race 2000*."

Even with his interest in film, Mosier felt his attention lagging. "I've always been underwhelmed by school, and I got bored and stopped going at a certain point. I didn't like living in L.A. anymore, and it was becoming obvious I wasn't going to get a degree. I wanted to go home to Vancouver [British Columbia], where my parents had moved, live at home and go to this tech school, and they'd help me pay for it."

So Mosier set about enrolling in the Vancouver Film School. "I called the school and they had two slots left. I said, 'Yeah, I'll take it.' The program was full time for eight months and I was like, 'I can handle this...' which I barely did."

And it was there, at film school, that Kevin Smith and Scott Mosier first met. But contrary to expectations, it wasn't exactly love at first sight.

"Initially we weren't crazy about each other," Mosier acknowledges. "I think I looked like I'd been in L.A. at that point. And he looked strange to me. I wasn't impressed—it wasn't magic. There was no instant connection."

A friendship formed nonetheless. "Once we started taking classes and were split into groups, we started talking about things we had in common, being Americans. He'd read a lot, and I read a lot of *Film Threat* and *Variety*, so we'd read the periodicals. And that was sort of the beginning, where we separated ourselves from everyone else by having seen certain independent films. After that, we were hanging out all the time."

In fact, Kevin Smith and Scott Mosier teamed-up for a class project—their first official co-production. The students planned to shoot a ten-minute documentary together, but things didn't quite turn out as planned.

"Everybody in the class splits into groups of two," relates Mosier, "and Kevin's idea was to make a movie about a pre-op transsexual. But we weren't being very serious about it. I think he'd gone out somewhere and talked to some girl. He was in the city all the time, and I lived out in the suburbs with my folks, so sometimes he had nothing to do, and he met this transsexual before I did."

"So he said, 'Let's do it,' and we did a proposal. Before we pitched, we met with Mae [the subject], and she invited us to this thing called The Seven Deadly Sins, this sort of Transvestite Ball. So we borrowed a camera, and Kevin and I went to the Transvestite Ball in downtown Vancouver. We hung out backstage with her and got some footage we thought we could use later on. We watched the show and it was pretty fun.

But then the two fledgling filmmakers had to sell their instructors and classmates on their notion. "We had to pitch it to all of the students and the teachers, and they would pick four out of twelve groups that would get to make their movies," Mosier describes. "We sat outside before the pitch and created something very sincere. It was a good pitch, but underneath it all, I don't know how much we really wanted to do it. It was more like preparing for a competition; we both just wanted to win.

"When the teachers said we could do it, Kevin and I were a little bit disappointed; like, 'Oh, really?' So we had to pick our crew, and I guess you could say that our person [the transsexual] wasn't really nailed down. We weren't really prepared to do it, and basically, the crew didn't like us. And, at the last minute, when things were going badly, we couldn't get in touch with this girl.

"We just didn't really have a plan," Mosier concedes. "We finally got together and shot one night with our subject, Imelda Mae, and then she blew [out of] town. She flaked on us. And were like, 'Oh shit!' So Kevin and I came up with the idea of doing a documentary about how everything fell apart. We went in and proposed it to the teachers, and they told us we'd fucked up, but we were fairly defiant and our attitude was we should be able to do what we wanted. This wasn't fucking high school; we'd paid our money, we should get to do it.

"Then Kevin wrote this spine for it, these scenes with us backlit. That was all scripted by us. Then we shot it and compiled it, and it became easy. It became fun at that point, because it was all about amusing ourselves. Once we did that, we were totally interested. How could we make ourselves laugh? Then we went forward full-bore."

The resulting project, *Mae Day: The Crumbling of a Documentary*, has become something of a legend at Vancouver Film School. "I've heard a lot of things," Mosier notes. "I know they show it a lot. I can't remember if they show it as an example of what to do, or as a cautionary tale of what can happen. I guess the cautionary tale would be: don't let the two most sincere guys do something, because they're full of shit. That's the lesson to be learned on that."

After the *Mae Day* documentary, the film program at Vancouver was just about half over. "That was the four month mark," Mosier explains. "It was a period where you worked on two separate short films, and that's when Kevin left. He was going to save the rest of his tuition. If he went another day, he'd have to forfeit his money, so he sort of bailed and put that money to use in *Clerks*."

Smith returned home to New Jersey, resumed work at the convenience store and R.S.T. Video, and began writing the screenplay for his first film.

While he wrote, he also did what Quentin Tarantino would later report doing: he became the undisputed master of the video rental.

"I used to stop at the video store and rent movies from Kevin," Jeff Anderson remembers. "It was great, because nobody ever went to this video store. I would get all the latest releases and Kevin would never charge me. He was sort of my Roger Ebert. He'd point to a movie, and I'd get it and go, no charge. He'd tell me to bring it back when he was working.

"When I was returning movies, I'd always hide the movies under my shirt to see if he was there. It's not an overly big store, so if I saw somebody else, they'd say, 'Hey, do you have movies there?' I'd say, 'No, no,' and come back when Kevin was back."

In Canada, life went on like normal, for a while.

"I was working at a stock room in The Gap, and working on some short films as an editor," Mosier remembers of that period. "And right when school was over, Kevin sent me the script for *Clerks*."

The rest, as they say, is history.

NOTES

1. Claudia Ansorge, "Kevin Smith—Star Wars: This Generation," *The Two River Times*, http://www.viewaskew.com/press.trt.html

2. Chris Smith, "Register Dogs," *New York*, October 24, 1994, p. 50.

3. Stephen Lowenstein (Ed.), *My First Movie: Twenty Celebrated Directors Talk About Their First Film* (New York: Pantheon Books, 2000), p. 73.

4. "The Monster That Ate Hollywood: Interviews: Kevin Smith." *Frontline*, p. 1, http://www.pbs.org/wgbh/pages/frontline/shows/hollywood/interviews/smith.html.

5. Rick Lyman, "Watching Movies with Kevin Smith: The Thrill Is Just Talk." *The New York Times*, July 20, 2001, p. 13.

6. Fred Topel, "Kevin Smith's Final Strike," *Entertainment Today Feature Story*, August 24, 2001, p. 4, http://www.ent-today.com/8-24/smith-feature.html.

7. Steve Ryfle, "On Fart Jokes, *Planet of the Apes* and the Making of *Jay and Silent Bob*," *IFilm: the Internet Movie Guide*, August 22, 2001, http://www.ifilm.com/news_and_features/feature/0,3536,608,00.html

8. Kenneth M. Chanko, "A Lot Happens at a Convenience Store," *The New York Times*, October 16, 1994, Section 4, p. 20.

Clerks (1994)

"I'M NOT EVEN SUPPOSED TO BE HERE TODAY!"

Just because they serve you, doesn't mean they like you.

CAST & CREW

VIEW ASKEW PRODUCTIONS PRESENTS *CLERKS*

WRITTEN AND DIRECTED BY: Kevin Smith

PRODUCED BY: Scott Mosier and Kevin Smith

CINEMATOGRAPHY BY: David Klein

CAMERA OPERATOR: David Klein

ASSISTANT CAMERAMAN AND CAT WRANGLER: Vincent Pereira

EDITED BY: Scott Mosier and Kevin Smith

SOUND EDITORS: Scott Mosier and James Van Buelow

SOUND MIXERS: Scott Mosier and James Van Buelow

SYNCHRONIZATION: Joia Speciale

MUSIC SUPERVISOR: Benji Gordon

POST-PRODUCTION SUPERVISOR: Charlie McClellan

M.P.A.A. RATING: R

RUNNING TIME: 92 minutes

STARRING:

Brian O'Halloran | *Dante Hicks*

Jeff Anderson | *Randal Graves*

Marilyn Ghigliotti | *Veronica*

Lisa Spoonauer | *Caitlin Bree*

Jason Mewes | *Jay*

Kevin Smith | *Silent Bob*

Scott Mosier | *Willam Black, the Idiot-Man-Child*; *Angry Hockey Playing Cutomer*; *Angry Mourner*

Walt Flanagan | *Woolen Cap Smoker, Egg Man, Offended Customer, Cat Admiring Bitter Customer*

Scott Schiaffo | *Chewlies Gum Rep*

Al Berkowitz | *Old Man*

Ed Hapstak | *Sanford; Angry Mourner*

Lee Bendick | *#812 Wynarski*

David Klein | *Hunting Cap Smoking Boy; Low IQ Video Customer; Hubcap Searching Customer*

Pattijean Csik | *Coroner*

Ken Clark | *Administer of Fine; Orderly*

Donna Jeanne | *Indecisive Video Customer*

Virginia Smith | *Caged Animal Masturbator*

Betsy Broussard | *Dental School Video Customer*

Ernest O'Donnell | *Trainer [Rick Derris]*

Kimberly Loughran | *Heather Jones*

Gary Stern | *Tabloid Reading Customer*

Joe Bagnole | *Cat Shit Watching Customer*

John Henry Westhead | *Olaf Oleeson*

Chuck Bickel | *Stuck in Chips Can*

Leslie Hope | *Jay's Lady Friend; Angry Crowd at Door*

Connie O'Conner | *'Happy Scrappy' Mom*

Vincent Pereira | *Hockey Goalie; Engagement Savvy Customer*

Ashley Pereira | *'Happy Scrappy' Kid*

Erix Infante | *Bed Wetting Dad, Cold Coffee Lover*

Melissa Crawford | *Video Confusion Customer; Candy Confusion Customer; Angry Crowd at Door*

Thomas Burke | *Blue Collar Man*

Dan Hapstak | *Door Tugging Customer*

Mitch Cohen | *Leaning Against Wall; Angry Crowd at Door*

Matthew Banta | *Burner Looking for Weed*

Rajiv Thapar | *Cut-Off Customer*

Mike Belicose | *Customer with Diapers*

Jane Kuritz | *Customer with Vaseline and Rubber Gloves*

Grace Smith | *Milk-Maid*

Frances Cresci | *Little Smoking Girl*

Matt Crawford | *Angry Crowd at Door*

Sarla Thapar | *Angry Crowd at Door*

Brian Drinkwater | *Hockey Player*

Bob Fisler | *Hockey Player*

Derek Jaccodine | *Hockey Player*

Matthew Pereira | *Angry Smoking Crowd*

Frank Pereira | *Angry Smoking Crowd*

Carl Roth | *Angry Smoking Crowd*

Paul Finn | *Angry Smoking Crowd*

THE STORY SO FAR...

IN LEONARDO, NEW JERSEY, Dante Hicks, a direction-less twentysomething, is called into work at the Quick Stop Grocery Store on his day off. Dante reluctantly reports to duty, only to be confronted by the worst day of his life.

To start with, someone has jammed gum in the locks of the store's metal shutters. Worse, one of his first customers is a Chewlie's Gum representative who calls him a death merchant for peddling cigarettes. Adding insult to injury, Dante learns that his current girlfriend, Veronica, has performed oral sex on some 37 boyfriends.

Then there are the problems with R.S.T. Video, next door. Randal, the slacker who works there, is late as usual and customers are angry. When Randal finally does arrive, he pisses off the customers and debates with Dante about a variety of minutiae. Dante pays little attention, as he learns that his old girlfriend, with whom he would like to reconcile, has just announced her engagement to an Asian Design Major in the newspaper.

Outside Quick Stop Groceries, two stoners, the hyperactive Jay and the taciturn Silent Bob, ply their trade and are visited by Bob's cousin Olaf from Russia. Olaf wants to be a metal singer and has written a ballad called "Berserker." The lyrics, however, lose something in the translation.

The day wears on and Dante and Randal continue to debate trivia (such as the ending of *Return of the Jedi*), and serve a variety of colorful customers. The Idiot-Man-Child Willam Black, the Egg Man (a deranged guidance counselor searching for the perfect dozen eggs), and a woman who manually masturbates caged animals for artificial insemination, all come and go.

Before the day is over, Randal and Dante have closed the store to play a hockey game on the roof, inadvertently sold cigarettes to a minor, and disrupted the wake of Julie Dwyer, an old girlfriend of Dante's who died of an embolism. Even worse, Dante's relationships with former love Caitlin Bree and current girl Veronica are shaken by a series of bizarre events and Randal's endless meddling.

At the end of a trying day, Dante and Randal reflect on their choices, and ask important questions about their lives. A little wiser, Dante and Randal part ways for the evening, and Dante closes the convenience store.

SILENT BOB'S WORDS OF WISDOM:

"There's a million fine looking women in the world, but they don't all bring you lasagna. Most of them just cheat on you."

THE STORY BEHIND THE MOVIE:

In this world, there are thousands (if not millions) of dreamers who believe they can make a movie, but few actually get beyond the fantasy. Even fewer deliver a professional, feature-length film to a festival (let alone Sundance) and walk away from the party sporting a deal from a prestigious operation like the Weinsteins' Miramax Films. Yet that's precisely what Kevin Smith, producer Scott Mosier and fledgling View Askew Productions accomplished in 1993 with Smith's celebrated first film, *Clerks*.

There's an old adage that authors ought to write "what they know" and perhaps that proverb is the best entrée into the world of Kevin Smith's films. With *Clerks*, Smith successfully transformed a minimum wage job jockeying the counter at Quick Stop Groceries in Leonardo, New Jersey into cinematic gold. Using tales of the convenience store (and its partner operation, R.S.T. Video) as fodder for his comedy, Smith drafted a 164-page screenplay for *Clerks* in thirty days, in early 1993.

The resulting script, concerning a day in the life of two disenfranchised young adults of Generation X in dead-end customer service jobs came replete with elements that would become Smith's hallmark—particularly witty and ribald dialogue. It might be stretching the truth to say that *Clerks* was autobiographical, but there was no doubt that Smith's work experience played a role in its creation.

"I think movies are usually one step behind the story teller," Producer Scott Mosier suggests. "You can't project into the future, so Kevin was making a film about his own previous experience, and maybe Dante's fear of being trapped in that time and place was something that Kevin, by writing this script, had already conquered."

Only the script's conceived ending, a tragic and fatal turn of events for Dante Hicks, hinted at a deep nihilism bubbling beneath the slacker angst. Smith later reported to John Pierson in *Spike, Mike, Slackers & Dykes* that the film's fateful climax was inspired at least in part by Spike Lee's *Do The Right Thing*, one of Smith's five favorite films.

> The tone of that movie was humorous and then it
> turned. And I thought I'd like to do that in a movie.
> Humorous, then turn it.[1]

But even before *Clerks*'s surprising ending had been crafted by Smith, the *Clerks* script had gone through a great many developments, as View Askew historian Vincent Pereira explains: "We were driving home from seeing *Slacker* and right on the spot Kevin thought of something based on *Slacker*'s opening scene, where Linklater is talking about the Schroedinger's Cat."

As aficionados of Linklater (and quantum mechanics) may recall, the Schroedinger Cat paradox was an idea first put forward in 1935 by Erwin Schroedinger. Briefly summarized: if a cat is deposited in a box and thus no longer observed, can it rightly be said to exist? Or—until observed again— is it actually non-existent? Schroedinger's Cat idea was also brought up in another film of the same vintage, John Carpenter's 1987 horror picture, *Prince of Darkness*. The concept isn't mentioned by name in *Slacker*, but the film opens with a character (portrayed by Linklater) contemplating parallel realities and the vicissitudes of perceptions and dreams.

"It was a very Lynchian sci-fi type of film," Pereira confirms of Smith's first idea. "Kevin then wrote a one-page synopsis of what he wanted to do with *Clerks*, which at the time was titled *In Convenience*. That plot line had to do with a guy working the midnight to 6:00 a.m. shift in a convenience store, and all the bizarre people who came in. It was very Lynchian, and Kevin didn't write it in a linear fashion; really just scenes. And at one point he handed me fifty pages of scenes that were sort of in order, and that was the first time I knew he was writing a straight comedy. It was very funny."

Forecasting the dark ending, Smith had even included an action-chase subplot that landed protagonist Dante in great danger. "In one of the pre-drafts there was something that never made it to the first draft," Pereira remembers. "There was a character who, in Kevin's words, was loosely based on me. I was kind of a hot-tempered guy at the time, and this character was going to be the mob boy at the convenience store who gets fired and is scoping out the bank with a rifle because he knows Dante is going there to deposit the money. So he's going to kill Dante and steal the cash. There was this whole subplot where Randal is watching events unfold on the TV at the convenience store, with Dante being chased all over town."

Pereira liked the interlude, but realizing money would be tight, voiced his reservations about the set piece. "Kevin asked me what should be cut and, first and foremost, I thought that subplot should go because it would have been really expensive to shoot. Even though it was very funny."

Once the *Clerks* script was written and then pared down to a manageable 135 pages, Smith and his cohort from film school, Scott Mosier, set out to produce the film. Making *Clerks* was not an easy task for two young students with little cash and even less experience, but they both dove in, head first, to make the film a reality.

"I didn't really know how to start the process of making this movie at all. Based on going to school, I wasn't prepared to do it," Scott Mosier remembers of the producer's job. "I understood the broadest of strokes, and I sort of broke it down in a practical way. I knew I needed to rent equipment and so forth. In *Filmmaker Magazine*, Peter Broderick used to do these articles about low budget films, like *Laws of Gravity* and *Slacker*, and print their budgets. So I used those articles as a sort of template of what the categories were. We needed cameras and lights, and this and that."

And, at that point, another important decision was made. Shooting the film would be David Klein, a native of Idaho and classmate whom Mosier had befriended at Vancouver following Smith's return to New Jersey. "When Kevin left, I started hanging out with David a lot," Mosier explains. "He became the next person. I had talked to him throughout the class and we'd gotten along, but once Kevin left we finished the class together."

According to Mosier, it was important to him that Klein shoot the film. "I talked to Kevin about Dave and said, in a selfish way, that I wanted to work with someone of our age and experience level so we'd all feel comfortable. I didn't really want to hire somebody from New York who had shot a bunch of short films because I felt we'd be better off being in our little bubble and doing things the way we wanted. The whole movie might have been a disaster because we were so isolated, because we were just dealing with the basic knowledge each of us had. I knew how to record sound, not to say well, but I took the foundations of what I knew and did it. Dave did the same thing. Kevin did the same thing."

In the pre-production phase of *Clerks*, Mosier's most important job became determining the production equipment needs. "I'd get up in the morning on the West Coast at about five a.m., because long distance was cheaper, and I'd call all of these New York facilities to get cameras and make a plan of how much we would have to spend. And Dave came up with a list of the things he thought he would need. It was a little unnerving because we were afraid we would get to the set and realize we'd forgotten something. It seems so simple: get three cameras, a Nagra, a boom, a mike, and a light. You think it can't be that simple, but in truth, it really was that simple."

The budget for *Clerks* was an issue, of course, but nobody set out with a defined ceiling on the project. "*Slacker* cost $24,000," Mosier compares, "but making *Clerks* was simply about spending as little as possible. Kevin really carried the financial risk of the project."

Smith not only sold his comic book collection to finance the picture, but according to Mosier, he "took a loan of $3,000 from his parents at the outset, and put the rest on his credit cards. And at the end, my parents loaned us $3,500 for the final print. But it was Kevin who took the brunt of the financial risk. If it didn't work, he was in for it."

Smith's credit card approach, already modeled successfully by Robert Townsend and the film *Hollywood Shuffle*, allowed the film's final budget to reach $26,685.

On Smith's end, permission was secured to film the movie in the video and convenience stores after closing time, from the owners, Tralochan and Sarala Thapar. It was at that point that casting began in earnest for the picture.

Interestingly, not everybody who hoped to be involved was certain that Smith's intention to make a movie was for real. "I remember the first time Kevin told me he wanted to make a movie," Jason Mewes remembers. "He said, 'I wrote this script, I want to shoot this movie, and I wrote a character for you.' My other friend, Kevin Horvath, and I had gotten those little Fisher Price video cameras that had little black and white cassettes for

Christmas. We used to make these funny little movies, so when Kevin said he'd written a script, I just thought it would be the bunch of us messing around with those cameras."

Jeff Anderson, who eventually came to play the wisecracking Randal, remembers how he first learned of *Clerks*. "I hung out with Ernie O'Donnell's roommate, and Ernie told me that Kevin was making a movie. When I visited him at the video store, Kevin was always at his word processor working on the script and we talked about it some. But then Ernie showed me the script, and told me Kevin had written it, and I thought this was totally unheard of. A movie? This was out in the woods! *Moving pictures?*

"Ernie told me that Kevin was holding auditions at the local playhouse [The First Avenue Playhouse]. He said I should go because there would be a lot of attractive girls there. So I went along with Ernie's roommate to watch Ernie audition for *Clerks*."

From there, Jeff Anderson watched actors come and go, and remembers being particularly impressed by Marilyn Ghigliotti, who eventually played Veronica. "I mean, we were at a playhouse in Atlantic Highlands, and the actors weren't terribly impressive, but Marilyn did this crazy audition where she was crying and doing all kinds of emotional things and I thought, 'My god, this chick can act.' After she was done, it was just quiet. Even I was impressed, and I was only there to mock Ernie. We were all thinking, 'Wow, that was really some acting...'"

By a strange twist of fate, Jeff himself ended up on the stage that day. "We were at the playhouse looking at all the girls and Ernie was on stage reading with some of them," Anderson describes. "We thought Ernie's reading had gone badly so we really started mocking him after he finished. 'How long have you had that script? I don't think you've ever looked at it!' And he said that he didn't see us reading any parts, so I grabbed the script, went up on stage and read for the part of Jay, which was pretty funny.

"Kevin told me I could audition for Jay, but I'd have to wait until the owner of the playhouse left the premises. I asked why, and he told me to look at what Jay was saying [lots of cussing]. Kevin was getting this play-house for free and didn't want the owner to think he was doing a piece of trash. So as soon as the owner walked out, they stopped whoever was auditioning and told me to go on. So I ran up on stage and spouted all these expletives. Then the owner walked back in and they stopped me. That was my big audition."

In the end, Anderson didn't get the role of Jay—he was destined for something else. Instead, the role went to Smith's young friend and some-times housemate, Jason Mewes. A talent with raw energy to spare and a screen presence that *Entertainment Weekly*'s Owen Gleiberman later described as "Dana Carvey's Garth stoked with Eminem's street rage and the raunch of Al Goldstein...the cinema's original suburban hip-hop id."[2]

"Kevin wrote the character of Jay because he, Walter, and Bryan thought I was funny," Jason Mewes reveals. "They liked the way I acted, and Kevin was always curious if other people would find it funny, or if it would just be our circle of friends. So he wrote the character based on me."

Contemplating the character, Mewes reflects on how much of Jay is actually him. "That's how I was when I was younger, when I met Kevin, when I was thirteen. I'm still like Jay, maybe about 60 percent, but in about eleventh grade I realized I had to straighten up, and that there are boundaries. The difference is that now I understand boundaries. I feel people out, and I know who can take a joke. And I don't pull my pants down anymore. I used to pull my pants down a lot."

Also attending the auditions for *Clerks* was an accomplished young actor named Brian O'Halloran, born in the Bronx, who had appeared in stage productions of *Dracula* (as Renfield), *Charlotte's Web,* and *Wait Until Dark.*

"I went down to the playhouse," O'Halloran explains, "and I saw Vincent Pereira with a video camera, and Kevin was there, and maybe Walter too. I filled out a questionnaire form that Kevin had printed up for the auditions, and then asked how many principals there were. They said six, but the roles had already been taken, so I was really auditioning to play an extra. But I went up and did this monologue from *Wait Until Dark.* I was the villain in that show and was really intense, and a couple of days later I got a call from Kevin inviting me for a callback.

"So I came back, he handed me two or three script pages, and I read the scene. Then I came back for another callback, and he asked what I thought about Dante. I said 'Dante's funny, but his friend is funnier.' Then Kevin told me I had the part and I didn't believe him, because I thought all the principals were taken. He told me not to worry about it, and gave me the script to read. He asked me if I wanted to do it, and I said yes."

The key to playing Dante, according to O'Halloran, was sympathy. "I could relate completely to what Dante was going through. I'd been working in the service industry [at a grocery store] for the last four years, so I knew about dealing with customers. I think I just brought sympathy to the character. If you could make him sympathetic, he wouldn't be whiny, and he just became a very loveable character."

As the fidelity-challenged girlfriend to Brian O'Halloran's long suffering protagonist, Kevin Smith cast Lisa Spoonauer after seeing her in a performance during a class at Brookdale Community College.

The fledgling filmmaker wasn't above a bit of nepotism either, recruiting his sister Virginia to portray a woman who stimulates caged animals for artificial insemination. His mother Grace was also brought in to portray a "milk maid," though she later complained that the finished sequence made her hips look "too big."[3] In one scene Smith's girlfriend, Heather Loughran, played opposite Ernie O'Donnell's chick-magnet, Rick Derris.

As for Jeff Anderson, he didn't score with his audition of Jay. "From my first audition, I got a smaller role," he reveals. "It was actually the role that Kevin's sister ended up playing in the movie, only at the time the character was killing chickens for the railroad. That character had several occupations over time, and that one [animal masturbator] was just the one that got left in. Anyway, I read for that smaller part, and the next day Kevin called me and asked what I was doing. He wanted to come over and have me look at another part.

"So he came over to my house, and that night we sat on my couch and he said, 'Listen, let's read through the script just you and me, and I want you to read for this Randal guy.' And then we just sat there and read the script and when it was over, Kevin said, 'You're my Randal.'"

Except it wasn't that easy.

"I said to him, 'I am *not* your Randal! I don't have that good a memory! I can't spout all this out!'" Anderson laughs. "But Kevin thought I could do it and told me we'd do it a little at a time. He asked me to come to rehearsals and said we'd read the script just the way we did there, on the couch."

Ironically, it was during the rehearsal process that Kevin Smith almost "lost his Randal," according to Anderson. That first night, Brian O'Halloran, Marilyn Ghigliotti, Jeff Anderson, and Kevin began rehearsals in the convenience store after hours.

"We sat on the coolers where the Salsa Shark scene takes place. I met Marilyn and Brian and they asked me what I'd been in. I thought, 'Oh dear Lord, I've never done anything.' And they were a little shocked by that. When they read me their resumes, I knew I was in trouble.

"So we did a read-through and it went okay. Then we did a rehearsal. And the next night, we did another rehearsal and Lisa [Spoonauer] came in and I thought, 'Oh my, this is looking up, she's really hot!' So we did a read-through with Marilyn, Brian, Lisa, myself, and Kevin. At the end of it, Kevin closed the script and told us it was pretty good, and that we'd just keep plugging away at it.

"But then Marilyn piped up and asked to say something. Kevin was like, 'Sure.' And Marilyn says, 'Uh Kevin, I don't think he's going to be able to do this,' and she pointed right to me. I was mortified. She said, 'He's never acted before, and he doesn't sound good.' She said this in front of every-body! It wasn't in a private conversation, and I just turned twenty shades of red. Kevin assured her I would be okay by the time we got to shoot."

But the damage was done, and Anderson's confidence was shot. "I went to work the next day, and now I was dreading going to rehearsal. I finally decided not to do the movie. So on the way home from work, I stopped at the convenience store and gave my script back to Kevin, saying, basically, 'Thanks, but no thanks.' I told him I meant no offense, but I wasn't being paid for this. I was just doing it as a kick, and now it wasn't very much fun.

"Kevin was very definite, telling me not to quit. He said he would rehearse Marilyn and me on different days. But I didn't want to do that either, because I didn't want to be some problem where now Kevin had to schedule us apart. I just wasn't comfortable. As it was, I was uncertain about acting, but to have her eyes on me — I was just afraid I'd mess up."

Though Kevin Smith convinced Anderson to stay aboard the project, Jeff remembers how his experience with Ghigliotti reinforced his feelings about actors. "Acting people always struck me as so serious. She was sure I couldn't do it, and there was no tact in the way she said it. It was in front of everybody and I thought, 'Man, this girl is brutal.'"

So, Anderson admits, it was sweet when time came to film Randal's one scene with Veronica. "The first scene we actually shot on *Clerks* was the one with me and Marilyn. We never rehearsed it, but Kevin told me to do the scene with her, and I'd never have to see her again. I remember the first take of that scene: she messed up her line. I was so happy, I thought, 'Thank God!' And from there it got better. I harbor her no ill will."

Pereira also recalls the lengthy rehearsal process leading up to pro-duction, which stretched throughout February of 1993. "Kevin would get the actors together and go through the script until the actors were as off the book as possible. Kevin worked in the store till about 10:30 p.m., and the actors would start showing up at 10:00 p.m. I have this image of driving back from a showing of Peter Jackson's *Dead Alive* in Toms River one night, and seeing Kevin at the store rehearsing. These people were just sitting on the freezers, going over the lines."

But if rehearsals lasted well into the night, shooting the film itself became an ongoing marathon of all-nighters. "We were young," Mosier comments, deadpan. "I was 20 or 21 at the time, and the thought of sleeping on the floor for two hours a night didn't seem that bad. I lost weight because we just smoked and drank coffee and shot all night long for three weeks. Sometimes we'd sleep two hours a day, and we shot seven days a week, except for Easter. Kevin was just working insane hours. He'd work at the convenience store and sleep sometimes while we were setting up. Then Dave and I would sleep a few hours in the video store in the morning. If somebody proposed to me to do it now, at my age, there'd be certain things I'd need. Like a bed. And a certain amount of sleep to function. Today, I wouldn't last more than a few days."

Playing against type, Jeff Anderson was anything but a directionless slacker at the time *Clerks* was made, a fact that complicated his schedule. "At the time, I worked for AT&T. I was supervisor of a mailroom in charge of three different locations of 50 people. I'd work from 7:30 in the morning to 4:30 in the afternoon. Then go to school to study architecture and design from 5:00 p.m. to 7:00 p.m., and then be down at the store by 11:00 p.m. and shoot until 6:00 a.m. in the morning. Randal was pretty different from me: I was working in a professional environment, and I could only wish to lash into people the way he did."

The aggressive shooting schedule of *Clerks* in March of 1993 also took its toll on the hard-working Smith, who continued to toil at the Quick Stop to augment the film's budget. He gained 30 lbs. in 21 days and smoked one-and-a-half packs of cigarettes a day.[4] Some of the stress he must have felt at the time may have resulted from the fact that some of his performers were not completely dependable. Many simply forgot to show up.

"For *Clerks*, every single character I did was a last minute thing," Walt Flanagan, who played Egg Man and other bizarre Quick Stop patrons, recalls. "We were waiting for actors to show, and the whole movie was shot after hours so we'd be scheduling a scene at 2:00 in the morning for an actor to come in and buy cigarettes. So we'd wait and we'd wait and then realize this guy just wasn't going to show up. So Kevin would turn to me and ask if I wanted to do the part. I would say, 'Kevin, I just did a character.' But he'd make me look different each time and I'd be all right."

Wearing hoods, suits and ties, glasses, caps, and wigs, Walt Flanagan was quickly dubbed the "Lon Chaney of the '90s" by Kevin Smith for his versatility and dependability.

While shooting *Clerks*, everybody in the Quick Stop had to learn to chip in, just like Walt, because there were few hands available, as Pereira remembers. "Originally, I was going to be the camera assistant, but David didn't have enough time to teach me how to change magazines and all that. When you were there in the store, you just did whatever needed to be done. So usually I helped, because there were maybe five or six people there. I left early some nights, but I was there for most of the shooting."

The old axiom "never work with animals" also proved true for the crew of *Clerks* during production when the black cat appearing in the film bolted between shots. "That was a stray cat from the area who started coming to the store," Pereira notes. "Kevin put him in the script. Basically, we were shooting a take and somebody opened the door, and the cat was getting agitated by the lights, and the people in the store, so he just bolted. We went out after him and called for him, but he wouldn't come back. He eventually came back, but we were all outside at around four in the morning trying to find this black cat—which was hard to see in the dark!"

Another hurdle in shooting *Clerks* involved Jason Mewes's confidence level. Simply put, the young man felt uncomfortable being in front of the camera and performing Jay's outrageous stunts. "I was so nervous," he confides. "Every day before shooting, they had to go buy me a bottle of blackberry brandy. I had to get really drunk to do the part, and then I'd make everybody go inside that didn't need to be out there. Usually, it was just Kevin, Scott, and Dave. Kevin would stand next to me, Dave was the DP, and Scott was doing the sound. But if I could avoid having anyone there at all, besides those three, I would do it."

For Jeff Anderson, the filming went fine, though he was still anxious about his first performance. He feels that to some extent the situation affected his work with Brian O'Halloran. "I like Brian," he stresses. "But after the Marilyn thing, I put my guard up against Brian because I knew he and Marilyn were friends and had done theater together, and I guess I found them intimidating. I shouldn't have done it, because Brian had nothing to do with it. But at the time, I thought he was one of them! So when we shot *Clerks*, it was just like, let's get through this, and Brian and I didn't pal around a lot."

On the technical side of the process, only a few shots had to be re-staged when it was learned that some footage of Mosier (as Willam, the Snowballer) was ruined by film burns. That turned out to be nothing, however, compared with Mosier's worry that things could have been a lot worse.

"We didn't have enough money for dailies, and when we got done shooting and it was time to synch everything up I had a pit in my stomach," Mosier recollects. "I thought, 'Holy fuck, am I going to be able to synch this?' Through the whole shoot I wondered about that. It was one of those things that I knew other people would worry about too if I told them, so I just kept it to myself and bore the brunt of it. That was the only thing that stressed me out."

What Pereira remembers about the shooting of *Clerks* is that even at that protean stage of his directing experience, Kevin Smith had already found his chops. "His main focus was on the actors," Pereira recalls. "In comedies like *Clerks*, Kevin is big on line readings. The screenplay reads a certain way, he hears it in his head, and then listens to the actor's delivery. Then he brings the two readings closer together. He likes David Mamet, who does that kind of stylized dialogue, and he loves fast-talking 1930s comedies, like *His Girl Friday*. Howard Hawks stuff."

For O'Halloran, he and Smith spoke the same language, which made their working relationship a comfortable one. "I could really relate to Dante, and to Kevin in general. We had similar upbringings. He had older siblings, I have older siblings. He comes from an Irish-Catholic background, and so do I. He was an altar boy, and I was an altar boy. I understood his humor immediately. It has the whole twang of Jersey-ness to it.

"I could really relate to Kevin, so when we talked about a scene we understood each other. Direction-wise, we talked mostly about intonation. He writes with so many words, and when I had big chunks of dialogue, he would give me my pauses, and tell me what marks to hit. His writing has a great flow to it. He uses all those words we got in English class and hoped we'd never have to see again. But man, the guy has a large vocabulary and isn't afraid to use it."

After *Clerks* finished shooting in March of 1993, it was finally time to put the pieces together and edit the film. "So much of it was just picking the takes, because the film is basically a series of two shots and static shots," recalls Scott Mosier. "It wasn't like we were cutting so much as choosing takes. One shot in there is seven minutes long. You could put 20 minutes together and do only four cuts.

"I had more experience on the flatbed, so I synched all the dailies and started the process of cutting. Then I got exhausted and brought Kevin in. I would work all day, he'd watch what I was doing, then I'd work in the store while he cut. But a lot of it was just Kevin watching the takes and telling me which ones he wanted to use."

In the case of *Clerks*, there wasn't a whole of lot of excess footage to litter the cutting room, er, video store floor. "It was just a matter of cutting things down," Pereira observes. "The draft Kevin shot was about 135 pages, and even that cut together to 105 minutes for the first cut. It was interesting, because you always read that one page equals one minute of screen time, but being a comedy, the dialogue was so fast-paced that it ran much quicker. The first cut of the film was 105 minutes and contained about 99 percent of the shooting script."

O'Halloran remembers checking in on the editing process and being pleasantly surprised. "They were editing in the video store on a Steenback editor, where you literally take the negative, cut it, put it together, tape it, and run it. So I asked how it was going and Kevin and Scott showed me some scenes and it was really funny. It looked good."

Perhaps one of the most controversial aspects of *Clerks* first cut was the original ending. Dante was shot dead from the gun of a mysterious customer in a beautifully executed final sequence. Filmed as a tracking P.O.V. shot, a la John Carpenter's *Halloween*, the ending gave the film one powerful jolt of a climax, and re-cast the meaningless events of Dante's day in a whole new — and rather disturbing — light.

"I thought the script was funny, but I hated that ending," O'Halloran admits. "I never thought it worked. I just thought it was too quick of a twist. I remember going to Kevin, and I believe I told him I didn't like the ending. But we did it anyway, and in the end, it got taken out."

"It was a massive change of tone from the rest of the film," Pereira acknowledges, "but Kevin shot that scene so well. On the DVD they messed it up. If you watch it on DVD or laserdisc, as Dante is laying there on the floor, the sound of the convenience store fades and the picture goes to black, but that's not how it was originally mixed. If you saw the original tapes, what Kevin and Scott did was to bring up all the background noise of the store to be really loud. The sound ramps up and up and then it cuts to black and silence. It was very powerful."

By the same token, Pereira admits that the grave initial denouement, cut before the film's showing at Sundance, would have changed the tone of the Kevin Smith film series rather substantially. "If *Clerks* was just going to be *Clerks*, then the ending might have worked, having Dante die. But it became this whole series of movies, and it would have been strange to have the specter of Dante's death hanging over the sequels. Could you imagine *Jay & Silent Bob Strike Back* with Randal alone in the convenience store?"

With their film cut together, many of those involved with *Clerks* thought that would be the end of the project. "I didn't even think anything about it," Mewes admits. "I continued to go to work; I was roofing at the time. We ate some chips and watched the movie in the video store one night, me, Kevin, Scott, and Dave. Then Kevin told me he was going to try to get it distributed."

On that front, Kevin Smith and Scott Mosier paid $500 to enter *Clerks* in the Independent Feature Film Festival held on October 3, 1993 at the Angelika Film Center in Manhattan. The *Clerks* showing was programmed at Sunday morning at 11:00 a.m., and was, euphemistically stated, sparsely attended.

"There were about twelve people in the audience, and about eight of them were us," Mosier remembers. "There were four others, and a few who wandered into the back to watch a little then leave. That happens a lot in these things. But we had spent all week trying to get people to go, and it was pretty hard because we didn't know what else we could do. But Bob Hawk was in the audience and told us he worked for Sundance."

The View Askew team's response?

"We didn't quite believe him," Mosier admits. "He didn't have any credentials, and I was just depressed. I wanted to leave. But then he started telling a bunch of people about the movie, pushing this little snowball down the hill, and it started getting bigger and bigger."

Robert Hawk, who attended the screening that day, was indeed a highly influential independent film consultant and member of the nominating committee on the Sundance Film Festival. He loved *Clerks* and began making calls to influential critics and film people on its behalf.

Before long, further interest in *Clerks* came from *The Village Voice*'s Amy Taubin (an early champion of Linklater's *Slacker*). Eventually word got back to film representative and marketing genius John Pierson, the undisputed guru of indie films, that he should take a look at *Clerks*. There was only one problem: Pierson wanted out of the business.

"I didn't really want to rep films anymore," Pierson acknowledges. And for good reason. He'd just come from an especially unpleasant experience working with the colorful Rob Weiss, director of the independent film *Amongst Friends*, and had no desire to get back in the game. It was his wife and long-time business partner, Janet Pierson, who finally swayed him.

"I was away speaking in Louisville, Kentucky, and Janet saw the film first. And it was just like seeing *She's Gotta Have It* and saying 'I have seen the future of cinema and his name is Spike Lee.' She told me flat out on the phone, 'If you don't want to rep films anymore, you shouldn't watch this.' And I came back and watched *Clerks* and fell off the chair laughing."

"I watched the film three times," Pierson continues, "and I'm laughing harder and harder each time. Sometimes, if you watch a movie repeatedly, you see nothing but the dead spots. But with *Clerks* I had exactly the opposite experience. It was effortless to let the dead spots just fly by."

Still, Pierson was reluctant to jump back into the repping game unless *Clerks* and its makers met three very important criteria. The first was that Pierson had to like the film; the second was that he had to believe it was marketable; and third, he had to feel as though he could work with the team who had made the film.

On the first criterion, there was no problem; Pierson loved *Clerks*. On the second, he had reason to hope. "I've been involved with people since the get-go who are fantastic self-promoters, and I think Spike is the first example of this. He was a fantastic salesman for his work, with a really good back-story, even before his first feature."

Rob Weiss, another of Pierson's clients, was also a brilliant self-promoter. However, unlike Spike Lee or Kevin Smith, his film work was hardly exemplary, and his relationship with Pierson was a rocky one. After his one and only film as a director, *Amongst Friends*, ballooned from a $250,000 to a $600,000 budget, Weiss faded quickly from celebrity, despite media reports that, like the gangsters of his flick, he may or may not have been involved in criminal activity.

"Weiss tried hard," Pierson offers another example. "He was already post-modern about that sort of thing. He was just desperate to make a name for himself and be a tough guy—and maybe he killed somebody and maybe he didn't. Instead of making a movie like *Mean Streets*, it's like he *was* a character from *Mean Streets*. But that was so self-conscious and so annoying and so counterproductive in the end that it made me re-consider how essential it was for people to have a great, self-promoting back-story."

And Kevin Smith, the talent who had earned his keep in convenience stores before writing his ode to them? "His story was great," Pierson affirms. "He did have this great self-promotion, and a couldn't-be-better-if-you-made-it-up-in-thin-air back-story."

Even better, Pierson liked him. "He's a fantastic person, one of my favorite people I ever met in my life. You couldn't find a more upstanding citizen, or just a great human being."

He felt the same way about Mosier. "Kevin doesn't really need a stabilizing force, because he's a very stable person on his own, but everything is that much more solid and rooted because Scott doesn't get worked up in a tizzy about things. He's just extremely confident."

But, just because its behind-the-scenes talents had admirable character traits, that didn't mean selling *Clerks*, a low-budget, black-and-white film with no recognizable actors, was going to be an easy proposition.

"Pierson told Kevin he wasn't sure what he could do with *Clerks*," Mosier remembers. "He liked it, but wasn't sure how to sell it. But he got us a lawyer, John Sloss."

Even more dramatically, John Pierson hooked Kevin Smith up with C.A.A. (Creative Artists Agency)[5] and agent Tory Metzger. Almost immediately, even before *Clerks* had gone to the Sundance Film Festival, Kevin Smith was attending pitch meetings in Hollywood for his next writing assignment. He was offered the opportunity to script a number of bizarre projects, including a comedy called *Beer Money* and a Michael Jackson "vehicle" entitled *Hot Rod*, which saw the gloved one blessed with the ability to transform into a super car and befriend children in need.

There was also talk of a second project related to *Clerks,* to be called *Busing*. Basically, it was *Clerks* in a restaurant.[6]

"I rolled out to L.A. with Kevin to these strange meetings where people were pitching him weird scripts," Mosier describes. "I just sat there thinking that it was all intensely stupid. But we were able to go to all the studio lots, like 20th Century Fox, and even if nothing happened, it was fun."

Back east, John Pierson was working harder than ever to make things happen for *Clerks*. He felt strongly that Miramax would be the perfect outfit to distribute the film and had worked with them before.

Miramax Films, a company that had formed in 1979 after brothers and co-chairmen Bob and Harvey Weinstein acquired a film called *The Secret Policeman's Ball* from the Cannes Film Festival, had become known in the intervening dozen years as a house where quality films were distributed. Named after the Weinstein brothers' parents, Miriam and Max, Miramax distributed the controversial documentary *The Thin Blue Line*, as well as Steven Soderbergh's first film, *Sex, Lies and Videotape*. More recently, it had distributed the scandalous Madonna documentary *Truth or Dare*, and the nearly X-rated *The Cook, The Thief, His Wife and Her Lover*, directed by Peter Greenaway.

In 1993, Miramax was purchased by Disney, but the Weinsteins' dedication to the distribution of high quality films continued. In its many years in business, Miramax movies like *Good Will Hunting, Pulp Fiction, The Crying Game, Wings of the Dove, Shakespeare in Love,* and *Life is Beautiful* have earned more than three dozen Academy Awards, and more than 130 nominations. Its chairmen, Bob and Harvey Weinstein, are reputed to be among the most powerful and influential men in Hollywood.

"Miramax and I had been through the sale of *Working Girls, The Thin Blue Line*, and the attempted purchase of *Anna*," Pierson reports. "They were really pissed that Vestron got that one [*Anna*]. If I hadn't gone to a studio, they would have had *Roger & Me* too, which was like a week's worth of negotiating."

So it was with some confidence that Pierson helped to orchestrate a showing of *Clerks* at Miramax in mid-December of 1993 with the full support of executive Mark Tusk, an admirer of the film from Miramax. "That was the only nerve-wracking time on *Clerks* with Miramax. It didn't play out exactly like we planned."

As Pierson describes the problem, chain-smoker Harvey Weinstein didn't appreciate the anti-cigarette tone of the Chewlies Gum Rep scene and bailed out of *Clerk* after just under a quarter hour.[7] "That was like,

'Oh shit,' because I thought it was a good orchestration," Pierson considers.

Miramax's failure to purchase *Clerks* near Christmas of 1993 meant one thing: the fate of Kevin Smith's first film would be decided at the Sundance Film Festival.

When *Clerks* and its filmmakers arrived in Park City, Utah for Redford's 1994 film festival, word-of-mouth about the film began to grow. The film not only won the Filmmaker's Trophy for the year, but instant popularity.

"We had four screenings at Sundance and I heard it was the first film to sell out there," O'Halloran comments. "I took a trip out to Sundance and saw people scalping tickets for it. That's when things really started to get weird for me. We had sell-out audiences, and we went to these screenings and people were just dying. Hearing an entire theater filled with laughter was great and, afterwards, people would run up and ask us for autographs."

John Pierson had just one more opportunity for Harvey Weinstein to see the picture and purchase it for Miramax. There was one last *Clerks* showing during the festival.

"That was one of those things where you set something up with your fingers crossed, and then just hope it works," Pierson explains. "You could feel the momentum for that film building throughout the week. And though Kevin isn't a big fan of [producer] Cary Woods, Cary and Mark Tusk were instrumental in making sure that Harvey was there and well-positioned in the middle of the theater for that screening, where he was both absorbing all the laughter and increasing the laughter on his own. But the pump had really been primed. Had he seen the first show, the first weekend, on the first Saturday, it would have been a really different experience."

"There was fantastic momentum in having that deal happen," Pierson further elaborates. "It lead up to critic's week selection for Cannes, New Directors, and having all this focus in the international news and media, Connie Chung going to the Quick Stop, and all that stuff. It was the perfect moment for that to culminate."

But that didn't necessarily mean that things were going to work out. "We weren't the hot property of the festival," Mosier notes with modesty. "There weren't a dozen people bidding on us. A lot of people didn't know what to do with a foul-mouthed, black-and-white grungy movie."

But at a restaurant called the Eating Establishment, over an after-dinner plate of potato skins, Harvey Weinstein [brother Bob did not attend Sundance that year], Miramax executive David Linde, and Mark Tusk sat down at a table with John Pierson, Kevin Smith, and Scott Mosier. In short order, a deal was cut to buy *Clerks* and then distribute it.

"Harvey had those potato skins, and wanted to buy the movie,"

Pierson reports. "We agreed on the outline, and he left, and David and I wrote it up."

Miramax paid $227,000 to purchase *Clerks* outright. The deal included a theatrical release of the film, and the distribution agreement began a long-standing relationship between View Askew and Miramax.

Pierson thinks the deal was a matter of serendipitous timing. "It was probably the last time in their [Miramax] corporate history that they ever would have gotten involved with that kind of film. So there does seem to be something resembling fate involved in things coming together at that moment."

"It was pretty amazing," Mosier acknowledges. "That was the beginning of this whole ride that started in 1994."

At Cannes 1994, the ride accelerated. *Clerks* garnered an International Critics Week Prize. It was also nominated for three Independent Spirit Awards, including Best First Picture, Best Debut Performance (for Jeff Anderson), and First Screenplay (Kevin Smith).

But with a major release slated for fall of 1994, there was still much work to be completed on *Clerks*. Fifteen minutes were cut from the film between its Sundance showing and its theatrical run. Gone for good was that pesky ending that saw Dante killed in the line of counter duty.

"It was a key moment for me after watching the film three times, when I realized it didn't have to end in a blood bath," reports Pierson. "Crossing that bridge was just a complete light bulb going off."

When Pierson suggested trimming the ending, removing Dante's death, Smith was receptive. "He was immediately prepared to do it," Pierson remembers. "As he's said, that was his reach for greater meaning. That was his *Do the Right Thing* ending."

"And frankly, there's still about ten percent of his audience—the smarter, educated, intellectual, existential crowd—who think that *Clerks* should have had that original ending. But they're dead fucking wrong," Pierson asserts. "I appreciate the fact there is always going to be a certain number of people who go for purity. But I thought that the ending was tagged on. It wasn't like the last gasp of existential horror. I think Kevin knew that, and I think that's why it was easy to give away. I just happened to say it first, but I know Larry Kardish at the Museum of Modern Art, who is the main proponent of New Directors, New Films, felt a huge relief when he knew the end was going. You can't fall in love with these characters and then kill them."

So, to Brian O'Halloran's relief, Dante lived, and *Clerks* rolled on. Clever trailers of the film were run before screenings of Quentin Tarantino's

Pulp Fiction, and Kevin Smith shot a music video for *Clerks* for $15,000. He walked the band Soul Asylum through a rooftop hockey game, mirroring the film's events. The resulting video, "You Can't Even Tell," was the first opportunity for fans to see the Quick Stop, Randal, Dante, Jay, and Silent Bob in color.

Other tunes were added to the film including the very funny "Chewbacca" by Supernova (played, appropriately, during Randal and Dante's debate about *Return of the Jedi*) and "Got Me Wrong" by Alice in Chains.

It was during this period of hard work that Smith and the View Askew people realized that their $227,000 check from Miramax would not necessarily make the filmmakers rich men. "Once the movie got bought at Sundance, Kevin came back and laid out all his credit card bills and saw what it was, had things not worked out," Mosier remembers. "The price of the film had grown from interest to over $30,000."

And there were bills yet to be settled. "A hundred thousand went to finish the movie," Mosier tabulates, "and around $34,000 went to paying off the credit card debt. So essentially you were talking about $93,000 back, but then Kevin immediately paid all the actors and crew, and I got a paycheck out of that. By the time I was done living without a job for over a year, I just basically broke even. I had enough money to pay down my debt, but I still had to get a job at the Banana Republic as a stock room guy. I had to make money, because there really wasn't much left after it all got divided up."

Today, Pierson will occasionally second-guess the Miramax deal. "The issue I have, years later, is that they've been slow to pay the overages on that film, and it's made a ton of money over time. And I'm sitting here thinking, 'It's great that we got $227,000 then, but maybe we should have gotten $527,000.' It's one of those things that you turn over in your head."

Yet, as Mosier is quick to point out, *Clerks* was a worthy investment. "It was scary, but to put it in context, how much is NYU a year? *Clerks* was a kind of school for all of us, and at the end of the day we made a product that gave us careers."

With the theatrical release of *Clerks* approaching, Kevin Smith and his friends must have believed the gods were favoring their freshman effort, but a controversy soon occurred that would, in some ways, set the tone for Smith's career.

Before *Clerks* was released, it was submitted to the Motion Picture Association of America for a rating. Though the film featured neither violence nor sex, the M.P.A.A. slapped it with an NC-17 rating, the kiss of death from a marketing standpoint. Few theaters are willing to play an NC-17 feature, and even fewer newspapers are willing to advertise them.

The chairman of the Motion Picture Association of America, Jack Valenti, went so far to declare, in relation to *Clerks*:

> There are millions of Americans who become hysterical about the kind of bad language that may be de rigeuer around dinner tables in the East Side of Manhattan. But in the cities and villages and towns across this free and loving land, it's not that way at all.[8]

In response to the unexpected broadside, Miramax tapped famed defense attorney Alan Dershowitz to appeal the M.P.A.A.'s decision, though the O.J. lawyer didn't actually end up arguing the case in court. But the decision was eventually reversed, and *Clerks* was awarded an R rating in time for its October 19, 1994 opening in the Big Apple. In late 2001, a similar battle with the M.P.A.A. was waged over the content of *Jay & Silent Bob Strike Back*, Smith's fifth film.

Ironically, the colorfully worded script of *Clerks* was also something of a concern for some of the film's stars. "My initial perception was, 'My God the language!'" O'Halloran relates. "But it was so funny!"

In particular, Jeff Anderson remembers shooting the scene wherein Randal orders a gaggle of pornographic videotapes (such as *Men Alone: The KY Connection*) from a distributor as one instance of the film's racy nature. "We were filming *Clerks*, and it's a foul-mouthed little movie. I didn't think anybody was going to see it beyond a videotape that I would throw in at parties. But I did know that at some point my parents would want to see it. And I think, 'My mother can't hear all this!'

"So we're doing the scene where I order the videotapes on the phone. I had read it in the script, and was just dreading it. And when we got to it, there were these titles written down on a piece of paper. We ran a rehearsal and I asked Kevin if it was really necessary to read all those titles. I thought you'd get the picture after three or four, and asked if we could tone it down a little, since my mother was going to watch this.

"Kevin said, 'Absolutely, I understand.' So I handed him the piece of paper, and people were fixing the lighting and we got ready to shoot. Kevin called action and as he handed the paper back to me, I saw he had added four titles to it. So I'm reading this list and I think: 'Kevin, you bastard!'"

"When we went to the premiere," Anderson continues, "my parents were with me. *Entertainment Tonight* was following me around for the day and I thought this would be the perfect opportunity to let my parents see the movie because they were all wrapped up in what was going on and I didn't even think they'd notice the film. I sat next to my mom until that scene, and when it started, I got up and left the theater. But she never called me on it. She said I was acting, and I hadn't written it, so it was okay.

"Well, cut to Vulgarthon [a View Askew convention] a few years later and my mom comes to see a showing of my movie, *Now You Know*. There's an interesting scene of a transvestite with a bottle up his ass—and I *did* write that movie!"

After *Clerks* premiered, the reviews rolled in, and nobody seemed much bothered by the language that had vexed Jack Valenti. In fact, the movie garnered raves from every media outlet in the States. Carrie Rickey noted that the film was "extremely raw and extremely funny."[9] *Newsweek's* David Ansen enthused that Smith's "chatty, affectionate salute to brainy guys in brainless jobs exhibits a deadpan mastery of verbal timing any veteran director might envy,"[10] and *The New York Times's* Janet Maslin called *Clerks* an "exuberant display of film-student ingenuity.[11]

Some critics even went so far as to indicate the film's profanity was a real plus. Jeff Gordinier for *Entertainment Weekly* noted that "the strategic use of a raunchy rant gives an artist a kind of literary panache" and compared Smith to Henry Miller.[12]

After *Clerks*'s successful release, it was time to take it around the world. "We toured with *Clerks* forever," Mosier remembers. "Miramax just sent us all over the place. The Sundance Institute took five award winners over to Tokyo and all the filmmakers had screenings. It was us and David O'Russell from *Spanking the Monkey*. Victor Nunez [director of *Ruby in Paradise* and *Ulee's Gold*] was there. Laura San Giacomo [of *Nina Takes a Lover*] was there. David [Siegel] and Scott [McGhee] from *Suture* and *The Deep End* came along.

"We had a great time and the Japanese people sort of thought we were a sensation. We were a cool film, I think. We represented youthful America, and there's such a large youth culture in Japan that embraced us. We were on TV, and it was a blast. Then we went to France and Munich and toured the States forever."

It was a great time for the cast and crew of *Clerks*, basking in critical praise and pop-culture popularity. But the canny Smith understood it would not always be so. In a bit of prophetic self-examination, he noted that expectations were so low on his first film that "I don't think any movie I'll ever make will be as well-reviewed as *Clerks*."[13]

Still, Kevin Smith, Scott Mosier, and a team of dedicated filmmakers had beaten the system. They created a brilliant first movie on a shoestring budget, saw it distributed by prestigious Miramax, and then won the hearts of audiences across America. And, in another ironic bit of good news, *Clerks*, by grossing some $2.5 million by January of 1995, became the highest-grossing movie of 1994 on a pure percentage basis·[14]

"Having said all that," Pierson contemplates, "you can easily ask the question, and Kevin and I often talk about this, if Miramax hadn't bought the film immediately after that screening, what would have happened? I can tell you, of all the serious, major players, nobody was going to buy the film right then. That doesn't mean Kevin Smith doesn't happen or that *Clerks* goes away, because it was already headed to New Directors, and it was already going to be reviewed in *The New York Times*. Assuming that Janet Maslin reviewed the film the way she reviewed the film, I don't think there was any doubt that one of the holdback companies from earlier, or even Miramax, would have come back knocking."

Summing up the *Clerks* experience, Scott Mosier reports that "it was the most fun ever. There were some testy moments [shooting] when people were tired or when someone was hanging out while the rest of us were working, but overall it was the best experience ever. All we could do is ask ourselves if the movie was making us laugh, and it was. We were just in the clouds, having fun, and didn't know enough to be scared."

THE GRUNGE GODOT?

Kevin Smith is usually the first person to tell interviewers that his films are nothing but "dick and fart jokes," but anybody who watches his films with an observant eye understands that his work speaks to much more than body function humor. Smith is a modest and unpretentious fellow, so you're not likely to find him uttering whispered truths about *mise-en-scène*, post-modernism, Pirandello, Biblical interpretations, or other heavy subjects. Nonetheless, his films concern many weighty "human" and existential dilemmas. What makes Smith so unusual and worthwhile a voice is that he tackles these subjects in a non-academic, clever way instead of a remote, didactic one.

Without too much difficulty, it is possible to view *Clerks* as a work of art more sophisticated than a foul-mouthed paean to the travails of minimum wage workers. For instance, Margot Hornblower dubbed Kevin Smith's film "The Grunge Godot" in *Time*.[15]

Those among us who survived drama classes in college remember Godot, *Waiting for Godot* actually, a play by Samuel Beckett about the utter meaninglessness of life. The play was set in a strange locale (a long stretch of barren road) and it involved two fellows named Vladimir and Estragon. These odd folk were waiting for the arrival of the enigmatic "Godot," who many scholars believe represented God.

The following review does a good job of expressing the feelings the play evoked in many audiences:

> Many spectators complained that the play made no sense. It lacked physical action, and the plot didn't seem to tie the events together. The mixture of philosophy, Biblical references, broad comedy and nonsense dialogue confused many people.[16]

Interestingly, the above-noted clip might also adequately serve as a review of *Clerks*. There's virtually no physical action dramatized in the film (but for a food fight and a hockey game) and most of Dante and Randal's adventures are merely discussed, not dramatized (such as Randal's casket tipping incident at Julie Dwyer's funeral).

Does the plot tie the events of the film together? Perhaps, but it also ends with many questions left unanswered. What will become of Dante's traumatized lady-love, Caitlin Bree? Or Veronica? Will Dante learn to "shit or get off the pot?" Will he return to school, or stay in a dead-end job because he is afraid of change? None of these issues are resolved, as they would be in, for example, a comedy by Shakespeare.

Additionally, *Clerks* mixes philosophy (including Randal's theory of a ruling class, his debate with Dante about free will versus personal responsibility, and whether title dictates behavior, or vice versa), broad comedy (the Egg Man, the food fight) and, yes, even nonsense dialogue ("Did he say 'making fuck'?").

And then there's Vladimir and Estragon, the two tramps living out their meaningless existence. In *Chasing Amy*'s opening moments, Smith compares Jay and Silent Bob's iconic alter egos Bluntman and Chronic to these literary characters. Yet for the purpose of *Clerks*, the Godot duo is more likely represented by Dante and Randal, two characters who don't really know or understand what they are waiting for. Both young men are smart, thoughtful, and teeming with potential, yet both choose to stay put on their intellectually barren stretch of road, the Quick Stop and R.S.T. Video store. They could attend college, seek better employment, or even embrace traditional cultural and romantic ideals like a committed relationship. Yet they don't. Instead, they dwell in a world of absurd minutiae, re-hashing and over-thinking simplistic movies like *Return of the Jedi*.

On a much less literary level, *Clerks* also reflects the time in which it was created, the early 1990s. America had just come out of a recession in 1992, and Generation X was graduating from school to discover there were not so many great job opportunities out there. After the yuppie prosperity of the 1980s, this new generation learned the hard way that it might be America's first to make less money and be less successful than its predecessors.

This realization led to a kind of disenfranchisement among an overeducated group of youngsters who, thanks to the benefits of a liberal arts education, had enough perspective to understand their dilemma. Their English degrees provided them the knowledge to quote Shakespeare, but their job opportunities were often limited to the question, "Do you want fries with that?" In essence, Gen Xers were educated enough to bemoan their situation. That's the zeitgeist of *Clerks*.

"I hate this fucking place," Dante notes helplessly, early in *Clerks*, and Veronica replies that he should be going to school because he has "so much potential that's going to waste in this pit."

But Dante does nothing.

Smith escaped that minimum wage trap by sheer ingenuity and determination, but *Clerks* is a cautionary tale about bright people who haven't been so lucky. It would probably be over-the-top to call *Clerks* "the wake up call" for a generation, but it remains the film that best exemplifies the "deflated" feeling of this specific generation as it left school in the early '90s and became embittered by the lack of opportunity. And in his examination of this time and feeling, Smith is surprisingly even-handed. He doesn't let the generation off the hook. He sees these young adults, at least to a certain extent, as their own worst enemies.

"Go ahead, keep cracking wise," a customer (#812, Wynarski) warns Dante. "That's why you're jockeying a register in some fucking local convenience store instead of working on a steady job." That line better exemplifies Gen Xers than just about any dialogue in the film. These young people are smart and witty, but they turn that intelligence to whining and sarcasm rather than improving their lot. That so many Gen Xers are seen smoking in the film is another curiosity that speaks to the contradictions of these characters. They are better educated than any previous generation about the hazards of cigarettes, and yet they continue to smoke. What's that about? Why is there such a self-destructive impulse among this generation?

David Fincher's *Fight Club* is one of the few films, other than *Clerks*, that looks at this phenomenon, and it draws much the same conclusion. Gen Xers are reluctant to assimilate into the American mainstream society because it seems to have failed them — repeatedly. Politics are corrupt, science is fucked, and nobody is taking care of the environment. A generation that grew up after Watergate and Vietnam, that witnessed the accident at Chernobyl and the destruction of the Challenger, would rather comment sarcastically about society's failings than embrace that society. *Fight Club* expressed this idea in terms of violence, *Clerks* does so in terms of ennui and cynicism.

"When it comes down to it, I think *Clerks* represents a moment in this generation when we didn't know what we wanted to do," O'Halloran says shedding light on the meaning behind the film. "We just wanted to live and get by, without really having any direction, yet we still had to deal with regular, every day jobs, which didn't necessarily sit well. Dante is definitely afraid to take a chance, to go beyond what makes him comfortable. That whole monologue that Jeff has after the fight scene says it so perfectly. That's the whole point of the film, right there."

The black-and-white, documentary look of *Clerks* only enhances the film's sense of crushing authenticity. As more than one critic noted, audiences might as well be watching these events unfold on a convenience store security camera. It seems real, not like some product from the dream factory.

Perhaps more to the point, Kevin Smith stages *Clerks* almost like a theatrical play. Klein's camera often shoots from a "head on" perspective in scenes at the counter, and even at the exterior of the Quick Stop and R.S.T. Video Store. Rarely does the audience see this scenery from an "askew" angle, and this dedication to a "straight" theatrical dimension makes the settings appear almost like the sets of a play.

Ultimately, this approach works well for the film, since it is the dialogue and characterization, not necessarily the sets, that are important. It's surprising that no one has yet adapted *Clerks* to the Broadway stage. It's a natural, with so few central characters and limited settings.

But what makes *Clerks* so funny? In the final analysis, it isn't merely the rapid-fire, brilliantly crafted dialogue; it is Kevin Smith's adherence to a long-standing comedic film tradition. Specifically, he often holds the camera back, limiting it frequently to long shots, medium shots, and two shots. There are few outright close-ups in the film, and that decision makes abundant sense in a comedy. The old rule about comedy is that audience identification must be limited. If a fellow slips on a banana peel, the audience doesn't want to see it in close-up, because that angle will foster identification with the character's pain when he hits the pavement.

But pull the camera back a bit, and the same tumble is considered funny, because the audience has sufficient distance from the pain.

The camera in *Clerks* is distinctly removed from much of the action, so the audience can laugh at Dante and Randal, Jay and Silent Bob, and the rest of the *dramatis personae* without necessarily feeling sorry for them. Imagine how disturbing it might have been to see Caitlin Bree, reacting in horrified close-up, to the fact that she had just copulated with a corpse. It wouldn't be funny; it would be sickening and disturbing. (By contrast, imagine how David Lynch or Wes Craven might stage such a sequence.)

But in *Clerks*, the scene is shot from far enough back that it becomes intensely humorous, despite the character's obvious dismay. Bracketed inside the frame by a disturbed Dante on the left and a non-plussed Randal on the right, Caitlin's plight is represented by three perspectives, not just the victim's, and identification is lessened.

People might complain the movie appears cheap, or lacks visual panache, but it seems that Smith (and Klein) hit on a style that is both efficient and artful. For instance, the lack of many cuts and the inclusion of long dialogue sequences also enhance the theatrical aspects of *Clerks* and generate a real sense of camaraderie among the characters, a factor that would have been sacrificed if there had been more use of coverage. As these scenes play now, they have rhythm and pacing, and cutting into that "space" would have only sacrificed those qualities.

In the end, it is always up to the individual viewer to judge a film. One can look at *Clerks* as a "grunge Godot," a reflection of its unique historical context, as a well-shot, almost theatrical comedy, or merely a very funny film.

"Bob Hawk can write that it's a wail of ennui, and I'm glad that was in the catalog, and maybe it helped give *Clerks* a greater weight," Pierson notes. "It's great there's subtext there, but to me, the reason it's successful is that it's funny."

For Scott Mosier, the appeal of *Clerks* is also simpler than any film theory: "My perception of that movie is that it's about friends. It was always about friends. A lot of it is sketch comedy, but in the end it does become a meditation about friendship, about these two guys who were both in that place and time where they didn't know what would happen, if they would commit to something bigger, to growing up. In that moment when Dante and Randal are sweeping up together, nobody's doing any talking for the first time, and that's a sign of friendship. They can just hang out and be friends."

ASKEW VIEWS:

BERSERKER! The character of Olaf, a Russian "metal head" who sings "Berserker" for the band Fucking Yankee Blue Jeans (and who is immortalized on Jay's T-shirt in *Jay & Silent Bob Strike Back*), is based on a character improvised by Walt Flanagan.

"Kevin, Bryan Johnson, Ed Hapstak and I were at the mall in Jersey and there was this mannequin in J.C. Penny that had this really strange wig on it," Flanagan explains. "So I snagged it and put it on, but it looked so odd, because I was wearing it backwards, and the bangs were like halfway above my head.

"So we walked into this store and ran into these two seventeen or eighteen year-old girls, and the guys were saying that I was Russian and couldn't speak English, but wanted to be a rock star. The girls bought it hook, line, and sinker. I was just trying to keep a straight face because I didn't even know what a Russian accent should sound like. I'd just grunt and groan, and they bought every minute of it."

Still, that didn't mean Flanagan was ready to play Olaf in the movie. "My initial response was that I didn't want to do it. I was uncomfortable singing in front of people even though Kevin wanted me to play Olaf. I said no because I was just too self-conscious."

INFIRMITY: Brian O'Halloran fell ill during the shooting of *Clerks*, as he recalls. "I think it was the last five days of shooting, so we'd done the majority of the principal shooting, and I had this bad head cold. I think it was only apparent in one scene. After Caitlin leaves, Dante is leaning against the counter with Randal next him, and I think you can hear me sniffling and talking at the same time. I was miserable, but you can't say 'Hey, stop,' because they're renting this camera, and time is literally money."

WHERE'S STEVE-DAVE? A familiar face missing from *Clerks* is *Vulgar* director Bryan Johnson, the actor who plays Steve-Dave in *Mallrats, Chasing Amy, Dogma,* and *Jay & Silent Bob Strike Back.*

"When Kevin came back from film school, we had a falling out," Bryan Johnson recalls. "Many different circumstances led to it, and we were both being hard-headed. That's why I wasn't in *Clerks.*"

But out of the blue, things changed. "Kevin went off and made *Clerks,* and then went to this self-help seminar called The Forum that encourages you to expand your horizons and see things that maybe you hadn't seen before; to build yourself up as a person. One of his tasks was to call someone who he hadn't spoken with in a long time, and didn't really want to talk to. I guess I fit the bill.

"So I was at home watching TV, the phone rang and I answered it. He said, 'Bryan Johnson?' I said, 'Kevin Smith?' And my initial thought was that Kevin must really be in a lot of trouble if I'm the only person he can turn to. But then he explained to me what he was doing, the idea of The Forum. Fences were mended and we shot the Soul Asylum video [for *Clerks*] some time that fall." Ironically, the character in that video was not Steve-Dave, according to Johnson. "I think he was just hockey player #3."

YOU CAN SMELL IT: The sickly respiratory organ a Chewlies Gum representative throws on the Quick Stop counter isn't actually a lung at all. "I think we used a calf's brain or tripe," O'Halloran recollects. "It was horrible. They ground in cigarette butts and all sorts of stuff to make it look nasty. It was there on the counter for probably a good hour-and-a-half by the time we got the coverage we needed. It smelled really bad."

SYNTAX: Kevin Smith often calls his movies a collection of dick and fart jokes, but John Pierson, for one, doesn't like the descriptor.

"I hate that he sums it up that way. I know it works as shorthand, but you'll never hear me use it. One of the reasons I hate it is that there aren't that many fart jokes. I know it's a category of humor. There's a huge number of dick jokes, but not that many fart jokes. Even the stink-palm isn't really a fart joke. It's a hand in your ass joke. There are more anal sex jokes than fart jokes.

"I've been in rooms where he's said that so many times, and people laugh. Kevin is a modest person, but on the other hand, he knows he has talent. So it isn't false modesty, but it's not like he's naïve. The shorthand really works for him when he's trying to be humble."

CONTINUITY: Rick Derris (portrayed by Ernie O'Donnell in *Clerks*) is a character referred to in *Chasing Amy*. The girl who dies in the pool, Julie Dwyer, motivates much of the action in *Mallrats*, and if one listens closely, even Alyssa Jones, the character portrayed by Joey Lauren Adams in *Chasing Amy*, is mentioned by name in the scene with Rick Derris.

THE ULTIMATE NUMBER: The number 37 is one that recurs in the films of Kevin Smith. In *Clerks*, it is the number of men on whom Veronica has performed oral sex. The number re-surfaces twice in *Jay & Silent Bob Strike Back* and twice in *Chasing Amy*.

HOSANNAS: *Clerks* is dedicated to three giants in the history of independent films: John Cassavetes, Jim Jarmusch, and Spike Lee.

KEVIN SMITH ON CLERKS:

"*Clerks* was born out of working for three years in that fucking store...Things like the Milk-Maid and the Egg-Man came directly from register-jockeying experience, as does the spirit of most of the discussions Dante and Randal share. When you're bored...you begin talking about some inane and meritless shit, just to get you through the day."[17]

NOTES

1. John Pierson, *Spike, Mike, Slackers & Dykes: A Guided Tour Across a Decade of American Independent Cinema* (New York: Hyperion and Miramax Books, 1995), p. 80.

2. Owen Gleiberman, "Smooth Mewes, As half of the dopey duo in *Jay and Silent Bob Strike Back*, Jason Mewes plays a rebel without a pause," *Entertainment Weekly,* September 7, 2001, p. 134.

3. Linda Lee, "A Night Out with Kevin Smith: Not the Dogmatic Type," *The New York Times*, November 14, 1999, Section 4, p. 3.

4. Stephen Lowenstein (Ed.), *My First Movie: Twenty Celebrated Directors Talk About Their First Film* (New York: Pantheon Books, 2000), p. 89.

5. Eileen N. Moon, "A Store Clerk's First Film Earns a Festival Showing," *The New York Times*, January 30, 1994, New Jersey Section, pp. 1, 9.

6. Chris Smith, "Register Dogs," *New York*, October 24, 1994, p. 53.

7. Pierson, p. 287.

8. Peter Travers, "*Clerks*—Dangerous Talk," *Rolling Stone*, November 3, 1994, p. 104.

9. Carrie Rickey, "*Clerks,*" *Knight-Ridder/Tribune News Service*, November 2, 1994, p. 110.

10. David Ansen, "Dante's Day in Jersey Hell, Convenience Store Blues," *Newsweek*, October 31, 1994, p. 67.

11. Janet Maslin, "At a Convenience Store, Coolness to Go," *The New York Times*, March 25, 1994, p. C10.

12. Jeff Gordinier, "The Directors," *Entertainment Weekly*, November-December 1997, p. 65.

13. Beth Pinkser, "Filmmakers in the Fast Lane," *Entertainment Weekly*, June 23, 1995, p. 26.

14. Robert Strauss, "Jersey Boy Makes Good and Comes Back Home," *The New York Times,* December 5, 1999, New Jersey Section "On the Town," p. 2.

15. "Waiting for Godot," *World Book Online Americas Edition*, March 14, 2002, http://www.aolsvc.worldbook.aold.com/wbol/wbPage/na/ar/co/748633.

16. Margot Hornblower, "Great Xpectations," *Time*, June 1997, p. 68.

17. "Kevin Smith: breaks the silence," *Verbosity*, Issue no. 3, 1996, http://www//verbositywiw.org/issue3/ksmith.html.

Mallrats (1995)

A LAUNDRY LIST OF COMPLAINTS

They're not there to shop. They're not there to work. They're just there.

CAST & CREW

Universal Studios and Gramercy Pictures Present an Alphaville Production, in association with View Askew Productions

Written and directed by: Kevin Smith
Produced by: Sean Daniel, James Jacks, and Scott Mosier
Cinematography by: David Klein
Edited by: Paul Dixon
Music: Ira Newborn
Line Producer: Laura Greenlee
Production Designer: Dina Lipton
Casting: Don Phillips
Costume Designer: Dana Allyson
M.P.A.A. Rating: R
Running Time: 94 minutes

STARRING:

Jeremy London | *T.S. Quint*

Jason Lee | *Bruce Brodie*

Shannon Doherty | *Renee Mosier*

Claire Forlani | *Brandi Svenning*

Ben Affleck | *Shannon Hamilton*

Joey Lauren Adams | *Gwen Taylor*

Renée Humphrey| *Tricia Jones*

Jason Mewes | *Jay*

Kevin Smith | *Silent Bob*

Ethan Suplee | *Willam Black*

Stan Lee | *Himself*

Priscilla Barnes | *Ivana*

Michael Rooker | *Mr. Jared Svenning*

Brian O'Halloran| *Gil Hicks*

Bryan Johnson | *Steve-Dave*

Walt Flanagan | *Fanboy*

THE STORY SO FAR...

DUMPED BY THEIR RESPECTIVE GIRLFRIENDS,
the stolid T.S. Quint and his buddy, Bruce Brodie, drown their sorrows by
visiting the local mall. There, they run into a variety of colorful patrons,
including rage-aholic Willam Black, a fifteen year-old sex-researcher
"Trish the Dish," obnoxious comic book fans Steve-Dave and Fanboy, and
stoner duo, Jay and Silent Bob.

When T.S. learns that his girlfriend, Brandi Svenning, is appearing
on a game show called Truth or Date at the mall that very night, because
her Dad is the producer, he vows to stop the program. But Brodie has
problems of his own: his girlfriend, Renee, is courting Shannon Hamilton,
the "date-rapist" manager of a store called Fashionable Male.

Evading mall security with the help of Jay and Silent Bob, Brodie,
and Quint set out to reclaim their girlfriends and bring down Mr. Svenning's
game show. They use every weapon at their disposal, including a mal-
odorous weapon Brodie calls "the stink-palm."

Before the night is over, romantic relationships are restored, Gil Hicks (Dante's cousin, and a game show contestant) is humiliated on stage, Svenning's show is in shambles, Brodie has met his hero, comic book legend Stan Lee, and Mr. Svenning continues to suffer the debilitating effects of Brodie's nefarious stink-palm.

SILENT BOB'S WORDS OF WISDOM:

"Adventure? Excitement? A Jedi craves not these things!"

THE STORY BEHIND THE MOVIE:

In 1995, mere months after *Clerks* was released to critical raves and financial success, director Kevin Smith and his View Askew team resurrected slacker anti-heroes Jay and Silent Bob for a bigger budgeted ($6.1 million), Universal Studio-financed sequel. *Mallrats*, the second movement in what Smith soon announced would become the "New Jersey Trilogy," was a more colorful, more mainstream, action-packed romp than its black-and-white predecessor.

Although the end credits of *Clerks*—in James Bond style— announced that Jay and Silent Bob would return in a movie called *Dogma*, the two Jersey slackers were to take a trip to the mall first. And director Kevin Smith was to take a detour into the morass of studio politics and critical expectations. The result was a film that made little money, satisfied few critics, and even prompted a public apology (actually a joke) from Smith—but then went on to become an unqualified, monster hit on the DVD and home video markets. Today, *Mallrats* is lovingly regarded as a popular cult film and as a valuable addition to the Askewniverse at large.

The idea to write and direct *Mallrats* actually came to Smith following the showing of *Clerks* at the Sundance film festival in Utah. There, he and Scott Mosier were introduced to producer James Jacks (late of another cult hit, *Tremors*, and eventually producer of *The Mummy* and *The Mummy Returns*).

Jacks liked *Clerks* and thought there was an opportunity to repeat the same material, essentially as a big "A-list" picture that dramatized all (or most of) the wacky adventures which Randal and Dante only talked about in the low budget film.

"We met Jim Jacks at the closing ceremonies of Sundance," reports Scott Mosier, "and he entertained the idea of remaking *Clerks* in color. He asked us what we wanted to do next, and Kevin came up with the idea for

Mallrats. Then we went to Los Angeles in April [1994] to pitch it. So before *Clerks* ever came out, based on our meeting with Jim Jacks, we generated our second project. By the time *Clerks* was playing in October, we were already in development on *Mallrats.*"

With *Mallrats* on the boards, much of the View Askew team reunited. Mosier was producing, Klein was behind the camera, Smith was writing and directing, O'Halloran was playing a supporting role (as a different Hicks), and Smith's friends Vincent Pereira, Walt Flanagan, and Bryan Johnson planned to go to Minnesota (where the film was to be lensed) to work as production assistants.

With his team ready, and a new script he'd fashioned in 60 days, Smith set out to create a mainstream comedy that payed homage to the teen films of the 1970s and 80s. Those were films Smith had admired growing up; from John Landis's *Animal House* to the works of John Hughes, such as *Sixteen Candles.*

As for Jacks and Universal Studios, there was a slightly different model that was considered worthy of emulation, and *Mallrats* quickly became dubbed a "smart *Porky's.*" Still, everyone agreed on one thing: the film would be an R-rated youth comedy.

But developing a studio film with a budget of $6.1 million was a drastically different ball game for View Askew, much different from shooting *Clerks* for roughly $27,000.

As Scott Mosier succinctly puts it: "Producing *Clerks* meant nothing. A lot of the stuff I did on *Clerks* I no longer had to do. On *Mallrats*, I had to learn the job all over again, and that meant being more of an overseer. On *Clerks*, I made the calls and rented the equipment, and suddenly I didn't do that anymore. My role was to be a real producer and I had to learn how to do that. I was a little overwhelmed."

Though Smith and Mosier both believed they could make *Mallrats* for an amount significantly cheaper than their allotted budget, they quickly learned that cheap was not necessarily the name of the game in Hollywood.

"Once you enter the process of making a movie at a certain level, there's a whole world of things that are dictated to you because you have $6 million to spend," Mosier explains. "You have to make a union deal. You have to hire a certain amount of drivers. You need to have a certain number of trucks. Then technical people come in and tell you that they need this, that and the other thing. You have to attack it all from a different place.

"On *Clerks*, all we could afford was three lights. On *Mallrats*, if you wanted to light an entire mall, you couldn't fucking use three lights. And you couldn't call up these vendors and complain that you have no money and need a break. They'd very quickly remind you that you're a Universal film and that Universal has money—$6 million, in fact."

Thrown into a new world of higher budgets, Mosier knew the best thing he could do was simply soak up the landscape. "My attitude was to shut up and learn as much as I possibly could. I was Kevin's partner, the guy who was always in his corner, no matter what anyone else thought. He never had to feel like he was alone. That's really all I could do. On *Chasing Amy*, all that changed. By the end of *Mallrats* I knew things, but for the time, the biggest role I could play was to support Kevin and remind him that I was as much a neophyte as he was, and tell him that I'd back him up, no matter what.

"The line producer on *Mallrats*, Laura Greenlee, also did *Dogma* and *Jay & Silent Bob Strike Back*," relates Mosier. "I sat down with her and told her I didn't know what possible use I could be, because I didn't even know how to read a budget. I didn't even know what a fringe was [things that get added into departments, like union dues and medicare]—I just thought it was something that hangs off a jacket. Even though I was her boss, I told her I'd do whatever she wanted me to. We got along and I learned."

While Mosier developed the skills that transformed him into what Smith has often called "an über producer," the studio had concerns about the script for *Mallrats*. Namely, Universal complained that some sequences were too raunchy, and that there was too much swearing.

"It was originally a lot more vulgar, a lot rougher," Vincent Pereira says of Smith's now-legendary first draft (which featured the oral sex scar scene that was later to be such a hit in *Chasing Amy*). "The studio reigned it back and wanted more plot, more action."

"My opinion of the first draft was that it seemed more like *Clerks*," Mosier considers. "It just had that meandering quality to it, and injecting all of this plot wasn't really necessary. Our thought was that the movie should just be as funny as possible."

There was also one scene that never made it to the shooting stage, in which a body fluid (later popularized in 1998's *There's Something About Mary*) was splashed around the mall by none other than Silent Bob.

But if Smith and Mosier came out of the script meetings for *Mallrats* feeling bruised, the battles over casting must have been scarring. Of all things, the big problem was the break out star of *Clerks*, Jason Mewes. In portraying the strutting stoner named Jay, Mewes had delivered big-time laughs in *Clerks* and a high-degree of authenticity too, and that apparently scared the studio higher-ups.

Mewes was excited about the prospect of resurrecting the character. "I was so psyched about *Mallrats*. I thought, 'Ooh, another movie!' And I was going to get paid this time, because I didn't get paid for *Clerks*."

But then Mewes learned that executives at Universal had reservations about him, and his excitement quickly turned to anxiety. "I was nervous," he says, "because it would have sucked if I didn't get the part. And in a way, I knew they were right. I didn't have any training or anything. I mean, I was nervous about acting in front of a bunch of my friends for *Clerks*, and these guys were saying that this time it would be no joke. There would be forty people around me on the cast and crew."

Despite Universal's misgivings, Smith stood behind his decision to re-enlist Mewes as Jay. The studio, like the Galactic Empire of *Star Wars*, struck back. It temporarily okayed Mewes as Jay, but then imposed a plethora of conditions and restraints.

First off, the studio refused to pay for Mewes's air flights, his hotel room, or even his participation during the rehearsal period of the film. Then, the studio demanded that Smith and Mosier audition other actors for the role, including Seth Green (of *Austin Powers*, *Buffy the Vampire Slayer*, and *Greg the Bunny*).

On Mewes's first day of shooting, studio suits were ready on the set to fire the young actor should they assess his performance as not passing muster.

Aware of the pressure, Kevin Smith took Mewes aside and talked to him. "He told me I had to do it," Mewes remembers. "And I decided I wasn't going to give up the chance, and told Kevin I'd get over my fear quickly. I'd gotten through the auditions, but I was still on trial. My first day, the two producers were there and they were sitting watching me. Kevin said, 'Yo, there they are; they're watching! You've got to do this. You can't be nervous. Just go with it and do your best.'"

Mewes took the advice to heart and went all out. "We did one scene, then another right after it, and when we were done, Kevin pulled me over and said the producers had left, and that they'd said I was perfect. They laughed. It felt so great."

In fact, the studio execs made an abrupt about face. They didn't just like Jason Mewes, they loved him. "They sent the dailies to the producers, and everyone at Universal would sit there, watch my scenes, and crack up," Mewes reports. As a result of his efforts, the film's eventual advertising campaign was built largely around the character of Jay and his new catch-phrase: "snootchie bootchies."

Universal also reportedly interfered in the remainder of the casting. It wanted Ethan Hawke, Mike Myers, Chris Farley, or Adam Sandler to head-line in *Mallrats*,[1] all choices that Smith and Mosier deemed inappropriate because of their age.

"At the time, I wondered if they could really be suggesting Mike Myers, but now, with perspective, I realize these lists are generated without thought," Mosier explains. "The top five names might have some thought; the rest don't. You realize the studio doesn't necessarily want you to cast Mike Myers, they're just looking at anyone of a certain age group and a little popularity. At the time, we wondered what the fuck was wrong with these people. Couldn't they look at Mike Myers and see that he was too old? But distance changes your perception. Now I understand that they were just throwing an idea out, and even they probably knew it was absurd."

"Your first experience reading notes is the same way," Mosier goes on. "Some of the stuff seems ridiculous, but you learn along the way how to deal with it. The ideas the studios actually want are the ones they bring up a second time. The ones that come up just once are probably filler."

One actor who was cast in *Mallrats* was Ethan Suplee, who had worked recently on the TV series *Boy Meets World* and later went on to acclaimed performances in *American History X* and *Blow*. Suplee came into the acting profession honestly: his parents had met while performing *A Streetcar Named Desire* at Carnegie Mellon. His dad was Stanley; his mom was Stella. In later years, Suplee was further encouraged to pursue acting by a friend one grade up, actor Giovanni Ribisi. *Mallrats* was the first movie he auditioned for.

"I had an agent and he picked up a script for *Mallrats*," Suplee explains. "A friend of mine, Danny Masterson, who's on *That '70s Show*, was there while I was reading it, and told me that this guy, Kevin Smith, had a movie playing and that I had to see it.

"He took me to the art-house theater on Sunset, and the movie [*Clerks*] was hysterical. You could tell immediately it wasn't a studio film at all, yet at the same it had so much more going for it than a lot of studio films. So I went in and met the casting director. Then I had a meeting with Kevin and Scott, and I remember it was pretty cool because after I read for him, Kevin applauded. He clapped for me and I thought, 'Wow, that has to be a good sign.'"

Suplee was auditioning for the role of Willam Black, the "snow-baller" of *Clerks* fame (essayed by Mosier), but the character underwent a radical re-think for *Mallrats*, becoming angrier and far less mellow. Smith has thus postulated the "Willam of Two Worlds Theory" to explain the differences. Fans of *Star Trek*'s mirror universe, or *Superman*'s nemesis and opposite, Bizarro, will grasp the reference: Willam of *Clerks* and Willam of *Mallrats* inhabit alternate realities.

But all that mattered to Suplee was that he deemed the script terrific. "I loved the shit-palming. And I loved the joke about fucking the girl in an uncomfortable place. Everything Jay did in that script was awesome."

After his audition went so well, Suplee was invited to a casting party that later become notorious.

"There was this thing called the Don Phillips Pizza Party where he [the casting director; Phillips] got together three or four choices for each part in *Mallrats*, and they had a day, like a whole Saturday, with all of these actors," Suplee sets the scene. "The casting area was just overflowing with young actors — probably thirty people — and they were all reading for the same parts, so it was crazy."

"Everybody got in at about 10:00 a.m. and it was announced that only one part was taken: the role of Willam. So I was sitting there in front of all these actors, knowing I had the part, wondering if I should go home. But they still had me read with people. It was funny, because throughout the day I would meet people and think how nice it would be to work with them, and then they wouldn't get the part."

One of the actors who made the cut that day was a pre-stardom Ben Affleck, who went on to achieve Oscar glory with his screenplay (co-authored with Matt Damon) for *Good Will Hunting*, as well as superstar status with *Armageddon*, *Pearl Harbor*, and *Changing Lanes*. Affleck would be playing the role of the nefarious Shannon Hamilton, Bruce Brodie's most powerful nemesis, and rival for girlfriend Renee's affections.

Actress Joey Lauren Adams, a native of Little Rock, Arkansas, had been promised the role of Renee in *Mallrats*, but in the end settled for the supporting role of Gwen Turner before appearing in such films as *Michael*, *Chasing Amy*, *Big Daddy*, and others.

British actress Claire Forlani (who starred with Brad Pitt and Anthony Hopkins in *Meet Joe Black* in 1998) and Shannen Doherty (late of *Beverly Hills 90210* and *Charmed*) represented female leads Brandi and Renee, respectively. Of Doherty, Smith reported that the reputed bad girl "was a dream" and that her "reputation may be unmatched...but people grow and change."[2]

Michael Rooker, the star of the chilling *Henry: Portrait of a Serial Killer* and *Cliffhanger*, would appear as the film's menacing adult antagonist, Mr. Svenning, after William Atherton passed on the role (to appear in *Bio-Dome*).

The two male leads, ironically, were among the hardest roles to cast. For a time, Brian O'Halloran, the star of *Clerks*, had his eye on one lead. "I did audition for *Mallrats* because I wanted to play T.S. They were holding auditions in New York with Kevin and Scott, and when I went in, Kevin pretty much told me he wanted me to play somebody else instead. I think the studio really wanted at least one "name" person in one of the lead male roles, so they brought in Jeremy."

The Jeremy that O'Halloran speaks of was Jeremy London, of the Fox network TV series, *Party of Five*. O'Halloran instead got to "once again play the straight man," Gil Hicks, a character related to the Quick Stop's Dante. But to essay that role, O'Halloran decided it was time for a makeover. "I needed a departure from Dante, because he was such a memorable character to so many people, so I went into *Mallrats* with a different look. I grew my hair long and cut off the van-dyke."

In the end, O'Halloran ended up shooting in Minnesota for the better part of eleven days, and thoroughly enjoyed his stint. "It was fun working with Jeremy and Jason [Lee] during the game show scene. We had a lot of laughs filming that, and it was just so strange and amazing going from *Clerks* for $27,000 to *Mallrats* for $6.1 million. It was a huge leap."

Casting the critical role of Brodie (a character based in part on Kevin Smith's friend, Walt Flanagan) was also a difficult task. Kevin Smith and Scott Mosier had their eye on a young skateboarder, Jason Lee, who had never worked in film before, but there was initially some resistance.

Suplee remembers the situation. "I was already friends with Jason Lee. After they told me I could go home from the casting party, I stuck around, and it was down to the wire with Jason. Everybody else was gone and we didn't think Jason was going to make the cut, but they finally pulled the trigger and announced that Jason had the part."

It was a good decision, for Jason Lee not only inhabited the role of Bruce Brodie, he became a regular and beloved contributor to View Askew films, appearing in *Drawing Flies*, *A Better Place*, *Chasing Amy*, *Dogma*, and *Jay & Silent Bob Strike Back*.

O'Halloran recalls that even on the set of *Mallrats*, the neophyte Lee was able to nail his scenes. "He was an absolute pleasure to work with. I understood it was his first film, and that he came from a skateboarding background, but he had it. He had such a natural, innate talent for delivering Kevin's dialogue, as well as great timing."

Not surprisingly, it wasn't long before Lee became a full-fledged star, headlining in films such as *Mumford*, *Almost Famous*, and *Big Trouble*, among others.

Making a cameo appearance in *Mallrats* was perhaps the biggest star of the bunch, comic book icon Stan Lee, the creator of *The X-Men*, *Spider-Man*, *The Incredible Hulk*, and *The Fantastic Four*. Smith is an unabashed fan of Lee's creations, and has gone on record noting that Lee is "right up there" with George Lucas and Steven Spielberg; that he is a "modern myth maker."[3]

Walt Flanagan, who now runs the comic book store *Jay & Silent Bob's Secret Stash* in Red Bank, New Jersey, loved meeting the soft-spoken, beloved creator of so many Marvel classic heroes in the flesh. "He was an extremely nice guy to every single person. It didn't matter if you were a star or anybody else. He was friendly and willing to share whatever he could remember."

Though its screenplay was set in New Jersey, it was in Eden Prairie, Minnesota where principal photography on Mallrats commenced. The mall in Eden Prairie was largely vacant and the proprietors were open to the idea of a movie company taking advantage of the empty space. Thus production designers went to work building special, fictional shop-fronts.

Among these so-called "low rent" mall store sets were Rug Munchers (a carpet outlet store run by two very successful businesswomen) and Burning Flesh Tanning Salon (a former Arthur Treacher's Restaurant, Brodie's birthplace). Then there was Fashionable Male (where Ben Affleck's evil character, Shannon Hamilton works as a manager) and Popular Girl (where starlet Adams repeatedly disrobes, much to the delight of Silent Bob).

Replete with a food court, a cookie bakery (ideal for "mid-mall snacking"), a pet shop (advertising "Gerbils! Gerbils! Gerbils!"), and a prominent elevator (in which Brodie and Renee would catch a passionate quickie), the mall proved to be a perfect microcosm by which Smith could satirize the aimless existence of a new group of Generation Xers.

But behind the scenes of *Mallrats*, unbeknownst to some, an interesting phenomenon was occurring. Vincent Pereira, Walt Flanagan, and Bryan Johnson had trucked out from New Jersey to work on the film as production assistants. Unfortunately, they met with some intense jealousy from other members of the crew, who quickly dubbed this trio of Jerseyites "The F.O.K.s" — Friends of Kevin.

"We had no idea what being a production assistant on a film would be like," Johnson acknowledges. "We thought it was going to be fun, that we would hang out, drink soda, and get paid. Mosier told us we'd get to carry walkie-talkies, and for me that was practically like being a movie cop! But once we got to Minnesota the job was the most hellish experience you can ever imagine. It's like you're nothing, the lowest person on the ladder. You eat after everybody else eats. You pretty much get stepped on, shut up, and spit on. For easy-going people like Walter and me it just wasn't for us.

"The first day was fifteen hours of running around being man servants to the whole crew. At the end of the day, I remember Walter just collapsing on his bed and ordering this $17 piece of chocolate cake from room service. Vincent was the only one who lasted the whole time. I lasted five days. But then I heard people refer to us as the F.O.K.s—the Friends of Kevin, and I just thought, whatever."

"I lasted a day," Flanagan admits. "I hated it. It sucked so bad. People were just yelling and screaming all the time. 'Bring coffee! Do this! Bring that!' So I decided to quit, hang out, and just do my scene. I had no idea what I was getting into."

Still, Johnson remembers that the *Mallrats* experience had some funny moments despite the fraternal rivalry. "On Walter's day as a production assistant, he was assigned to help Craft Services, the lady who provides the snacks. She constantly complained about everything, even to the point where she walked up to Kevin and said, 'See this?' and pointed to a cold sore on her mouth. She told him it was from the stress of production, but she'd only been on the set maybe a day or two.

"Anyway, Walter was her assistant, and she had an eight-foot table with tons of food on it and this coffee urn that must have held five gallons. She had to move it around a lot to accommodate the shooting, and so she takes this wagon and puts one end of the table on it, and then tries to pull it from the other end. I'm watching from about ten feet away, and almost in slow motion I see the table twist and start to fall. And there's shit everywhere! Five gallons of coffee went on the floor, mixed with potato chips and candy. I thought it was hysterical. Then maintenance came out and gave her this mop that looked like a Playskool mop, like My First Mop. It had the smallest head, and here's the Craft lady trying to clean up five gallons of coffee with it. It took her forever."

Ethan Suplee, for one, enjoyed getting into his comedic character. In particular, he found that his first scene on *Mallrats* dictated the direction that the "new" Willam would take. "If you watch *Clerks*, Willam is not an angry guy. He's kind of the opposite; he didn't really do any yelling," Suplee notes. "But the first thing I shot on Mallrats was the scene with Willam exploding at the little kids."

The scene grew organically out of the shooting situation, according to Suplee. "I've got to tell you, these children were the most annoying kids you've ever met. You know; little stage kids who are always projecting and emoting and enunciating every word. And they had the biggest, phoniest smiles. It's kind of creepy, like those Little Miss Pageants they have out west somewhere. And their parents were following them around constantly fixing their hair and stuff. And I guess I got a little irritated with the kids and their sparkling white teeth, and felt like instilling the fear of God in them. So I let 'em have it once, and Kevin liked it. Then we kicked it up even more. It just kind of stuck."

For Jason Mewes, *Mallrats* was the opportunity to play more broad physical comedy than he had in *Clerks*, and even perform his own stunts. "We got stunt bumps!" he enthuses. "We got extra money for performing our own stunts. I would ask them to let me do all the stunts, because I wanted more money, but studios won't let you do everything, because you can get hurt."

In particular, Mewes remembers hanging in mid-air with Kevin Smith for the scene in which Jay and Silent Bob use Bob's "bat grapple" to evade mall security and the villainous La Fours. "We weren't up in the air that long. They'd pull us up and shoot it, then bring us down really fast. We did it twice, and I remember the first time Kevin got a little nervous because we were strapped together up in the air and he saw his harness was kind of slipping slowly through the clip. It was just adjusting, they told him when we got down, but up there he was pretty scared. It wasn't too scary for me, because there were pads beneath us, plus I had Kevin to break my fall."

Replete with action and comedy (and some brief nudity), *Mallrats* promised to be a fun film, and the feedback coming from Universal on the production's progress was encouraging, as Mosier explains. "They were enthusiastic all the way to the end. They liked the dailies; they liked the cuts. [Exec] Tom Pollock said to Kevin when he saw the Stan Lee/Brodie material that it reminded him of Wolfman Jack and Richard Dreyfuss in *American Graffiti*. We heard that on the set, and it was amazing. The previews went well too, but then it all blew up."

One bone of contention between Universal and the filmmakers involved the opening act of the film. In the original script, Smith had written an effective (and economical) opening act on a local game show, one that was filled with verbal comedy (regarding geography, of all things) and would bookend nicely with the game show sequence at the film's climax. But the studio wanted the opening of *Mallrats* to be bigger and more elaborate than what Smith had engineered.

Pereira remembers the change. "Kevin followed the studio instructions, and wrote and shot all of this new material."

The new opening of *Mallrats* occurred at a fancy Governor's Ball, and saw the clumsy T.S. accidentally shooting a blank (from a Revolutionary War musket) at the New Jersey Governor (a Christine Todd Whitman figure). In the process, he embarrassed Mr. Svenning, who was seeking to acquire state funds so as to continue his game show.

"It was quite elaborate and long," Pereira notes of the re-vamped opening, "but I liked the scene—not just because I was in it. It looked really good. There was this opening crane shot, which was beautifully executed, and Michael Rooker's character certainly would have benefited from the scene, because his dislike of T.S. makes more sense with that opening."

When preview audiences saw the new, almost half-hour-long opening of *Mallrats*, they weren't nearly as impressed. "Kevin and I had done a two hour and seventeen minute cut," Mosier confides. "It was a disaster. That's when we cut off the new opening. The studio never even got to see it in there, but we said, 'Trust us, it doesn't work.'"

"It's funny," Pereira remarks. "The preview audience said the movie was called *Mallrats*. Why don't they get to the mall in the first half-hour? So Kevin had to cut the opening and make it much more like his original, low-key opening."

This created some problems since the events at the Governor's Ball were referred to frequently in the remainder of the film (notably in Jay and Silent Bob's introductory sequence in front of the pet store, and a short scene late in the film in the mall's parking lot). When the opening was deleted, the actors had to loop new lines that reflected the changes, but which ended up sounding flat-out weird.

"There was some crazy A.D.R. because of that," Pereira reports of the deletions. "In the first scene with Jay and Silent Bob, Brodie says the word 'excellent' for no reason. In the original script, he'd been correcting T.S., noting that Brandi was his 'ex-girlfriend.' It made no sense."

When *Mallrats* completed principal photography, the film premiered at the 1995 Comic-Con International in San Francisco, and the reviews were universally positive, though that crowd was probably geared to appreciate Smith's comic-book vision of 20-something life.

But Vincent Pereira, for one, was afraid that the studio was not really marketing the film effectively. "It seemed like a weak sell. I remember seeing the trailer for the first time and thinking it was weak. If I knew nothing about the film, I probably wouldn't go to see it based on the trailer. And the tagline was: 'What else would you expect from the director of *Clerks*?' Well, *Clerks* made about $3 million in theaters, and I just don't think you can sell a big studio film to an audience solely on the basis of *Clerks*." Furthermore, Pereira notes that the early posters for the film were "terrible."

When Mallrats opened in general release near Halloween of 1995, it became clear that Kevin Smith's sophomore effort was not being received like another *Animal House*, or even a *Porky's*. On its first weekend, *Mallrats* played on 650 screens nationwide, and the one-night money tally signaled the overriding disinterest to come. Grosses were dismal: less than half-a-million dollars ($400,000) on Friday night, traditionally the strongest night of the weekend (at least for teens).

Adding insult to injury, critics were unkind. Kenneth Turan called the film a "numbing and dispiriting experience."[4] Michael Medved wrote that the film was "so cheerfully mindless, so proudly puerile, that it defeats all attempts at reasonable criticism."[5] J. R. Taylor of Entertainment Weekly categorized *Mallrats* as "hopelessly stupid."

Despite the brickbats, *Mallrats* did receive some nice notices. Writing for *Time* magazine, Richard Corliss noted that *Mallrats* was a "50s teen flick for the 90s" and that Smith was "flouting the sophomore slump.[6] Gary Dauphin noted in *The Village Voice* that Jason Lee was "a perfect slacker hero," and Janet Maslin of *The New York Times* similarly commented that Lee "has the grunge and surliness to give him credibility... but also a sweet, funny indignation over life's little outrages."[7]

"Kevin has all the clipping of the reviews for Mallrats and they aren't as devastating as some would have you believe," Pereira reports. "Obviously, Roger Ebert hated it. But it's not like the film was universally reviled, just on the whole it was not received nearly as well as *Clerks*. The real failure of that film was at the box office. Kevin wasn't expecting great reviews for *Mallrats*; he was making a very broad comedy that he hoped would connect with a large audience."

"I think *Mallrats* was designed to be a commercial hit," John Pierson considers. "To me, Kevin's talent is way beyond that. That's just one side of him. I think there's some pretty lousy stuff in *Mallrats*, and some really funny stuff in *Mallrats*. I just think when a film is designed to be a money making machine, there's something really deflating about it not working out that way."

Reflecting on the *Mallrats* experience, and the differences from the *Clerks* experience, Scott Mosier is thoughtful. "Now, producing was a career and there are all of these people standing around, and there's a studio watching the dailies, and that changes the face of things. Your enjoyment is no longer the only thing to consider; it gets spread out over all these people. And suddenly there are all these other opinions and, whether you give a shit or not, they're important.

"The guy at the studio can make life hard on you. Sometimes you don't respect his input, but the fact is that if he likes what you've done, your life is easier. Sometimes you become anxious wondering what people will object to; whether there's too much cursing or whatever. Now, because I'm getting paid to produce, I have certain obligations. I have to answer to people, even though I don't want to. It's the name of the game, and it does taint the process. You have to use precedents from other movies to defend your case for doing things a certain way."

Smith was also thoughtful about the lessons learned on *Mallrats*:

> I tried to do something different, and I didn't have anything to say at that point, so I just made a John Hughes movie.[8]

John Pierson, Smith's friend, confidante and booster from the days of *Clerks*, may have parsed the experience best:

> You cannot get from *Clerks* to *Chasing Amy* without something like *Mallrats* in between. Where do you think the cast for *Chasing Amy* came from?[9]

Elaborating, Pierson asks: "Would he have had any access to those actors immediately after *Clerks*? I don't think so. Maybe in 2002, he might. But not in 1995, 1996. No way."

Scott Mosier is quick to reiterate that statement. "As much as *Chasing Amy* was a transitional film to *Dogma*, kind of instilling new confidence in us, *Mallrats* was a transitional film to *Chasing Amy*. The learning process started with *Mallrats*. It was a film where we were dealing with a new environment. *Chasing Amy* — the budget level and money spent on it — was a much more realistic step to take than going from $27,000 to $6 million."

Many of the key participants in *Mallrats* were shocked when the film failed to find an audience, and the test of time has borne out their perspective. "Everyone I know who sees it, likes it," Jason Mewes stated on the collector's edition DVD release of the film.

Indeed, the home video and DVD market gave *Mallrats* a huge reprieve. Smith's second film quickly became a popular cult hit and has consistently ranked high on Amazon.com's best-seller list (often in the top 100). It is now an acknowledged classic of the teen comedy genre. The stink palm, no doubt, is immortal.

A MID-MALL'S DREAM

Looking at *Mallrats* today, some seven years after its theatrical release, one might easily determine the reasons why, among many critics, *Mallrats* is not the most favored of Kevin Smith's five films. It is not the blunt-faced, sharp-witted revelation that *Clerks* was. Nor is it the human, authentic love story that *Chasing Amy* is. It lacks the overtly provocative, social and intellectual stirrings of the ambitious *Dogma*, as well as the celebratory, satirical style of that lunatic rant, *Jay & Silent Bob Strike Back*. Yet, in its own way, *Mallrats* is a solidly crafted work, and a really good time at the movies.

Mallrats passes the most important test of any comedy: it is relentlessly funny. And then there's Jason Lee's brilliant performance holding it together. He makes Brodie a sarcastic, humorous B.S. artist with the heart and humor to go side by side with his more caustic qualities.

And, even if critics found the scripted material low brow, Brodie's "stink-palm" schtick is still one of the funniest (and most disgusting) sequences in any teen comedy of the 1990s. Watching Michael Rooker's pompous Mr. Svenning lick that melted chocolate pretzel off his hand, and knowing what else he is ingesting is, well, a stomach-churning riot.

Though reviewers will no doubt barbecue me for saying so, *Mallrats* is a film that was really ahead of its time. The "gross out" comedy sub-genre was not really popular with American audiences again until the Farrelly brothers struck gold with the megahit *There's Something About Mary* in 1998. Then came *American Pie* in 1999, followed shortly by S*cary Movie*, *Road Trip*, and the inevitable (and unfortunate) *American Pie 2*. All of those films championed lowbrow, gross out body humor, often to surprisingly good reviews and big money. Are any of those films as good or better than *Mallrats*?

Mallrats's perceived critical failure might simply be a result of nothing more significant than timing. Today it would most likely be viewed as a rather funny and valuable companion piece to *American Pie* or *There's Something About Mary*, being similarly loaded to the gills with outrageous dick and tit jokes. If *Mallrats* had been released, say, in the summer of 1999 or 2000, would the reviews have been so persistently negative? One has to wonder.

It is true that Jay and Silent Bob come off as a bit more toothless and inoffensive in *Mallrats* than in other View Askew outings, but to its credit, *Mallrats* nicely opens up the parameters of their world. It makes the case for the stoner duo not just as verbal comedians, but as physical ones to boot. Bob's imitations of the Dark Knight, or rather the *Dork Knight*, are not only funny, they jibe nicely with Smith's on-going inclusion of comic book and superhero references in his films. Approve of these slapstick hijinks or not, they're consistent with Smith's oeuvre.

A few years ago, a friend of my wife complained that Martin Scorsese was always making gangster movies; that *Casino* wasn't really much different from *Good Fellas*. I reminded her that one sign of a true artist is consistency. A fine filmmaker will return to similar ideas, worlds, and themes, because it is often enlightening to compare different perspectives on like material. The same argument is true of *Mallrats*. It is filled with pop-culture references (like *Clerks, Chasing Amy,* and *Jay & Silent Bob Strike Back*), and features two buddies of a certain "maturing" generation (like *Clerks* and *Chasing Amy*). So *Mallrats* isn't some freakish anomaly in the View Askew canon. It's like *Clerks*, only more mainstream.

Mallrats has some other nice qualities too. It's a movie with some emotional sincerity, not just glitzy young actors going about their shallow business (like *She's All That* or *Summer Catch*). And it is nicely energized by its musical score, featuring The Goops ("Build Me Up Buttercup"), Elastica ("Line Up"), Weezer ("Susanne"), and even K.C. and the Sunshine Band ("Boogie Shoes"). Good laughs, good performances and a good score —what's not to like? Did reviewers actually walk into a movie entitled *Mallrats* expecting a thoughtful, Ingmar Bergman-style introspection? If so, no wonder they were disappointed.

Also, I would be terribly remiss if I did not report that at least a few critics found considerable depth in *Mallrats*. Graham Fuller, of *Interview* magazine, for one, saw fit to compare the film to the works of Shakespeare:

> Just like *Midsummer Night's Dream*, it's got two couples...who repair to a mystical haven: Only in this case, it's a New Jersey shopping mall instead of the Athenian woods. *Mallrats* also has an agent of misrule entrusted with reconciling these quarrelsome lovers and constantly botching it: He's played by Kevin Smith himself, who makes a low-rent Puck alongside Jason Mewe's Gen X Oberon."[10]

So, with just two films under his belt, Smith's work had already been compared to *Waiting for Godot* and a Shakespearean comedy.

Making the comparison to *A Midsummer Night's Dream* a bit more apt, it may be prudent to remind people that critics didn't happen to appreciate Shakespeare's comedy very much when it "premiered" either. It was called "the most insipid, ridiculous play"[11] by one self-satisfied critic. Scholars would also have us acknowledge that it was not until the latter half of the 20th century that *A Midsummer's Night Dream* became recognized as a "complex and exacting work of art."[12] *Mallrats* may never be a critical darling, but neither has it waited some 400 years for popular acclaim.

Actually, as strange as it may sound, Kevin Smith's films do have elements in common with the comedies of Shakespeare. As Dwight Ewell, the classically trained actor who portrays Hooper in *Chasing Amy*, cleverly notes: "In most of the Kevin Smith monologues, there is a rhythm there, you just have to find it. Reading Shakespeare is the same way. He uses iambic pentameter, which means when you're reading the lines you don't have to push to get the meaning out, you simply do the melody and the audience gets the meaning. Kevin's words are the same way. As an actor you don't have to do much—it's all in the words. Kevin's words are so lyrical and beautiful."

Brian O'Halloran agrees. "Thank god I had theatrical training, where you have to memorize an entire play, because Kevin's words have this great flow. If you listen to him, you can almost hear it in his conversational speech. His dialogue becomes very story-like, and you can almost feel the peaks and valleys. It is very song-like, very melodic, and there's always a point. It sort of works like this: let me give you the point, now here's the point, now here's the punch line to the point."

Jeff Anderson also suggests the dialogue of Kevin Smith is complex, purposeful and exacting. "It is like music. Once I start doing it, if one little word trips me up, my mouth keeps going and I'm lost."

Even in *Mallrats*, ostensibly a broad teen comedy, the dialogue, not unlike the Bard's, is a delightful dance, and it is amusing not merely because of the delivery, but because of the very words themselves. The beast with two backs? The back of a Volkswagen? There isn't a whole lot of daylight between those concepts.

"Some actors can't handle the dialogue," Ewell notes confidentially of Smith's writing, "because they don't trust themselves." But when it's done right, the Smith cadence is charming, amusing and downright Shakespearean. "Ben Affleck is very good with that dialogue," Ewell notes appreciatively. "Very good."

Not surprisingly, considering the precision with which he selects his words, Kevin Smith is renowned throughout Hollywood as a director who strongly discourages improvisation on his sets. And that is precisely because his words are so carefully chosen.

Ethan Suplee explains the rule. "He wrote the lines, and that's what you're supposed to say. I never saw him give anybody a hard time about that, but there's a distinct pattern to how Kevin Smith writes, and if you improvise other things it throws off the prose aspect of it. It's cut and dry, and he writes really well. It's intelligent, so there's no real need to change any of it."

"Kevin has a firm grip on the script and the characters," affirms Jeff Anderson. "I later found out, [while shooting *Now You Know*] that actors generally don't like to be given line readings, but when Kevin and I work together, Kevin would always do his director's thing and say, 'Do it like you're feeling anxious.' But I'd just tell him to read me the lines how we wanted me to say them. He'd give me the line, and I'd give it right back. We'd cut to the chase."

"Kevin is big on line readings," Pereira repeats. "He does that a lot with Jason Lee. Jason can listen to a line, internalize it, and give it back perfectly."

No actor would dare attempt to improvise lines in a Shakespeare play, and it's interesting that Kevin Smith holds his performers to the rigorous standard, respecting the written word to such a high degree.

On a lighter note, Shakespeare is also renowned for (presumably) writing 37 plays, the selfsame number that crops up often in Kevin Smith movies! But more importantly, both Shakespeare and Kevin Smith are known to have at least two other qualities in common: the ability to turn a naughty, bawdy phrase with the best of them, and a rather keen understanding of human nature.

Though Shakespeare wrote about kings and other noble figures and Kevin Smith writes about more common characters — like those in service industry — the colorful humanity of these *dramatis personae* is something both authors explore. In its core structure, love of language, ribald humor, and human characters, Graham Fuller is right about *Mallrats*: it isn't that far removed from *A Midsummer's Night Dream*. Both productions have been dismissed as trifles, but in the final analysis, such is the enduring fate of comedy. Most people think it is easy to make people laugh, and for some reason don't always take that ability seriously.

As in so many cases, the reviewers really just needed to lighten up when they watched *Mallrats*. As Jason Lee says on the DVD edition of the film: "Critics, shmitics!"

ASKEW VIEWS:

MAGIC EYE: Though Ethan Suplee plays a character vexed by those Magic Eye Posters that once dotted mall landscapes, the actor took the popular art somewhat less seriously.

"When I first saw those things, I had no idea you were supposed to look at it and some other image comes out of the chaos of the design. I never let myself get frustrated through, and thought if somebody did see something hidden there, they were creating it themselves. Then finally, someone said to me, 'Cross your eyes.' Not actually cross them, but let them relax until they naturally cross. Then I saw the picture, and it was this miraculous revelation."

ORIGIN: *Mallrats* heralds the first appearance of another favorite Kevin Smith comedy duo, Fanboy (Walt Flanagan) and Steve-Dave (Bryan Johnson). The more verbose of the duo, Steve-Dave, is based on a real person.

"He's the guy who actually used to own the comic book store before Kevin did," Johnson reveals. "Walter and I used to go there, and Kevin went there, and Walter could never remember if the guy's name was actually Steve or Dave. So the name Steve-Dave was coined. He wasn't an angry guy, like the character I portray."

As for Fanboy, Walt Flanagan has a pretty good idea of who the character should be. "He's the fan boy to the nth degree." Then Flanagan pauses with insight. "I'd imagine all he cares about is comics, but if you watch the movies it seems that all he cares about is Steve-Dave. He's constantly pumping up Steve-Dave's ego. Maybe he's more Steve-Dave's fan boy than anything else."

Johnson agrees, with delight. "Fanboy is needed to re-affirm everything Steve-Dave says. He's the ultimate bootlicker. It was Kevin who came up with that idea. He wanted the eternally outraged Steve-Dave, and then Fanboy always cowering behind him shouting 'Yeah!'"

BRENDA: During one scene with Shannen Doherty, Ethan Suplee's Willam looks at her with a piercing gaze and calls her "Brenda," the name of Doherty's character on the Aaron Spelling series *Beverly Hills 90210*.

"I did that take once," Suplee remembers, "and then Kevin whispered in my ear. He said I should call her Brenda. And I said 'What?' And he said, 'Yeah, call her Brenda.' To my knowledge at the time, she had no idea it was coming. I think that afterwards I found out she did know, but it was still pretty funny."

WALT FLANAGAN'S DOG: This is, perhaps, the ultimate of the Kevin Smith in-jokes. During a chase sequence in *Mallrats,* Jay notes of a pursuer that he is "faster than Walt Flanagan's dog." The line came from an event that happened during shooting. After Flanagan had quit his brief tenure as production assistant, he had lots of free time.

"I was in Minnesota for four weeks with nothing to do. I'd be on the set for hours doing nothing but walking around different stores, and I saw this dog in the pet store that was so small. I think everybody on the crew had gone in to see it, because it was a pocket-sized rat terrier.

"I'd always wanted a dog, so I purchased it with about three weeks left in the shoot, which wasn't the smartest thing to do because then I had to keep a puppy in the hotel against hotel rules for three weeks. The people I was rooming with had kept their jobs on the film and were working these weird hours. They'd start at 6:00 p.m. and work till 6:00 a.m. and then they'd come home, and the dog would wake up.

"It wasn't the best conditions to train a new puppy. But I let her out in the mall, which was closed down for the shoot, and I'd go to an empty part of the lot and let her off the leash. She'd just tear around and looked like a little hockey puck, because she was so fast. That's where the joke came from. I don't know how it happened. It was such an inside joke, I guess Kevin just decided to keep it."

For the record, the dog's name is Brodie, and according to Flanagan, "She's a total lap dog," and is "still doing great."

CONDIMENTS: The character of Willam Black, the Idiot-Man-Child, undergoes a drastic transformation in *Mallrats*. Instead of Scott Mosier, Ethan Suplee portrays him. And, to Suplee's dismay, he's become a slob!

"I was in wardrobe and make-up and they said they were going to dirty me up," Suplee explains. "I thought it would be fine, but then this lady whips out a bottle of mustard. Then on top of that they dump on soy sauce, vinegar, and ketchup, and I started to wonder if a little colored water wouldn't have done the trick instead. I mean, did I actually have to stink? The audience wouldn't be able to smell me, but I sure did. It was a pretty messy operation."

REFERENCES: *Mallrats* is chock full of references to Smith's favorite films, television shows, and comic books, including *Smokey and the Bandit, Jaws, Star Wars*, and *Superman* (particularly the Man of Steel's need for a Kryptonite condom if he wishes to have sexual intercourse with a mere mortal).

GENEOLOGY: As *Mallrats* opens, Brodie (Jason Lee) reflects on some messy anal fun and games played by his relative Walt. This is the same character Randal discusses in *Clerks* as having suffocated on his own genitals. Since Walt is cousin to both buddies, that makes Brodie and Randal related.

CONTINUITY: At the end of *Mallrats*, Jay and Silent Bob are seen walking down a long stretch of highway accompanied by an orangutan, as the song "Susanne" plays on the soundtrack. Their adventure with the simian Susanne is the subject of *Jay & Silent Bob Strike Back*.

Also, Silent Bob makes use of a bat-grapple gun in *Mallrats*, and that toy, as well as his Dork Knight utility belt, re-appear in *Jay & Silent Bob Strike Back*.

KEVIN SMITH ON MALLRATS:

"It was liberating making a movie that failed on such a grand level...You reach the point when the reviews are so horrendously bad and the critics are particularly vicious, that it's like, 'Where can you go but up?'"[13]

NOTES

1. Cindy Pearlman, "Rat Patrol," *Entertainment Weekly*, November 11, 1994, p. 16.

2. "Star Brenda," *Entertainment Weekly*, June 9, 1995, p. 12.

3. Christopher Allan Smith, "Smith talks to Stan Lee," *Cinescape Online: DVD News*, April 15, 2002, p. 1, www.cinescape.com

4. Kenneth Turan, "*Mallrats*, No Match for Ultra-Low-Budget *Clerks*," *The Los Angeles Times*, October 20, 1995.

5. Michael Medved, *The New York Post*, October 20, 1995.

6. Richard Corliss, *Time*, "*Mallrats*," November 6, 1995, p. 78.

7. Janet Maslin, "Whiling Away the Day at the Shopping Center," *The New York Times*, November, 1995, p. C8.

8. Graham Fuller, "Mr. Smith Goes to Emotion," *Interview*, April 1997, p. 42.

9. Monica Roman, "Indie's Prodigal Son (independent film producer Kevin Smith)," *Variety*, January 26, 1998, v369, n11, p. 3.

10. Graham Fuller, "*Mallrats*," *Interview*, November 1995, p. 48.

11. *The Riverside Shakespeare* (Boston, MA: Houghton Mifflin Company, 1974), p. 217.

12. Ibid.

13. "Interview with Kevin Smith," *Independent Film Channel*, June 1998, http://www.newsaskew.com/ifc.-Kevin/.

Chasing Amy (1997)

"I FINALLY HAD SOMETHING PERSONAL TO SAY..."

Finally, a comedy that tells it like it feels. Sex is easy. Love is hard.

CAST & CREW

MIRAMAX PRESENTS A VIEW ASKEW PRODUCTION, *CHASING AMY*

WRITTEN AND DIRECTED BY: Kevin Smith
PRODUCED BY: Scott Mosier
ASSOCIATE PRODUCER: Robert Hawk
LINE PRODUCER: Derrick Tseng
EXECUTIVE PRODUCER: John Pierson
CINEMATOGRAPHY BY: David Klein
EDITED BY: Kevin Smith and Scott Mosier
MUSIC: David Pirner
PRODUCTION DESIGNER: Robert "Ratface" Holtzman
COSTUME DESIGNER: Christopher Del Coro
BLUNTMAN & CHRONIC/CHASING AMY ARTWORK: Mike Allred
M.P.A.A. RATING: R
RUNNING TIME: 111 minutes

STARRING:

Ben Affleck | *Holden McNeil*

Joey Lauren Adams | *Alyssa Jones*

Jason Lee | *Banky Edwards*

Dwight Ewell | *Hooper X/Lamont*

Jason Mewes | *Jay*

Kevin Smith | *Silent Bob*

Ethan Suplee | *Fan*

Scott Mosier | *Collector*

Casey Affleck | *Little Kid*

Guinevere Turner | *Singer*

Carmen Lee | *Kid*

Brian O'Halloran | *Exec #1*

Matt Damon | *Exec #2*

Alexander Goebbel | *Train Kid*

Tony Torn | *Cashier*

Rebecca Waxman | *Dalia*

Paris Petrick | *Tony*

Welker White | *Jane*

Kelly Simpkins | *Nica*

John Willyung | *Cohee Lundin*

Tsemach Washington | *Young Black Kid*

Ernest O'Donnell | *Bystander*

Kristin Mosier | *Waitress*

Virginia Smith | *Con Woman*

THE STORY SO FAR...

BLUNTMAN & CHRONIC COMIC BOOK co-creator
Holden McNeil is blindsided at the Comic Con in Manhattan when he meets
Alyssa Jones, a beautiful and feisty comic artist. When Holden learns that
Alyssa is a lesbian, he must re-calibrate his traditional views about the
sexes. But as his friendship with Alyssa deepens, Holden's partner, roommate and long-time friend, Banky Edwards, begins to grow jealous of the
bond forming between them.

When Holden and Alyssa's friendship deepens to romantic love,
Banky uncovers a secret about Alyssa's past that shatters Holden's confidence. Despite sage advice from a black friend and artist named Hooper X
(who writes the comic book *White Hating Coon*), Holden breaks up with
Alyssa over the matter.

Jay and Silent Bob, seeking money from Holden because his comic
book is based on their likeness, set McNeil straight in matters of the heart.
But Holden draws the wrong conclusion, and in a tense summit with Banky
and Alyssa, brings the matter to an unfortunate conclusion.

SILENT BOB'S WORDS OF WISDOM:

"No, idiot. It was a mistake. I wasn't disgusted with her, I was afraid. At that moment, I felt small, like I lacked experience, like I'd never be on her level, like I'd never be enough for her or something like that, you know what I'm saying? But what I did not get—she didn't care."

THE STORY BEHIND THE MOVIE:

After the disastrous reception heaped on *Mallrats* during its release in the closing months of 1995, many in the film industry wondered what would become of Kevin Smith. The story was an all-too-familiar one. A talented young filmmaker brimming with ideas goes to Hollywood only to see his edge blunted, his individuality reigned in, and his creative muse tempered by interfering studios. The same "hot" director, once the talk of the town, retreats to obscurity, dreams shattered.

Fortunately, this was not to be Kevin Smith's story. Not by a long shot.

Instead, Kevin Smith and his View Askew colleagues simply went back to basics. They produced a small budgeted ($250,000) independent feature with the same team that had pulled it off so well before, including producer Scott Mosier, and cinematographer David Klein.

Also along for the ride was a stable of talented actors who hadn't yet peaked, but were hungry to sink their teeth into meaningful roles, including Ben Affleck, Jason Lee, Joey Lauren Adams, Dwight Ewell, Ethan Suplee, and Brian O'Halloran. The result of the combined effort was a comedic and romantic masterpiece, and one of the ten best films of the 1990s, *Chasing Amy*.

Funny and tender, touching and sharp, *Chasing Amy* was the movie that changed everything for Kevin Smith (again). It made a huge profit, won rave reviews, and became View Askew's new calling card to Hollywood at large.

"*Chasing Amy* made *Dogma* possible," producer Scott Mosier explains. "A lot of talented actors saw it, and it made them think about working on *Dogma. Mallrats* was not a great calling card to the Alan Rickmans of the world. But a film like *Chasing Amy* says that Kevin Smith can write great scenes and create an environment for actors where they produce good work. That's the kind of thing that is very attractive. *Chasing Amy* elevated us on all levels; as far as audiences, within the industry, and financially as well."

But before the film that has become known as Kevin Smith's "come-back" picture was released, there was an interesting period of development. At one point, the movie was set to follow hard in *Mallrats* footsteps as a broad, somewhat juvenile teen comedy.

Ethan Suplee remembers how he first heard about *Chasing Amy*. "A lot of Kevin's friends who worked on *Clerks* in some capacity came out and worked in Minnesota as production assistants on *Mallrats*. Some of them were into making movies too, and one, Vincent Pereira, was planning an independent film [*A Better Place*]. That happened really soon after shooting *Mallrats*. So I went back to Jersey and stayed at Kevin's house while I did a couple of scenes in Vinnie's movie.

"Then Kevin took me aside and said 'One day, all this will be yours,' and he was actually referring to a very early draft of *Chasing Amy* that took place in high school. I was going to play one of the main characters. But then *Mallrats* came out and did so poorly that Kevin totally rewrote *Chasing Amy*. But the vibe was still there that I would work with Kevin whenever he worked."

Vincent Pereira picks up the story from there. "I don't think I ever read that earliest version. I think Kevin only wrote a few scenes for it. But he had this idea that he was going to make a PG-13 movie that his mother could watch. Well, you've seen *Chasing Amy*, and that obviously didn't happen. But the original idea, before *Mallrats* was released, was to go down the same path and play it very broad.

"If I remember correctly, Jay and Silent Bob were trying to live as if they were really superheroes. Ethan was going to play a character that has two different gorgeous women on his arms every time you see him. He was going to be this real stud, and I think Kevin only wrote maybe two scenes of that version. Then, after *Mallrats*, he decided to go in a more subtle direction."

According to Pereira, once Kevin stayed on that path, *Chasing Amy* underwent relatively few changes in the scripting process. "There was going to be a subplot involving Holden and his ex-girlfriend, who happened to be a teacher, and that sequence had many of the characters Kevin introduced in the early version of the script. But those ideas were dropped very early on."

Interestingly, some sequences that were dropped from earlier View Askew films were resurrected for *Chasing Amy*, including the oral sex scars scene (which had appeared in the original draft of *Mallrats*). "The funny thing about *Amy* is that a lot of the good stuff in there came out of other scripts. Kevin found a notebook where he'd written some preliminary scenes for *Clerks*. He lost it before he actually wrote the screenplay, so he forgot all about it. About a year or two later, he found the notebook again and there's that wonderful deleted scene in *Chasing Amy* where Holden and Alyssa are at the dartboard talking about true love. That sequence was in the notebook, but it was a discussion between Dante and Randal. It was the exact same sequence, except with the two of them at the Quick Stop counter. I wish that scene were still in the film. That's the one thing Kevin's cut out of his movies that I believe should have stayed in."

Bringing *Chasing Amy* to final draft also involved opening up the story. "Miramax read it and sent a note to open it up a bit," Pereira recalls. "The whole confrontation scene in the hockey rink took place over dinner in an apartment, but Miramax said, 'Let's have them go out somewhere instead.' But the last draft wasn't tremendously different from the first draft."

The final script, a focused tale about a heterosexual comic book artist falling hard for an avowed lesbian, has been speculated about in the press for years. Some people believe it is an autobiographical work; that Kevin Smith wrote it as a love-letter to his then-girlfriend, Joey Lauren Adams, who had acquired more relationship experience than he had.

But other sources, including *Entertainment Weekly*, indicated there might be a more dishy story to uncover. An article by Allison Gaines pointed to the fact that Kevin Smith and Scott Mosier became chummy with lesbian director Rose Troche and writer Guinevere Turner (director of *Go Fish*) during their stay in Utah during Sundance in 1994. The article vaguely intimates that either Smith or Mosier were infatuated with the lovely Guinevere Turner (who appears in *Chasing Amy*) and that somehow it all ended up on the screen.[1]

When questioned on the subject, Mosier was non-committal about the details. "It was in an *Entertainment Weekly* article. The information that's in there is fine."

Regardless of the story's beginnings, the final shooting script by Smith was a polished, yet blunt piece of work that seemed to understand the pain of the most intense human relationships and emotions. Ethan Suplee, for one, loved the results. "It was very honest in dealing with a much more intense subject matter than what Kevin had done before. It was much more true than I expected."

With a screenplay in hand, Smith, Mosier, and executive producer John Pierson made a deal with Miramax's Harvey Weinstein to finance the project.

"We went down to breakfast in Sundance with Harvey Weinstein," Pierson recounts, "and within a short amount of time, everybody agreed Kevin should make this movie, make it for very little, make it with exactly the cast he wanted, and exactly the way he wanted to do it."

And Pierson's role in the negotiations? "I was just sitting at the table nodding. I would love to hear an audiotape of that meeting, because I can't really call it up. I know Harvey was wearing this ridiculous skiing outfit..."

According to Pierson, the executive producer credit he eventually received on *Chasing Amy* was merely another example of Kevin Smith's kindness of spirit. "That was just Kevin being generous towards me, because I was very generous to him on *Clerks*. I didn't care about the money; I thought it was a great film, and I had a feeling this was going to be someone I would really like knowing. And I pretty much told him the first time I met him that I had a book idea and somehow he was going to be a part of it. Because of his participation in *Spike, Mike, Slackers and Dykes* — which to this day helps sell the book — I always felt our deal was complety fair.

"But that credit was him continuing to thank me. I love having my name on that film. I always thought it was a fantastic script, and he did a knock out job bringing it to life. But I don't make the slightest claim that I was around to have an influence on that film. He was just really generous with the credit, and I'm happy to have it."

So, with $250,000 dollars to spend on production ($2,000 of which went to the creation of an authentic looking comic book convention), producing *Chasing Amy* felt almost like old home week to the team, including producer Mosier.

"Once again we were in more of an isolated environment," Mosier says. "Unlike *Mallrats*, we were surrounded by people of our age, people of the same experience level, and so we were much more comfortable exploring exactly what we wanted to do and how we wanted to go about things. That was true from both of our standpoints: how I wanted to run a movie and how Kevin would direct it. We were able to grow and feel more confident about what we were doing. On *Mallrats*, we'd made mistakes here and there, but it was a good film to learn on because the mistakes aren't necessarily as apparent."

Smith too felt free and confident enough to go for broke on *Chasing Amy:*

> Clerks had been over-praised. Mallrats had been over-bashed. We'd been at both ends of the spectrum. The third time is always supposed to be the charm so we were able to approach Chasing Amy from a very liberated position: what better could they ever say about us than they did the first time, and what worse could they ever say about than they did the second time?[2]

The cast of *Chasing Amy* rehearsed for nearly a month (always Smith's preference when shooting a comedy wherein the dialogue and characterizations are so important). Though Miramax had pushed for a well-known female lead in the film, Smith fought to keep Joey Lauren Adams on the project. Previously known primarily as the girl who "deflowered" Bud Bundy (David Faustino) on Fox's *Married with Children*,[3] Adams soon came to inhabit the once-in-a-lifetime part of Alyssa, in the process creating a memorable character, and even writing a sexy torch song for one scene. Months later, the heartfelt performance would garner her a Golden Globe nomination.[4]

Joining the cast on *Chasing Amy* was a new face to the world of Kevin Smith cinema: Dwight Ewell. Born in North Carolina but raised in New Jersey, Ewell is a powerful and charismatic African-American performer who persevered through a difficult childhood. "My story is not very different from a lot of young black men," he says. "I had dreams of becoming something, but because of things happening in my environment, people told me I wouldn't amount to shit, or that I was just dreaming. I'd be one person out on the street, but then I'd come home and go read Shakespeare, like *A Midsummer's Night Dream*."

For Ewell, the decision to pursue acting came at an early age, and was cemented after one particularly harrowing incident. "I ran away from home and went to Philadelphia when I was sixteen. I hooked up with a drug dealer and he tried to kill me. I got in a car with him; I just didn't know any better. He offered me a joint, and when I couldn't feel my legs I realized it was laced with something. And he started saying, 'Isn't it a shame: so young, so far away from home, don't you know I could do anything to you, and nobody would know where you are?' I was scared, but I had street savvy and I didn't let him see how frightened I was. I don't remember what I said to that man, but I got out of that car and decided I wanted to go back to school."

After studying at SUNY-Purchase, where Parker Posey, Stanley Tucci, and director Hal Hartley had attended, Ewell graduated well-trained and "sounding like a Shakespearean actor." He soon won roles in films such as Hartley's 1995 film *Flirt*, and in the short years since has appeared in more than thirty independent films. When interviewed for this book, Ewell had just finished shooting three films, including *Pagan*, *The Guru* (with Heather Graham and Marisa Tomei), and *Wheel Men*.

Ewell recalls with good humor his first meeting with Kevin Smith. "He came over to the house of a friend, and met me there. It was a really hot day so we went to sit out on the fire escape and I was reading from this book called Linda Goodman's *Love Signs*. It's sort of the bible of horoscopes, and Kevin and his girlfriend started laughing. It was then that my friend told me that Kevin was a filmmaker. I told him I'd just finished a film with Hal Hartley, and Kevin kind of interviewed me about the experience of working with Hal, and I told him everything I knew.

"Later on, Kevin and I joked about this conversation, because at the time he thought I was trying to school him on film. But I would never do that. I was just telling him about my particular experience. He had *Clerks* out at the time, and I'd never seen or heard of it. '*Clerks*?' I thought, 'what's that?'

"Meanwhile, my film was premiering that night so I asked Kevin and his girlfriend if they wanted to come, so Kevin could meet Hal. So they came to the screening, met Hal, and after the movie was over, Kevin said to me, 'I liked you in the movie, but I don't think he used you properly.' Next thing I knew, it was a year later and I received a call saying that Kevin wanted me to read his new script. They mailed it to me and I loved it."

With one caveat. "I liked the script a lot," Ewell clarifies. "Hooper is really funny, but I told Kevin there was just one thing that should be changed. Hooper seemed to be used as comic relief, only one-dimensional. All of the other characters talked frankly about their sexual encounters except for him. And Kevin understood immediately and said, 'Forget about that, I'm going to write something else.' Well, he came back with that scene in the record store and I loved it. Now I thought the character was really three-dimensional. I loved Hooper because you can't tear him down, even with words. He always has a reply to everything. He's not a victim. He wants to diss everything out, so people can't laugh at him."

Interestingly, Ewell based his interpretation of Hooper on an acquaintance. "I met this guy through a friend. He was black, 40 years old or so, and had this very dry sense of humor. On the outside he appeared very masculine; there was something very hard about him. But when he loved somebody, you could just feel it. He had a gruff voice, but you could tell he wanted to help people. It was a strange dichotomy. He was part of Hooper, the part who maybe hadn't seen his dreams fulfilled."

Also back in the saddle for *Chasing Amy* were Steve-Dave and Fanboy, the obnoxious comic book fans that had hassled Bruce Brodie at the comic book store in *Mallrats*. This time around, they would open the film, haranguing comic book writers Holden McNeil and Banky Edwards about the overtly "commercial" nature of their "juvenile" creation, *Bluntman & Chronic*.

To augment the reality of the scene, Kevin Smith actually used a negative review of *Mallrats* to formulate the blistering critique.

"Kevin showed me that review and was like, 'Can you believe this shit?'" Bryan Johnson remembers. "People are so full of venom."

How did Johnson find the necessary vinegar to play his vitriolic role so well? "I just thought of a person who is stunted in their own career, because it seems like there are a ton of jealous people out there who want to take other people down."

Walt Flanagan remembers it was difficult to maintain his composure as Johnson so expertly dressed down co-stars Affleck and Lee. "It was hard to keep a straight face, because we'd get to a certain point, crack up, and have to start over again. It was tough to keep going."

Unfortunately, this very funny sequence, which Johnson terms Steve-Dave and Fanboy's "finest hour," ended up on the cutting room floor. "The movie originally opened with Walter and me giving Ben and Jason shit," Johnson describes. "But then in the next scene, Mosier was giving them shit at the convention, so our scene had to go. It was too repetitive."

The shooting of *Chasing Amy* by all accounts went quite smoothly, save for a few incidents. For the scene of Alyssa Jones emotional break-down outside a Jersey hockey rink, Joey Lauren Adams did sixteen takes, becoming increasingly effective and emotional each time.

And, at one point during the shoot, Scott Mosier nearly found himself in trouble with the long arm of the law for too closely following the tenets of guerilla filmmaking. "On *Chasing Amy*, we didn't have a production staff, so I did a lot of the physical work to get things done," he explains. "We were in a location we weren't supposed to be in, on a holiday, I think."

"It wasn't like we broke in, but we kind of tried to do something, hoping nobody would drop by. But we got busted, and for a minute the people who owned the building were threatening to have me arrested because I was in charge. The incident was a little more flavorful than that, but I don't think I should go into too much detail. We just had no money, and had to take some risks. Basically, I was a little more willing to take those risks then than I would be now."

For his part, Ewell enjoyed shooting *Chasing Amy*, except for his favorite scene in the script: the scene with Holden and Hooper gabbing in the record store. "That was uncomfortable. I had tape on the bottom of my boots so they wouldn't make any noise, a body mike inside my leather jacket, so I couldn't move, or it would rustle. And then on top of that, I had all of these CDs in front of me wrapped in plastic. If I picked them up, they'd rustle and the mike would pick up the sound. So I could only pick up the unwrapped CDs, which was difficult. I remember feeling very uncomfortable and insecure about that scene, but Kevin assured me that it flows."

Brian O'Halloran was a bit surprised to learn that his character, an MTV executive, went though some changes during the film's shooting. "Initially, Matt Damon wasn't in that scene with me, it was just my character," he recollects. "But when Ben became involved, he wanted to get Matt in the picture and it was late in the casting, so Kevin didn't have a role for him. So he divided the executive part into two, and my agent called to tell me there was a change. My agent said there would be someone else with me, and I was like, 'Who?' And the agent said 'Matt Damon.' And I said, 'Who the fuck is Matt Damon?' I'd never heard of him, but when I met him he was such a nice guy, and he had this beautiful girlfriend at the time. Matt is really a great and giving actor, and it was fun shooting with Ben and Jason Lee again."

Perhaps because the tone of *Chasing Amy* was more serious than *Mallrats*, old favorites Jay and Silent Bob only appeared in one scene in the film, offering sage advice to Ben Affleck's character, Holden. Though their appearance was brief, the scene remains one of the most important in the film.

Jason Mewes remembers a funny incident shooting the sequence: "I didn't know this until after we shot, but Kevin had told the crew guys to be patient with me. He told them I hadn't worked in a while, and said that we might be there all night because I had a long, long monologue. Kevin even thought we might have to do a line then cut, then do another line of my dialogue, then cut. But I breezed right through my stuff.

"Then Kevin's 'Chasing Amy' speech came up and we ended up doing *thirteen* takes because Kevin kept forgetting his lines. Afterwards, the crew started saying, 'Oh yeah, Kevin, we better watch out for this Mewes character; we're gonna be here all night...'"

After shooting the film, Scott Mosier and Kevin Smith repeated their editing collaboration, which had worked so well on *Clerks*, and David Pirner contributed an understated and highly effective musical score. The completed opening credits montage, like *Mallrats* before it, featured comic book creations, this time Jay and Silent Bob's alter egos *Bluntman & Chronic*, given life courtesy of Mike Allred. He also drew the more "personal" work of Holden McNeil, the comic book seen in the film's final frames, *Chasing Amy*.

What emerged from all of View Askew's hard work in spring of 1997 was a deeply emotional, touching, and very funny film that was beloved by audiences and critics alike. Kevin Thomas of the *L.A. Times* called it a "little movie with big truths," and a work of "fierce intelligence and emotional honesty." *Newsweek's* David Ansen reported that the film's characters were seductive with "their blunt and heartfelt eloquence." Also supporting the film were *Time's* Richard Schickel, who found the film "smart and truthful" and Smith's old supporter, Amy Taubin, who thought *Chasing Amy* was the "funniest, most honest" sex comedy she'd ever seen. Financially, the film was a huge hit, raking in more than $12 million dollars on a meager investment of $250,000.

Even more delightfully, this was a Kevin Smith film that touched the heart as well as the funny bone. As Roger Ebert pointed out in his review, falling in love is often a painful experience. *Chasing Amy* speaks to the pain inherent in the situations where human beings try to connect in a meaningful way. Holden's confession of love (in the rain no less) is touchingly performed by Ben Affleck. And Alyssa's breakdown after her realization that Holden really is breaking up with her is also deeply sad, gut-wrenching even. The nice thing about the film is that it was championed as a success by critics, but also judged as a positive contribution to society.

The gay community, in particular, welcomed Smith's efforts to portray it even-handedly and fairly, and Kevin Smith even made a prophetic statement in *The Advocate*, one that would take on ironic new meaning in 2001: "I'm sure there's a GLAAD award somewhere in my future."[5]

View Askew Historian Vincent Pereira was one of the many viewers who thought that *Chasing Amy,* so funny and yet so poignant, best expressed Kevin Smith as a creative artist. "I think it's Kevin's best film; his masterpiece. I think every director has a defining film. For right now, *Chasing Amy* is it. The only people who express problems with *Chasing Amy* are some of Kevin's youngest fans, who are more into the wild comedy. You go back to Woody Allen and it's the same syndrome: Why don't you make your earlier funny movies anymore?"

Dwight Ewell agrees that *Chasing Amy* has transcended its time and place to become something of a classic. "I believed in the messages the movie sent. There hasn't been another movie like it. A lot of people have tried to duplicate *Chasing Amy*, but no one can. It's a timeless piece, and I'm grateful that Kevin Smith saw I had the ability to be funny. I'm very leery of doing stuff where the humor is so forced and predictable, but Kevin's sense of humor is very intelligent; he doesn't spoon-feed it to you."

For Scott Mosier, *Chasing Amy* represented a mature look at complex relationships, ones that don't end with typical Hollywood predictability and pretense. As poignant as the film is, he feels it also carries a positive message. "Ultimately, if you look at the film from my perspective, it has a happy ending because it comes from a place of learning. Holden is a better person for being through that experience. That's what the end of that movie represents: that he's stronger and better and touched because of his relationship with Alyssa.

"Then, because of that, he's in a position to go out in the world and not make the same mistake. While it's emotionally sad to see that stupid mistakes made it impossible for Holden and Alyssa to be together, in the end the fact that he has grown through the experience is very positive.

"At the end of the movie you feel Holden gets it. He's going to be okay. I think it's a film about a guy who's trying to grow up and become a man. And finally he does."

THE NEXT SCORSESE?

In Spring of 2000, *Esquire* magazine ran a series of articles in which prominent critical voices looked at the next generation of filmmakers. One of those voices belonged to Andrew Sarris, the renowned film critic of *The New York Observer* and a professor of Film at Columbia University. In a brief, but pointed article, Sarris selected Kevin Smith as "the next Scorsese," a title which is quite an honor.

At the same time Sarris championed Kevin Smith as a filmmaker, he also noted his irritation with the young director for, basically, being so self-deprecating in his public persona:

> I would be happier...if he stopped giving faux-naïf interviews about his alleged shortcoming as a "visual" director...For one thing, he shouldn't be providing ammo to reviewers who couldn't recognize visual style if it conked them on the noggin. For another, it is disingenuous... to claim that he is uninterested in the visual dimension of the cinema when he is...addicted to comic strips, a sure sign of an artist as much obsessed by how things look as how people talk. *Chasing Amy*...works on all cylinders, visual as well as verbal, to deliver its explosive climaxes.[6]

The interviews Sarris referred to were the ones in which the genial Kevin Smith off-handedly put down the look of his films.

In one piece, Smith called *Clerks* "shitty-looking," and in others he berated himself for being unable to vet any material except for dialogue. Both those perceptions, with all due respect to the artist, are flat-out wrong. Regardless of cost, *Clerks* has a charm and visual style all its own, a real authentic character and quality; and *Chasing Amy* is quite accomplished in its lighting, editing, and composition.

Vincent Pereira thinks he understands why Smith tends to belittle his own work in print. "It all comes down to his belief that if he bashes himself, then other people can't bash him for the same things. But I think he's gotten savvy to the fact that he has to stop it. If he doesn't bring it up, nobody else does either. It bugged me personally when he did it with *Dogma*. They went out and shot *Dogma*, and it had a bigger look. And then Kevin started bashing the visual style in interviews, and I thought, 'Oh Kev, you've got to quit it.' I think if people didn't know that Kevin Smith had a 'reputation' of not having a good visual style, you could sit them down in front of *Chasing Amy* and *Dogma* and it would never dawn on them in a million years to criticize his work."

Part of the problem, Pereira admits, may have stemmed from Smith's over-reported critical remarks concerning *Magnolia* in early 2000. The major news media picked up Smith's e-mail comments about the Paul Thomas Anderson film and things took off from there:

> They sent me an Academy screener DVD…I'll keep
> it right on my desk, as a constant reminder that a
> bloated sense of self-importance is the most
> unattractive quality in a person or their work.[7]

Smith also noted that watching the three hour-plus *Magnolia* was the movie equivalent of "root canal."

Almost immediately, there was a backlash among some film buff sects, and a number of Paul Thomas Anderson fans went on the offensive.

"When this whole *Magnolia* flap came up, Kevin never said that he hated Paul Thomas Anderson or his films," Pereira clarifies. "He just didn't like *one* of his films. He loves *Boogie Nights*. But he didn't like *Magnolia*, and it was like this huge controversy. But then a lot of Paul Thomas Anderson fans were posting on the net saying how dare Kevin Smith say that about *Magnolia* when his films are technical disasters. And I'm thinking, 'technical disasters?' Where do they get that? How can you look at *Chasing Amy* and think that? Look at *Amy*, which cost $250,000, compared to *American Pie 2*, which probably cost $30 million, and tell me which film looks more accomplished."

John Pierson is able to put the controversy into a historical perspective. "The writer-directors who came of age in the 1980s — Spike,

Jarmusch, the Coen brothers—they had been to film school and had either learned from classic films, or just had a more visual orientation. They figured out how to make films that looked great and had distinctive visual motifs that carried through their work.

"The current generation is not so much like that. There's a number of them, and I put Kevin, Todd Solondz [*Welcome to the Dollhouse* (1995), *Happiness* (1998), *Storytelling* (2002)], and Neil La Bute [*In the Company of Men* (1997), *Your Friends and Neighbors* (1998)] in the same category. I think all three are writers way before they're visual directors. I think they write their lines, and they've all worked with great actors, and they've all gotten great performances, but they want those actors to say those lines in a particular way, and they're much more concerned about that than exactly how it looks."

Jennifer Schwalbach, Kevin Smith's wife and confidante, concurs that visual style isn't nearly as crucial to the director's palette as what is on the page.

"The movies aren't his children," she explains. "They're movies, and they're very close to him, but when he looks at them, he's a writer first. He is a very emotional filmmaker who would rather have people focus on what the actors are saying, and the emotions they are getting across, than how cool a set is. He's not trying to make a *Moulin Rouge*."

And yet *Chasing Amy* is a beautifully composed film, boasting visuals that effectively highlight the emotional story. Attentive viewers will note how a deep blue light, a cool shading, colors the funny and intimate scene with Alyssa and Holden in bed together as she discusses her motives for being with a man in general, and this particular man specifically.

That same blue light informs the later sequence in the hockey rink parking lot, but on its second appearance seems harsh and chilling rather than mellow, given the intensity of Alyssa and Holden's angry conversation. The identical lighting in the two sequences links them together in a subtle way.

Thematically, the scenes are purportedly opposite: intimacy versus anger, togetherness versus rejection and betrayal. But the reappearance of the blue light hints there is a connection; that the later sequence is an extension of the first—that whispered secrets and confidences sometimes give way to shocking turnarounds.

The hockey game also grants the film a touch of amusing visual panache. As Holden verbally corners and "checks" Alyssa, confronting her about her checkered past, the film promptly cuts to players on the ice literally checking each other in physical opposition. Funny too how the bells and whistles of the game punctuate especially powerful moments in the argument.

In *Clerks*, Smith maintained an appropriate distance from the humorous characters so that their turmoil came off as funny rather than sympathetic or even painful. In *Chasing Amy*, Smith's *modus operandi* is to make the audience closely identify with every scintilla of pain and yearning Holden feels. So Smith pulls a switcheroo on his established technique. Watch for Holden not in comforting medium shot, but in tight emotional close-ups as he confesses his love to Alyssa during a raging storm. Or notice his face when Alyssa rejects his invitation to a *ménage-à-trois*. The audience sees in agonizing proximity how a tear forms in his eye and rolls down his cheek.

These moments are deeply affecting for two important reasons. One is that Ben Affleck is a powerful and honest actor seemingly incapable of insincerity. Secondly, the situation is universal. We've all been in love and remember how much it can hurt, how deeply it can bruise. But frankly, neither of these two potent elements would work nearly as powerfully if Smith didn't understand where the camera should go; if he didn't have a keen sense of visualizing the drama.

Pereira also appreciates the manner in which Smith handled his third film (and the manner in which Mosier and Smith cut it). "In the case of *Chasing Amy*, Kevin played out a lot of the scenes in two-shot. Kubrick would do that a lot too. Look at *Eyes Wide Shut*; that film is composed of nothing but long shots. There's very little coverage in that film. It's two-and-a-half hours long, and it's a series of three-minute takes. The way Kevin shoots *Chasing Amy* is kind of similar. Look at that scene in the bar with Holden and Alyssa sitting at the table after Hooper and Banky go to look at *Archie* comics. It's a three-minute sequence that just plays itself out in two-shot. It doesn't cut, by why should it have to? What's interesting there is to see the chemistry between the two characters, to see them play off of each other. If you cut, you would lose that rhythm of the actors actually responding to one another.

"I get annoyed with movies nowadays that seem so cut happy. It's good to use coverage where appropriate, but today everything is covered to death, and there is so much cutting that it is actually distracting. *Lord of the Rings* was like that. In dialogue scenes, Jackson just kept cutting, not to different shots, but from one close-up to another close-up of the same actor from a slightly different angle. And I wondered why he couldn't let the dialogue play out. It kind of defeats the purpose of epic filmmaking.

"If you watch a great epic film like *Lawrence of Arabia*, it doesn't cut constantly. The whole point of having a wide frame is to let things play out, but a lot of filmmakers have forgotten that. It's distracting as hell. But

Chasing Amy is subtle in the way it uses the frame; there's some nice camera stuff going on. It's just a really poetic film, in the use of music and everything, and I love the acting."

Other viewers found the film rewarding not just visually, but thematically too. Terry Teachout writes *Front Row Center*, a column about the performing arts for the magazine of the Library of Congress, *Civilization*, and penned an interesting column about *Chasing Amy* for *The New York Times*, noting the film was deeply Catholic in its approach to morality:

> ...I was struck by...Alyssa's unexpected use of the
> word "sated"...it seemed to sum up the peculiar
> atmosphere of the film, all of whose principal charac-
> ters are searching for valid moral coordinates in a
> post-moral world. Then I realized that Alyssa was
> speaking the language of conversion—one becomes
> sated with sin—and I asked myself, is there more
> going on here than meets the eye?[8]

In the remainder of her piece, Teachout expresses the idea that a relationship needs more than love to work, it also requires "grace." She even makes note of the fact that several characters in the film, including Silent Bob, identify themselves as being Catholic. This is a pretty interesting reading of the film, and knowing Smith's religious background, one that's nearly impossible to resist exploring.

Yet *Chasing Amy*, as Teachout also notes, is a secular film, though perhaps informed by a Catholic mind-set. There may be a striving for grace in it, but, importantly, also a real lack of righteous judgment. Holden may feel inferior to Alyssa, and believe that she's been unforgivably promiscuous, but he never indicates she's a sinner in the eyes of God. Religions are prone to making just such pronouncements. In *Chasing Amy*, being gay is okay (notice that Holden has "zero" problem with Alyssa's homosexual experience), and that's not likely an attitude endorsed by the Vatican.

In contrast to Teachout's interesting and informed reading, one might argue equally cogently that *Chasing Amy* concerns a generation that is building its own morality out of the ruins of the old one, but having a hard time getting rid of some baggage, namely religious doctrine. Alyssa provides a perfectly reasonable explanation for homosexuality: Why rule out fifty percent of the population in selecting a mate? Isn't that dumb? Interestingly, the film doesn't refute her argument.

But it does note that religious upbringings (that of Silent Bob, and perhaps of Holden), may limit some people's ability to accept the decisions of others. It is that indoctrination in dogma, that judgmental quality of so many organized religions, that renders Holden (or Bob, in the case of his romantic quarry, Amy) unable to accept a woman who is forthright and honest about her sexuality. The movie is, like Scott Mosier noted, about guys who have to move past their stupidity and grow up.

Another rewarding element of *Chasing Amy* is certainly the deliberately self-reflexive nature of its screenplay. Kevin Smith, recently off a commercial project (*Mallrats*), now finds himself vetting a very personal film. In the screenplay, Holden McNeil finds himself similarly disliking his commercial art (*Bluntman & Chronic*) and finding career redemption in a personal project called *Chasing Amy*.

And, one of the best and most pointed moments in the film occurs when Holden asks Jay if he and Bob shouldn't be hanging out at the mall, and the loud-mouthed stoner replies: "We stopped that shit years ago." Nice.

ASKEW VIEWS:

WE'RE GOING TO NEED A BIGGER BOAT: In *Chasing Amy*, Alyssa and Banky discuss "war wounds," scars received while performing oral sex, as an incredulous Holden watches. The set design, the staging and the discussion of old wounds all ape the famous "Indianapolis" scene between Robert Shaw, Richard Dreyfuss, and Roy Scheider in Steven Spielberg's 1975 film *Jaws*.

Observant eyes will note that the lamp hanging over the restaurant booth in *Chasing Amy* looks virtually identical to the one aboard the Orca in the film adaptation of the Peter Benchley best seller. "It's paying tribute to his influences, and Kevin is a huge *Jaws* fan," Vincent Pereira notes. "That scene was originally in *Mallrats*."

WALT FLANAGAN'S DOG: A comic book seen in the convention at the end of *Chasing Amy* advertises a book named *Walt Flanagan's Dog*, after the spunky rat terrier named Brodie who Flanagan trained in the Minnesota mall on the set of *Mallrats*. A comic book publisher in the films is named View Askew Comics.

THE DIVIDED ARTIST: *Chasing Amy* depicts Kevin Smith's third set of twenty-something buddies. In *Clerks*, it was the backwards-hat wearing

Randal and Dante. In *Mallrats*, it was the stolid T. S. and the dixie-cup-bearing Bruce Brodie. In *Chasing Amy*, it's the backwards-hat wearing Banky and love-struck Holden.

"I think that they represent Kevin's comment on his friends," Pereira suggests. "He *always* has a friend with him. We worked at the Quick Stop together, and sometimes it was Kevin and Walter, and sometimes Kevin and Bryan. But he always has a real close male friend, and when he writes those characters, it's a riff on that."

Interestingly, Pereira suggests an alternative interpretation. "It's also a division of himself. One side of Kevin is the serious side, one is the slacker side."

IT'S A SMALL WORLD AFTER ALL: For a film that stands on its own so well, *Chasing Amy* is surprisingly rich in Askewniverse lore, and Smith's script refers to characters often mentioned or seen in the previous films. Alyssa mentions the Eden Prairie Mall by name, a reference to *Mallrats*. The screenplay also makes note of Caitlin Bree and Rick Derris (characters seen in *Clerks*), Brandi Svenning, Mr. Svenning, Shannon Hamilton, and Gwen Turner (characters seen in *Mallrats*), and even pauses for a brief sequence (with Cohee) outside Leonardo's Quick Stop.

Scott Mosier is happy, however, that despite cross-references, *Chasing Amy* has retained its own identity, and is only mentioned in passing in *Jay & Silent Bob Strike Back*. "It was better just to leave that alone," he considers, "and let *Chasing Amy* be what it was; let it end the way it did."

A LONG TIME AGO IN A GALAXY FAR, FAR AWAY: Just about every Kevin Smith movie ever made features overt reference to *Star Wars*. *Chasing Amy* boasts perhaps the funniest *Star Wars*-themed conversation of all: Hooper's racially-motivated diatribe against the Holy Trinity, noting that it is really about "gentrification."

"We shot that *Star Wars* dialogue in one day," Ewell remembers. "Some actors think there's a lot of film in that camera, so they can just keep doing take after take, and I don't think people thought I was going to get through it so fast. But it went really well. If we had to stop at all, it was to fix the lights or the sound."

THE ULTIMATE NUMBER: That number, thirty-seven, pops up again in *Chasing Amy*, this time in the opening credits. Banky and Holden's first comic was titled *37*, and in headlines that open the picture, "Local Pair

Have Drawing Pair" and "37 Pair Headed to Contender," the ultimate number appears.

A SPOONFUL OF SUGAR: If you watch Jay and Silent Bob's scene in *Chasing Amy* closely, you'll notice that in the background, Jay (Jason Mewes) is pounding down spoonfuls of sugar.

"Kevin wanted to do the sugar thing in *Clerks*," Mewes reports. "There was a scene where Jay was eating sugar, and then I spit out this big mouthful of it, but it got cut. So during *Chasing Amy*, Kevin was thinking of all this stuff to keep us busy, and he brought back that little thing from the first script. When I could, I would spit the sugar out..."

KEVIN SMITH ON CHASING AMY: "Holden was definitely the character closest to myself I'd ever written. Here's a guy who's a typical Nineties liberal male, who's like, 'Yeah, I'm from the suburbs, I got myself a black friend, me and my friends do this underground comic-book thing, I've got this girl I like and I'm very OK with her homosexual past.' It's in the arena where you imagine he'd be the most comfortable in—the heterosexual arena—that he completely malfunctions."[9]

NOTES

1. Allison Gaines, "Chasing Down the Rumors: Did Kevin Smith Date a Lesbian?" *Entertainment Weekly*, November 28, 1997, p. 87.

2. Kevin Smith, *Chasing Amy Liner Notes*, September 20, 1997, http://www.godamongdirectors.com/smith/amystory/shtml.

3. David Hochman and Jessica Shaw, "Clip'n'save (profiles of actress Renee Zellweger, Joey Lauren Adams, and Jewel)," *Entertainment* Weekly, June 13, 1997, n383, p. 12.

4. Deanna Kizis, "Joey Lauren Adams," *Cosmopolitan*, July 1999, v227, p. 156.

5. Gregg Kilday, "Straight Outta Jersey," *The Advocate*, July 4, 2000, p. 62.

6. Andrew Sarris, "The Next Scorsese: Kevin Smith," *Esquire*, March, 2000, p. 218.

7. Chris Willman, "Biting Criticism: *Dogma* Director Kevin Smith disses *Magnolia*," *Entertainment Weekly*, January 27, 2000, p. 1, http://www.ew.com/ew/report/0,6115,84950~1~~00.html

8. Terry Teachout, "Moving from Carnal Bliss to Something Truly Divine," *The New York Times*, May 25, 1997, pp. 9, 12.

9. Stephan Talty. "The Clerk, the Girl and the Corduroy Hand Job," *Playboy*, Volume 45, no. 12, December 1998, p. 1, http://www.newsaskew.com/playboy.

Dogma (1999)

LEAVE IT TO THE CATHOLICS TO DESTROY EXISTENCE

Get touched by an angel.

CAST & CREW

LIONS GATE FILMS PRESENTS A VIEW ASKEW PRODUCTION OF *DOGMA*

WRITTEN AND DIRECTED BY: Kevin Smith
PRODUCED BY: Scott Mosier
CO-PRODUCER: Laura Greenlee
EXECUTIVE PRODUCER: Johathan Gordon
CINEMATOGRAPHY BY: Robert Yeoman
EDITED BY: Scott Mosier and Kevin Smith
PRODUCTION DESIGNER: Robert "Ratface" Holtzman
MUSIC BY: Howard Shore
MUSIC SUPERVISOR: Randall Poster
COSTUME DESIGNER: Abigail Murray
VISUAL EFFECTS SUPERVISOR: Richard "Dickie" Payne
SPECIAL MAKE-UP AND CREATURE EFFECTS DESIGNER AND SUPERVISOR:
    Vincent J. Guastini, Vincent J. Guastini Productions
STUNT COORDINATOR: Gary Jensen
M.P.A.A. RATING: R
RUNNING TIME: 130 minutes

Prepare thyself.

STARRING:

Linda Fiorentino | *Bethany Sloane*

Ben Affleck | *Bartleby*

Matt Damon | *Loki*

Alan Rickman | *Metatron*

Salma Hayek | *Muse/Serendipity*

Chris Rock | *Rufus, the Thirteenth Apostle*

Jason Lee | *Azrael*

Jason Mewes | *Jay*

Kevin Smith | *Silent Bob*

George Carlin | *Cardinal Glick*

Bud Cort | *John Doe Jersey*

Alanis Morissette | *God*

Jeff Anderson | *Gun Salesman*

Brian O'Halloran | *Grant Hicks*

Janeane Garofalo | *Liz*

Betty Aberlin | *Nun*

Dwight Ewell | *Kane*

Guinevere Turner | *Bus Station Attendant*

Walter Flanagan & Bryan Johnson |
   Protestors — Steve-Dave and Fanboy

Jared Pfennigwerth, Kitao Sakurai & Barrett Hackney | *Stygian Triplets*

Dan Etheridge | *Priest at St. Stephen's*

Ethan Suplee | *Voice of Noman/Golgothan*

Ratface Holtzman | *Officer McGee*

THE STORY SO FAR...

WHEN GOD—PLAYING SKEEBALL in New Jersey—
is incapacitated by demonic Stygian Triplets, the supernatural forces of
good rally to rescue the divine entity before chaos reigns. The problem is
St. Michael's Church in Red Bank, New Jersey, and a new publicity campaign
to revitalize interest in Catholicism (*Catholicism Wow!*). By offering a
plenary indulgence—a chance to wipe away all sin—on the Church's
anniversary, the avaricious Cardinal Glick has inadvertently opened the
door for two exiled angels, Bartleby and Loki, to return to Heaven and
thereby undo creation.

Metatron, the voice of God, recruits Bethany Sloane, a divorced
abortion clinic worker in Illinois, and stoner "prophets" Jay and Silent Bob
to stop Bartleby and Loki before it is too late. But on their quest to reach
Jersey, these unlikely saviors of mankind encounter a variety of friends
and foes, including Rufus, the Thirteenth Apostle; Serendipity, a muse
turned stripper; the Golgothan, a monstrous shit demon; and even the
architect of the treacherous plan, Azrael the demon.

As Bartleby and Loki cut a swath of destruction across America, from corporate board meetings to mass transit, a faithless Bethany is forced to confront her religious beliefs, as well her secret role in the scheme of things. As Metatron reveals, she has a special lineage, and one that she must rise to honor.

HE STORY BEHIND THE MOVIE:

Kevin Smith, a Catholic who once flirted with the Pentecostal Church and Calvary Ministries, and an avid reader of Milton and Dante, wrote the screenplay for *Dogma* in the August of 1994 for Miramax. The 148-page script, a satire about religion and a heartfelt statement about faith, would eventually lay the groundwork for Kevin Smith's most controversial film.

Like his other projects, *Dogma* went through a long process of development before arriving on the silver screen. At one point, the screenplay was set to be a high school story, along the lines of *Mallrats* or the first proto-draft of *Chasing Amy*. Kevin Smith noted (in the liner notes for the special edition DVD) that some of his original thoughts on the project (conceived in Vancouver Film School, well before *Clerks*), included a male protagonist (a "jock"). But even early on, he knew *Dogma* would be a story of angels and demons, and biting, provocative humor.

"Originally it was an idea Kevin called *God*," Vincent Pereira relates, "but by the time he finished the script it was called *Dogma*. Kevin told me about some scenes in it. In the original draft, the main character, Bethany, was a stripper—and that's how she met Jay.

"She was a stripper in Chicago, and Metatron came to her and ordered her to wait for someone who would 'come like Moses and identify himself as a prophet.'

"So the next day, she's working, getting ready for her striptease in front of these little booths, where the partition slowly rises as the customer puts his money in. Her boss tells her she's got a customer, and it's Jay. He's already been there five times that day, and the boss warns that he's got a real mouth on him. So Bethany begins her routine, and as the partition slowly rises, Jay is already telling her everything he wants her to do. And finally, he says, 'I want to cum like Moses, and you can make yourself a profit.' She puts it together, asks him out to dinner, and he thanks God."

The script for *Dogma* was to have the longest gestation period of any View Askew production. It was, fans will notice, announced as the next picture at the end of *Clerks*, and later *Chasing Amy*. The reason for the delay was that there was some reluctance on the part of writer/director Smith and producer Mosier to tackle so grand a project early in their careers.

"I think Kevin knew we were going to make *Mallrats* second, but he'd written scenes for *Dogma*," Scott Mosier describes. "What happened was that Miramax had an option, and that was going to be *Dogma*, and *Mallrats* was this side thing where we were going to do this commercial film. There was no way we should have done *Dogma* second. We needed a movie in between to know what it was like to have an actual crew and the rest. The decision was mutual. I think we both knew there was no way we'd get the cast and money we needed for *Dogma*, so *Chasing Amy* became our transitional film."

When the script was completed, Miramax reviewed it and decided that, like *Chasing Amy*, some adjustments in settings might benefit the picture. "It was again a case of making things bigger," relates Pereira. "In the first scene, the dialogue between Bartleby and Loki occurs in a coffee shop, but Miramax told Kevin to give it more scope, and he switched it to an airport. The Golgothan and the Stygian Triplets weren't in the first draft either. They were all added to give the film more action, but thematically it was very consistent from start to finish."

The reaction to the script was very strong from all quarters. Ben Affleck read the script on a plane trip from New Jersey to Boston, before shooting *Chasing Amy*, and developed a fascination with it, becoming determined to play the part of the renegade angel, Bartleby. Another actor who loved the screenplay was Ethan Suplee.

"To me, that script was — and still is — the greatest thing ever written," Suplee enthuses. "There was a point in it where the Golgothan actually had dialogue scenes with Serendipity and talked about where he came from. Golga or Calvary, where Jesus was crucified, was also a site in that part of the world where they crucified criminals. And when they died, their excrement was released as their bowels opened up, and all that shit flowed into a pit. Out of that pit, the Golgothan was born. I remember reading and wondering, 'Who can come up something that good?' It was the best script I'd ever read."

Furthermore, Vincent Pereira felt that Smith's intention in writing *Dogma* was noble. "Kevin is Catholic and his inspiration for writing *Dogma* was, I think, that he had in his life a priest who was very dynamic. He was an earthy guy, a great speaker, and Kevin realized religion could be fun, something that people aren't just obliged to go to because of guilt, but because they feel genuinely inspired. That's what *Dogma* was about. It wasn't anti-religion; it wasn't even anti-Catholic."

Smith sounded off on his intentions as well:

I think for me, the flick was my own celebration of faith...I just wanted to do something that was pro-faith and expressed my spirituality—my Catholicism. And in the process I figured, you know, a few dick and fart jokes wouldn't hurt.[1]

Working with their largest budget yet—$10 million—View Askew Productions ramped up to shoot *Dogma*, even as Smith and Mosier were aware that some audience members might consider the subject matter of the film offensive.

If any actors worried about being associated with a controversial film, it didn't stop them from appearing in *Dogma*, and the film boasted Smith's largest and most experienced cast yet. Although the role of Bethany was originally designed for Holly Hunter, and then Emma Thompson was briefly cast (before begging off to have a baby), it was Linda Fiorentino, the femme fatale of *The Last Seduction*, who signed on as the troubled protagonist and "last scion."

Alan Rickman, Hans Gruber of *Die Hard* fame, agreed to portray the voice of God, Metatron. Ben Affleck recruited *Good Will Hunting* co-writer and friend Matt Damon to play Loki, Bartleby's angelic partner in crime. The hilarious Chris Rock signed on as Rufus, the thirteenth apostle, while indie-darling Janeane Garofalo was cast as a friend of Bethany's at the abortion clinic and View Askew favorite Jason Lee was back as the film's antagonist, the rejected muse turned demon, Azrael.

In a small but significant role, comedy legend George Carlin made quite an impression in *Dogma* as the self-serving Cardinal Glick, and later returned for *Jay & Silent Bob Strike Back*. He's already agreed to appear in *Jersey Girl*, Smith's upcoming project. Lovely Salma Hayek (star of *From Dusk Till Dawn* and *Desperado*) took on the role of a muse turned stripper, and Dwight Ewell also returned to the View Askew fold, along with Ethan Suplee, playing gang leader Kane and the Golgothan, respectively.

Clerks stars Brian O'Halloran and Jeff Anderson also appeared, the latter for his first role in a Kevin Smith film in more than five years. This time out, O'Halloran played another Hicks cousin, a reporter named Grant, and Anderson had a cameo as a gun shop owner visited by Loki and Bartleby. And, in a move that proved quite controversial, God was cast as a woman; singer/songwriter Alanis Morrisette.

"*Dogma*, to me, was our first movie with really big stars," Jason Mewes notes of the impressive cast. "It was Chris Rock, Alan Rickman, and Salma Hayek. I didn't really know Alan's work that well, but Kevin told me before we started shooting that I couldn't mess up my lines and forget my dialogue because Rickman was a British actor. He said to me that British actors are *serious*; that they're the ones who invented acting. So he told me to memorize my stuff."

Mewes took the advice to heart and memorized the entire script. Not just his own part; but all the parts interacting with Jay. But it wasn't just actor's pride that motivated Mewes to learn the dialogue. He ended up spending a lot of time in Pittsburgh, where much of the film was shot, because of a new friend — a girl.

"Kevin and I went out to Pittsburgh while pre-production on *Dogma* was happening," he relates. "We were scouting out locations, to look at the church there and see if Kevin liked it. I think we stopped at a college and Kevin did a Q & A, and we signed some stuff. But during those two days, I met this girl at a comic book store. While I was in there, I talked to her the whole time, because Kevin was shopping for laserdiscs, and when he does that it takes a really long time. So I ended up talking to her for a half-hour while Kevin shopped, and she was really cute.

"When we were leaving, she gave me her number and Kevin said, 'Invite her back to Jersey.' I said, 'No, she'll be scared.' But I did call her and asked if she could get off work for three days and come back to Jersey. She came back with us, and we hung out for four days. Then she took a train back to Pittsburgh, and we talked on the phone every night for two weeks.

"Anyway, I went back to Pittsburgh to hang out with her, and that was another reason I learned the script. There was nothing to do out there. So I would check out the sets being built and just read the script. Kevin and I rehearsed it, and suddenly I had memorized all of the dialogue."

Despite Mewes's extensive preparation for *Dogma*, dealing with the large, famous cast turned out to be something of a headache, at least from one person's perspective. "*Dogma* was a scheduling nightmare," reports Scott Mosier. "Actors can go from one set to another in L.A., but once you start flying people to Pittsburgh, you have to block it out like a week at a time. You can't have actors flying back and forth across the country fourteen times to be in a movie."

Another complication on *Dogma* involved visual effects. The film featured angels with wings, demons with horns, burning flames (heralding Rickman's supernatural arrival), people in flight, and not a small helping of blood and gore. This was the first time that a View Askew film prominently featured digital effects and prosthetics.

For Mosier, dealing with special effects added a whole new dimension to the producing game.

"It's all about hiring the right people," he says. "If you get the right people, they know what they're doing, and I don't really have to learn anything. If I have to learn a whole lot about CGI or digital effects then I haven't done my job right."

"My job really changes from film to film," Mosier contemplates. "It's mostly reactionary. You bring in a bunch of different people and then they generate a bunch of problems or what not for me to react to. Being a producer is like being a director of practical things; answering questions. I'm constantly making decisions and looking around, making suggestions. Mostly though, I'm in my office fielding telephone calls from different people, having meetings with the production staff and dealing with things so far as post-production. As the job goes on, I do more with talent, actors, and scheduling."

One of Scott Mosier's "right people," who designed and created many of the stunning "creature" effects in *Dogma*, is Vincent Guastini, a veteran of films such as *Virus*, *Requiem for a Dream*, and *Hannibal*. After working with Bryan Johnson on *Vulgar*, Guastini came to *Dogma* with one mission: to create the best angel wings yet depicted on film.

"Kevin called me into his office, and said, 'Listen, I'd really like to go all out on this. I didn't like the wings in *Michael* [starring John Travolta], because you barely ever got to see them move.' Then he told me about the money." Guastini remembers. "It was decent. It wasn't horrible, but I knew it was definitely going to be a challenge."

The angel wings that emerged were based on Smith's notion they should look like those appearing in the *Justice League of America* comics. "It was a tall order," Guastini considers. "The main frame of the wings are aluminum, machine parts, welded metal with gears, and they were fully cable operated.

"On top of that was a foam build-up for the muscles, and on top of that, we had a stretching material called spandex which went over the wings to simulate the skin going over muscle. And all those giant feathers on the wings? They weren't feathers. You can't get them that big, so we had to sculpt them. We had three or four different sets of feather sculptures, and from those we took a mold and had them vacu-formed. So we vacu-formed as many feathers as we would need to build the main frame of the wings, and on top of that, each feather had a little spine that went down the center. It had to be sculpted and reproduced, and each feather had to have its own spine. Then we mixed in real feathers like you'd get at a feather supply place. It was all blended in, plus airbrushing and dyeing, so the real feathers would match the fake feathers in a seam- less blend, and the wings would look absolutely authentic."

But even that wasn't the end of the process. "Kenny Walker was the main mechanical designer on the wings, and my animatronic supervisor, Gregory Ramoundos, put a team together and engineered how the wings were going to work," Guastini continues. "Usually, most wings only do one function. It's always a cheat. But these could not be cheat wings. They had to do everything at once. We had a second pair to back-up the first pair, in case one set went down. On top of that, any time you see someone flying over the steeple, with a double or Ben coming down, we had an open or "static" pair of wings. And those are the ones we actually used later, to blow up, so we didn't damage the animatronic wings. Due to movie magic and clever editing, it looked like those wings were really getting beat up.

"And towards the end of the shoot, I came up with this little mechanism, this little wing stump, to really get across the pain Ben was going through. I thought it would be really cool to have this bloody stump and a bone hanging out, while blood is coming out. People always comment about how painful that stump looks."

When complete, the angel wings in *Dogma* weighed some sixty pounds, and cost a considerable amount of money. Though Guastini notes that the wings were "economical," he is also quick to point out that the $5,000 price tag for them, related in the commentary of the *Dogma* DVD, is way off. The actual cost was much, much higher. "I'm a miracle worker," he notes, without going into specifics, "but I'm not that good."

Beautifully designed and executed, the heavy angel wings were nonetheless untested when it came time to shoot them.

"It was a situation where we wondered if they were going to work," Guastini remembers the first time the angels were deployed on set. "It wasn't that the wings were big and clunky, it was that no one had worked with effects before, and you have to keep practicing and adjusting, and all of that takes time. We had very little time to build the wings at all, and now we were on the set puppeteering them, and we'd never had a chance to work with Ben on them."

It was Kevin Smith, according to Guastini, who first managed to wrangle the wings. 'Kevin got behind the wing controls and started playing with them. And he got it! He said, 'Oh I see, you have to practice this.' And I said, 'Yeah.' You have to get magic moments—magic accidents—where it just all works, if you can catch it on film. And if you get it on the third take or the first take, you edit that moment into the film and you're on. Kevin was able to understand that. He turned around to me and said he wanted a puppeteer credit. And when a director wants a puppeteer credit, he gets it!"

Though the angel wings are no doubt the most extraordinary ever developed for the movies, they did have a downside, particularly in regards to Alan Rickman. The actor had a bad back and wasn't sure he could wear the sixty pound accouterment. Though for a time there was the possibility that the wings could stand on their own, on an aluminum stand stationed behind the actors, Smith felt that they wouldn't look attached that way. And, since Ben Affleck had worn the wings, Rickman was game to try too. Unfortunately, after shooting a few scenes, he aggravated an old injury and pulled his back out. A trip to the hospital was the result.

The Golgothan, the shit demon, was the second major special effects piece in *Dogma*. "Kevin wrote that into the script, and he's a big fan of *Batman*, so he wanted the Golgothan to look a little like Clay Face," Guastini explains. "I tried to approach the character as part of a comic fantasy. I took a little inspiration from *Ghostbusters* too. I took the funny and slimy characteristics from Slimer, and used the Marshmallow Man for bulk, and had Clay Face in there too. Then I added some shit horns, since it was a demon. And then we had to mechanize the whole suit and mimic dialogue. On top of everything else, we had to make shit talk and walk."

Attentive eyes will notice that the shit monster looks wet. That was also by design. "We had a local guy leading the Golgothan team, named Craig Hicks, and he was in charge of making different consistencies of shit," Guastini remembers. "It was made out of oatmeal and vegetables and all kinds of stuff. He had names for all of the shit too: baby poop, runny poop, all colors and varieties. But every time we had to put a stuntman into the suit [with the shit] it would really stink.

"We would store the shit in this warehouse in these big oil cans and during heat and condensation some of the containers would explode and shit would run all over the floor. There was no time to mix new stuff, so it smelled really bad. It was a mess, because everybody had to wear rain gear and ponchos every time we dealt with the shit monster. We had a shit team that just dealt with the monster after we locked the stuntman into the suit. He had on an animatronic helmet on it with all these radio-controlled servos, then we had to drop the shit on him, and it was just a nightmare."

At least some critics of *Dogma* complained that the Golgothan was too comedic-appearing, and somehow out of synch with the tone of the rest of the film; a rather unsubstantiated claim, considering the film's humor and comic book approach. Guastini has heard the feedback, but it doesn't concern him. "If people say it looks like shit, I win, because it's supposed to look like shit..."

Guastini's other contributions to the film were many, and not always

The View Askew Brain Trust: Director Kevin Smith and producer Scott Mosier, circa *Clerks* (1994).

Left — An askew view: A publicity still of the *Clerks* dramatis personae. From left to right: Brian O'Halloran, Kevin Smith, Marilyn Ghigliotti, Lisa Spoonauer, and Jeff Anderson.

Below — "I'm not even supposed to be here today!" A close look at *Clerks*'s put-upon protagonists, Dane Hicks (O'Halloran) and Randal Graves (Anderson).

Above — The sting of friendship (and F.D.S.): Dante (O'Halloran) and Randal (Anderson) reconcile a messy food (and feminine product) fight in the denouement of *Clerks*.

Right — "A generalization about broads..." Dante (O'Halloran) paints Veronica's (Ghigliotti) fingernails as the couple debates their sexual histories.

Stoners Jay (Jason Mewes) and Silent Bob (Kevin Smith) enjoy their regular digs in front of the Quick Stop.

No more worlds to conquer... Brodie (Jason Lee) and Quint (Jeremy London) survey the breadth of their shopping domain in *Mallrats* (1995).

Shannen Doherty strikes a pose (and attitude...).

Breaking up is hard to do: Renee (Doherty) and Brodie (Lee) discuss the division of their mutual assets.

Above — Silent Bob (Smith) peruses John Pierson's best selling *Spike, Mike, Slackers and Dykes* while his hetero life mate Jay (Mewes) selects less intellectual reading material.

Below — Feel the force flow from within. Kevin Smith directs stars Doherty and Lee on the set of *Mallrats*.

Gerbils! Gerbils! Gerbils! Quint (London) and Brodie (Lee) catch up with Jay (Mewes) and Silent Bob (Smith) in front of the pet store.

"There is no Easter Bunny!!!!" Willem (Ethan Suplee) rages against shopping children.

Just cross your eyes. Mallrats Quint (London), Willem (Suplee), and Brodie (Lee) search for the secret image in a kiosk poster.

That's a wrap: Kevin Smith and Jason Mewes review a take behind the scenes on *Jay & Silent Bob Strike Back* (2001).

RIght — Cut and Print! Chaka (Chris Rock) shoots the stirring finale of *Bluntman and Chronic: the Movie*.

Below — Cat women of the world unite! Left to right: Eliza Dushku, Ali Larter, Shannon Elizabeth and Jennifer Schwalbach (that's Kevin Smith's wife to you!) strike seductive poses.

Above — Snootchie Bootchies! Jason Mewes
"macks" on co-star Shannon Elizabeth on the
Mooby set.

Below — Something tells me they're not in
Jersey anymore. Stoners Jay & Silent Bob
turn the Miramax lot upside down

Above — A bunch of savages in this town! Randal (voiced by Jeff Anderson) peruses a nudie magazine while Jay (voiced by Jason Mewes) causes trouble in *Clerks: The Animated Series*.

Right — Men in black seize Randal for a top-secret assignment while Dante plans to coach a pathetic little league team in episode #5.

Randal and Dante discover reality isn't what it used to be when the series's artist magically re-draws them in a gay bar in the final episode.

as noticeable as the poop demon. His production team was responsible for Ben Affleck's metal chest armor (which one technician sanded for sixteen hours one day just to make smooth). Guastini Productions also engineered and built an animatronic Ben Affleck torso and head that ultimately didn't make it into the final film for the spectacular, exploding head shot that heralded Bartleby's exit from existence.

Guastini's team also crafted some thirty-to-thirty-five corpses (of Bartleby's victims) to litter the scene of the St. Michael's massacre. "Each of those victims had carefully designed heads and were painted," Guastini notes, "but nobody really gets to see all that work. There are people broken in half in cars and buses, and bodies on top of the cathedral."

While working on the effects for *Dogma*, Guastini heard an interesting revelation from Kevin Smith. "He told me he wanted to be a make-up effects guy before he was director."

And that would be fine with Guastini. "When I'm in dialogue with Kevin and we're talking about effects in his office, out at lunch, or on the set, he is so easy going, but also so precise in what he wants. He's a big fan boy, as big a fan boy of stuff from the 1980s as I am. When he writes his scripts, he interjects as many 1980s inspirations as he can into them, and that's why we click. We were both brought up by movies, especially 1980s movies, and it's a perfect marriage. He loves fantasy films and monsters."

One actor who got to work up close with the many special effects on *Dogma* was Brian O'Halloran. "*Dogma* was my first experience getting bloodied on film. I'd been in *Dracula* on stage, and the blood really flew there, but this was my first opportunity to do it in a movie. There was a lot of amazing stuntwork in *Dogma* too. There was this whole ending scene with the reporter [Grant] that was bigger—a wider shot— than what you saw. It was the first thing to be shot on the film. Stuntmen were being flown around and dropping from the top of the building behind me. I don't know what happened to those shots, but we had stuntmen and I had to coordinate how I would walk backwards. I'd take three steps back, then pause, and it was a lot of fun seeing these guys on rigs being thrown off the top of a church and hitting these bags below. There was a lot of set-up time on that."

Before it was finished filming, the production team of *Dogma* had shot at the Pittsburgh airport, St. Michael's Church, and back in Jersey. The opening sequence, which saw God ambushed by the Stygian Triplets, was shot at the Asbury Park Boardwalk, and the Bootlegger, a bar in Highlands, N.J., doubled for a bar in Chicago.

During the shooting of *Dogma*, Kevin Smith had to leave the set to do some publicity rounds for *Good Will Hunting*, the film he and Scott Mosier had executive produced for Affleck and Damon (for which he was later honored with a Humanitas Prize). He flew to Los Angeles on one such publicity run, and his life suddenly changed.

It was in the City of Angels that Smith first met a beautiful 25 year-old reporter from *USA Today* named Jennifer Schwalbach. It was a Saturday, and the reporter for the paper's Life section didn't think the assignment would be anything special. In fact, she was a little peeved she had to do the interview on her day off.

"I had seen his films," Schwalbach relates, "but I wasn't some über-fan that was super-excited to go interview him. I liked *Chasing Amy* and vaguely remembered the other ones. This was before *Dogma* came out, so I didn't remember *Clerks* and had only the vaguest recollections of *Mallrats*."

But Schwalbach and Smith hit it off. And fast. "It was love at first sight," she explains. "I interviewed him for about an hour, and I started packing up my stuff, and he asked if I wanted to hang out and shoot the shit. And I said, 'Sure,' but I was secretly wondering if he was super creepy, or just a really nice guy, because we were in his hotel room. But it wasn't weird at all. We talked for hours and got to know each other. We really just connected, and laughed and traded stories, and told secrets. I walked out of there feeling giddy."

She wasn't alone. Smith was so taken with the reporter that when he next returned to Los Angeles, approximately a month later, he asked her out on a date. "He asked me to the Independent Spirit Awards, where he won for *Chasing Amy*, and we had a really fabulous time," Schwalbach remembers.

"It was weird for me, because I hung out with a totally different group of people. I wasn't really into film as much as I was into music. And then suddenly I'm at the Independent Spirit Awards sitting at a table with Harvey Weinstein and his wife. And they said to Kevin, 'You brought a journalist to sit at our table? She'll listen to our conversations! How can you do this to us?' And Kevin said, 'No, it's a date.' And they were really upset. 'Oh my god, he's dating a journalist! This is a nightmare for us!'"

Kevin remained in Los Angeles with Jennifer overnight, much to the chagrin of those still studiously lensing *Dogma* back in Pittsburgh, where he was expected back. "He was kind of M.I.A.," Schwalbach relates. "He was supposed to fly out to L.A., grab his award, and head back to Pittsburgh. And he just went missing. They expected him to be filming the next day, and I kept asking if he needed to check in with anybody, and he said no. It was wonderful."

From then on, Jennifer Schwalbach and Kevin Smith conducted a long distance romance, commuting back and forth from L.A. to Pittsburgh.

Finally, when filming was finished, they knew it was time to put the frequent flyer miles behind them and get together. As post-production began, Jennifer was introduced to the glories of Jersey life for the first time.

"It's heaven for Kevin there, and he loves it," she reports. "His friends are there and the 'burbs are like home to him. But I was an outsider. There just wasn't anything there for me. I didn't know a soul, I didn't have a job, and Kevin was living in this little apartment, and there was ratty-ass college furniture and boxes everywhere. He'd been so busy, he hadn't even made the time to make a home for myself."

While Jennifer adjusted to the Garden State, *Dogma* was prepared for release. In post-production, Scott Mosier and Kevin Smith edited the film, and ended with a comic fantasy that lasted a whopping three hours and seventeen minutes. Thus it was not only the most expensive, most elaborate, and grandest of Smith's films to date; it was also the longest. But the editors knew they couldn't release a three-hour plus comedy, so they had to whittle away at the film, and pull it back in. The standard rule for comedy is that ninety minutes or less is a good length. *Dogma* had overshot that by quite a bit.

"The man was editing *Dogma* from the moment he woke up in the morning to 4:00 a.m. the next day," Jennifer Schwalbach, then a new arrival in Jersey, remembers of that period. "He didn't have time to take me on a tour of the 'burbs, or tell me where the best pizza place was; he was working all the time."

"Scott and Kevin did an absolutely great job of cutting it down from three hours to two hours," Pereira notes. "The film has a breakneck pace, and when some people argue that it's too long, I wonder what they would have cut out. The only way to cut the film would have been to drop whole sequences, and then I don't think it would have been coherent. But when people criticize the film, it's easiest for them to say it's too long."

Indeed, in many ways, *Dogma* is Kevin Smith's *J.F.K.* or *Malcolm X.* It's a big, sprawling film; an epic adventure packed with esoteric but fascinating information on a variety of religious subjects. For some viewers, however, it was a bit too ambitious a trip, and some of the wordy, technical information about matters such as the Last Scion, plenary indulgences, and transubstantiation were simply too much to process in one viewing.

Published reports on such matters indicate that on a first viewing, audiences only "register" about 80 percent of what actually happens on screen. In a fast-talking, dialogue-laden movie like *Dogma,* that may not have been enough to make the story comprehensible to some.

"I have a whole theory about *Dogma*," confides Pereira. "It's not that's it too long. It's that it's too short. There's so much information that's given to the audience, and the two-hour cut removes any chance for the audience to breathe. The audience tries to process it all, and sometimes people feel there's something off about the pacing; that it's too long.

"In fact, it needs to be 20 minutes longer. The original cut of the film had some transitions that got cut out; some chances for the audience to breathe and take it all in. I think if the film still had those moments intact, and the audience were able to sit back and let the information sink in, the film would feel shorter because you're getting the chance to process."

"*The Deer Hunter* was three hours long," Pereira argues. "In the book *Final Cut* [the 1999 book by Steven Bach, subtitled *Art, Money and Ego in the Making of Heaven's Gate, the Film That Sank United Artists*], he talks about how the studio previewed a two-hour version of the film, and the audience didn't like it. Then they previewed the three-hour version and the response went way up. Even though the movie was longer, it needed that length to breathe. I think *Dogma* may have suffered from that. Of all Kevin Smith's films, it's the one that would have benefited from a bigger budget. It needed another $5 million and another 20 minutes of running time. I still think it's a great accomplishment, but it was hugely ambitious considering the scope the budget allowed it to have."

Since *Dogma's* release, many Kevin Smith fans have pined away for a new special edition of the film, the original Mosier-Smith three hour, seventeen minute cut. In Hollywood today, people don't always give audiences credit for being willing to sit three hours in a theater. However, under the right circumstances, like *J.F.K.*, *Malcolm X*, *Lord of the Rings*, or even *Dogma*, many moviegoers are willing to commit that much time because the director's vision is a thoughtful one.

It is important to note, however, that even at two hours long, *Dogma* was released in 1999 to great acclaim. The sound mix from Skywalker Sound was impressive, and Howard Shore's brilliant, rousing score made the action seem even bigger. Indeed, if you call the View Askew offices and get put on hold, you'll hear Shore's score and be drawn into its majesty. Considering his fine work here, and on *Lord of the Rings*, Shore's 2001 Oscar for best score was definitely earned (and probably many times over).

On the critical front, Roger Ebert gave *Dogma* "thumbs up," *Entertainment Weekly* heralded it as one of the "ten best films of the year," and *The New York Times*'s Janet Maslin again waxed enthusiastic about View Askew's work. But, as most people who lived through the experience recall, the film also attracted more than its fair share of negative publicity.

Months before *Dogma* was even released, in the early summer of 1999, it was attacked by conservative elements of the far religious right. The Catholic League, the group responsible for pressuring ABC to cancel *Nothing Sacred*, a TV series about a progressive man of the cloth, made Kevin Smith's fourth film its latest target.

Leading the charge of moral indignation and outrage was William A. Donohue, the president of the Catholic League for Religious Civil Rights. Importantly, Donohue hadn't even bothered to see the film before condemning it.

Apparently, originality isn't important to self-appointed guardians of morality, because Donohue's strategy to protest *Dogma* appeared cribbed from Billy Graham's old play-book. A quarter century earlier, it was Graham who had vigorously objected to William Friedkin's film version of *The Exorcist*—claiming it was evil, and even causing people to become possessed by Satan. In equally fiery terms, Donohue laid out his objections to the movie:

> Joseph and Mary have sex and a descendent of theirs
> is a lapsed Catholic who works at an abortion clinic;
> God is played by a singer known for her nude videos
> and songs about oral sex; the Thirteenth Apostle
> resembles Howard Stern, the Mass is compared to
> lousy sex.[2]

Disney, the parent company of Miramax, which planned to release the film, had faced this kind of censorship before and buckled.

"Disney is an easy target for this kind of protest. It's their Achilles' heel,"[3] noted Harvey Weinstein. *Nothing Sacred* was not the only precedent. In 1994, the same year *Clerks* ran in theaters, Miramax released a British film called *Priest*, about a gay Catholic man of the cloth, and it too was picketed. Disney deemed the film "inappropriate" because of its content involving "Roman Catholics," and didn't release it under a Disney imprint.[4]

When it looked like Disney was again going to cave to censorship (allegedly at the behest of Michael Eisner, who may not have wished to see theme park attendance drop because of protesters), the resourceful brothers Weinstein swooped in. They put up $12 million of their own cash to buy the rights to *Dogma*, so Disney would no longer be attached to any of the controversy. The Weinsteins then shopped for a new distributor, and after turn-downs from Columbia, MGM, and Universal, the film was sold to Lion's Gate Films, an outfit headquartered in Vancouver, BC.

Though his screenplay won an Independent Spirit Nomination for the year, Smith had other things to worry about. For one thing, the CBS television network objected to the film's ad line, "Get Touched by An Angel," claiming it infringed on the copyright of their white-bread inspirational series, *Touched by an Angel*.[5] But more disturbingly, the protests were reaching a fever pitch.

"It was terrifying," Schwalbach explains. "It was so shocking to me that we needed armed bodyguards — when I was pregnant — if we ever went out in public. We'd get all these horrible little suggestions from Miramax, like, 'Be sure to look under your car before you get in it. Look behind you when you go anywhere.' And I thought, 'This is horrible, are you serious?' When Kevin would walk out on stage, they'd tell us, 'You don't know who is in the audience, so you might want to have a guard.' But it was just a movie! Then the hate mail started coming, and we couldn't have mail sent to our house or the office because of mail bombs, and I was just disgusted and very angered by the entire experience."

Donohue's Catholic League picketed *Dogma* during its premiere in the New York Film Festival in October of 1999, but the attacks only emboldened Kevin Smith, according to his wife. "Kevin is never one to hold back about what he's feeling, so we poked back a little bit."

What did Smith do to "poke back?" He joined the opposition.

"The movie came out at our local theater," Schwalbach explains. "And it was on the news that some people were going to protest *Dogma*. So we said, 'Let's go,' and started making signs that read 'Dogma is Dogshit' and things like that. It was Bryan Johnson, myself, and Kevin. I started throwing back drinks before we left because I thought the protesters would immediately recognize Kevin and we'd be chased out of town. But it was completely the opposite. There were five yokels there singing, and we walked up...and they wouldn't let us use our sign because it said 'shit.' They were just hooting and hollering, and had no idea who Kevin was."

Then the first news team arrived.

"A reporter came up and asked if Kevin was Kevin Smith. He said, 'Oh God no, I get that all the time. I'm here to protest this movie, it isn't right.' And she looked at him, then a picture of him on her clipboard, and just didn't put it together. Basically that was the point. The protesters and others were trying to stir up a controversy, but hadn't even seen the movie enough to recognize Kevin. How can you be so offended by something that you haven't seen, and aren't educated about? But the whole thing was tired. It went on for months, and people wanted to sue us. It was really ridiculous."

Ironically, the controversy surrounding *Dogma* only made more people see the film. By 1999, Ben Affleck was a huge and influential movie star, and he used his authority and popularity to support the film:

> Dogma is a lot more accessible than any sermon.
> This movie has a real chance of getting younger
> people talking about faith. If the Inquisition were
> around, they would undoubtedly brand Kevin a
> heretic and light him on fire.[6]

Other collaborators were just as quick to come to Smith's defense. "I did anticipate the protest," notes Pereira, "because I'd seen what the same people did to *The Last Temptation of Christ*, which was probably the most pro-Christian movie ever made, and these idiots shot themselves in the foot by protesting it."

O'Halloran also feels bad that people couldn't understand what Smith was trying to do, and instead saw only their own fear. "When these mini-controversies come up about Kevin, like GLAAD and the Catholic League on *Dogma*, he isn't really intending what these people are thinking. They don't realize that it really does bother him that people take things the wrong way and lose their sense of humor when it comes to comedy. They forget what comedy means. All Kevin is doing, all we're doing, is questioning; that's all. But some people don't like that."

Interestingly, many religious sources crossed Donohue and actually supported Kevin Smith's film. Richard A. Blake, writing for *America*, praised the film:

> He [Smith] has created a profoundly spiritual film, but
> he does not speak the church language of those of us
> who have absorbed several decades of dull, unimagi-
> native sermons and ponderous ecclesiastical
> abstractions. Dogma takes aim at an audience that
> has not yet learned to take the suffocating face of
> religion as the norm.[7]

Douglas LeBlanc of *Christianity Today* also found some things to admire. He noted the film was "flawed, but oddly touching" and that "Kevin Smith shows nascent gifts as a visual stylist and a storyteller."[8]

Still, there were some holdouts that objected to *Dogma*, not because of the controversy—but merely because they found the film to be weak. "The real problem is that *Dogma* isn't as funny as it thinks it is. The speechifying about religion is dull to a surreal degree," wrote Jeff Giles of *Newsweek*.[9] "*Dogma* is a smugly gory film," complained Karl Stevens in *The Christian Century*. "The violence seems to be incorporated only because it is part of the common aesthetic of Smith's generation."[10]

Worst of all, *Entertainment Weekly's* Bruce Frett wrote a column entitled "Unholy Mess" on December 1, 1999, in which he devised a new holy commandment, one dictating that Kevin Smith "shalt not" direct any more films.[11]

As is typical of the witty Scott Mosier, he had a pithy response to all the controversy and negative vibe surrounding *Dogma*. "People took it awfully seriously for a movie that had a rubber poop monster in it."

In this case, View Askew really did have the last laugh. Not only was the film highly regarded by America's mainstream critics, it generated more than $30 million at the box office, making it Kevin Smith's most profitable movie yet. It was also the third-highest grossing film the weekend of its release. Accordingly, Smith and Mosier re-upped with Miramax in an "expansive three year, first-look deal" covering film and TV projects.[12] In addition, Smith was awarded the "Defender of Democracy" award from the People for the American Way for his efforts to shepherd the controversial *Dogma* from page to stage, to theaters.

Thanks, Mr. Donohue.

MORALITY PLAY IN FOUR COLORS

When it was released theatrically in 1999, Dogma commenced with a disclaimer noting that it was not the filmmaker's intent "to offend." Ironically, Smith's disclaimer was highly amusing because it gently mocked disclaimers in general, noting they were designed to "save one's ass." That's the essence of Smith's self-deprecating comedy style and in many ways the perfect opening for Dogma. The disclaimer releases tensions, makes one laugh, and leaves one ready for the silliness—and intelligence—that follows.

Despite the Catholic League's protestations to the contrary, *Dogma* seems to be a highly pro-faith and moral film. In fact, it is a post-modern morality play, cloaking its overt didacticism in a slew of very funny fart and dick jokes.

More than five centuries ago, the morality play was a school of theater that in essence represented "dramatized sermons."[13] The common theme of the morality play was the war for control of the immortal human soul; the battle between good and evil, God and the Devil. Characters in morality plays often had names that expressed their vital traits, such as Gluttony, Sloth, Chastity, Virtue, Vice, et al.

It isn't a stretch to see how *Dogma* fits into this long-standing tradition. Bartleby and Loki, for instance, take great glee in turning humans to "the dark side," convincing a nun (Betty Aberlin) to leave behind her vows, and then punishing them for their infractions. In doing so, they endanger the human soul and chock up one more score for evil.

And look at the names of the characters in *Dogma*. Salma Hayek's muse is called Serendipity, and Bethany and friends run across her at a strip club by pure happenstance, only to learn important information about their quest from her. *Serendipity*, of course, is defined as the faculty of making valuable discoveries by accident. So in a very real sense, the role the character Serendipity plays in saving the world is dictated by her very name.

Loki, the angel played by Matt Damon in *Dogma*, also lives up to his name. In Norse Mythology, Loki is known as a terrible troublemaker, a mischief-maker, a trickster, who is ultimately punished by the gods for his behavior (an unsanctioned murder). In *Dogma*, Loki is the more playful of the two angels. As he torments the head of the Mooby board of directors, he presents him a voodoo doll and leads him to fear that it possesses supernatural powers. Of course, Loki is really deceiving him. "I don't believe in voodoo!" he laughs playfully.

On the bus journey to New Jersey, Loki takes great amusement in his entrapment of a young adulterer (Scott Mosier). He toys with him before killing him, thus sharing the same characteristics as the mythical Loki, and in fact, suffering his very fate: exile. Only here, *Dogma*'s Loki is punished for his unsanctioned decision not to commit murder. He once (a very long time ago) showed mercy, at the behest of Bartleby.

Metatron, played by Alan Rickman, represents the voice of God, a necessity in interactions with humanity because man's frail ears could not withstand the sound of the divine voice. *Meta* is a prefix that means "transformation or change" and *tron* is a Greek suffix denoting an instrument. Put those two together and you have an "instrument of transformation." Of course, that perfectly suits Rickman's character because he hears the word of God in one ear, and then must transform (or translate) it with his own instrument, his voice.

The other characters are similarly named to represent Christian symbols or characteristics. Bethany may be named after Mary of Bethany, a character in Luke (10:39) who listened to the teachings of Christ. It is

Bethany's job, in *Dogma*, to hear the will of God, and heed those teachings.

The Golgothan is named for a place, a terrible site where criminals died, and in the process voided their bowels. Thus the Golgothan is literally emblematic of his birthplace's primary characteristic: he is composed of shit.

Even Cardinal "Glick" seems to be a play on two words: *glib*, meaning "superficial" and *click*, meaning a sort of unpleasant, short sound. This fits his character because this is, after all, the man trying to dumb-down Catholicism to make it more "user-friendly." His words, though not merely clicks, are unpleasant sounds that have little significance.

Then of course there's Silent Bob. His name speaks for itself.

Perhaps more significantly, *Dogma* might be considered a modern morality play because its purpose is didactic. Kevin Smith's screenplay explains the importance of faith, decries how an idea can become first a belief, and then, ultimately, dogma. In the end, the film is pro-faith most simply because the characters that ultimately work against creation, and therefore against God, are punished for their trespasses. Bartleby commits the mortal sins of vanity and hubris. He can't conceive that God might prefer man to angel, and so is ready to betray God and un-write the universe in defiance of that preference. His punishment, like something out of David Cronenberg's *Scanners*, is an exploding head.

Another interesting facet of the film is the ambiguous climax. Do the murdered men and women at St. Michael's (including Cardinal Glick?) remain dead, or does God restore them to life when she "cleanses" the crime scene? And, what of Bartleby and Loki? What will be their "eternal" punishment for nearly destroying creation? By leaving those answers to the viewer's imagination, Kevin Smith is permitting a personal interpretation of *Dogma* (and again establishing that he prefers the realistic school to the formalist school of filmmaking). If audiences believe that God is a wrathful, punishing entity, they can believe the guilty are punished. Contrarily, if audience members believe in a loving and forgiving God, there is an opening for their view as well. Much of *Dogma* is similarly open-ended.

Despite some provocative and positive messages, *Dogma* remains a controversial work of art because Kevin Smith is not willing to equate "dogma" with "faith." He sees and describes an important difference. He believes one can have faith without necessarily believing in every edict handed down from the Vatican (or any organized religion).

In *Dogma*, for instance, a savior is found in an unusual place: an abortion clinic. Homosexuality is not a sin, yet the disowning of another human being is. The New Testament is "false" in that it ignores a black apostle, and hence it is bigoted too. And finally, the very act that saves all of creation is one that would make Jack Kevorkian and other advocates of euthanasia proud — pulling a terminal patient (John Doe Jersey) off of life support. Each of these issues — abortion, homosexuality, racism, and euthanasia — is a hot-button one for the Church, and by confronting them head-on, Smith seems to be expressing a critical point: Faith in God does not necessarily mean an unquestioning support of everything espoused by man's organization, the Church. God's laws and man's "dogma" are separate things.

It's probably also fair to state that Donohue and the Catholic League didn't appreciate Smith's attempts to make Jesus Christ an understandable, sympathetic and, yes, likeable figure on pure human terms. But that was Smith's bag, to make a film that "celebrated" faith and didn't treat it like a "funeral."[14] In the superhero mythos, the best and most popular figures are those who have some flaws, some connection to humanity. Batman has his anger, Peter Parker his angst, and so forth, and without these characteristics, the heroes would be boring — invincible drones with whom no one would identify. In *Dogma*, Smith discusses Jesus as if he is the ultimate superhero.

When Metatron speaks of the young Jesus Christ, who had to face his fate — to die on the cross for all mankind — it is strongly suggested that Jesus rebelled against the notion; that he had moments of self-pity and agonizing doubt. Sadly, that level of pure humanity flies in the face of a rigid dogma that wants people to consider Christ wholly divine, infallible, and nobler than the best in human nature. Of course, that interpretation leaves Jesus wholly unbelievable and unsympathetic. Smith takes the opposite approach, relating how Jesus was really the culmination of all man's best characteristics — graced with divinity — but still identifiable as a human being.

Smith's understanding of superhero mythos is ideally suited for this material, and *Dogma* succeeds because of this radical re-characterization of a religious "super" hero.

That Smith re-writes common Church beliefs with humorous new interpretations (a thirteenth apostle, a female God, and the idea that Hell is a place where *Mrs. Doubtfire* plays continuously) no doubt fails to win him new friends among the religious right. Religion is, for these folks, something to be treated only with righteous solemnity and reverence, and comedy's goal is always to make one laugh, to be irreverent. There is probably no religious comedy in the world that would satisfy the Catholic League, but that's okay. Comedy remains accessible; religion not necessarily so.

Dogma is also a great and funny adventure. In many senses, it is filmed like the most majestic comic book ever imagined, filled with colorful angels, monstrous demons, and an outrageous shit monster that could challenge the Incredible Hulk. This "comic book" interpretation of religious concepts fits in with Smith's earlier films and makes *Dogma* a more accessible film than it might have been, despite a screenplay that is, alas, more knowledgeable about Christianity than most viewers are.

Before this crazy ride is over, the audience is expected to have processed ideas such as Divine Mandate, Plenary Indulgence, Transubstantiation, Papal Sanction, and the Last Scion, a wordy chunk of material. For that reason, *Dogma*, already a good film, improves dramatically on repeated viewing. And, one has to admire the audacity of Smith's common-man, genre approach. His comic book background reduces difficult religious conceits to concepts no more arcane than the Fortress of Solitude or the Phantom Zone. It's clever and endearing, and grants an all-together new perspective on faith. If the Bible were a (Marvel) comic book, it might very well look and play like *Dogma*.

Yet it is the quieter moments in *Dogma* that speak most clearly of Smith's evolving sense of film style. The scene in which Metatron walks on water, approaching the despondent Bethany on the shore of a quiet lake by moonlight, is nothing less than wondrous. The location is perfect and idyllic, and the shot is beautifully composed. As the soundtrack reaches an emotional crescendo, the film rises to and honors its important subject matter. It may seem belittling to compare a quasi-Biblical scene of cosmic importance to a pop culture movie, but for me, this scene always evokes the grandeur of *Star Wars*, when a wistful Luke Skywalker awaits his calling under the setting suns of Tatooine.

Kudos also to Matt Damon. His character goes from angel of death to doubting Thomas with great skill. "I've heard a rant like this before," he reports in a stunning scene with Bartleby, and Damon finds exactly the right pitch for the material. Loki wants to return home to Heaven, but he understands that there are limits. That there is something greater than his own needs and that he and Bartleby can only go so far.

On the down side, Bethany is an interesting character, but it may be a mistake that she is never permitted to be funny. Linda Fiorentino is a fine actress, but her performance ranks as the least interesting of the "straight man" characters in the View Askewniverse. Like Jeremy London in *Mallrats*, she doesn't seem totally in tune with the cadences of Smith's dialogue, and often comes across as whiny or mopey.

By contrast, Brian O'Halloran and Ben Affleck have really mastered this style of "straight man" character, bringing a solid foundation of self-awareness and *joie de vivre* to their similar roles in *Clerks* and *Chasing Amy*. Granted, Bethany is facing remarkably tough stuff in *Dogma*, but the audience is not completely on her side; at least not in the way it identifies with Rufus, Jay or Silent Bob, or even, for that matter, Bartleby and Loki.

It may just be the so-called superhero syndrome. Being "special" (or super) may be a drag for a time, but wouldn't it also be really cool to be invisible, super-strong, or the savior of all humanity? Fiorentino's portrayal seems to have no joy in it, and that's a shame. Bethany, unlike Smith, seems to treat faith as a funeral.

Dogma is an ambitious, entertaining, and thought provoking movie, and many critics and audiences found it to be Kevin Smith's best motion picture yet. This author is firmly in that camp that prefers *Chasing Amy*, but it would be impossible not to appreciate and respect the audacious nature and beautiful execution of *Dogma*.

ASKEW VIEWS:

SACRED COW: One of the best sequences in *Dogma* involves Bartleby and Loki punishing idolaters who worship the golden calf named Mooby. The star of TV, film and other media, Mooby the Cow also sports a line of fast food restaurants (seen in *Jay & Silent Bob Strike Back*, as well) and a gaggle of merchandising to boot. Many viewers and reviewers assumed that Mooby symbolized Mickey Mouse, and by proxy, Disney. But that wasn't necessarily the intent, as Vincent Pereira explains.

"Mooby wasn't a jab at Disney per se, it was more a jab at corporate America. People speculated that it was about Disney, especially after everything that went down, but I don't believe that was Kevin's intention. He was just showing people how little kids are brainwashed by corporate America into buying things they don't really need."

PUT 'EM UP: In a complete departure from his role as Hooper, Dwight Ewell plays a violent gang leader named Kane in *Dogma*. One of the requirements of the role was a scene (eventually cut) that involved firearms.

"It was cool playing Kane, but I hate working with guns," Ewell reveals. "In that scene, they had policemen on the set and everything, standing all around you. As soon as you fire the weapon, you have to freeze in that position. After the takes are over, they rush in and get the gun out of your hands."

METHINKS THEY PROTEST TOO MUCH: Bryan Johnson's Steve-Dave and Walt Flanagan's Fanboy make their strangest appearance yet in *Dogma*, picketing at an abortion clinic in Illinois.

Johnson explains how that came about. "Realistically, where are you going to put Steve-Dave and Fanboy in *Dogma*? Maybe they were traveling together and were so full of piss and vinegar that they stopped at this abortion protest.

"It's funny, because if you notice, we're set apart in that scene. Everybody else is gathered together in support of one another, and we're just off by ourselves, having our own personal protest."

THE STRAIGHT POOP: Those listening closely to the monstrous Golgothan may recognize the tones of actor Ethan Suplee. "There was some computer enhancement of my voice," the actor says. But nonetheless, he regards the demon as his favorite character in the View Askewniverse. "There's just a special place in my heart for an excremental shit demon..."

A LONG TIME AGO IN A GALAXY FAR, FAR AWAY: The *Star Wars* references fly fast and thick in *Dogma*. One scene in a dinner featuring Jay, Silent Bob, and Bethany evokes the famous Mos Eisley cantina scene from George Lucas's space opera. Another cut sequence sees Matt Damon's character Loki pontificating (with hilarious results) about the religious significance of such Lucas characters as IG-88 and the Ewoks.

NO TIME FOR LOVE, DR. JONES: Other than *Jaws* and *Star Wars*, the *Indiana Jones* films are those most referenced in the cinema of Kevin Smith. In *Clerks*, Randal quoted *Temple of Doom*'s sidekick, Short Round. In *Dogma*, Silent Bob throws Bartleby off the moving train and then deadpans "No ticket." This is the same line Indiana Jones spouted in *The Last Crusade*, when throwing a Nazi officer from an in-flight dirigible.

In the *Clerks* cartoon, the fifth episode re-stages the *Temple of Doom*, making Randal slave to an Egyptian, quasi-Thuggee cult until rescued by Dante and his little league team.

HE'LL TAKE YOU FOR A RIDE: Keen eyes will notice that the bus line in *Dogma* is named Derris, after that chick-magnet from *Clerks* and *Chasing Amy*, Rick Derris.

A VERY VIEW ASKEW WEDDING: Kevin Smith & Jennifer Schwalbach tied the knot while *Dogma* was being mixed at the Skywalker Ranch and

Schwalbach was eight months pregnant.

"I'm not a very traditional person," Schwalbach notes, "and wasn't very concerned with the details. We'd been up to Skywalker so many times during *Dogma*, and the last time we were up there it was so beautiful and breathtaking. We were there with Mosier and his then-girlfriend Monica. And we said, 'Let's do it,' and put it together in a day. It was exactly what we wanted and from what I understand, we were the second couple ever to be married there.

"Kevin and I had a special moment that I hope everyone who gets married goes through. We had thrown our lives together, we were having a child, and we didn't think we could become any closer. It was more than I ever expected or hoped for, and he feels the same. We just love being married."

KEVIN SMITH ON DOGMA: "...It was just kind of an offering up of what I consider myself to be, a contemporary Catholic. I'm Catholic, I go to church, but I'm not one of these people who condemn others for not believing in the same thing I do. So isn't it possible to be a guy who makes a movie chock-a-block full of dick and fart jokes and still have faith in God?"[15]

NOTES

1. Michael Atkinson, "Kevin Smith Stirs It Up," *Interview*, October 1999, p. 180.

2. Dave Kehr, "Deflator of the Faith? Director Begs to Differ," *The New York Times*, August 1, 1999, pp. 7, 12.

3. Jessica Shaw, "A Hollywood Dogfight," *Entertainment Weekly*, April 23, 1999, p. 9.

4. Bernard Weinraub, "Disney and Miramax Collide Over Church Issues in New Film," *The New York Times*, April 8, 1999, p. C4.

5. *"Touched by an Angel* objects to *Dogma's* ad Campaign," *CBC Radio Arts, Iculture*, November 18, 1999, p. 1
    http://www.infoculture.cbc.ca.archives.filmtv/filmtv/11171999_angelsbattle.phtml.

6. John Brodie, *Gentleman's Quarterly*, November 1999, p. 208.

7. Richard A. Blake, "Fallen Angels," *America*, December 4, 1999, p. 20.

8. Douglas Le Blanc, "Dogmatically Anti-dogma," *Christianity Today*, January 10, 2000, p. 80.

9. Jeff Giles, "Knocking on Heaven's Door," *Newsweek*, November 15, 1999, p. 88.

10. Karl Stevens, "Old Dogma," *Christian Century*, December 15, 1999. v116, p. 1235.

11. Bruce Frett, "Unholy Mess," *Entertainment Weekly*, December 1, 1999, p. 1.

12. Oliver Jones, "Dogma duo re-ups 3 years at Miramax (continuation of Miramax contracts for producer and director Scott Mosier and Kevin Smith)," *Variety*, November 22, 1999, v377, p. 17.

13. Albert Wertheim, "Morality Play," *World Book Online, Americas Edition*, March 1, 2002, http://www.aolsvce.worldbook.aol.com/wbol/wPage/na/ar/co/37070

14. "Kevin Smith: Stirring Up *Dogma*." *CBC Radio Arts, Iculture*, November 19, 1999, p. 1, http://www.infoculture.cbc.ca/archives/filmtv/filmtv_11181999_kevinsmith.phtm.

15. Cliff Stephenson, "Chasing Kevin: An Interview with Kevin Smith," *DVDFile.com*, May 1, 2000, http://www.dvdfile.com/new/special_report/interviews.

Jay & Silent Bob Strike Back (2001)

A JAY & SILENT BOB MOVIE?
WHO WOULD PAY TO SEE THAT?

Hollywood had it coming.

CAST & CREW

DIMENSION FILMS PRESENTS A VIEW ASKEW PRODUCTION,
JAY & SILENT BOB STRIKE BACK

WRITTEN AND DIRECTED BY: Kevin Smith
PRODUCED BY: Scott Mosier
CO-PRODUCER: Laura Greenlee
EXECUTIVE PRODUCERS: Bob Weinstein, Harvey Weinstein, and Jonathan Gordon
CINEMATOGRAPHY BY: Jamie Anderson
EDITED BY: Scott Mosier and Kevin Smith
PRODUCTION DESIGNER : Robert "Ratface" Holtzman
COSTUME DESIGNER : Isis Mussenden
VISUAL EFFECTS SUPERVISOR : Joseph Grossberg
SPECIAL MAKE-UP AND CREATURE EFFECTS : Vincent Guastini Productions
MUSIC: James L. Venable
CASTING: Christine Sheaks
M.P.A.A. RATING: R
RUNNING TIME: 103 minutes

STARRING:

Jason Mewes | *Jay*	Amy Noble | *Baby Bob's Mother*
Kevin Smith | *Silent Bob*	Harley Quinn Smith | *Baby Silent Bob*
Ben Affleck | *Holden McNeil/Himself*	Ever Carradine | *Baby Jay's Mother*
Jeff Anderson | *Randal*	Brian Andrew Saible | *Baby Jay*
Brian Christopher O'Halloran | *Dante*	Gavin Brooks | *Baby Jay Voice*
Shannon Elizabeth | *Justice*	John Willyung | *Passerby*
Eliza Dushku | *Sissy*	Jake Richardson | *Teen #1*
Ali Larter | *Chrissy*	Nick Fellinger | *Teen #2*
Jennifer Schwalbach | *Missy*	Vincent Pereira | *Customer*
Will Ferrell | *Marshal Willenholly*	Ernest O'Donnell | *Cop*
Jason Lee | *Bruce Brodie/Banky Edwards*	Marc Blucas | *Guy*
Judd Nelson | *Sheriff*	Matthew James | *Dude*
George Carlin | *Hitchhiker*	Jane Silvia | *Bookish Girl*
Carrie Fisher | *Nun*	Carmen Lee | *Redhead Beauty*
Seann William Scott | *Brent*	Dan Etheridge | *Deputy*
Jon Stewart | *Reg Hartner*	Diedrich Bader | *Security Guard*
Jules Asner | *Herself*	Scott Mosier | *AP; Willam the Idiot-Man-Child*
Steve Kmetko | *Himself*	Jason Biggs | *Himself*
Tracy Morgan | *Drug Dealer*	James Van Der Beek | *Himself*
Gus Van Sant | *Himself*	Bryan Johnson | *Steve-Dave*
Chris Rock | *Chaka*	Walter Flanagan | *Fanboy*
Jamie Kennedy | *P.A.*	Renée Humphrey | *Trish*
Wes Craven | *Himself*	Joey Lauren Adams | *Alyssa*
Shannen Doherty | *Herself*	Dwight Ewell | *Hooper*
Mark Hamill | *Himself/Cocknocker*	Alanis Morrissette | *That Woman*

THE STORY SO FAR...

RANDAL GETS JAY & SILENT BOB ARRESTED

for peddling pot outside the Quick Stop, and the two stoners complain about their situation to Bruce Brodie, who is now running a comic book store in Red Bank. He informs them that a movie is being made by Miramax, one based on Holden McNeil and Banky Edwards's old cult comic book, *Bluntman & Chronic*. Jay and Silent Bob know nothing about the deal, and haven't been paid for their likeness rights.

The stoners visit Holden McNeil, who tells them about the Internet and a site called *Movie Poop Shoot.com*, where nerds are blasting Jay and Silent Bob and the *Bluntman & Chronic* project. Jay and Silent Bob are angered about the rap against their good names, and decide the only way to stop the online bitching is a pilgrimage to Hollywood to shut down the movie.

Jay and Silent Bob hitchhike cross-country, and after a few harrowing adventures with a hitchhiker, a nun, and the cast of *Scooby Doo*, stop at a Mooby restaurant to eat breakfast. There they meet Justice, a beautiful girl who claims to be from S.A.A.C. (Students Against Animal Cruelty). She and three friends, Sissy, Missy, and Chrissy, are on their way to a pharmaceutical company in Boulder to free animals from captivity. But that's just a cover. Justice is actually part of a gang of jewel thieves who plan to use the Garden State stoners as patsies.

Before long, Jay and Silent Bob have stolen an orangutan named Susanne, had numerous run-ins with the law (and a Federal Wildlife Marshal, Willenholly), and disrupted the Miramax Studio lot. Masquerading as Bluntman and Chronic, Jay and Silent Bob finally catch up with Banky Edwards, even as Willenholly and the jewel thieves close in on them.

SILENT BOB'S WORDS OF WISDOM:

"As we are not only the artistic basis, but also obviously the character basis for your intellectual property, *Bluntman & Chronic*, when said property was optioned by Miramax films, you were legally obliged to secure our permission to transfer the product to another medium."

THE STORY BEHIND THE MOVIE:

In the dog days of August 2001, the last film of Kevin Smith and View Askew's "New Jersey Chronicles" appeared on the screens across America and took the weekend box office by storm. Replete with a gaggle of celebrity cameos and a laugh-a-minute pace, *Jay & Silent Bob Strike Back* was essentially a big budget ($20 million) party, a celebration of all things Jay and Silent Bob. Featuring state-of-the-art CGI special effects and satirical looks at movies such as *Scream, Good Will Hunting, E.T.*, and *Planet of the Apes, Jay & Silent Bob Strike Back* brought the five-strong film franchise to a close with hilarious style.

"After *Dogma*, and how stressful it had been, we thought we were safe with *Jay & Silent Bob Strike Back*," reports Jennifer Schwalbach. "Kevin needed to make a movie like *Jay & Silent Bob* that was very funny and irreverent and light-hearted and ridiculous."

"I thought the script was hysterical," adds Brian O'Halloran. "A road trip with scenes from *Scooby Doo* and *Planet of the Apes* was great. You could tell that it was a movie made for the fans, and yet it could still stand up on its own."

And stand it did. *Jay & Silent Bob Strike Back* won the weekend box office sweepstakes (a first in View Askew history), raking in over $11 million. It also poked wicked fun at a current phenomenon in contemporary

America: fan boy posters on the Internet.

Alas, it's a fact of life in the 21st century. Movie fans of all ages now flock to message boards and chat rooms to bash films, albums, TV series, and books. These attacks are often misspelled, inappropriately capitalized, poorly worded, and launched behind the all-protective veil of anonymity. People can say anything on the net, with no consequences or accountability, and unfortunately some people have exploited the freedom the technology offers merely to vent personal frustrations.

For artists working in this environment, the negative, persistent, and often thoughtless assaults are hugely frustrating. And, yes, Kevin Smith has been the target of some of the crap (to wit: the *Magnolia* flap). So, to the delight of many, *Jay & Silent Bob Strike Back* seems tailor-made to skewer those "militant" movie fans who hide behind jocular handles and lob attacks at filmmakers. To its credit, the film does so in the funniest manner imaginable. Specifically, Smith reveals these accomplished "critics" to be twelve year-old boys; or better yet, people with the mentality of twelve year-old boys.

"The Internet is a great communications tool," explains Vincent Pereira, "but everybody suddenly thinks they can be a film critic. And their idea of criticism is to come up with the best one liner as they bash something. There are a lot of personal attacks, and for some people, it's become a tool to let out their pent-up frustration. The anonymous attacks are hard to deal with."

Kevin Smith seems to be of two minds when it comes to the net. He has lauded it as being a "valuable" tool to build and communicate with his audience,[1] and is known to be a rabid surfer of the web. But at the same time, one senses he is not particularly pleased that some users of the Internet have resorted to irresponsible, inaccurate attacks:

> When people say negative things about me on the
> Internet, I kind of lose my cool and basically hire P.I.'s
> to track these people down, because they always hide
> behind anonymous names.[2]

Accordingly, it is one such attack on the good name of Jay and Silent Bob at the web-site *Movie Poop Shoot.com*—a dead-on parody of Harry Knowles's popular, controversial and ground-breaking *Ain' t it Cool News* movie site and its "talk backers"—that precipitates the wild events of Smith's latest film.

This "hook" then introduces a series of cameo performances from the likes of Carrie Fisher, George Carlin, Marc Blucas, Tracy Morgan, Deidrich Bader, Matt Damon, Gus Van Sant, Shannen Doherty, James Van Der Beek, Jason Biggs, Jon Stewart, Seann William Scott, Chris Rock, Jamie Kennedy, and Mark Hamill.

Playing the supporting roles in *Jay & Silent Bob Strike Back* are *American Pie*'s Shannon Elizabeth, Ali Larter (of *Varsity Blues* and *Final Destination*), *Buffy the Vampire Slayer*'s rogue slayer, Eliza Dushku, and *Saturday Night Live's* comedic powerhouse, Will Ferrell. In the ultimate in-joke and reference to 1970s television, Ferrell is named Marshal Willenholly — a tribute to the three leads in Sid and Marty Krofft's *Land of the Lost*: Marshal, Will, and Holly. Another *Land of the Lost* reference: Chris Rock's character is named "Chaka" — the handle of the Pakuni ape boy from that '70s Saturday morning classic.

Before Jay and Silent Bob have finished their wacky odyssey across America, Miramax, Hollywood, and even films adapted from comic books are thoroughly roasted. On that last count, Hollywood's inability to produce a "faithful" film from a comic book is noted with specific references to *Batman & Robin*.

"I think Hollywood tries to make films for everybody," notes Walt Flanagan of the superhero movie quandary, "and when you try to make things for a wide audience, you take a risk of watering them down; changing the aspects that appeal to certain people in the first place. If you're really in love with a character and want to do the movie, I don't understand why Hollywood wants to change it."

On hand for the less-than-successful premiere of the fictional *Bluntman & Chronic* movie are the many stars of Smith films past. Dwight Ewell returns as Hooper, Joey Lauren Adams is back as Alyssa, Renee Humphreys re-appears as Trish the Dish, and Scott Mosier re-creates the role of Willam "Snowball" Black. And, of course, Bryan Johnson and Walt Flanagan make a triumphant re-appearance as the forever-discontented Steve-Dave and Fanboy. Star Ben Affleck also returns to the fold playing Holden and himself, and fan favorite Jason Lee performs double duty as Banky and Brodie.

One of the few familiar faces missing from this grand bash is actor Ethan Suplee. "I was working and couldn't get out of what I was doing," Suplee notes with disappointment. "I was working on a movie called *The First 20 Million is the Always the Hardest.*"

Despite Suplee's absence, shooting the film proved to be something of a class reunion for many View Askew stars. For Brian O'Halloran and Jeff Anderson, the stars of *Clerks*, it was a chance to play Dante and Randal again, and to return to the Quick Stop — the setting where the whole adventure began, after more than eight years earlier.

"Returning to the Quick Stop to shoot was a lot of fun," O'Halloran reminisces. "It was strange though. This time we had tractor-trailers of equipment, dressing rooms, and people taking your costume. It wasn't just five of us in the store going, 'Ready? Yeah, let me finish my Gatorade.' It was a little overwhelming."

"They could have literally built that store on a soundstage in L.A.," O'Halloran acknowledges. "But I'm so glad Kevin went back to Jersey. It was nice coming back and doing scenes in the store. It was like coming home."

For Jeff Anderson, it was a little disconcerting to return to the familiar setting, but with so many changes. "Good Lord, it was a different scene! I'd missed my plane the day before, so I had to take a red-eye. I flew in, and had to film that morning, so I asked the driver to take me to the store so I could see what time I needed to come back.

"We pulled into the U-turn and I saw police cars blocking the street, and there were groups of people standing there, and trucks and trailers. And I thought, 'This is definitely different.' I came back to shoot around ten in the morning and the crowd was three times larger. It was maybe 200 feet from my trailer to the actual store, and I was just signing autographs the whole way, and people were snapping pictures.

"I even remember that at one point in the convenience store, between set-ups, I counted 60 people crammed inside. I turned to Brian and said, 'Do you remember doing *Clerks* when we actually had to clap the scene and throw the clapper on the floor because we had no available hands to clap?' Now the store was packed with people, and I didn't know what half of their jobs were."

But if shooting *Jay & Silent Bob Strike Back* was a reunion for some, it was a new ball game for others, specifically Jennifer Schwalbach, who was cast in the film as sexy "tech girl" and jewel thief, Missy.

"I had never acted in my life," she reveals. "I had never even taken an acting class. But I thought, 'If Bryan Johnson and Walt Flanagan can act, I can too.' At the time, I knew that Kevin would be on the set all day, and wanted to be included in some way so I could see him. I wanted to be in the movie and Kevin asked me if I could handle it. I said, 'Of course I can!' Bryan, Walt, and Mosier — they all just jump in there, and I don't see them in acting classes. So I wanted to be one of the girls. I picked Missy, Kevin was happy, and Miramax was supportive."

But, Schwalbach admits, some folks were a teensy bit worried there would be trouble with a director's wife on the set of a major film production every day. "I tend to be a little sassy, and I'm constantly getting into trouble telling somebody off," Schwalbach says. "The Miramax people were terrified I'd go on the set and that Kevin and I would fight when he tried to tell me what to do. But that couldn't have been further from the truth. I didn't know what I was doing. I didn't even know camera right. So I didn't give him any guff at all, and I think everyone was completely shocked and thankful for that. I went in terrified, and was so grateful for any direction or rehearsal time Kevin gave me."

Jennifer also found support from her co-stars, Eliza Dushku and Ali Larter. "The other girls were so amazing, and that's not a line of shit. They were incredible."

Which might not have been the case. "Kevin gave me this whole speech going in. 'The other girls may not like you and might be really mean to you because you're my wife and because you're not an actress. You know, who does this chick think she is, the director's wife?' So I went in terrified.

"But I started spending time with Ali and Eliza, and we immediately hit it off. We threw back a couple of beers, tossed a football around the parking lot and had an instant bond. If it hadn't been that way, it would have been a terrible experience, because I spent so much time with them. We would work all day together, and then go out at night. And they'd play with Harley. Eliza taught Harley how to do her first high-five."

Jennifer also remembers the shooting of *Jay & Silent Bob Strike Back* as being something akin to a revolving door, because so many performers dropped in for a day or two, finished their parts, then left. "There was a new actor on the set every day: Ben and Matt, and Jason Biggs and James Van Der Beek, and so on. So Kevin had no time to coddle me through my performance. 'Get your clothes on and get your ass out there and do it!' I was at the bottom of the totem pole. My close-ups were shot last; everything for me was shot last. I didn't get any special treatment at all because I was his wife."

But, at least for Scott Mosier, the scheduling of *Jay & Silent Bob Strike Back*'s large celebrity cast was not as much of a stumbling block as scheduling *Dogma*. "It was not hard, because we shot in Los Angeles," he relates. "Everyone lives there, so it was easy to deal with the cast. There's much more freedom surrounding L.A., than say, Pittsburgh, because there you had fly actors in and fly them out. You'd lose days here and there."

For Jason Mewes, who now resides in L.A., shooting the film there was a great experience. "It was nice to work every day. When I'm out-of-town shooting other movies, I don't have anything to do because I don't know everybody. So usually I'd sit in a motel and not do much, but this was cool. I loved watching the other actors. Will Ferrell was so much fun. It was great to work with him, but it was also great to just sit back and watch him work too."

While shooting *Clerks*, way back in 1993, Kevin Smith and his crew had dealt with a wily cat who escaped the Quick Stop, but on *Jay & Silent Bob Strike Back*, they not only worked with animals, but children too. Unfortunately, in this case, it was his own child, Harley Quinn Smith, who proved the most difficult to direct.

"It was a complete nightmare," Schwalbach remembers of the scene in which Harley was tapped to portray a young Silent Bob in front of the Quick Stop. "I wanted her to play that part, for obvious reasons. It was a once-in-a-lifetime opportunity for her to play her father, and I thought it would be wonderful to have that on film for the rest of her life. So I insisted that there be no back-up baby actors.

"So there we were in New Jersey, and it was early in the morning; it was freezing cold and it was raining. And Harley is a bit like me: she wanted to do her own thing. She didn't want to sit in the stroller, she wanted to talk, and we kept telling her to stop. After months of us begging her to talk, she's chattering away, but has to play a silent character. So she's yammering away, and wouldn't wear the hat.

"It was so frustrating, but Kevin and I learned a good lesson about parenting that day. We had not only the entire crew, but all of these onlookers, his fans, who came out to watch. And we tried to keep our cool as parents in front of this huge crowd. She wasn't even two. But it was raining, and was probably about 35 degrees out. And it was 6:00 in the morning. And it just took hours. At one point, they were even considering switching kids and having Harley play Jay. She would not shut up! But I really wanted her to play her father, so they finally got it together, and it was a genius bit of editing that did it. If you watch closely, you'll see that Harley is holding a bagel in one hand during part of it, and then not in another. They had so few seconds where she was behaving that they just left the bagel in. They had no choice during editing!"

One of the main characters in *Jay & Silent Bob Strike Back* is an orangutan named Susanne. For Jason Mewes, it was both fun and difficult working with the simian. "That ape was cool! It was neat to watch how she interacts with people. But it also sucked because we weren't allowed to play with her or mess with her. Her trainer said that when you mess with an ape that's trained, you confuse them. They have to work with you, so you're like a prop to them. If you start messing with them, all they want to do is play, and they won't act.

"So we had to do a scene with her and they had to take her away. Every once in a while, Kevin and I would forget the rule and start messing with her. Then we'd remember to watch it. But we'd slap her hands and she'd slap you back."

In the film, Jay imagines a *Planet of the Apes*-style scenario in which Randal is hunted by gorilla soldiers, and Dante undergoes experimental brain surgery at the hands (and scalpels) of two chimps. For Brian O'Halloran—who wore a head appliance featuring an exposed brain in that scene—it proved to be a bit harrowing to shoot.

"I had to get up really early to be in make-up for two-to-three hours putting on that brain skull," O'Halloran sets the scene. "It was amazing how they were able to match my hair color and make it look so real. So anyway, I came to the set with my exposed brain and there were a lot of *Hannibal* jokes, because the movie had come out not long before.

"So I approached the trainer and asked if I could meet the chimps, because I was nervous about working with live animals. In fact, it wasn't until that morning I knew there would even be live chimps. I thought it would be guys in costumes like in *Planet of the Apes*, like Zira and Cornelius, poking at me. Jeff had taped his scenes a week earlier and told me about these stunt men in *Planet of the Apes* costumes so I just assumed that's how it would be with me."

It wasn't.

Instead, O'Halloran was to work with a brother and sister team of chimpanzees. "They had been training these chimps with a plastic brain, teaching them to touch it. And they did really well, so when they saw me with my exposed brain, they immediately wanted to touch it. So I went up to Jonah [the male] and they put him in my arms. He was really heavy; I mean he was solid muscle, like a small adult. Then I went over to his sister to say hello and Jonah got really jealous that I'd put him down, and started jumping up and down on a cabinet."

Jonah's temper tantrum got O'Halloran thinking, and made him a little nervous. "They were supposed to have surgical implements in their hands, and I was going to be tied down on the autopsy table. The trainer told me he'd be just out of camera if anything went wrong during the scene, but that didn't really help. If something went wrong, he'd be too far away. But the make-up guy who was watching my brain told me that if anything happened, he'd get me out. I told him just to cover my face, because I didn't have my hands free to cover my eyes in case they wanted to poke them.

"So we're ready to go for picture and they roll action and tell me to scream. So I scream, and it freaks out the apes. They won't touch my brain. At one point, as I'm screaming, Jonah puts his hands over my mouth. But they just won't touch my brain. So they tell me not to scream, and I just pretend—mouthing the scream—and the chimps still won't go near the brain.

"By now we're all starting to get nervous that these chimps are freezing up. And I wonder if there's anything they might like instead of the slime on my brain. And I ask if there's honey on the set, and they bring it over from craft services. So they pour honey on my brain, because apes like honey.

"On the next take, Jonah really starts going for the brain. The sister didn't want anything to do with it, but then they started poking me with their fingers. At one point, Jonah leans in and licks my head."

The *Planet of the Apes* parody also proved interesting for Jeff Anderson. "It was their first day of shooting, I think, for *Jay & Silent Bob Strike Back*, and we went out to some field in California, and it was early in the morning, and it was cold. I was in my trailer eating breakfast and they bring me my hockey shirt, all ripped and torn. Then they take me out to this field, and I remember I'm standing there and here come the *Planet of the Apes* characters on horsebacks, and they have mechanical [animatronic] faces that move.

"So they line me up with a dozen or so slave people. And Kevin gives the direction: 'Let the slaves go first, and then Jeff, you run up from behind, pass them, and run through this field.' The field was pretty much cropped and cut down, so we all line up, Kevin calls action, and the slaves start running. But they stop after about five feet into the field.

"I started running into the bushes, and I'm wondering why these guys stopped. So I keep running and suddenly I'm in these sticker bushes. But these poor slaves are only wearing loin clothes, and they're impaled on these branches. And here I am, still in my old *Clerks* mentality, thinking 'Don't waste film! It hurts like hell, but keep running!' I actually ran out of one of my sneakers, and these bushes were just chewing up my feet. When I stopped, they yelled cut, and everybody was wondering what was up with the slave people—and they were breaking out in hives already."

Then came the rub. "I walk out of the bushes and there's this guy dressed like me. He was my stunt double! And I think, 'Now you tell me?' I've been jumping into the pricker bushes, I'm all cut up, and I have a stunt double sitting and watching this on the monitor?"

Another film referenced none-too-subtly by *Jay & Silent Bob Strike Back* is one of Kevin Smith's all-time favorites: *Star Wars*. In fact, Carrie Fisher (Princess Leia), and Mark Hamill (Luke Skywalker) appear in the film, and Smith even gets to indulge in a light-saber-style duel. As Hamill told *USA Today:*

> As we were filming the movie, and I'm in this outfit, I said 'Kevin, this is your big, giant play set — and I'm your action figure…Kevin had gone from playing the ersatz toy versions of *Star Wars* characters in New Jersey to a big Hollywood set. Now he was playing… on the grand scale.[3]

As for working with Carrie Fisher, Smith had this pithy remark: "Won't say the words Star and Wars in the same sentence. Not in the same paragraph — even if they're separated by 98 words."[4]

For the climactic battle between Jay (as Chronic) and Mark Hamill (as Cocknocker), *Jay & Silent Bob Strike Back* featured a dramatic bong-saber duel, like something out of *Star Wars* and *The Matrix* combined. Jason Mewes, for one, was thrilled at one more opportunity to perform stunts.

"For that flip where Jay says, 'Call me Darth Balls!', they put me in harness with cables, and were trying to teach he how to flip," he explains. "That was fun, but really tough. I thought it would be easier than it was. We did it a few times, and I got it, but not that good. It just didn't pan out."

Another scene that didn't quite pan out was the parody of cartoon favorite *Scooby Doo*. According to f/x guru Vincent Guastini, the scene in the original script was far different, and much more outrageous than what eventually appeared. "*Dogma* had the angel wings, and that was the effect everybody would talk about," Guastini recollects, "and when I read *Jay & Silent Bob Strike Back*, I felt that the *Scooby Doo* scene would be the show stopper, so it was my main concentration.

"The scene was that Jay gets high and hits the dog's dick with a bong. The dog gets a hard-on and basically attacks Jay. Jay and Silent Bob try to get away from it by hiding in a van, and the dog hops on the windshield and starts humping the window. The dog's eyes go crazy and it blows its load all over the windshield, and the dog flies off while they're driving. It was the most hysterical scene in the whole film, as far as I was concerned."

To make it happen, the artist built an elaborate, animatronic dog for the sequence. "I made the dog's tongue come out and touch its nose; I made the eyes bulge. It had every single movement that a real dog would have, plus five more on top of that. It was so highly-detailed that the testicles on the dog actually swelled, the shaft swelled, and the dog could blow its load.

"So I kept asking, 'Are you guys sure this is going to make it into the movie?' Then, the day before we were going to shoot the thing, I'm hearing about lawyers getting nervous about the *Scooby Doo* image and licensing. So, in one weekend, they were going to make a decision. By Monday, the dog would either be in or out.

"Well, Monday came and the word arrived: the dog was out. I'll be honest, I cried. I cried like a big baby. That's how personally I take my work. Kevin and Scott saw me on the set and hugged me and told me they were really sorry."

And, to this day, Guastini is convinced the movie would have been funnier with the original Scooby-attack. "As great and funny as the movie was, I thought the Scooby scene needed that."

Legal issues were also a concern for Guastini while creating the gorilla soldiers for the *Planet of the Apes* satire. "I was in something of a quandary, because Miramax was a little worried, and I believe I was hearing through them that 20th Century Fox wanted to make sure that I didn't come too close to what Rick Baker was doing on the *Planet of the Apes* remake. But they also didn't want me to get too close to the old movies, so I had to come in somewhere in between.

"My main inspiration was *Planet of the Apes 2* [from the art book *Millennium*], which had very 'heavy metal'-style apes [rendered by artist Luis Roya]. I wanted to go heavy metal, and the main gorilla in the film is actually animatronic, with moving eyebrows, but it went by so quickly that you didn't get to see it that much. It wasn't about the effects on *Jay & Silent Bob Strike Back*, it was about getting the point across quickly in funny little gags."

That said, the ape hunt was no picnic. "It's one thing to have a stuntman in a hot mask in the California sun, out in field, it's another to have animatronics and servos on top of that. The gorilla had a battery pack on too. And then you had to coordinate with a horse galloping across a field. It has to stop on cue, on a dime, the camera has to zoom in, the gorilla has to make an expression, then take a shot with a rifle. It was a really difficult thing to coordinate, but we just went for it. I could have just put a rubber mask on the rider, but that's not me. It's too easy. That's what I'm always killing my crew on: giving more than what's asked for."

Other Guastini effects in *Jay & Silent Bob Strike Back* included an orangutan "suit" to double for little Susanne. An eight year-old boy (son of another stuntman) wore the suit in some sequences, such as *The Fugitive* riff at the dam.

At other points, a foam body was sewed into the suit for more dangerous stunts, such as the *E.T.*-style bicycle flight on the Miramax lot (past a sign that reads "Ben Affleck **IS** the Moonraper").

Guastini's firm also designed Cocknocker's oversized, maniacal fist (laden with acrylic nails), Dante's exposed brain, and Sean William Scott's rather unattractive braces.

By all accounts, shooting the effects-laden *Jay & Silent Bob Strike Back* was nothing less than a hoot. "Everybody who worked on that movie was crying when it was over, saying it was the best experience they'd ever had," Schwalbach reports with pride. "We had barbecues at our house, and we'd invite the entire crew over, and they'd say, 'My God, the director never has the crew to his house!' But everybody walked away from that movie having a wonderful experience, and we benefited completely. Our daughter got to be on the set everyday, and Eliza Dushku played with her, and trainers would let her play with the monkeys, and all kinds of stuff."

According to Schwalbach, the experience of being in a Kevin Smith movie also increased her respect for her husband. "I had never really been a part of something Kevin had worked on. I visited the setsof *Dogma,* or when he was doing a commercial, but never really paid that much attention. But having been in the movie was a really wonderful thing for our marriage, because I understood why he couldn't come home for lunch. I understood why he was working twelve hours a day.

"I got it before, but now I really got to see with my own two eyes the experience that Kevin has making a movie, the incredible pressure that he has on his shoulders: writing it, directing it, acting in it, and having to deal with the problems and joys of everyone on his set. I really admired him for being able to handle it so gracefully. There's always a line of 45 people wanting to ask him a question or two. It was really a very healthy thing for me to have been a part of that."

In all, it was a joyous send-off for that stoner duo, Jay and Silent Bob. And make no mistake, that's what it was; a send-off. "I think this is it. I'd rather get out while the getting's good,"[5] Kevin Smith noted in an interview for *Hollywood.com*. Later, he admitted he'd miss the duo, but really had no choice except to leave them behind:

> If I had any balls whatsoever, I'd make nothing but Jay
> and Silent Bob flicks for the rest of my life. However,
> being a critical whore, I've gotta move on and "grow"
> beyond those characters. But no matter what I wind
> up making in the future, a part of me will always yearn
> to make another flick with Jay and Silent Bob.[6]

Released by New Dimension, Miramax's sister "genre" arm, *Jay &
Silent Bob Strike Back*, the stoner swan song, screamed into theaters on
the weekend of August 28, 2001, facing off against the work of other cult
directors including Woody Allen (*Curse of the Jade Scorpion*) and John
Carpenter (*Ghosts of Mars*). But, for a film that was supposed to be fun and
games, it ended up stirring perhaps the strangest controversy of Kevin
Smith's career. Even before the film was released, there was another protest
not unlike the one that had dogged *Dogma*.

Specifically, Scott Seomin, the media director for the Gay and Lesbian
Alliance Against Defamation (GLAAD), complained that *Jay & Silent Bob
Strike Back* was a film that was hostile and derogatory to the gay commu-
nity. "I've never seen something so horrific,"[7] he reported in one periodical.

In a letter addressed to Kevin Smith, dated July 26, 2001, Scott
Seomin went further. He wrote:

> We were overwhelmed by the potential negative
> impact for the film with what we would assume is a
> large share of its target audience: teen and young
> adult males. We will be public and aggressive in our
> condemnation and will provide substantiation for our
> opinions.[8]

Seomin's comments were picked up all throughout the media, and
before long, a Kevin Smith film was again at the center of a publicity firestorm.

"It's getting to the point in this country you can't make a joke," Smith
fired back to *The Washington Post*. "You're always offending somebody."[9]

But Seomin and GLAAD were firm in pursuing their belief that the
Smith film portrayed gays in a bad light. They believed the film's humor
came at the expense of a stereotyped people, that it promoted the ridicule
of gay men, that it offered new defamatory vocabulary to use against gay
men, and that the movie substituted the word "gay" for things seen as
stupid or wrong.[10]

Feeling that the movie could not adequately address the concerns
of GLAAD, Scott Seomin and the group instead requested a $10,000 check
from Smith, to be donated to the Matthew Shepherd Foundation.

"Kevin and I are the most gay-friendly family that could exist,"
Jennifer Schwalbach says. "We have so many gay people in our lives, and
we're so thankful for them. It was so shocking and offensive to us that we
had Scott Seomin, the head of GLAAD, and the person who started this
whole shit storm, come over to talk to us about it. I needed to confront

him, I was so offended. With the Catholic protest, I wasn't affected by it because religion isn't a part of who I am, but this really hit me. My family has a lot of gay people in it, and I was outraged. I insisted Malcom film the entire thing, because it was a scam job. It was extortion. We gave them $10,000 dollars out of our pocket. We would have gladly done so in a more natural setting, but this was like, 'We're going to twist your arm for cash.' And he [Seomin] came in, and I had to tell him how I felt, and it was really emotional, and he didn't do anything or say anything to make me feel any better about it. But at least I got to vent. I'd been venting to Kevin, who was equally outraged.

"It was pointing the finger at the wrong person. As a woman, I have to be able to laugh at myself; at the jokes that people make about women, and if they're not mean-spirited, go along with it. Because if you can't laugh at yourself, you'll probably have a mighty sad existence. And I think that was the case here. It was too bad. It was mean-spirited."

Vincent Pereira also believed that the wrong target had been selected by GLAAD. "Kevin is not a gay basher. You can see it in *Dogma*. One of the greatest and most subtle moments happens during the Mooby scene. Bartleby is going through the offenses of the various executives on the Mooby board. And the one offense that damns this executive is that he disowned his gay son. An angel sees that act as an unpardonable offense. You can't get any more pro-gay than that."

On the other hand, Vincent Pereira does believe that there are some people who don't understand Smith's humor, and misinterpret the jokes in his films. "Kevin is not a homophobe, but reading his web site, GLAAD may have had a point so far as a few people were concerned. Some of his younger fans perhaps didn't understand that the film is satire. I know absolutely that it is not Kevin's intention to put people down, and that intelligent people can see that *Jay & Silent Bob Strike Back* isn't a gay bashing movie at all, but there are those people who don't see the satire. It's flared up a couple of times on the web site, and people get banned very quickly, but it is terribly disheartening to see kids bashing gay people. They think it's cool."

"But," Pereira adds, "I thought *American Pie 2* was much more homo-phobic than *Jay & Silent Bob Strike Back*, and nobody protested that."

The controversy surrounding *Jay & Silent Bob Strike Back,* like the *Dogma* protest, may have merely drawn more attention to Kevin Smith's film. It had a big opening weekend, and continued to play well into September, before the tragic terrorist attacks that left a nation stunned on September 11. When the film was released on DVD and VHS some months later, on February 26, 2002, it topped the rental and purchase charts for several weeks.

Jay and Silent Bob — always a magnet for controversy — "had left the building."

ALL GOOD THINGS...

Jay & Silent Bob Strike Back is the curtain call for two of cinema's true originals, the New Jersey stoner duo played by Jason Mewes and Kevin Smith. Their final adventure is a film with not much on its mind but out- and-out fun. In some interesting ways, the film speaks to its historical context (the advent of the Internet's down side; the proliferation of entertainment news channels and programs; the slew of uninspired Hollywood sequels and remakes, etc.), but it's really just a knock down, drag-out funny film. For fans of the View Askewniverse, it is nostalgic (and sometimes touching) to see Randal, Dante, Brodie, Hooper, Banky, Holden, and the rest of the gang back in action.

In the years to come, *Jay & Silent Bob Strike Back* may be of primary interest, surprisingly enough, for its visual aplomb. The first scene of the film features one of the greatest visual jokes to come down the road in years.

Outside the Quick Stop in the 1970s, Jay's mother says "fuck" about 200 times, and as her child takes tentative baby-steps out of his stroller with momentous effort, Jay voices the word for himself for the first time. Then the film dissolves to 20 or so years later. It's the exact same shot, and a grown-up Jay is standing in the very same place, singing "fuck" in a variety of original ways.

It's the comedy equivalent of Stanley Kubrick's masterful transition in *2001: A Space Odyssey*, as primitive ape first picks up a bone and uses it as a tool, and then tosses it into the air. The bone, through a jump cut, transforms into a spaceship in Earth's orbit centuries later. All of man's technological development, from primitive ape to space-shuttle-piloting human being, is encapsulated in that single cut.

In the Kevin Smith film, Jay's transformation from infant to adult charts a similar evolution, only the tool in this case is a cuss word; a cuss word the adult Jay has mastered like no other man alive. It's a funny, funny moment, and the perfect use of the dissolve brings roars of laughter every time the scene is shown.

Jay & Silent Bob Strike Back also features the best damned *Planet of the Apes* satire yet put to film. In fact, it's a hell of a lot better than Tim

Burton's weak "re-imagining." The scene with Jason Mewes on the beach before the ruined Statue of Liberty (intoning "Damn youse! Damn youse all to Hell!") is so faithful in composition and art design to the original 1968 film that it's actually difficult to tell the two apart. And Vincent Guastini's gorilla soldier on horseback is full of character and invidivuality, a more convincing villain than any seen in the remake and a nice alternate interpretation of the Apes characters. *Spaceballs* executed a *Planet of the Apes* joke like this back in 1987, but Smith's crazy parody blasts Mel Brooks' version off the pop cultural map.

As far as "gay bashing" is concerned, *Jay & Silent Bob Strike Back* is really pretty innocuous. Kids have been substituting the word "gay" for "stupid" since before Kevin Smith was a kid on the playground. It may not be nice or even PC, but it is reflective of the truth in our culture. Sometimes women get termed "bitches," men are called "dicks," and "gay" is substituted for the word "stupid," so just about everybody can complain about something if they look hard enough. It is far worse to censor an artist (for mirroring real life, to boot) than to endure a few jokes like this. And, it's a little sad and disconcerting to see a progressive, helpful organization like GLAAD seeking to assert control over artistic content simply because said content doesn't favor the organization's preferred world view.

Those who complained about the movie might be wise to review some of the film's dialogue. "Don't be so suburban," George Carlin's hitchhiker chides Jay and Silent Bob. "It's the new Millennium. Gay, straight, it's all the same now. There are no more lines."

That, it seems, might have been a point GLAAD would be happy to see made in a mass entertainment.

And really, why look to anti-heroes Jay and Silent Bob to model appropriate behavior anyway? That's like asking the Three Stooges to legislate public policy.

With a joke-a-minute pace, a wicked and witty premise about Hollywood and the Internet, and more celebrities than your eyes can register, *Jay & Silent Bob Strike Back* is the most enjoyable comedy of 2001, and a stylish send-off.

ASKEW VIEWS:

KITTY LITTER: Those sleek, black cat suits worn by Missy, Sissy, Chrissy, and Justice looked terrific on film, but were difficult to wear, according to Jennifer Schwalbach.

"It was freezing cold all the time, and these cat suits were so thin.

They were like nylon suits. They were some cheap-ass material and we'd be out at 4 a.m. running around in them, freezing to death. And we could not get too close to the heaters, otherwise the suits would go up in smoke."

Making matters worse, there was only one suit per jewel thief; no back-ups. "Those suits are not easy to get on, and not easy to get off." She reports. "And since there's only one, you have to move very carefully. Mine, they had to alter, so they stitched me into it. Unfortunately, I had the worst stomach flu in my life, and was having to go the bathroom literally every ten minutes. So they'd stitch me in, then rip the suit off to me, I'd go to the bathroom, get back into the suit, and get sewed back in. It was a nightmare. I was so sick I didn't even care that 200 people on the set knew I was living in the bathroom."

RAP MEWES-IC: Fans of the New Jersey Chronicles will note that Jay's profanity-filled raps have become more elaborate over the course of five films, and that's fine by Jason Mewes. Even though he's never done any professional singing, he reports that he's written songs and would like to pursue his interest in music.

But even if the first rap in *Jay & Silent Bob Strike Back* was easy to master ("It just flowed."), Mewes found the later one, eventually cut from the film, more difficult.

Mewes explains, "If you watch the outtakes, you can see the one they didn't show, at the convenience store out west. 'Balls, balls, in your mouth! Balls! Where? In your mouth!' That was tough, and I had to do it a few times. At one point, I messed up and said, 'Where, where? In *my* mouth!' And then I realized what I said and was like, 'Yuck. I messed up.'"

DAME DENCH: One of the funniest lines in *Jay & Silent Bob Strike Back* is Dante's exasperated remark that he can't believe the filmmakers behind the *Bluntman & Chronic* movie hired "Judi Dench" to play him. But that was just one permutation, as O'Halloran remembers.

"It was either that, or 'I can't believe they got Freddie Prinze Jr. to play me.' But I think it was better with Judi Dench."

TOGETHERNESS: The fact that Walt Flanagan and Bryan Johnson are good friends sometimes adds to the impression that Fanboy and Steve-Dave are constantly together. Unknowingly the actors encouraged this notion on the set of *Jay & Silent Bob Strike Back*.

"In the movies, we're constantly portrayed as hanging out together," explains Johnson. "So I wonder if people look at us and say, 'These mother-fuckers really do hang out all the time!' Every time we're seen, we're together.

"When we did *Jay & Silent Bob Strike Back*, according to SAG rules, the production has to pay for a room for each of us. But we didn't know that. So I signed in at the hotel and just assumed that Walter and I had one room. So Walter stayed in my room for three days. Then someone asked us why we didn't take Walter's room, and we were like, 'Walter has a room?' People must really think we can't stay away from each other. He had his own room, but we had to sleep side-by-side."

FREEZE FRAME: The colorful, 1960s TV version of *Batman* starring Adam West and Burt Ward is the basis for some of the *Bluntman & Chronic* sets in *Jay & Silent Bob Strike Back*. In particular, the Bluntcave resembles the Batcave of that classic series, down to a similar "atomic pile" in the background.

"It was stunning to see how much work they'd put into the set," Walt Flanagan notes. "But you don't see it that much in the movie. All that effort and you don't even get a real panoramic shot of the Bluntcave! But you can see it great on DVD."

THE ULTIMATE NUMBER: The number 37 crops up repeatedly in Kevin Smith's films. In *Jay & Silent Bob Strike Back*, a poster at their condo heralds Missy, Chrissy and Sissy's "37th" successful jewel heist. Later, on the set of *Bluntman & Chronic*, Jay and Silent Bob appear during, according to the clapper, Scene 37.

SHE AIN'T ALL THAT: Early in *Jay & Silent Bob Strike Back*, it is noted that everything went downhill for Miramax after its release of *She's All That*. According to John Pierson, that joke relates to a real-life incident:

"When *Dogma* started test market screenings, at least two were in Philadelphia, and *She's All That* had either just opened big or was about to open big. The fact of the matter was that it was thrown in Kevin's face. 'Look, you're getting okay scores here, but it's no *She's All That*.'" Pierson pauses before continuing, "How could anybody compare *Dogma* to *She's All That*?"

KISS-KISS, BANG-BANG: One of the spicier moments from *Jay & Silent Bob Strike Back* was cut from the theatrical version (and restored for the DVD outtake section). Specifically, it was Jennifer Schwalbach's steamy kiss with co-star Ali Larter.

"Ali and I had become such good friends, and we knew from the beginning we would have to do it," Schwalbach explains. "The worst stuff got cut out and wasn't even on the DVD. It was that bad. It was...dirty. And I thought 'Good God, no.' But they had cleared the set, and it was just Kevin and Mosier and a few other people, so it wasn't hard or awkward. We just did it. Then Kevin started to get paranoid that everybody thought he was a total pervert. But the whole thing was un-pervy and sterile. There wasn't porn music playing in the background to get us in the mood, and no one was plying us with drinks."

But if the love-scene was easy to do, stunts were a killer. "Ali accidentally whacked me in the face with her fake gun," Schwalbach reveals. "In fact, I got hit in the head by several things during the filming of that movie. A light would fall, find me, and then hit me. It was the most random thing. But the movie was so fun, a blow to the head didn't even matter."

KEVIN SMITH ON JAY & SILENT BOB STRIKE BACK:
"We were trying to do a live action *Looney Tunes* with more dialogue.... Scott Mosier, my producer summed it up best. He said, it's kind of like *The Muppet Movie* on acid."[11]

NOTES

1. "Is it Theft Or Is It Freedom? Seven Views of the Web's Impact on Culture Clashes," *The New York Times*, September 20, 2000, p. 42.

2. "Kevin Smith is Moving On," *CNN.com, ShowbizToday*, August 21, 2001, http://www.cnn.com/CNN/Programs/showbiz.today/featured.story/0108/21/html.

3. Andy Seiler, "Kevin Smith is seldom 'Silent,'" *USA Today*, August 24, 2001, p. 1, http://www.usatoday.com/life/enter/movies/2001-08-24-kevin-smith.html.

4. William Keck, "On Nuns, Star Wars & Evil Designers," *Esquire*, August 2001, p. 30.

5. Stacie Hougland, "Kevin Smith Breaks the Silence," *Hollywood.com*, http://www.hollywood.com/celebs/features/feature770297/page 2.

6. Eugene Hernandez, "Kevin Smith Strikes Back," *Indie Wire*, August 30, 2001, p. 2, http://www.indiewire.com/film/interviews/int_Smith_Kevin_010830.html.

7. Rebecca Asher-Walsh, "Reel World: News From Hollywood," *Entertainment Weekly*, August 10, 2001, p. 46.

8. Scott Seomin, "Scott Seomin's Letter to Kevin Smith, Writer/Director of *Jay & Silent Bob Strike Back*," *G.L.A.A.D. Documents*, July 26, 2001, p. 1, http://www.glaad.org/org/publications/documenta/index.html?record=2814.

9. Teresa Wiltz, "Silent Bob's Last Words; Director Kevin Smith Takes the Scenic Route for His Final 'Jersey Chronicle,'" *The Washington Post*, August 23, 2001, p. C01.

10. Seomin, p. 1.

11. Rob Blackwelder, "Silent Bob Speaks Out: Writer-director Kevin Smith kisses his famous cameo character goodbye in new Hollywood farce," *SPLICEDwire*, August 2, 2001, http://www.splicedonline.com/01features/ksmith.html.

Clerks (2000)

THE ANIMATED SERIES

CAST & CREW

FROM MIRAMAX HOME ENTERTAINMENT.

BASED ON CHARACTERS CREATED BY: Kevin Smith
DEVELOPED FOR TELEVISION BY: David Mandel, Scott Mosier & Kevin Smith
PRODUCED BY: John Bush
CO-PRODUCER: Chris Bailey
SUPERVISING PRODUCER: Brian Kelley
EXECUTIVE PRODUCERS: Bob Weinstein, Harvey Weinstein, Billy Campbell, David Mandel, Kevin Smith, and Scott Mosier
FILM EDITOR: John Royer
ART DIRECTOR: Alan Rodner
ANIMATION PRODUCER: Saerom Animation Inc.
EXECUTIVE IN CHARGE OF PRODUCTION: Bob Osher, Miramax Television
MUSIC: James L. Venable
VOICE CASTING: Jamie Thomason
FROM WOLTZ INTERNATIONAL PICTURE CORPORATION AND TOUCHSTONE TV.

FEATURING THE VOICE TALENTS OF

Brian O'Halloran I *Dante*
Jeff Anderson I *Randal Graves*
Jason Mewes I *Jay*
Kevin Smith I *Silent Bob*
Alec Baldwin I *Leonardo Leonardo*

THE STORY SO FAR...

EPISODE I

TELEPLAY BY: David Mandel and Kevin Smith

THE STORY: The construction of a new deluxe "Quicker Stop" by billionaire megalomaniac Leonardo Leonardo threatens Dante and Randal when it looks like R.S.T. Video and Quick Stop will be closed. The clerks break into Leonardo Leonardo's ofice by night and team up with Jay and Silent Bob, now selling fireworks, to destroy the competition.

GUEST VOICES: Charles Barkley

EPISODE II

TELEPLAY BY: David Mandel and Kevin Smith
STORY BY: Paul Dini, David Mandel, and Kevin Smith
DIRECTED BY: Nick Filippi

THE STORY: Randal and Dante lock themselves in the Quick Stop milk room freezer after the store is robbed. Bored and cold, they reminisce about previous adventures. When they run out of old stories, they resort to flashing back to sitcoms like *Happy Day*s.

GUEST VOICES: Charles Barkley, Gwenyth Paltrow, Gilbert Gottfried

EPISODE III

TELEPLAY BY: David Mandel and Kevin Smith
DIRECTED BY: Chris Bailey

THE STORY: After introducing a new African-American character to the show named Lando, Randal and Dante mishandle a container of frozen burritos and visit a new pet shop next door. When Leonardo Leonardo samples the rotten burritos and becomes violently ill, Randal thinks the monkey at Patrick Swayze's pet shop — Gerbils, Gerbils, Gerbils — is responsible for the outbreak.

GUEST VOICES: Charles Barkley, James Woods, Gilbert Gottfried, Al Franken

EPISODE IV

TELEPLAY BY: Steve Lookner, David Mandel, and Kevin Smith
STORY BY: Steve Lookner
DIRECTED BY: Steve Loter

THE STORY: Dante and Randal challenge each other to switch jobs for a day, but Randal has trouble with the Quick Stop. When Jay slips on Randal's spilled soda, he gets a high-priced lawyer to sue Dante and Quick Stop in the People's Court, presided by Judge Reinhold.

GUEST VOICES: Judge Reinhold, Kenny Mayne, Dan Patrick, Charles Barkley, Grant Hill, Reggie Miller

EPISODE V

TELEPLAY BY: Brian Kelly
DIRECTED BY: Nick Filippi

THE STORY: Dante and Randal attend their high school reunion, but run afoul of Leonardo Leonardo and Randal's old girlfriends, all of whom have become lesbians. When Randal gets the high score on an old arcade game called "Pharoah," the government abducts him and forces him to work as slave labor. Dante's pathetic little league team saves the day and rescues Randal.

GUEST VOICES: Michael McKean, Charles Barkley

EPISODE VI

TELEPLAY BY: David Mandel and Kevin Smith
DIRECTED BY: Steve Loter

THE STORY: Dante and Randal go to a convention and are deluged by fans that think the *Clerks* cartoon is a sell-out! The duo vows to take the series back to its independent film roots, come hell or high water. Meanwhile, a fair is in town and Caitlin Bree is cheating on Dante again. And some mysterious guy named Morpheus keeps telephoning Dante and calling him "Neo."

GUEST VOICES: Kevin McDonald, Mark McKinney

THE STORY BEHIND THE SERIES

In the summer of 2000 *Clerks: The Animated Series* came—briefly—to network television. Though it was pulled by its host network ABC after just two half-hour episodes, the series has since been released on DVD and VHS and has, like virtually all Kevin Smith productions, acquired a rabid cult following. There has even been talk of a big-screen resurrection: an animated *Clerks* feature film to be called *Clerks: Sell Out.*

However, if things were just a little different, *Clerks* would never have been a cartoon at all. Instead, it would have been a live-action series—a sitcom— and Kevin Smith, Scott Mosier, and View Askew would have most likely had nothing whatsoever to do with it.

"When we were shooting *Mallrats*, ABC was interested in doing a *Clerks* TV show," Scott Mosier recalls of this strange chapter in View Askew history.

But the notion of a 22-minute, live-action *Clerks* sitcom was news to Jeff Anderson. "It was after *Clerks* came out, I guess, and they were shooting this live action pilot. I had just come out to L.A. for the Spirit Awards, and it was my first time there. I met up with these agents—and they were all asking where I'd been. They wanted to know if I wanted to audition for the *Clerks* TV show. And I was like, 'What the heck? Sure!' So they set up an audition, but then told me that the part of Randal had already been cast. So I actually went in and auditioned as Dante."

"We both auditioned as Dante," Brian O'Halloran notes with amusement. "Because Jim Breuer from *Saturday Night Live* had been cast as Randal."

Or rather a pseudo-Randal.

"He was named Randal, but he wasn't really like Randal at all; more of a new, third character," Mosier reports of Breuer's interpretation. "And they added all of these new locations to the show, like an ice cream parlor and a tanning salon."

Jeff Anderson continues the story. "At the time, a CNN news crew was following me around town for the *Showbiz Minute* and were doing a kind of 'young actor comes to Hollywood' story. Probably on my second or third audition for the part, the news crew cleared it with the people I was auditioning for that they could come in and tape it. So it was my third audition ever, I'm reading for Dante in the *Clerks* TV show, and it's all happening on CNN. No pressure there!

"I went in and I'm sure it was the world's worst audition, because I was laughing. I read the part of Dante, but not as the Dante you saw in the movie. I did my own Dante, which was kind of a pain-in-the-assy Randal— which is exactly what I wanted to do. I didn't get the part.

"Kevin heard through me, I think, about the pilot, because I told him I was auditioning for it," explains O'Halloran. "He got involved with it at that point as an executive producer. But he read the script and didn't like it at all."

"I called Kevin about the show," adds Anderson. "Miramax owns the name *Clerks*, I guess, and they did this pilot without Kevin. After I auditioned, Kevin and Scott came to town and were attached to the pilot as consultants. Later, I called Kevin again and told him that my audition was terrible, and that the script was terrible. And Kevin said, 'Yeah, Scott and I are out now.' They were in for about four days before they bailed out!"

"Kevin had a different sensibility about it," Mosier notes diplomatically, then on further thought adds, "The pilot was terrible; almost unwatchable."

O'Halloran's description is less flattering. "It was such an abortion of a show. They set it in a 7-11 type of convenience store. It was a very big, corporate type of place. And the set looked like a bubble gum set you'd see on *Saved by the Bell*. You could tell it was a fake set."

"I saw the pilot later," adds Anderson, "and boy was I glad I didn't get the part. It really was like *Saved by the Bell*. It was sort of edgy, but everyone was acting as though it were a kid's show. I was glad not to be associated with it."

But the idea of a *Clerks* TV show done well was one that still carried major appeal to many producers in Tinsel Town. And at least one old friend. "Harvey Weinstein wanted there to be a TV series," O'Halloran reports, "even after that one was aborted. He was hot on the idea, and I think it was then that Kevin first offered the idea of doing a cartoon, because he wanted to do bizarre scripts, have more freedom, and not do a sitcom version."

"This is the PG material that my mother always wanted me to do."[1] Kevin Smith told *The New York Times* of the proposed series.

But Jeff Anderson wasn't so sure that a cartoon would work either. "I thought everybody had lost their minds about this movie. But then Kevin called me again and asked me to play Randal on the animated show. I thought it would be bizarre, but wonderful."

"I was ecstatic," O'Halloran notes of the concept. "I'm a huge cartoon fan to begin with. I just love animation so much, so when I heard we would be doing a cartoon I knew the potential it had to offer was enormous."

"And then I heard that the show was going to air on ABC in prime time and thought, 'Holy crap!' I thought it would be a Saturday morning show, not a *Simpsons*-type thing. Then it clicked, and I realized how long *The Simpsons* had been on. I knew if it came off, and was popular, which I thought it would be, this could be huge."

Others shared that belief, and there was something of a bidding war to see which network would finally carry the show. "When UPN made their initial offer, they were going to purchase thirteen episodes, with all thirteen going to air, but we wanted to go with ABC because it was a bigger network," O'Halloran explains.

Indeed, in the year 2000, ABC seemed like a good, solid bet. "At the time, it was in third place, and seemed to be doing more edgy television," Scott Mosier explains. "I guess they figured if they were in third, they had nothing to lose. So they had a show set in a mental institution, *Wonderland*, and they were going to do the *Clerks* cartoon."

Writing the scripts for the new series were Kevin Smith, *News Radio* scribe Brian Kelly, and *Saturday Night Live* alumni Steve Lookner and David Mandel.

"We went to ABC and did the first table reading for the cartoon," recounts Anderson. "It was my first time in the situation where we were doing our *Clerks* thing in front of guys in three piece suits, who had befuddled looks on their faces."

"We were reading the scripts to the bigwigs at Disney and ABC," O'Halloran joins in. "We'd met Steve Lookner and David Mandel at that point, and the scripts were a little longer than 22 minutes. They're usually about 35 minutes, so you have enough material to trim down from, and we got a really great response."

The result of the readings was a deal for a TV series. There would be a *Clerks* cartoon, and it had a guarantee of six episodes. From that point, it was a matter of transforming Dante, Randal, Jay, and Silent Bob into animated characters.

"When it came to production, we went out to L.A. and I saw the production offices, and there were these great start-up sketches," O'Halloran describes. "The artists were looking at me, taking photos, and we discussed what they wanted. They did all these passes on the characters and I loved Chris Bailey's style of animation. He had such a great idea and edge as to how he wanted to stylize those characters. There was something lovable about the animation."

"They locked down Brian pretty early." Anderson relates. "Jay went through a few changes. I kept asking to see myself, but I never saw the sketches. So I pulled the writers aside and said, 'Give Randal some muscles and a tattoo and some piercings.' Then I finally saw the drawing and thought, 'That's not me.' But everyone else said, 'Oh yes it is,' and I thought, 'Dammit!'"

One of the new characters created specifically for the *Clerks* cartoon was a millionaire arch-villain named Leonardo Leonardo. As O'Halloran recalls, the clerks' new nemesis wasn't easy to cast.

"They had originally hired Alan Rickman, I believe, to play Leonardo Leonardo. I think Kevin had based that character on Hans Gruber, the villain Rickman played in *Die Hard*. But for some reason it just wasn't coming across in the vocalizations. So they interviewed quite a few people, and I think they met Alec Baldwin up in Toronto. I never got to meet him, because it was late in casting, but I think he recorded the dialogue up there. He has such great comedic timing. People don't think of him as being really funny, but he is. His timing and vocalizations were great."

Anderson and O'Halloran agree that recording the scripts for *Clerks* turned out to be the most fun, and most hilarious, job of their careers. "Everybody believed in that show, and would tell you that it wasn't like work at all," Anderson confides. "We'd show up at the studio, horse around, and have all these cool people in there doing voices with us."

"Recording was so much fun," O'Halloran concurs. "We worked with so many people I admired, and the shows just got better and better. We got more comfortable, and we taped the shows in sequence, so we were getting used to the process. You don't realize how much, as an actor, you have to be animated for an animated series. There's got to be more fluctuation and emotion in a voice so that when you see the animation it goes together well; it isn't just a voice quietly saying a line."

"They should have left the recorder on constantly, because the things we'd come up with and just change on the spot...it was hard to believe I got paid to do that job," Anderson laughs. "Initially, I sort of read Randal how he would be in the movie *Clerks*, but once we got into actually recording the show, Kevin encouraged me to bring him up a little, to put more energy into him. I would always get a kick out of Kevin doing cartoon Randal. He'd get this kind of squeal to his voice."

"We had great directors," O'Halloran adds. "They always wanted to do a couple of takes to nail it down. David Mandel was the primary vocal director of the episodes, and he would encourage us to try new things and do things different ways. After about the third episode, we knew exactly what they wanted and were able to have an immediate sense of what the script required vocally."

As the stars, writers, and directors of the *Clerks* cartoon grew more confident about their work, the recorded scripts and storyboards were shipped to Korea to be animated. "It takes about eight months to put out an episode," O'Halloran notes. "So you have to do it in batches. You do all the recordings, and then send over all the episodes in a batch, and it still takes that long."

Unfortunately, the higher-ups at Disney and ABC began to perceive content problems with the show. In their eyes, it was simply too racy. ABC "reportedly gave Miramax a difficult time,"[2] according to the press, but that modest description was apparently an understatement.

"After our readings, they would tell us, 'You can't do that.' And it was pretty tame stuff they objected to. Then they'd finally okay it, the cartoon would get drawn, and when the network got the stuff back, they'd make changes again," Anderson explains with frustration. "You can't do that with an animated show once it's been drawn. You know you're way offtrack if you're making people re-draw scenes."

The result of this interference in the creative process? *Clerks* missed its debut. "For a long time we were going to premiere after the Super Bowl, so we believed ABC was really behind the show," O'Halloran remembers. "Then the Super Bowl got closer and the first episode wasn't even done because they were asking us to re-do scenes."

"They moved us back to the summer," Mosier reveals, "which meant we were on with reruns."

When *Clerks* finally did appear in the summer of 2000, it aired on Wednesday nights at 9:30 p.m. Unfortunately, it was pretty well ignored by viewers and poorly reviewed by the critics who took note. "Why put them on a broadcast network, where they can't talk nearly as dirty as they did in the movie?" questioned *People*'s reviewer, Terry Kelleher. "Can you say ill-conceived?"[3]

"That's like saying *South Park* is ill-conceived because the characters can't say 'fuck' on TV," notes historian Vincent Pereira.

Still, those who tuned in to the short-lived series found much to appreciate and chortle about. "The first night the show was on, I was out with a friend of mine and we were in a hotel lobby," Anderson remembers. "We ran into the bar and flipped on the TV, and when the show came on, we were just fascinated by it. I couldn't go anywhere; I just had to sit and watch the whole show."

With the addition of *Clerks: The Animated Series* to the ever-expanding View Askewnivese, the grungy, discontented register jockeys of the 1994 film *Clerks* were re-invented and re-tooled with one purpose in mind: to skewer popular culture (particularly film and television). Smith's films have always been laden with references to contemporary culture, but his *Clerks* cartoon is a rapid-fire barrage of zingers aimed straight at Hollywood. In many ways this approach signals the direction of *Jay & Silent Bob Strike Back*. That movie featured parodies of *Scooby Doo*, *E.T.*, *Scream*, *The X-Files*, and *Planet of the Apes,* to name but a few. Any one of those sequences would have been right at home in the cartoon.

Tracking the references in *Clerks: The Animated Series*, it's a little amazing to witness their breadth and scope. *Marathon Man, Silence of the Lambs, Access Hollywood, Aliens, The Secret Diary of Desmond Pfeifer, Batman* (all in episode 1), *The Flintstones, Schindler's List, The Real World, Happy Days* (all in episode 2), *Outbreak, Jaws, Dirty Dancing, Road House, Point Break* (episode 3), *The People's Court, Law & Order, J.F.K., Beverly Hills Cop, Pokemon* (episode 4), *The Last Starfighter, Indiana Jones and The Temple of Doom* (episode 5), and *The Matrix* (episode 6) are among the many productions parodied, often brilliantly, always mercilessly.

These self-aware jabs at Hollywood, this acknowledgment of Generation X pop-culture touchstones (like the *Happy Days* episode in which the Fonz jumps the shark), lands *Clerks: The Animated Series* in the realm of such hip programming as the much-missed *Mystery Science Theater 3000*. Straight, narrative content has been rendered secondary to a slew of canny references to the culture Gen Xers grew up worshipping. It is a hysterically funny TV series, but one undeniably aimed right at Smith's own age group. Those outside it, like the baby boomers, may not really get the jokes, because, ostensibly, they don't understand the significance of *Happy Days* to the audience that grew up with it in the 1970s.

But ABC didn't seem to get the jokes either. The racy material reportedly confused Bob Iger and Michael Eisner. ABC also objected to one of Smith's more colorful jokes about Dr. Seuss (and an erotica book called *Horton Hears a Hymen*), as well as comedic material about the Challenger explosion and the Holocaust.[4]

Even worse, ABC pulled *Clerks* from its schedule after airing only two episodes. Why? Between the time period the program was conceived and then finally ready to air, the network went from being last ranked to first with the help of Regis Philbin.

"This milquetoast game show, *Who Wants to Be a Millionaire*, was so successful and they didn't want to risk losing their first place," Scott Mosier notes. "It ended badly. We were all calling each other names."

"*Millionaire* changed the complete dynamic of what ABC was going for," O'Halloran explains. "They thought they could air *Millionaire* three times a week and it would be their savior, but now they're paying for that decision. They ran that show into the ground."

And, in the process, killed *Clerks* before it could find an audience. "If you watch those six episodes, you get the feeling it's the beginning of something good," notes Pereira. "Look at the first season of *The Simpsons*, and then what it ultimately became. The pacing was different, the design was a little different. I believe that had *Clerks* been given the chance to develop, it would have grown in the way *The Simpsons* or *South Park* did. I think by the fifth episode of the show, you could already see where it was heading."

O'Halloran and Anderson, who were having the time of their lives shooting the series, were dismayed by the way the series was treated. "They jerked us around," O'Halloran says. "It put a bad taste in our mouths. When you go into television, episodic work, you have to realize they can just pull you any second."

Anderson offers his own post-mortem. "Fox or UPN would have been the place for the show, because those networks really don't have anything else."

Others have suggested that Comedy Central might be the right home for the series, but O'Halloran isn't so sure. "At the time, Comedy Central didn't have the budget to spend on *Clerks*. The cartoon cost $750,000 to make per show."

Mosier puts it more succinctly. "If we'd been on Comedy Central, we all would have made about three dollars per episode."

O'Halloran was especially disappointed by *Clerks'* s cancellation, because he'd caught a glimpse of things to come. "When we fulfilled our six episode contract, I asked Kevin what was next and he gave me some of the synopses of future shows, and they were just so funny. It would have been great to be able to do it."

Still, fans shouldn't lose hope. The idea of a *Clerks* animated production—whether a TV series or a feature film—is not yet dead. "Harvey Weinstein is a huge fan of the series," O'Halloran reveals. "He would rather Kevin make an animated feature than *Jersey Girl*. He's saying we shouldn't worry; that once we do a feature film, we'll find another episodic outlet for the show, even if it's HBO. Cable is starting to become more and more a contender, sweeping the Emmys and such, and it offers more freedom."

"There is talk of doing an animated feature," Anderson confirms. "Kevin says that he and Mandel, who wrote the TV show, are working on the script. I'd love to do it. On the TV show, I was always waiting any minute for someone to bust in and close us down because we were having so much fun."

While the stars and fans of *Clerks: The Animated Series* wait for the feature, there's opportunity to reminisce about their favorite moments on the short-lived series.

"I always liked that Randal began referring to himself in the third person. If the cartoon went any further, it would have been the undoing of Randal. In the *Real World* episode [episode 2], he was saying, 'You kicked out Randal? You can't kick out Randal!' That's where it gets scary, when Randal starts referring to himself in the third. Kevin said if the Jay Leno shorts [short films starring Dante and Randal produced for the *Tonight Show*; see chapter eight] go further, that's where we're headed."

"I liked the fifth episode," O'Halloran reports. "Dante's little league baseball team and the *Temple of Doom* thing is just really funny. And I loved the idea of Randal's ex-girlfriends all becoming lesbians."

"I always liked the courtroom episode too," Anderson laughs. "That one actually made it on the air. I always appreciated the line: 'Show me where they touched you. Show me on the doll where they touched you...'"

ASKEW VIEWS:

TAKE THE FIFTH: In *Clerks*, episode 4, Randal represents Dante in court against Jay's attorney (named Pierson), and calls various personalities to testify, including filmmakers George Lucas, Woody Allen, Spike Lee, Joel Schumacher, and Steven Spielberg. He questions them about the quality of various productions, including *The Phantom Menace* and *Hook*. But if Jeff Anderson had his way, there would have been one other witness on the stand: Kevin Smith.

"I always said why the hell isn't Kevin testifying, so I could ask him what the hell was up with *Mallrats*?"

NC-17: The stars of *Clerks: The Animated Series* had so much fun recording their dialogue, that at one point they conceived a wicked idea, O'Halloran remembers. "It was the type of fun where Jeff and I got together and decided that if the show went on, we'd record an entire episode wearing only our underwear. Then we'd have the pleasure of knowing that people are watching this episode all over the country, and we were almost naked when we did our lines."

UN-PRESIDENTED: The *Clerks* cartoon, even more than Kevin Smith's films, are packed with references to popular films and television. One of the funniest such jokes occurs in episode 4, where there is a straight-faced riff on Donald Sutherland's powerful, information-laden scene with Kevin Costner in Oliver Stone's meditation on the murder of President Kennedy, *J.F.K.* In this case, Randal fills in for the Costner character.

Speaking of presidents, in episode 2, when Randal and Dante flash back to their first meeting at the Quick Stop in the 1980s, the character first seen walking down the street is none other than an animated Ronald Reagan. Likewise, in the 1970s introduction of Randal and Dante, the first character to appear is a cartoon version of Jimmy Carter.

WOMEN'S LIB: At the start of episode 3, a letter writer named Jen Schwalbach complains in a missive to Randal and Dante about the lack of substantive roles for women on the show.

Well, at least she didn't ask them for ten grand.

NOTES

1. Rick Lyman, "At the Movies: A Risque Kiss? So Very Quaint," *The New York Times*, September 17, 1999, p. E14.

2. John Dempsey, "Miramax rings Clerks in DVD key." *Variety*, August 14, 2000, p. 37.

3. Terry Kelleher, "Picks and Pans," *People Weekly*, June 5, 2000, p. 27.

4. Jeff Jensen, "'Night, *Clerks*," *Entertainment Weekly*, June 7, 2000, p. 1, http://www.ew.com/ew/report/0,6115.85266~3~~,00.html.

Kevin Smith Conquers
THE UNIVERSE!

Comic books, flying cars and Mr. Executive Producer.

KEVIN SMITH IS...

A REALLY BUSY FELLOW. In fact, he may be the busiest
man working in Hollywood today. During the interview period for this
book, Smith filmed a cameo appearance for the Affleck superhero film,
Daredevil (on April 2, 2002), and directed two commercials in Toronto.
He went on the lecture circuit, filmed several "Roadside Attractions" for
Leno's *The Tonight Show*, and completed the first draft of his next View
Askew feature, *Jersey Girl*.

A quick perusal of current video releases reveals more Smith,
everywhere. He appears in *Star Woids*, a documentary about fans
awaiting the premiere of S*tar Wars Episode I: The Phantom Menace*, and,
pending its May 3, 2002 premiere, a similar documentary about the
Spider-Man movie with *Mallrats* buddy, Stan Lee. The latter is a Columbia
Tri-Star Home Entertainment Release entitled *Stan Lee's Mutants, Monsters
& Marvels,* and it's a one-on-one interview between the ultimate fan,
Kevin Smith, and the revered creator of the best comic books the world has
ever seen.

Beyond all of these appearances in front of cameras, Smith is renowned and respected by both the comic book industry and its readers as the hottest writer working in that field today.

He has resurrected the slumping *Daredevil* and *Green Arrow* titles with exciting new story lines, and even brought four-color life to *Bluntman & Chronic* (for Oni Press), his crazy *Clerks*, and Jay and Silent Bob. In the matter of *Daredevil*, sales of the book sky-rocketed nearly fifty percent after Smith began writing. *Green Arrow*, Walt Flanagan's favorite title, has proven similarly successful under his guidance. For his comic book writings, Smith has received an Eagle Award, a Harvey Award, and a Wizard Fan Award.

Comic book fans are already drooling over Smith's anticipated summer 2002 book: *Spider-Man/Black Cat: The Evil That Men Do*. It's a four part miniseries for Marvel featuring the artwork of Rachel and Terry Dodson. And, in a late-night TV first, Smith will be promoting the comic during a visit with Jay Leno on *The Tonight Show* in late June of 2002.

> I'm as proud of my work in comics asI am of anything I've done on film, so I thought, 'Why not call up the folks at The Tonight Show and see if I could talk about Spider-Man/Black Cat on the show as a guest?[1]

For Smith, these comic assignments, toiling in the realms of heroes like Peter Parker, Daredevil, and Green Arrow, represents more than a dream come true:

> Before I became a filmmaker, I wanted to write comics, but was told it was too tough a market to crack, so I went into films, which oddly enough proved more accessible.[2]

Kevin Smith hasn't always been so lucky, of course. He was paid a substantial salary to write *Superman Lives* for producer Jon Peters and Warner Brothers, a screenplay that would have substantially and creatively re-imagined the Man of Steel's movie franchise for the 1990s. But Smith's efforts were "shitcanned" when *Batman* director Tim Burton joined the team and went in a different direction.[3]

Kevin Smith's much praised outline for a remake of 1970s TV series *The Six Million Dollar Man*, also looks unlikely to be the final word on that project, now reportedly in the care of the Farrelly brothers.

On the other hand, all indications are that Kevin Smith will one day write and direct *Fletch Won*, with either Ben Affleck or Jason Lee starring as the laconic detective first given cinematic life by Chevy Chase in the 1980s. "*Fletch* is waiting in the wings," Jennifer Schwalbach notes with optimism. "There are so many movies Kevin wants to make."

THE FLYING CAR

In the View Askewniverse at large, Smith remains as busy as ever. Most recently, he filmed *The Flying Car*, a *Clerks* short for Jay Leno and *The Tonight Show*. Starring Brian O'Halloran and Jeff Anderson, the ten-minute film was shot in New Jersey after *Jay & Silent Bob Strike Back*'s release in November 2001. It aired in late February of 2002.

"When Kevin first approached me to do it, the script was written for a Ford Company corporate meeting," O'Halloran reveals. "Then it got cancelled because the budget wasn't right or something. But Kevin had ownership of the script. Then, when Kevin was promoting *Jay & Silent Bob Strike Back* on Leno, *The Tonight Show* approached him to do a short film. It was such a funny little piece, and Kevin had had it for two years, so he brought it out. Shooting it was hysterical. We were back to the original style of dialogue we had in *Clerks*."

Jeff Anderson describes the premise. "In *the Tonight Show* piece, Dante and Randal get stuck in traffic because they're heading to a strip bar. The script was about nine pages, and the eighth page was a long monologue."

For Randal.

"At the time we shot *Clerks*, I would never have been able to do it," Anderson notes of the speech. "When Kevin faxed the script over, I wondered what he was trying to do to me. Randal was getting more and more wordy. I read the short three or four times, and then had a friend read it with me. Probably on my fourth reading, I nearly got the whole thing out."

"I have to hand it to Jeff," adds O'Halloran. "He has a great grasp of dialogue. Especially in *The Flying Car*, where he has so much dialogue and long, long diatribes. But it was weird how easy it was for us to fall back into our characters. It's very rare to have that chemistry as an actor, to work with someone who you can just pick it up with."

Shooting *The Flying Car* was so much fun for all the people involved because, for one thing, it offered Smith, Anderson, and O'Halloran the opportunity to reminisce about the short-lived *Clerks* cartoon while shooting it.

"Randal in the movie was this pain-in-the-ass, serious guy and not very animated," Anderson considers. "I even said to Kevin once, watch me get into Randal's character: all I do is put a piece of gum in my mouth, I chew the gum, and then just scowl like the gum tastes bad. Then I push my eyebrows together. It's all in the eyes and a forever furrowed brow."

But the cartoon had changed that forever, and Randal had developed into a more lively personality.

"So when we shot the short, the first take we did on the whole thing was a single shot on me. We went though the whole nine pages and I did it all how the movie Randal would have.

"Then we changed the set-up and did the two-shot and I did it the same way," Anderson describes. "Then it was time to shoot Brian. During that set-up, Brian and I were joking about the cartoon and our favorite moments. Then when we came to Brian's close-up, I started reading my lines as Cartoon Randal."

"I remember looking over at Kevin's face and he was laughing. That's when I knew he was going to come back to me. When we got done with Brian, he made me do my part again, this time as Cartoon Randal. So that's what's on the Leno show. My eyes are a little bulgy, my pitch is a little higher, and my hands are flying around. I became Cartoon Randal for real."

The Flying Car garnered such a positive response after its February 28, 2002 airing that O'Halloran, Anderson, and Smith are destined to return for further *Clerks* shorts on *The Tonight Show*.

O'Halloran thinks it would be fun to explore some material related to the original film, including Dante's love life. "We never really broached that subject on the cartoon. It was a very different approach. But I can't see Dante with either Caitlin or Veronica. Caitlin is just nuts and Veronica is now a woman scorned, so I see him starting fresh with someone new. Of course, he'll still have Randal messing things up, but at least he'll have a new woman."

"The next show is them at the strip bar," Anderson confides. "But you know it will be the same thing. They'll be at a strip bar, but they won't be paying attention to the girls. Dante will be unhappy he's there, and Randal will be tricking him into something. They'll be totally out of their element, yet still doing the same shit."

When asked if Randal and Dante had become a screen couple of sorts, or rather a screen duo, Anderson answered succinctly.

"Yeah. We're Gilligan and Skipper."

MR. EXECUTIVE PRODUCER

Everybody remembers how Kevin Smith helped out his pal and leading man, Ben Affleck, in 1997. *Good Will Hunting* co-authors Affleck and Matt Damon were having trouble with the powers-that-be and shepherding their project to the screen, and Smith stepped in, lead the actors to Miramax, and rescued the project. Executive-produced by Kevin Smith and Scott Mosier, *Good Will Hunting* eventually grossed over $100 million and earned Affleck and Damon a golden Oscar trophy for their screenplay.

What many people may not know about Kevin Smith is that this kind of help is simply a matter of course for him. He does it all the time. Perhaps cognizant of his own good fortune in the industry, Smith has made it a point in his career (along with that of über-producer, Mosier) to help those who had helped him. In the process, he has provided a creative outlet for several new and important filmmakers.

Walt Flanagan, who runs Smith's comic book store in Red Bank, New Jersey (Jay & Silent Bob's Secret Stash), has seen Smith's generosity up-close, and remains wowed by it.

"Here's a guy who has absolutely showered his friends with the ability to be a part of his success," Flanagan notes. "He's given other people a chance to make films, what with Bryan [Johnson], Malcom [Ingram], and Matt [Gissing], and Vinnie [Pereira]. He never misses an opportunity to share his success. I would like to say if it were me, I'd do it too, but I'm not sure I would. He gives so much back to his circle of friends."

"It's very bizarre, and kind of shocking," Jennifer Schwalbach notes of her husband's priority to help others. "He doesn't have an ego that interferes with his generosity. He wants to see his friends do as well as he has, or better. There isn't anybody who is excluded from his success. He's very self-deprecating, where he feels like if he did it, anybody can. And he wants to lend a hand in any way he can without expecting anything in return."

To wit: *Drawing Flies*, *A Better Place,* and *Vulgar*, three View Askew films executive produced and partially-financed by Kevin Smith and Scott Mosier. These small-budgeted films, not unlike *Clerks*, reveal burgeoning talent in suburban New Jersey, and the creative talents of new artists with distinct visions.

Of the three pictures, *Drawing Flies*, written, edited, produced and directed by Matt Gissing and Malcom Ingram, is perhaps the most evoca- tive of *Clerks* in terms of its look and theme. It's another black-and-white, perfectly-pitched, self-aware encapsulation of the Generation X experience as a group of directionless twenty-somethings, including Jason Lee, Renee Humprheys, Jason Mewes, Carmen Lee, and Martin Brooks leave behind a meaningless "party" life in Vancouver for a seemingly endless camping trip.

Unbeknownst to the group at large, their leader, Donner (as in Donner party), has become obsessed with the idea of finding Big Foot, or rather, Sasquatch. Where did he get such a peculiar notion? Why, in perfect Generation X fashion, of course, from watching a marathon of *The Six Million Dollar Man* reruns.

At times absurd, at times unnerving, *Drawing Flies* follows the degeneration of its lead character (portrayed ably by Jason Lee) as he goes progressively "native," *Apocalypse Now*-style, going so far as to ingest Sasquatch shit.

Shot immediately after *Mallrats* in 1995, the Gissing/Ingram film was finally released on DVD in 2002, and the 76-minute, black-and-white features cameos by Ethan Suplee, Kevin Smith, and Joey Lauren Adams. The film will also be of interest to Scott Mosier's female fans (and my wife assures me they are legion), because the producer appears in one scene wearing only a diaper.

Ambitiously shot, replete with great natural locales (including a really scary-looking suspension bridge), *Drawing Flies* is a quirky, amusing movie that speaks to some of the same ennui captured so memorably by *Clerks,* only with a different group of characters and a different comedic sensibility behind the camera.

Director Malcom Ingram, a close friend of the Smiths, recently collaborated with Jennifer Schwalbach on the set of *Jay & Silent Bob Strike Back* to shoot a documentary about Kevin Smith that will, hopefully, appear on the *Clerks* Ten Year Anniversary DVD Re-issue.

"The documentary Malcom and I worked on—we interviewed everyone, and I mean everyone who worked on *Jay & Silent Bob*, like Alanis, Ben, Matt, Chris Rock, and Shannen Doherty," Schwalbach reveals. "It was such a beautiful insight into how other people feel about Kevin. I think we have over 70 hours of film, but we haven't finished it yet."

Vincent Pereira's film, *A Better Place*, was also shot in New Jersey after *Mallrats* and before *Chasing Amy*. It marks the writing and directorial debut of this talented View Askew historian. It's the story of a teenage loner, Ryan, and his friendship with the new kid in school, Barret. At first, they share the status of "outsider," but before long Barret has made new friends, and starts to grow fearful of Ryan, who evinces a negative, and very violent, world view.

"Kevin was always the writer, and I wanted to be the filmmaker," Vincent Pereira remembers of the project's genesis. "I sort of said to myself that I wanted to make a film myself at the same age Kevin was when he directed *Clerks*. So I set the summer of 1995 as the time I wanted to make a movie. I think it was around the end of 1993 when I saw a *Nightline* about the Bolger case in Britain."

The story had made news around the world. On February 12, 1993, a two-and-a-half year-old boy, Jamie Bolger, had been abducted from a shopping mall in Liverpool by two ten year-old boys. They brutalized and eventually killed the smaller child. It was a stunning and horrible story.

"That case sparked something in my mind and I thought I should make a movie about teenage violence," Pereira explains. "*A Better Place* wasn't based on the case, but it got me thinking. I was kind of a hot head at that age. In high school, I was pretty angry and anti-social, and I thought it would be interesting to put those feelings into a movie.

"So I wrote this script about a fucked-up kid who makes his first friend in many, many years, and you think maybe he'll be all right, but things spiral out of control."

Participating in the View Askew films, it turned out, helped prepare Pereira to shoot his own movie. "I've learned a lot just from being on a film set. The best thing I learned from working with Kevin Smith was being on the set and seeing how it was all done. I think we have very different styles of directing. He writes such great dialogue, and my biggest stumbling block is dialogue. But he has a specific idea of how lines should be said and generally doesn't allow improvisation. I'm not nearly as confident a writer of dialogue as he is."

A Better Place went through two years of post-production and hit the festival circuit in the fall/winter of 1997. It received glowing reviews, but, alas, didn't go into theatrical release. "It was right around the time all those school shootings started," Pereira reports. "I guess it had been on the festival circuit for about a year-and-a-half."

Unlike *Clerks* or *Drawing Flies*, *A Better Place* is a distinctly darker vision of suburban life than one would expect from Kevin Smith, filled as it is with convincingly staged and well-shot violence. Like some of the early, almost visceral work of director Wes Craven in the 1970s, the film constantly surprises with its unexpected descents into bloody terror. Two deaths, in particular, are shot with such straight-faced bluntness that the audience is left feeling uneasy, almost sick.

And, there is an audacious edit during the film's final confrontation that bears mention. This "cut" heralds the unexpected appearance (or replacement) of one character for another, one tormenter for another, and is so courageous, so perfectly executed that one wants to stand up and applaud the film's brutal honesty. That scene and several others of equal intensity reveal a confident director exploring a theme that mainstream films are very reluctant to embrace.

A Better Place also benefits from a terrific sound mix. Pereira remembers how that came about. "*Dogma* was mixed at Skywalker Sound, and Kevin and Scott became good friends with the people there, and after some discussion found out that Skywalker occasionally does pro bono work for independent films. Scott suggested they could do a remix of *A Better Place* for its DVD release, and the guys at Skywalker really loved it. So Skywalker mixed it for free."

There was just one drawback. "It took us about two years to work on the DVD, because the remix had to be scheduled around Skywalker's schedule, but everything got finished in August [of 2001] and the film got some great reviews."

A Better Place is not only genuinely harrowing, it features some fine performances, especially from Robert DiPatri, as Barret, and Eion Bailey of *Fight Club* as the disturbed — but ultimately sympathetic — Ryan. Scott Mosier, Carmen Lee, Ethan Suplee, and Jason Lee all appear in small, effective roles, but in this case, it is the two leads that focus audience attention.

And then there's Bryan Johnson's *Vulgar*, another View Askew film executive produced by Smith and Mosier, and another twist down a strange, dark alley.

"It's kind of a mix of a psychological thriller and dark comedy, and it walks a weird line," says Johnson of his debut feature. "The way it came about was that Kevin, Walter, and I were hanging out at the Quick Stop. This was when Kevin was trying to maintain a job there even though he was a filmmaker, and Walter and I used to play basketball at night and we'd go down to the store afterwards to see him. And one night we talked to him about the clown [the View Askew Productions logo; first imagined and sketched by Walt Flanagan], and what his story might be. Kevin thought that it was an interesting idea, and that we should write a movie about the clown. I told him I wanted to take a shot at it and he said, 'Fine, but don't make it jokey and stupid.'

"So I went and wrote a few pages of the script and didn't think too much about it. Then, my girlfriend failed chemistry and needed to re-take it in the summer. She was studying every night and I had nothing else to do, so I sat down and wrote the script. It took about 28 days, I showed it to Kevin, and he loved it and said, 'We have to make this movie.'"

Smith also helped Johnson shape the material. "When I gave it to Kevin, he gave me a lot of good notes. He told me what he thought should be cut from the script, and then wrote a note on the cover saying that the notes didn't reflect quality, but rather quantity. 'A tighter movie means more showings at the Angelika,' he wrote, and at the time I was thinking, 'Yeah right. By the Angelika, he means my parents' living room…'"

Originally, *Vulgar* was to be shot before *Chasing Amy*, but then that film went to production and Johnson for one was glad to have some time for prep. "I had no idea how films were made, and we lifted a lot of the *Chasing Amy* cast and crew. I was glad we waited until [Kevin and Scott] could guide me through the process. At the time, Kevin had the deal with Miramax where they'd put up the money for smaller movies, so Miramax kicked in about $40,000 and Kevin kicked in about $40,000."

Vulgar stars Brian O'Halloran as a man who makes a living as a clown named Flappy. One day, he comes up with the idea to make more money (to pay for his mother's stay at a nursing home), and becomes this sort of erotic, specialty clown who wears lingerie, named Vulgar. But when he gets a gig as Vulgar, he's attacked and raped by a really messed-up father (Jerry Lewkowitz) and his twisted two sons (Ethan Suplee and Matthew Maher).

O'Halloran's character survives the terrifying experience, but that's not the end of the story.

"After he gets assaulted, my character saves a child and then becomes famous, but his past comes back to haunt him," O'Halloran reveals. "There's a lot of twists in it that I really enjoyed. It's a very, very dark, twisted movie, so it isn't like a Kevin Smith laugh-a-minute film. It really sucks you in and then disturbs you."

"I love O'Halloran," Johnson notes of his lead. "He's very good. He's an actor who pays attention to details."

"It definitely shatters the Dante image," O'Halloran notes of his roles in *Vulgar*. "It is really a complete departure from any of the other characters I play in View Askew films. It's a role that as an actor is extremely challenging. When I read it for the first time, it was so disturbing, I had to put it down. I wondered why I ever wanted to do it. Then, in the same breath, I was like, 'Wow, how can I ever turn this down?'"

Vincent Guastini's first job for View Askew Productions was *Vulgar*. "I thought it would be a good calling card. I would get used to them [View Askew] and they would get used to me until the *Dogma* shoot came along," Guastini remembers. "So I did this very violent death scene for Ethan [who gets shot in the face], and it was very effective in the movie; highly detailed and very realistic. I thought Bryan did a really great job for it being his first film and basically for very little money."

At the time of writing, *Vulgar* had gone into limited release at the Angelika theater on April 26, 2002, thereby promising to launch the career of another View Askew director. A good review in the *New York Post* praised the film, noting O'Halloran's "extraordinarily brave and moving performance" and comparing *Vulgar* favorably to the bigger-budgeted *Death to Smoochy*.

Outside of View Askew Productions, Jeff Anderson was also bitten by the directing bug. He recently finished shooting *Now You Know*, an independently produced romantic comedy he also wrote. Featured in the film are none other than Kevin Smith and his wife, Jennifer Schwalbach. "I think they have a great cameo piece," Anderson laughs. "She's playing a hooker, and let's just say that Kevin is interacting with her."

"I play a hooker, because I'm Kevin's wife," Jennifer clarifies. "I love Jeff Anderson and wanted to be in his movie. I don't want to be an actress, contrary to what many people think who don't like me, and who say I only married Kevin to become an actress. However, if one of my friends is making a movie, I'm probably going to be in it. Jeff asked me which role I wanted to play, and I said I wanted to be the hooker. He asked if I was sure, because I'd be wearing a little nighty, and I'm Kevin's wife, and he didn't want it to seem too seedy, throwing me out there in some scandalous get-up. But I wanted to do it, because I wanted to be in a scene with Kevin."

"And," she confides, "I didn't want him [Kevin] to make out with any-body else. I was there the day he kissed Linda Fiorentino in *Dogma* — it didn't make the final cut — and I didn't want to see that again."

"I just saw *Now You Know*, and it was really funny," Schwalbach reports. "I'm taller than Kevin anyway, and I'm wearing spiked heels in the movie, so I'm literally a foot taller than him. And he's having to step on his tippy-toes to kiss me."

Kevin Smith not only appeared in Anderson's first film, he offered the first-time director moral support.

"As we got closer to doing the film, I sent Kevin the script," Anderson relates. "He read it and called me back, and I think he was pretty surprised by it. He was great. He told me if I had any questions, I could bounce things off of him."

But Anderson didn't really have any questions, and production of the film went so well that director Anderson actually overslept the first morning of the shooting schedule. It wasn't until post-production, in fact, that Anderson got worried.

"The editing room was a bit of a nightmare. That's where we first got into trouble," Anderson relates. "The first time I saw the film at the raw stage with no background sound and music, I panicked. The producers hired a post-production supervisor, yet I never met her. I didn't know much about post-production, but good Lord, I do now. She was basically hired because she's well known around town and they used her name to get good deals, but she never physically came in and did post-production, so I did it. There were some dark days there. It wasn't until I started looking at the dailies tapes and pulling things together that I saw it was going to be all right. I'm very happy with how it all turned out."

Now You Know, in fact, had its world premiere at a Vulgarthon, a View Askew/Kevin Smith convention. "It was a beta copy that wasn't quite ready to be shown, but the crowd really responded to it. It's nerve-wracking to show your own film, and the first time Kevin saw it I wanted it to look its best and be its best," Anderson notes. "It's like showing it to your dad. But he never got the chance to see it, because he was doing something else in one of the other auditoriums."

Drawing Flies, A Better Place, Vulgar, and *Now You Know* are four independent films that have emerged, either directly or indirectly, from the cinematic experiences of Kevin Smith and View Askew Productions.

But Kevin Smith has proven himself a good friend to people outside View Askew too, giving selflessly of his time and his money. He recently served as a guest auctioneer for a non-profit charity organization called ACTOR (A Commitment To Our Roots) that supports comic book writers who have seen their fortunes fall with changes in the economy.

After the tragic attacks on the World Trade Center on September 11, 2001, Kevin Smith added his poetic voice to Alan Moore's and Todd McFarlane's by contributing words and thoughts to *Heroes*, a Marvel comic book benefit special. The proceeds went to victims of the tragedy, and the book has already raised several hundred thousand dollars.

And, Smith has also assisted John Pierson in making one of his personal dreams become a reality.

"There's nobody I'd rather help out, and/or help to be the moral con-science of than Kevin Smith, and I hope he does the same for me," Pierson notes. "And I feel like we've been intimately involved since *Clerks*, and I don't think anyone went to the mat to defend him more on *Dogma*, espe-cially with the Miramax bullshit, than me. I exposed myself in ways that could have been trouble for me, so I feel good about that."

But Pierson, recently turned 48, has been looking for new horizons, new directions, in his life. "Kevin knows I'm moving away from the old me, the producer's repping, financing John Pierson."

And he's been moving towards something else. Specifically, the island of Taveuni in the Republic of Fiji, and a movie theater called the 180 Meridian Cinema.

"The Fiji idea came up in the last season of the TV show [*Split Screen*]," Pierson explains. "We were looking for the world's most remote movie theater, to which we could bring some American independent films. 'How far could these movies travel? Could they go to the rain forest on a little island on the international dateline in the South Pacific, in the Republic of Fiji?' That was the gig, and we had a fantastic trip in February 2000, and something happened on that trip."

Pierson elaborates, "They put on a Three Stooges short, which had been screened there for 50 years, three generations of filmgoers, and it's the only one set in the South Pacific. And basically, 300 people lost their minds laughing at this movie. It was the most extremely moving experience you could have. Ever since that moment, I knew I wanted to go back there and write what it's like where there's no other entertainment, to find out what movies mean at the edge of the world.

"When I went back last summer to see how far I could take that idea, I learned that the man who owned the theater was getting ready to emigrate." Pierson details. "So I bought the theater. But once I bought it, I had issues of where the money was coming from. I'm in the process of writing a book derived from all this, and there's probably going to be an HBO documentary, but these things are still shaping up.

"In the meantime I went to the filmmakers I feel closest to, and I feel maybe I helped the most: Spike, Kevin, the *Blair Witch* guys, and Matt Stone from *South Park*. And they've all come through in just fantastic ways. But Kevin came forward first and foremost when I needed support — seed money, I guess you'd call it — to get this going. He was supportive, both financially and emotionally, in ways that make you tear up a little bit."

Of course, that doesn't mean people should expect to see Smith frequenting the 180 Meridian Theater any time soon. "Kevin says things like, 'There's too much dirt in the jungle.' You will not be seeing Kevin on an island where he can't be on the Internet 24 hours a day."

The only downside, Pierson admits, is that he'll be in Fiji, when *Jersey Girl* plays in theaters next year. "I'll want to be showing it at the 180 Meridian Theater as early as possible," he notes. "And at that time, I'm sure everybody will help me arrange that, so it'll probably be shortly after whatever major festival it premieres at. But the people in Fiji would love to see Affleck. Mosier and Affleck would be a great pair to go..."

The legacy of *Clerks* lives on.

NOTES

1. Christopher Allan Smith, "Kevin Smith to break ground on TONIGHT SHOW,"
    Cinescape Online: Comic Book News, April 17, 2002, p. 1,
    http://www.cinescape.com

2. Jeff Jensen, "Chasing Glory: Filmmaker Tries Hands at Comics,"
    Advertising Age, October 19, 1998, p. 24.

3. Tricia Laine, Dan Snierson, and Shirley Fung, "Flashes (brief reports on filmmaker Kevin
    Smith's comic books)," *Entertainment Weekly*, February 20, 1998, n8, p. 12.

4. Lou Lumenick, "Send in the Clown—If You Can Take It," *The New York Post*,
    April 26, 2002, p. 1,
    http://www.nypost.com/movies/41936.htm

Sneek Peek

JERSEY GIRL

KEVIN SMITH'S MUCH ANTICIPATED sixth feature film, and the first one that doesn't feature Jay and Silent Bob, is called *Jersey Girl*, and the writer/director has described it in print as a "chamber piece about fatherhood."[1] Set in the Garden State in the late 1980s (technically making the movie Smith's first period film), the movie will be produced by View Askew and distributed by Miramax. Smith finished writing the first draft of the script in early 2002.

"I expect to be working on *Jersey Girl* full time by summer [of 2002]," Scott Mosier reports. "It's a very funny script, and its closer in tone to *Chasing Amy* than anything else we've done. It's also very emotional."

Mosier confirms that View Askew favorite Ben Affleck is committed to play the lead role (after finishing *Daredevil*), and that comedian George Carlin—late of *Dogma* and *Jay & Silent Bob Strike Back*—has also signed on. Despite rumors to the contrary, it appears Joey Lauren Adams will not be involved in the film.

But Jason Mewes, now working on a movie called *The Last Kiss* co-starring Dennis Hopper and Christopher Walken, is still holding out hope that he'll appear in *Jersey Girl* in a non-Jay role. "I know Kevin wrote a character for me," he notes, "but I haven't talked to him, and he hasn't mentioned it."

"*Jersey Girl* is the movie I wanted Kevin to do after *Dogma*, because I thought it was that good," reports Jennifer Schwalbach. "It's really him expressing himself as a parent. And we don't think that anybody can be offended by it—though there might some group out there looking for money!"

Though John Pierson is quick to note that "Jay and Silent Bob can appear in every movie Kevin ever makes, and I would be very, very pleased to see that," he also believes it is time for Smith to grow, specifically "because he can." *Jersey Girl* is the vehicle that will help him do that. "It's the same thing as *Chasing Amy*, but at a higher level," Pierson reports.

Without revealing too many spoilers about the project, Schwalbach is able to offer some of the specifics. "It's a very quiet film. There are no stunts or bright colors or loud music, and it's very real. It may be the first and perhaps only PG-13 movie that Kevin does. There's little to no need for swearing, and there isn't anything racy or scandalous about it. Basically, if you're not crying within the first 30 pages, you're a robot. It's a tearjerker."

And the plot? "It tells this very beautiful story between a husband and his wife, but is basically about the husband facing life with his daughter, and not knowing what to do, kind of winging it, and learning on his own. It's him getting to know himself, and getting back to his roots to raise his daughter in the way he thinks his wife wants him to.

"It's Kevin's love letter to Harley. It sounds so ridiculous coming from me, his wife, to someone writing a book about Kevin, but I could not ask for a better father for my child. Kevin touches me so deeply when I watch him with her. Not only does she look exactly like him, but she has so many of his personality traits. The two of them are just two peas in a pod, and it's so wonderful to watch the two of them together. And he's so brilliant and funny, and a completely different parent than I am. It's so nice for me to sit back and watch him give her the things I never could. I'm the mom; and I put the band-aids on her boo-boos, but he brings out this very creative, very different part of her personality, and it's amazing to see. And I think she's going to grow up to be just like him.

"I think *Jersey Girl* is a peek into our love," Schwalbach continues, "but it's really so much more about fatherhood. I think he'll come back to us."

One View Askew cast member not returning for a co-starring role in *Jersey Girl* is Harley Quinn Smith, Schwalbach reveals with a laugh, remembering the difficulties on the set of the last Jay and Silent Bob picture. "She's very, very dramatic, and wants to be in the movie, but will have minimal responsibility."

Jersey Girl is currently slated for release in 2003, and was officially greenlit by Miramax in mid-April of 2002. In late June, Jennifer Lopez was cast opposite Ben Affleck, and a ten-week shooting schedule was slated for August in the city of Philadelphia.

NOTES

1. Mr. Smith Goes to Hollywood: The Voice Behind Silent Bob Weighs in On His Return to 'Mallrats' Culture," *Entertainment Weekly*, August 24, 2001, p. 104.

10

A Tribute to Jay & Silent Bob

THE WASHINGTON POST has dubbed them a sophomoric Greek Chorus and a Gen X Cheech and Chong. *Time* has called them Vladimir and Estragon, characters from Beckett's *Waiting for Godot*.

In chat rooms across America, Jay and Silent Bob have been compared to every comedy duo dating back to the beginning of the medium: Laurel and Hardy; Abbott and Costello; Bill and Ted; Wayne and Garth; even those lovable droids from *Star Wars*, R2-D2 and C3PO. But the fact remains, no matter who these guys remind us of, Jay and Silent Bob have become an important part of our contemporary pop-culture tapestry.

So far, they've appeared in six films (if one includes their cameo in *Scream 3*), a cartoon TV series, comic books, music videos, and TV commercials. They've done their "stoner schtick" everywhere, making it, in fact, "stoner chic." And people — especially those of Kevin Smith's generation — love them.

The question remains, why? What is it about this comedy team that is so appealing? The answers below come straight from the book's interviewees, and, as you'll see, run the gamut. There is some psychobabble, historical references, philosophy, and even discussion of the magical Jason Mewes, the actor who has made the vocal portion of the comedy team so memorable.

Just for safe measure, some participants in this discussion had more than one answer...

THEORY ONE

Jay represents the id; Silent Bob, the ego.
(Proposed by Vincent Pereira)

"Jay is everybody uncensored," says Pereira. "If you took everything that is built into a person by society, growing up: that you can't say certain things; that you can't tell people this or that, and then remove all that, what you've got left is Jay. He is the id. What you see is what you get.

"Bob is the silent conscience. Even though he hangs out with Jay, he has a little more wisdom. If Jay were alone, he'd have no one to talk to. He'd be ranting and raving to space and looking like a lunatic. So Bob is his built-in audience, and the one who holds him back."

THEORY TWO

Jay and Silent Bob represent wish-fulfillment.
They do what others only wish they could.
(Proposed by Walt Flanagan)

"Jay can pull off saying just about the crudest, nastiest dialogue, and yet not come across as threatening," notes Flanagan. "Instead, he comes across as almost cartoonish and likable. No matter what he's saying, even if he's calling Randal and Dante some derogatory name, he's no threat."

Flanagan has an additional thought: "I also gotta chalk it [their popularity] up to Jay's never-ending energy to get pussy or stoned. That just appeals to everyone."

Dwight Ewell subscribes to this theory as well. "I think for the most part, people are slackers. In essence, none of us want to work. We all want the good times and the great experiences, just like them."

THEORY THREE

Historical precedents.
(Proposed by Scott Mosier, Jennifer Schwalbach, and Brian O'Halloran)

"I think every generation has a duo like them," reports Scott Mosier. "Even Bob Hope and Bing Crosby to some extent. Bob Hope was always a little dumber, Bing Crosby a little more suave."

"The general consensus," Schwalbach notes, "is that they're Laurel and Hardy for Gen X."

"Everybody enjoys buddy movies," O'Halloran explains. "Jay is the stoner friend who goes back to the days of Shaggy on *Scooby Doo,* and I guess that makes Bob his silent buddy, Scooby. It's R2-D2 and C3PO. It's Laurel and Hardy. It's just that buddy dynamic that so many people seem to enjoy."

THEORY FOUR

Jay and Silent Bob almost seem real.
(Proposed by Bryan Johnson, Ethan Suplee, and Dwight Ewell)

"You know, these guys probably could exist," Bryan Johnson weighs in. "At their advanced age now, I'm not so sure, but those wacky hi-jinks are, for the most part, almost believable."

"They're like your cousins," adds Ethan Suplee. "You'd like to hang out with them maybe once a year. They're such the yin and yang, the silent genius and the crazy, outspoken lunatic."

"I don't know if it's because we worked together or something, but he [Jay] feels like my cousin," echoes Dwight Ewell. "He's like a relative."

THEORY FIVE

Jay and Silent Bob are actually very wise, yet also incredibly stupid.
(Proposed by Jeff Anderson)

"The thing that always gets me," says Anderson, "is that Jay and Silent Bob can come into a scene and be completely clueless, but then in the next minute become all-knowing. My favorite scene with them was in *Chasing Amy.* That was Jay and Silent Bob at their best. From scene to scene they can be dumb, and yet they still have all the answers to life's questions."

THEORY SIX

They are the thread that stitches together the fabric of the (Askew)niverse
(Proposed by Jennifer Schwalbach)

"I think people enjoy the consistency from movie to movie; getting to know these two characters; getting to know their relationship. It's fun seeing them go from *Clerks*, a black-and-white independent film, and evolving — if you can use that word in regards to Jay and Silent Bob — into something fascinating enough to make basically, a blockbuster movie where they're the stars."

THEORY SEVEN

It is the comedic genius known as Jason Mewes.
(Proposed by John Pierson, Dwight Ewell, and Brian O'Halloran)

"Jay Mewes in that role is such a loveable character," O'Halloran notes.

"Jason and I hung out a lot on *Dogma*. Jason is beautiful. Period," Ewell states emphatically. "He's not like what you think at all. He's a beautiful person, and you just want to take care of him."

"It's great how Kevin found him and decided he had the screen charisma the world is demanding," muses John Pierson. "Or, whatever it was *People* magazine said: 'Whatever rock this guy crawled out from under, let's hope there's nobody else under there.' I don't even if know if there's a character like Jay on a one-off basis in a movie, let alone a continuing character in a series of them. What's been interesting, of course, is that over time, you've seen the sweetness that goes along with this raunchy character."

Finally, in this discussion of Jay and Silent Bob we'll leave the last words to the fellow who always gets the last words in these movies: Jason Mewes.

"Everybody tells me that Jay says stuff that people want to, but can't. But I also hear a lot of times that people have friends who act just like Jay," Mewes notes. "I think Jay is just a kid people relate to. He smokes weed and a lot of the people who like the films smoke weed. And I also think [they are popular] because Jay and Silent Bob are into *Star Wars*, wreaking havoc, and just trying to get pussy."

For the record, this author's theory is that everybody in the world has either a Jay or a Silent Bob within; that the characters represent two basic, core human personality types. Keeping that in mind, the interviewees for this book were questioned about whether he/she had more in common with Jay or Silent Bob.

"I don't think you'll find many people who admit they're Jay," warned Vincent Pereira. "He's got no inhibitions."

For the most part, he was right. Jeff Anderson, Bryan Johnson, Scott Mosier, Brian O'Halloran, Walt Flanagan, Vincent Pereira, and Ethan Suplee all felt they had more in common with Silent Bob.

But, courageous Dwight Ewell and Jennifer Schwalbach bucked the trend by identifying themselves as being "closer" in real life to Jay.

That may be something the fans will be pleased to know; that the world's real Silent Bob (Kevin Smith) has ended up marrying a woman who identifies herself as being close to his alter-ego's hetero-life mate, Jay.

Epilogue

YOU'RE CLOSED!

THE ADVENTURES OF KEVIN SMITH began with a humble origin story. A bright, creative kid from the Jersey 'burbs fell in love with the movies. By the time he was a young adult, surrounded by a group of colorful friends, Smith was a keen observer of the human condition; one who was inspired by the low-budget ingenuity and intelligent presentation of Richard Linklater's *Slacker*.

Now, more than eleven years later, this situation has come full circle. To paraphrase Darth Vader in *Star Wars,* "the learner" has become "the master," and it is the triumphs and works of Kevin Smith that have served to awaken the creative urges of a new generation of young filmmakers.

"I've always said in terms of the whole independent movie boom, from 1995 to 2000, the second half of the '90s, the two most influential films—one for good and one for bad—are *Clerks* and *The Brothers McMullen*," John Pierson reports.

"These two films are very influential. The bad part is that the accessibility factor is really high. People look at those films and think, 'I can do that.' My opinion on the Burns front is that it's so crappy, you *can* do that. But on the *Clerks* front, it's hard to be that funny."

So often in the movie-making business, imitation is the name of the game, and few films have inspired as many low-budget wannabes as *Clerks*. "People would always say, I made the Canadian *Clerks*. I did *Clerks* in a graveyard," Pierson notes of the prolifrating knock-offs.

But the good news is that just as *Slacker* inspired *Clerks*, so has *Clerks* no doubt inspired another masterpiece, the powerful debut of another interesting voice. "Out of those 995 people who maybe shouldn't have been inspired by *Clerks*, there's maybe five who take the right lesson away from it." Pierson considers.

And in the end, that means five good films.

How else have Kevin Smith's films been influential? The names Ben Affleck and Jason Lee pop immediately to mind. These charismatic, gifted actors still have many great performances to give the world, and it is the cinema of Kevin Smith that nursed them to stardom in the mid-1990s.

Similarly, Jeff Anderson, Brian O'Halloran, Bryan Johnson, Malcom Ingram, and Vincent Pereira are just a few other talents who transformed their association with Kevin Smith, Scott Mosier, and *Clerks* into new and daring film visions.

On other fronts, Kevin Smith's films have been remarkably successful. *Chasing Amy* is one of those movies that stands the test of time, and has already become a perennial rerun on cable television. Rising from the ashes of its commercial failure, *Mallrats* is indisputably a cult favorite.

Thus it's no surprise that Smith's five-strong (soon to be six) film franchise boasts both a rabid and large fan following. These admirers of the View Askewniverse gather once a year at conventions called "Vulgarthons" to relive the crazy adventures of Jay and Silent Bob, collect comics, and buy DVDs.

In this regard, Kevin Smith, a fan boy himself, has brilliantly tapped the fan boy culture that loves *Star Wars*, comic books, and raunchy humor, and they've embraced him for it. In return — on his best days and in his best films — Smith has accomplished something more than making us laugh; he's made us think about ourselves, primarily about our everyday relationships. Relationships with God, significant others, best friends, and even, with the advent of *Jersey Girl*, our children.

And I truly believe it's for that emotional honesty and self-examination — not merely the fart and dick jokes — that generations to come will return to the films of Kevin Smith.

The Quick Stop may be closed for now, but Kevin Smith will return.

The More You Know...

IF YOU'D LIKE TO LEARN MORE about View Askew
Productions and The Films of Kevin Smith, log onto the internet and go to
www.viewaskew.com, the official website of Kevin Smith, designed by Ming
Chen. You'll find news on the director's latest adventures, read his latest
column in the British magazine *Arena*, and even get updates about *Jersey Girl*
and the animated feature *Clerks: Sell Out*. There's also a calender of important
events in the Askewniverse, as well as links to all sorts of available merchandise
(like a *Clerks* lunchbox, and action figures of Bluntman and Chronic). In the
archives, there are informative interviews with all the View Askew personnel.

Or, if you're in town, visit Jay and Silent Bob's Secret Stash, in Red
Bank, New Jersey, the last word on comics, sci-fi and fantasy collectibles.
You'll find the store at:

> 35 Broad Street
> Red Bank, New Jersey, 07701
> (732) 758-0020

And, if you're really lucky, you might get to meet Walt Flanagan.

Appendix

F@&%—ING BABY TALK: THE KEVIN SMITH LEXICON

KEVIN SMITH'S FIRST FILM, *Clerks*, features a number of "section breaks," or inter-titles between sequences, a technique sometimes used by Woody Allen. These breaks are marked by the display of very impressive vocabulary words (like "vagary") that nicely mirror the events, themes, and moods during that particular portion of the film. Included below is a listing of those words, and the way in which *Clerks* reflects their meaning.

Now if somebody will just step forward and reveal the derivation of snootchie bootchies, snootch to the nootch, or snoogans.

DANTE: Okay, everybody knows that Dante is the name of Brian O'Halloran's long-suffering Quick Stop character. But, it also happens to be the name of someone else, the author of *The Inferno*, an epic poem that looked at the various levels of Hell. Allegedly, an early version of *Clerks* would have featured very different inter-titles—not these tongue-twisters—but the nine levels of Hell; all equated with Dante and his job at the Quick Stop.

VILIFICATION: The act of speaking evil of someone. Of course, this title refers to a Chewlie's Gum rep's efforts to paint Dante (or 'vilify' him) as a "death merchant," to equate him with the Nazis because he sells cigarettes.

JAY AND SILENT BOB: I have no idea what this refers to. Seriously, this section of the film introduces our heroes as they take up their familiar position outside the Quick Stop. There, Jay makes the immortal remark, "I'll fuck anything that moves."

RANDAL: Ditto. The introduction of Jeff Anderson into the film, as Dante's best friend.

SYNTAX: is the way words are assembled into bigger constructions, like sentences. And, it is in this section that Dante attempts to re-define his relationship with Caitlin. Yes, she cheated on him eight-and-a-half times, but Dante re-structures the cheating in his mind so it isn't that bad. Also, Randal assembles a long batch of words (porno movie titles), to construct a totally offensive "whole" (not hole).

VAGARY: A vagary is a whim, and it defines Randal's unplanned response to a customer in the video store who attempts to pull an unexpected "ruse" on him. He bans her from the store.

PURGATION: This word means "the act of ridding of sin," but oddly, the term pointedly contrasts with the action in the film. Here, Randal sins most egregiously: selling cigarettes to a four year-old girl.

MALAISE: A vague feeling of depression settles on Dante as he realizes he is "ever backing down" and that his boss has gone to Vermont. Ostensibly, his hockey game with Sanford and friends should lighten Dante's malaise, but has the opposite effect.

HARBINGER: A harbinger is a forerunner or signal of things to come. In this section of *Clerks*, an old man goes into the bathroom with a porno mag, not to be heard from again, at least for awhile. But, inevitably, he will return, with catastrophic results for Dante and Caitlin. This section of the film signals what (and who) is to come during *Clerks*'s climax.

PERSPICACITY: This word means "clarity of understanding," and it is here that Randal explains to Dante how title does not dictate behavior, but actions do. To prove his point, Randal spits water on a customer. Dante immediately gets the point.

PARADIGM: A paradigm is an example or model, and during this section in *Clerks*, Rick Derris, the town stud, shows up to remind Dante how out-of-shape he is. Derris is clearly a physical paradigm. On the other hand, this is also the section in which Dante is fined for selling cigarettes to a minor, and so his (or rather, Randal's) behavior is a paradigm of bad behavior.

WHIMSY: A whimsy is a quaint or fanciful idea. There is nothing quaint about what happens in this part of *Clerks*: Caitlin screws the dead guy in the bathroom.

QUANDARY: Caitlin's activities in the bathroom leave Dante in something of a quandary. His dilemma: who was really back in that room with her? Also, the coroner has a quandary to contend with: what kind of a convenience store do these guys run, anyway?

LAMENTATION: A lamentation is an expression of sorrow, and in this section, we bear witness to Dante's self-pity party, wherein he stews abut his life and inability to improve his station.

JUXTAPOSITION: By comparing the loyal, supportive Veronica (who brought Dante lasagna for lunch) and the fickle Caitlin (who cheated on him 8 and a half times, got engaged to an Asian design major named Sang, and screwed a dead guy), Dante is juxtaposing his girlfriends. Jay and Silent Bob are especially helpful in this regard.

CATHARSIS: A catharsis is a release, a cleansing of emotions, and in this case, Randal and Dante get into a food fight. And though the FDS stings, at least according to Dante, the food fight leads the two best friends to an epiphany about their lives, a point of confrontation and cleansing.

DENOUEMENT: A more verbose way of saying, "You're closed!"

Bibliography

BOOKS

Brennan, Shawn (Ed.). *Magill's Cinema Annual 1996: A Survey of the Films of 1995* (Farmington Hills, MI: Gale Group, 1996).

Brooks, Tim and Earle Marsh. *The Complete Directory to Prime Time Network TV Shows 1946—Present* (Third Edition) (New York: Ballantine Books, 1985).

Ebert, Robert. *Roger Ebert's Movie Yearbook 2000* (Kansas City, MO: Andrews McMeel Publishing, 2000).

Katz, Ephraim. *The Film Encyclopedia* (New York: Harper and Row, 1979).

Lowenstein, Stephen. *My First Movie: Twenty Celebrated Directors Talk About Their First Film* (New York: Pantheon Books, 2000).

Magill, Frank N. (Ed.). *Magill's Cinema Annual 1995: A Survey of the Films of 1994* (14th Edition) (Farmington Hills, MI: Gale Group, 1995).

Pierson, John. *Spike, Mike, Slackers & Dykes: A Guided tour Across a Decade of American Independent Cinema* (New York: Hyperion and Miramax Books, 1995).

The Riverside Shakespeare (Boston, MA: Houghton Mifflin Company, 1974).

PERIODICALS

Abele, Robert. "Home is Where the Art Is: Whether making electronic music or hanging paintings in his fancifully furnished apartment-cum-gallery, indie-film ace Jason Lee is a man of many muses," *In Style*, September 1, 2000, v7, p. 511.

Ansen, David. "Dante's Day in Jersey Hell, Convenience Store Blues," *Newsweek*, October 31, 1994, p. 67.

Ascher-Walsh, Rebecca. "Reel World: News from Hollywood (portrayal of gays in 'Jay & Silent Bob Strike Back')," *Entertainment Weekly*, August 10, 2001, p. 46.

Atkinson, Michael. "Kevin Smith Stirs It Up," *Interview*, October, 1999, v29, p. 180.

Blake, Richard A. "Fallen Angels," *America*, December 4, 1999, v181, p. 20.

Brodie, John. "Mr. Smith Goes to Hell," November 1999, *Gentleman's Quarterly*, pp. 205–208.

Chanko, Kenneth M. "A Lot Happens at a Convenience Store," *The New York Times*, October 16, 1994, Section 2, p. 20.

Dempsey, John, "Miramax rings 'Clerks' on DVD key," *Variety*, August 14, 2001, v379, p. 37.

Driver, Minnie. "Joey Lauren Adams," *Interview*, June 2000, v30, p. 52.

Entertainment Weekly. "Star Brenda," June 9, 1995, n278 p. 12.

Etter, Jonathan. "Richard Anderson—How Gary Cooper Got Him Into the Movies," *Filmfax*, pp. 58–65, 90–92.

Fitzpatrick, Kevin. "Kevin Smith's Jedi Mind Trick: The indie filmmaker on Boba Fett and loving *The Empire Strikes Back*," *Star Wars Galaxy Magazine*, April 3, 1995, pp. 1, 2, http://www.fitzbrothers.com/writing/writing012/html.

Fuller, Graham. "Mallrats," *Interview*, November 1995, v25, n11, p. 48.

Fuller, Graham. "Mr. Smith goes to emotion," *Interview*, April 1997, v27, n4, p. 42.

Gaines, Allison. "Chasing Down the Rumors: Did Kevin Smith Date a Lesbian?" *Entertainment Weekly*, November 28, 1997, p. 87.

Giles, Jeff. "Knocking on Heaven's Door," *Newsweek*, November 15, 1999, p. 88.

Gleiberman, Owen. "Smooth Mewes: As half of the dopey duo in *Jay and Silent Bob Strike Back*, Jason Mewes plays a rebel without a pause," *Entertainment Weekly*, September 7, 2001, p. 134.

Gordinier, Jeff. "The directors (filmmakers Richard Linklater, Errol Morris and Kevin Smith are three top independent directors in the business)," *Entertainment Weekly*, November-December 1997, p. 65.

Gordon, Devin. "A Phatty Boom Batty Flick: With his new movie, director Kevin Smith says thanks to family, friends, and yes, those nutty fans on the Web," *Newsweek*, August 27, 2001, p. 55.

Hochman, David and Jessica Shaw. "Clip'n'save (profiles of actress Renee Zellweger, Joey Lauren Adams, and Jewel)," *Entertainment Weekly*, June 13, 1997, n383, p. 12.

Hornblower, Margot. "Great Xpectations," *Time*, June 1997, p. 68.

Jensen, Jeff. "Chasing glory: Filmmaker tries hand at comics," *Advertising Age*, October 19, 1998, p. 24.

Jensen, Jeff. "Mr. Smith Goes to Hollywood: The Voice Behind Silent Bob Weighs in On His Return to 'Mallrats' Culture," *Entertainment Weekly*, August 24, 2001, p. 104.

Jones, Oliver. "*Dogma* duo re-ups 3 years at Miramax (continuation of Miramax contracts for producer and director Scott Mosier and Kevin Smith)," *Variety*, November 22, 1999, v377, p. 17.

Keck, William. "On Nuns, *Star Wars* & Evil Designers," *Esquire*, August 2001, p. 30.

Kelleher, Terry. "Picks and Pans," *People Weekly*, June 5, 2000, v53, p. 27-28.

Kempley, Rita. "Silent Bob's Inside Joke; Kevin Smith Takes a Starring Role but No Chances in a Moronic Riff on Hollywood," *The Washington Post*, August 24, 2001, p. C01.

Kilday, Greg. "Straight outta Jersey," *The Advocate*, July 4, 2000, p. 62.

Kizis, Deanna. "Joey Lauren Adams," *Cosmopolitan*, July 1999, v227, p. 156.

Laine, Tricia, Dan Snierson, and Shirley Fung. "Flashes (brief reports on filmmaker Kevin Smith's comic books)," *Entertainment Weekly*, February 20, 1998, n8, p. 12.

Le Blanc, Douglas. "Dogmatically Anti-Dogma," *Christianity Today*, January 10, 2000, v44, p. 80.

Lee, Linda. "A Night Out with Kevin Smith: Not the dogmatic type," *The New York Times*, November 14, 1999, Section 4, p. 3.

Lopate, Phillip. "Snoochie Boochies, The Gospel According to Kevin Smith," *Film Comment*, November-December 1999, pp. 60–65.

Lyman, Rick. "A Risque Kiss? So Very Quaint," *The New York Times*, September 17, 1999, p. E14.

Lyman, Rick. "Watching Movies with Kevin Smith: The Thrill is Just Talk," *The New York Times*, July 20, 2001, pp. 1, 13.

Maslin, Janet. "At a Convenience Store, Coolness to Go," *The New York Times*, March 25, 1994, p. C10.

Maslin, Janet. "At Cannes, New Faith, Simplicity and Dignity," *The New York Times*, May 22, 1999, p. B5.

Men's Health, "A Few Words from Captain Clerk," June 2001, p. 112.

Moon, Eileen N. "A Store Clerk's First Film Earns a Festival Showing," *The New York Times*, January 30, 1994, Section XIII, p. 1, 9.

The New York Times, "Is it Theft Or Is It Freedom? Seven Views of the Web's Impact on Culture Clashes," September 20, 2000, p. 42.

Pearlman, Cindy. "Rat Patrol," *Entertainment Weekly*, November 11, 1994, n248, p. 16.

People Weekly, "Shelf Employed: Ex-store Clerk Kevin Smith turns a bad job into a hit movie, but still slacks off at his convenience," December 12, 1994, p. 156.

Pinkser, Beth. "Filmmakers in the Fast Lane (Erich Schaeffer, Rusty Cundieff, Robert Rodriguez and Kevin Smith)," *Entertainment Weekly*, June 23, 1995, n280, pp. 26–29.

Richter, Erin. "The view askew-niverse (www.viewaskew.com addresses works by filmmaker Kevin Smith.)," *Entertainment Weekly*, April 25, 1997, n376, p. 77.

Rickey, Carrie. "*Clerks,*" *Knight-Ridder/Tribune News Service*, November 2, 1994, p. 110.

Roman, Monica. "Indie's Prodigal Son (independent film producer Kevin Smith)," *Variety*, January 26, 1998, v369, n11, p. 3.

Sarris, Andrew. "The Next Scorsese: Kevin Smith," *Esquire*, March 2000, p. 218.

Shaw, Jessica. "A Hollywood Dogfight," *Entertainment Weekly*, April 23, 1999, p. 9.

Silberg, John. "Community Access (how director Kevin Smith has used the Internet)," *Variety*, December 18, 2000, 381 I5, p. S36.

Smith, Chris. "Register Dogs," *New York*, October 24, 1994, pp. 50–54.

Stevens, Karl. "Old Dogma," *The Christian Century*, December 15, 1999, v116, p. 1235.

Strauss, Robert. "On the Towns: Jersey Boy Makes Good And Comes Back Home," *The New York Times*, December 5, 1999, p. 20.

Teachout, Terry. "Moving From Carnal Bliss to Something Truly Divine," *The New York Times*, May 25, 1997, pp. 9, 12.

Travers, Peter. "Clerks — Dangerous Talk," *Rolling Stone*, November 3, 1994, p. 104.

Travers, Peter. "Jay and Silent Bob Strike Back," *Rolling Stone*, September 13, 2001, p. 115.

Weinraub, Bernard. "Disney and Miramax Collide Over Church Issues in New Film," *The New York Times*, April 8, 1999, p. C4.

Wiltz, Teresa. "Silent Bob's Last Words; Director Kevin Smith Takes the Scenic Route for His Final 'Jersey Chronicle,'" *The Washington Post*, August 23, 2001, p. C01.

Zahed, Ramin. "Indie farm team fields future H'wood stars. (independent filmmaker Kevin Smith)," *Variety*, February 23, 1998, v370, p. A14.

INTERNET

Ansorge, Claudia. "Kevin Smith — Star Wars: This Generation," *The Two River Times*, http://www.viewaskew.com/press.trt.html.

CBC Radio Arts, Iculture. "*Touched by an Angel* objects to *Dogma*'s ad Campaign," November 18, 1999, pp. 1, 2, http://www.infoculture.cbc.ca.archives.filmtv/filmtv/11171999_angelsbattle.phtml.

CBC Radio Arts, Iculture. "Kevin Smith: Stirring Up *Dogma*." November 19, 1999, pp. 1-3, http://www.infoculture.cbc.ca/archives/filmtv/filmtv_11181999_kevinsmith.phtml.

CNN.com.ShowbizToday. "Kevin Smith is moving on," August 21, 2001, http://www.cnn.com/CNN/Programs/showbiz.today/featured.story/0108/21.html

Frontline. "The Monster that ate Hollywood: interview: Kevin Smith," http://www.pbs.org/wgbh/pages/frontline/shows/hollywood/interviews/smith.html

GodAmongDirectors.com. "Kevin Smith: *Chasing Amy* Liner Notes," September 20, 1997, www.godamongdirectors.com/smith/amystory/shtml.

Hargrave, John. "Kevin Smith-o-Rama: The Zug Interview," *Zug*, http://www.zug.com/scrawl/ksmith/intview.html

Hernandez, Eugene. "Interview: Kevin Smith Strikes Back," *IndieWIRE*, August 30, 2001, http://www.indiewire.com/film/interviews/int_Smith_Kevin_010830.html

Hollywood.com. "Kevin Smith Breaks the Silence," August 21, 2001, http://www.hollywood.com/celebs/features/feature/770296/page/2

Jensen, Jeff. "'Night, *Clerks*," *Entertainment Weekly*, June 7, 2000, p. 1, http://www.ew.com/ew/report/0,6115.85266~3~~,00.html.

Lumenick, Lou. "Send in the Clown—If You Can Take It," *The New York Post*, April 26, 2002, pp. 1, 2, http://www.nypost.com/movies/41936.htm

Marsh, Tanya D. "Dogma: Episode I—The Catholic Menace," *The Buzz*, October 1999, http://www.the-buzz.com/dogma1.html

Mogil, Michelle. "An Evening—no, a NIGHT—with Kevin Smith," *14850 Today*, March 14, 2001, http://www.14850.com/today/kevinsmithmm.html

Phipps, Keith. "Kevin Smith," *The Onion a.v. club*: http://www.theavclub.com/avclub3115/avfeature3115.html

Project Greenlight. "Kevin Smith Answers Back," http://www.projectgreenlight.liveplanet.com/community/kevin_smith.jsp.

Ryfle, Steve. "On fart jokes, *Planet of the Apes* and the making of *Jay and Silent Bob*," *IFilm: the Internet Movie Guide*, August 22, 2001, www.ifilm.com/news_and_features/feature/0,3536,608,00.html

Schmitz, Greg Dean. "Jersey Girl," *Upcoming Movies.com*, http://www.upcomingmovies.com/kevinsmith20002.html.

Seiler, Andy. "Kevin Smith is seldom 'Silent,'" *U.S.A. Today*, August 24, 2001, http://www.usatoday.com/life/enter/movies/2001-08/24-kevin-smith.html

Scott Seomin. "Scott Seomin's Letter to Kevin Smith, Writer/Director of *Jay & Silent Bob Strike Back*," *G.L.A.A.D. Documents*, July 26, 2001, p. 1, http://www.glaad.org/org/publications/documenta/index.html?record=2814.

Smith, Christopher Allan. "Smith talks to Stan Lee," *Cinescape Online: DVD News*, April 15, 2002, http://www.cinescape.com

Smith, Christopher Allan. "Kevin Smith to break ground on TONIGHT SHOW," *Cinescape Online: Comic Book News*, April 17, 2002, http://www.cinescape.com

Sweeney, Jennifer Foote. "Grandma sees *Dogma*," *Salon.com*, November 9, 1999, http://www.salon.com/mwt/feature/1999/11/09/dogma/index.html

Topel, Fred. "Kevin Smith's Final Strike," *Entertainment Today Feature Story*, August 24, 2001, pp. 1–4, http://www.ent-today.com/8-24/smith-feature.html.

Willman, Chris. "Biting Criticism: Dogma Director Kevin Smith disses *Magnolia*," *Entertainment Weekly*, January 27, 2000, p. 1, http://www.ew.com/ew/report/0,6115,84950~1~~00.html

About the Author

JOHN KENNETH MUIR is the author of ten reference books published by McFarland (www.mcfarlandpub.com), including *Terror Television* (a 2001 Booklist Editor's Choice), *Wes Craven: The Art of Horror* (1998), *The Films of John Carpenter* (2000), and *Horror Films of the 1970s* (2002).

John has written for a variety of magazines, including *Cinescape*, *Filmfax*, and *Collector's News*, and recently wrote two original short stories for the *Official Farscape Magazine* (issues six and eight), entitled "That Old Voodoo," and "Make a Wish."

Since 2001, Muir has penned a popular monthly opinion column on genre film and TV for *Deep Outside Science Fiction, Fantasy and Horror* (www.deepoutsidesffh.com).

John has made personal appearances at genre conventions, was a guest on the Sci Fi Channel's short-lived series *Sciography*, and has appeared twice on the New York-based radio program *Destinies: The Voice of Science Fiction*.

New Jersey born and bred, John lives in the historic district of Monroe, North Carolina with his wife, Kathryn, and three cats.